A History of the Women Marines, 1946-1977 - Legislation, Korean War, Pepper Board, Snell Committee, Recruit and Officer Training, Uniforms, Promotions, Marriage, Motherhood, Husbands

* * * * * * * * * * * * *

U.S. Government, Department of Defense, U.S. Marine Corps (USMC)

* * * * * * * * * * * * *

Progressive Management

Questions? Suggestions? Comments? Concerns? Please contact the publisher directly at

bookcustomerservice@gmail.com

Remember, the book retailer can't answer your questions, but we can!

* * * * * * * * * * * * *

This is a privately authored news service and educational publication of Progressive Management. Our publications synthesize official public domain government information with original material - they are not produced by the federal government. They are designed to provide a convenient user-friendly reference work to uniformly present authoritative knowledge that can be rapidly read, reviewed or searched. Vast archives of important data that might otherwise remain inaccessible are available for instant review no matter where you are. There is no other reference book that is as convenient, comprehensive, thoroughly researched, and portable - everything you need to know, from renowned experts you trust. For over a quarter of a century, our news, educational, technical, scientific, and medical publications have made unique and valuable references accessible to all people. Our books put knowledge at your fingertips, and an expert in your pocket!

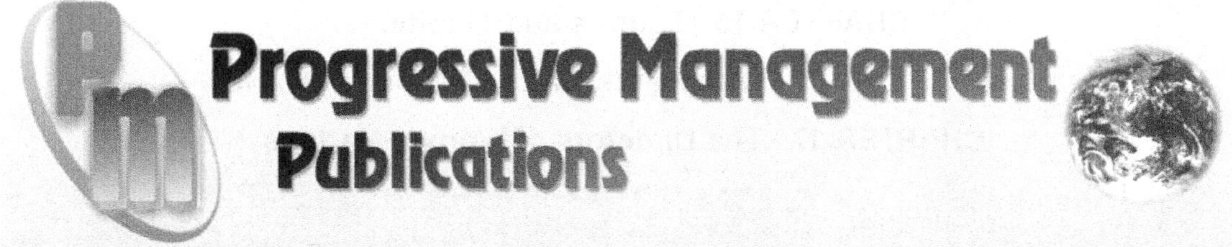

* * * * * * * * * * * *

CONTENTS

* * * * * * * * * * * *

* * * * * * * * * * * *

COVER: On 4 November 1948, the Commandant of the Marine Corps, Gen Clifton B. Cates administers the oath to the first three women to be sworn into the Regular Marine Corps. They are (left to right) LtCol Katherine A. Towle, Maj Julia E. Hamblet, and 1stLt Mary J. Hale.

* * * * * * * * * * * * *

A History of the Women Marines, 1946-1977

* * * * * * * * * * * * *

Colonel Mary V. Stremlow, U.S. Marine Corps Reserve

History And Museums Division

Headquarters, U.S. Marine Corps

Washington, DC. * 1986

* * * * * * * * * * * *

Foreword

Despite the acknowledged contribution made by the 20,000 women Reservists who served in the Marine Corps during World War II, there was no thought in 1946 of maintaining women on active duty or, for that matter, even in the Reserve forces. This volume recounts the events that brought about the change in thinking on the part of Marines, both men and women, that led to the integration of women into the Corps, to the point where they now constitute eight percent of our strength.

The project was the idea of Brigadier General Margaret A. Brewer, who, in 1975, as the last Director of Women Marines, noted that the phasing out of women-only organizations marked the start of a new era for women in the Corps, and the end of an old one. Further, she rightly reasoned that the increased assimilation of women would make the historical trail of women in Marine Corps difficult to follow.

The story is drawn from official reports, documents, personal interviews, and transcribed reminiscences collected by the author and preserved by the Oral History and Archives Sections of the History and Museums Division.

The pattern set during World War II of calling women Reservists "WRs" was followed after the passage of the Women's Armed Services Integration Act in 1948 by referring to the women as "Women Marines," or more often as "WMs." In the mid-1970s there was a mood to erase all appearances of a separate organization for women in the Marine Corps and an effort was made to refer to the women simply as Marines. When it was necessary to distinguish between the sexes, the noun "woman" with a lower case "w" was used as an adjective. Thus, throughout the text the terms "WR" and "WM" are used only when dictated by the context.

The comment edition of this manuscript was read by many Marines, men and women, who were directly associated with the events. All but one of the former Directors of Women Marines contributed to the work and reviewed the manuscript draft. Unfortunately, Colonel Katherine A. Towle was too ill to participate.

The author, Colonel Mary V. Stremlow, now a retired Reservist, has a bachelor of science degree from New York State University College at Buffalo. She counts three other women Marines in her family —two aunts, Corporal Rose M. Nigro and Master Sergeant Petrina C. Nigro, who served as WRs in World War II, and her sister, retired Major Carol Vertalino Diliberto. Colonel Stremlow came to the History and Museums Division in 1976 with experience as a company commander; S-3; executive officer of Woman Recruit Training Battalion, Parris Island; inspector-instructor of Women Reserve Platoon, 2d Infantry Battalion, Boston; instructor at the Woman Officer School, Quantico; and woman officer selection officer for the 1st Marine Corps District.

In the interests of accuracy and objectivity, the History and Museums Division welcomes comments on this history from interested individuals.

E. H. SIMMONS

Brigadier General, U.S. Marine Corps (Ret.)

Director of Marine Corps History and Museums

* * * * * * * * * * * *

Preface

A History of the Women Marines, 1946-1977 is almost entirely derived from raw files, interviews and conversations, newspaper articles, muster rolls and unit diaries, and materials loaned by Marines. There was no one large body of records available. In the course of the project, more than 300 letters were written to individuals, several mass mailings were made, and notices soliciting information were printed in all post and station newspapers, Leatherneck, Marine Corps Gazette, Retired Marine, and the newsletters of Marine Corps associations. More than 100 written responses were received and some women Marines generously loaned us personal papers and precious scrapbooks. Especially helpful in piecing together the events between World War II and the passage of the Women's Armed Services Integration Act were the scrapbooks of former Director of Women Marines Colonel Julia E. Hamblet, and former WR Dorothy M.

Munroe. Taped interviews were conducted with 32 women, including former Director of the Women's Reserve Colonel Ruth Cheney Streeter.

Researching this history was a challenge. Women's units were extremely difficult to find. Only those labeled "Women Marine Company" were easily identified. At times, days were spent screening the muster rolls of all the companies of all the battalions on a base looking for one with personnel having feminine first names. More recent unit diaries were even less useful since they are not signed by commanding officers and initials are used rather than first names. To add to the problem, the Corps had no system that permits a researcher to find a married woman when only her maiden name is known, or vice versa.

The author and the women Marines whose story is told in this monograph owe a special debt of gratitude to Master Sergeant Laura J. Dennis, USMCR, now retired, who from January to October 1977 voluntarily worked several days a week at the History and Museums Division, doing the painstaking research that resulted in the publication of much more material than would have been otherwise possible. Had it not been for her tenacity and dogged determination, easily 100 names, now documented for posterity, would not have made it to these pages. She tracked vague but important leads that the author, because of limited time allowed for the study, could not. Later, as a civilian volunteer, she shepherded the work through the comment edition stage and assisted in the search and final selection of photographs.

Master Sergeant Dennis also induced Colonel Agnes M. Kennedy, USMCR, to volunteer for the difficult task of indexing the manuscript. In the process, Colonel Kennedy further assisted in checking and verifying hundreds of names cited. Her own experience as a Marine officer enabled her also to make other valuable comments.

The manuscript was prepared under the editorial direction of Mr. Henry I. Shaw, Jr., chief historian of the History and Museums Division. Teacher and mentor, he encouraged the author to take the step from merely parroting a string of facts to presenting interpretations as appeared justified. More than 100 Marines reviewed the draft edition and, thanks in large measure to Mr. Shaw's expert guidance, few took issue with the historical facts or the interpretations of those facts.

The author also received valuable assistance from Mrs. Catherine A. Kerns, of the division's Publications Production Section, who prepared the typeset version of the manuscript, offering numerous stylistic suggestions in the process, and who was particularly helpful in the rendering of captions for photographs and in designing the tables which appear both within the text and in the appendices. Thanks also are due to Mr. W. Stephen Hill, the division's graphic artist, who is the book's designer, and who prepared all of the boards used in printing. His contribution has been to enhance the usefulness of the book by making its appearance especially attractive.

MARY V. STREMLOW

Colonel, U. S. Marine Corps Reserve

* * * * * * * * * * * *

CHAPTER 1 - A Time of Uncertainty, 1946-1948

A Time of Uncertainty

Postwar Women's Reserve Board

Termination of the Wartime MCWR

Retention of the WRs at HQMC

A New Director

The Volunteer Women's Reserve

4th Anniversary Celebration, 13 February 1947

The Women's VTUs

Plans for the Organized Reserve

* * * * * * * * * * * *

Introduction

"The opinion generally held by the Marine Corps is that women have no proper place or function in the regular service in peace-time. This opinion is concurred in by the Director of Marine Corps Women's Reserve, and a majority of the Women Reserves."1 In these words, Brigadier General Gerald C. Thomas, Director, Division of Plans and Policies in October 1945, stated the basic Marine Corps case against women on active duty. He elaborated his stand with the contention, "The American tradition is that a woman's place is in the home . . . ." and, "Women do not take kindly to military regimentation. During the war they have accepted the regulations imposed on them, but hereafter the problem of enforcing discipline alone would be a headache."2

The controversy over what to do with the women had been going on for months before the hostilities of World War II ended. It was a problem —an emotional one at that —which had to be faced. It was agreed that the Women Reserves (WRs) had successfully met the challenge of military service. At the close of the war, working in 225 specialties in 16 out of 21 functional fields, WRs constituted 85 percent of the enlisted personnel at Headquarters Marine Corps and one-half to two-thirds of the permanent personnel at all large Marine Corps posts and stations.3 It was generally acknowledged that it had been necessary to activate a women's unit for wartime duty; it was safe to assume that women would be called upon in any future, major emergency; most Marines, however, men and women, displayed a marked lack of enthusiasm toward the prospect of women in the postwar Marine Corps. The men were understandably reluctant to admit women permanently into one of the few remaining male-dominated societies, and the senior women officers were concerned about the type of women who would volunteer. Colonel Ruth C. Streeter, wartime Director of the Marine Corps Women Reserves (MCWR), believed that there was a difference in the women who enlisted for purely patriotic reasons due to the war, and those who enlisted after the G.I. Bill was passed —those who joined for what they could get for themselves.4

The pressure to give peacetime military status to women came from the other services, most notably the Navy. In the summer of 1945, the Secretary of the Navy, James V. Forrestal, made the statement, "The Navy favors retention, at least in cadre strength, of the WAVES, as well as SPARS and the Marine Auxiliary."*

* In 1943, when women joined the Marine Corps, the Director of Reserve, Colonel Littleton W. T. Waller, wrote to Representative Louis L. Ludlow of Indiana: ". . . these women will not be auxiliary, but members of the Marine Corps Reserve which is an integral part of the Corps and as . . . they will be performing many duties of Marines it was felt they should be so known." Col Littleton W. T. Waller, Jr., ltr to Hon. Louis L. Ludlow, dtd 8Feb43. (File 1535-55-10, Female Enrollment Marine Corps Reserve No. 1, Central Files, HQMC). Thus, the term auxiliary used by the secretary was incorrect.

Hoping to keep the Marine Corps out of any grand-scale plan for maintaining a women's corps in peacetime, Colonel Streeter developed a plan for an inactive Women's Reserve to be administered by no more than 10 women officers on active duty. On the accompanying routing sheet, she pencilled:

These comments are submitted at this time because there is considerable agitation in the Navy in favor of keeping WAVES on active duty in peacetime. It comes mostly from BuAir, Communications, and Hospital Corps. The WAVES themselves are much opposed to the plan.5

Colonel Streeter, tempered by her experience in building a wartime women's organization from nothing, took a very practical approach to the matter. She recognized that in planning a Reserve of women, wastage was going to occur because many of the women trained for military service would marry and have children, but this was a loss which would have to be accepted if women were truly needed. Indeed, if war threatened, even mothers could give a few months' active service for recruiting and training programs until enough new women Marines were ready to carry on.

By December 1945, General Thomas' division had developed a detailed plan for training a postwar, inactive, Volunteer MCWR (VMCWR) of 500 officers and 4,500 enlisted women, that would provide a nucleus of ready WRs capable of being expanded rapidly into a war-strength organization. In the introduction to this plan it was bluntly stated, "The arguments against retention . . . preclude any further discussion in favor of women being kept on active duty."6 In the eyes of the leading Marines, the case was closed.

* * * * * * * * * * * *

CHAPTER 1

A Time of Uncertainty, 1946-1948

A Time of Uncertainty—Postwar Women's Reserve Board—Termination of the Wartime MCWR Retention of the WRs at HQMC—A New Director —The Volunteer Women's Reserve 4th Anniversary Celebration, 13 February 1941'—The Women's VTUs—Plans for the Organized Reserve Release of the WRs Delayed Again — Stenographers Recalled

A Time of Uncertainty

At the end of the war in August 1945, the strength of the Marine Corps Women's Reserve was approximately 17,640 enlisted women and 820 officers. Demobilization procedures for women called for the mandatory resignation or discharge of all WRs, officers and enlisted. Demobilization was to be completed by 1 September 1946.

Colonel Streeter, who felt strongly that no woman should remain after she was no longer needed, asked to be released. She resigned on 6 December 1945 and, the following day, her assistant, Lieutenant Colonel Katherine A. Towle was appointed the second Director of the wartime Marine Corps Women's Reserve and promoted to the rank of colonel. To Colonel Towle fell the dual responsibility of overseeing the demobilization of the women and planning for a postwar women's organization.

In the spring of 1946 there was a steady flow of correspondence between the Chief of Naval Personnel, Vice Admiral Louis E. Denfeld, and the Commandant of the Marine Corps (CMC), General Alexander A. Vandegrift. The Navy was making plans for a WAVE organization with 1,500 officers and 10,000 enlisted women on active duty. The Army had already publicly announced its plan to give Regular status to the WACs.1 The Commandant, however, stood firm. The only women Marines on active duty during peacetime would be "Director, VMCWR; OIC [Officer in Charge], Personnel; OIC, Planning and Training; OIC, Recruiting; six officers, one officer assigned to each Recruiting Division."2

Recognizing that some sort of women's military organization was inevitable, and because legislation authorizing a women's inactive Reserve was pending, the Marine Corps no longer required WR officers to resign. Those still on active duty were allowed to request assignment to inactive status, and those already separated were sent a letter asking them to reenlist in the Reserve and reminding them of the privileges and responsibilities of belonging to the Marine Corps Reserve. Upon request, they could be reappointed to the permanent rank held upon resignation.3

Former colonel Mrs. Streeter was one of the women who applied for a Reserve commission, but her request was denied because of a legal restriction that precluded the appointment of more than one woman colonel in the Reserve. In fact, Mrs. Streeter, who saw the wartime Women's Reserve through all of its growing pains and its initial demobilization, had voluntarily given up terminal leave in order that her successor (then Lieutenant Colonel Towle) might immediately have the rank of colonel. The Commandant told Mrs. Streeter that he would recommend her to the Secretary of the Navy for reappointment in her rightful rank in the inactive Reserve, but the Navy Judge Advocate General held that there could be no exception. He later reversed his decision and Mildred H. McAfee Horton, the WAVE Director, was given Reserve status as a captain.*

* Subsequently, efforts were made by Colonel Towle, and two Commandants, General Vandegrift and General Lemuel C. Shepherd, Jr., to straighten out the matter. It was not until 1959, however, through the persistence of Colonel Julia E. Hamblet, that this situation was satisfactorily resolved. In a letter to the Chairman, Board for Corrections of Naval Records, the then Commandant, General Randolph McC. Pate, wrote: "Correction of Mrs. Streeter's records would erase an apparent inequity and allow her to be affiliated with the Marine Corps Women's Reserve which she was so instrumental in establishing. This correction would afford the Commandant of the Marine Corps great satisfaction." (CMC ltr to Chairman, Bd for Corr of NavRecords, dtd 31Mar59 [Postwar MCWR J File]). He also wrote to Mrs. Streeter and said, "In view of your outstanding contribution to the Corps, I sincerely hope you will not deprive me of the opportunity of recommissioning you as a Colonel in the Marine Corps Reserve." (Gen Randolph McC. Pate ltr to Mrs. Ruth C. Streeter, dtd 25 Feb 59 [Postwar MCWR J file}). And so, on 25 June 1959, Ruth Cheney Streeter was reappointed a colonel in the Marine Corps Reserve and retired.

Colonel Joseph W. Knighton, legal aide to the Commandant, advised General Vandegrift on 13 March 1946 of the Army's and the Navy's plans to keep women on active duty. They even allowed for women in their budgets —something that the Marine Corps was not to consider until after passage of the women's armed forces legislation in 1948. It was apparent that Admiral Denfeld was giving more than lip service to the support of women since he had instructed the Navy's judge advocate general to prepare a bill which would enable the Navy to have women in its Regular component. Colonel Knighton put two questions to the Commandant:

(1) Does the Marine Corps want women in its regular peacetime establishment?

(2) If the answer is negative, can the Marine Corps justify this stance if the Army and the Navy have come to the conclusion that women should be included in their permanent establishment?'1

In response, the Plans and Policy Division recommended that the Marine Corps be excluded from the provisions of Denfeld's proposed legislation to provide Regular status for women because ". . . the number of billets which could be filled to advantage by women in the postwar Marine Corps is so limited that the increased administrative overhead could not be justified." Although the Commandant approved this recommendation on 18 March, that was not the end of it.

Postwar Women's Reserve Board

Acting on a suggestion from Colonel Towle, on 28 March 1946, General Vandegrift appointed Colonel Randolph McC. Pate, Director, Division of Reserve, senior member of a board to recommend policies for administration of women in the Marine Corps postwar Reserve structure. The board convened at Headquarters, Marine Corps (HQMC) on 1 April and consisted of Colonel Pate, Colonel Richard C. Mangrum, Colonel Katherine A. Towle, and Major Ernest L. Medford, Jr., with Major Cornelia D. T. Williams and Major Marion Wing as additional members, and Captain Sarah M. Vardy as member and recorder.5

The report of this board, which was approved by the Commandant on 7 June, called for women to be included in both the Volunteer and Organized components of the Reserve. Enlisted women would be trained at unit meetings in home armories. Officers would train at an annual summer officer candidate school to be established at Quantico and then return home to participate in a Reserve unit. A total of 45 officers and 32 enlisted women —all Reservists—would be assigned to continuous active duty to administer the program. It was spelled out that no woman would be allowed to remain on active duty longer than four years, and summer training was not considered necessary even for the organized Reservists. At the time of the study, only the volunteer, inactive status was legally possible and many of the 40 recommendations were based upon the premise that legislation would be passed authorizing inclusion of woman in the Organized Reserve. Finally, the board recommended that a qualified woman Reservist of field grade be selected as soon as possible for the position of director and that she be appointed to the rank of colonel.7

Concurrence with the creation of a permanent women's Reserve was unanimous. The staff comments, for the most part, dealt with minor administrative details. Colonel Knighton, however, spotted the weakness which would eventually alter the opinions of the leading women officers. He recognized that the four-year active duty limit was impractical, and he stated:

. . . where can you find a woman, unless she happens to be unemployed and hunting for a job, who would agree to serve on active duty for a short period? In peacetime housewives will not volunteer, socialites will not be interested, and a woman who has to work for a living, unless she is temporarily looking for employment, will certainly not sign up for a few years of active duty in the Women's Reserve.8

Long before the board report was officially approved, Colonel Towle outlined its main points in a statement she prepared for the Joint Army-Navy Personnel Board on 17 April, and for the 9 May House Naval Affairs Committee Hearings on H. R. Bill 5919, "To amend the Naval Reserve Act of 1938, as amended so as to establish the Women's Reserve on a permanent basis . . . ." (See Chapter 2 for a more detailed discussion of the Women's Armed Forces Integration Act of 1948 (P.L. 625)).

By the time the bill was reported out of committee on 21 May, it had undergone some major changes. The next day, Admiral Denfeld wrote to Representative Margaret Chase Smith of Maine giving his views of what the legislation should embody. Due mainly to her efforts, the subsequent draft read:

All laws or parts of laws which authorize the appointment of persons to commissioned grades or ranks in the Regular Navy and Regular Marine Corps and which authorize the enlistment of persons in the Regular Navy and Regular Marine Corps should be construed to include the authority to appoint and enlist women in the Regular Navy and Regular Marine Corps in the same manner and under the same conditions as such laws or parts of laws apply to the appointment and enlistment of men.9

Now, like it or not, the Marine Corps was included. In the words of Victor Hugo, "No army can withstand the strength of an idea whose time has come."10

Termination of the Wartime MCWR

The office of the wartime MCWR was closed on 15 June 1946 when Colonel Towle began her terminal leave. Before leaving the Marine Corps to return to the University of California's Berkeley campus as administrative assistant to the vice president and provost, Colonel Towle proposed the name of Major Julia E. Hamblet to be director of the women's postwar organization. She wrote:

It is believed that Major Hamblet has all the attributes and qualifications desirable in a director of a postwar MCWR. She is a college graduate, about 30 years of age (which is considered a great advantage in appealing to volunteers among younger women, especially those of college age), of fine appearance, with a great deal of natural dignity and poise, and has an outstanding service record and reputation. She has had experience in both line and aviation assignments and has served in the present MCWR since her commissioning in the First Officers' Class in May 1943."

The recommendation of Major Hamblet to head up the postwar MCWR was acknowledged and held in abeyance.

Turning to another matter, Colonel Towle suggested that her assistant, Captain Mary V. Illich, continue duty in the Personnel Department to take care of the work incident to the termination of the office of the director. Captain Illich and one private first class were assigned the task of tying up the administrative details of the wartime Women's Reserve and were expected to finish by 15 July 1946.

Retention of the WRs at HQMC

It is ironic that only two months earlier, on 14 June, in a report on the state of the MCWR to the Director of Personnel, Colonel Towle wrote:

General morale during demobilization has been gratifyingly high. Part of this had been due to the definite stand the Marine Corps itself had taken from the beginning on MCWR demobilization, particularly in setting and maintaining 1 September as the terminal date of the wartime Women's Reserve. It had been a goal to work toward, and Marine Corps women have never had the uncertainty and confusion concerning demobilization which have occurred in some of the other women's services because of the shifting of date and changes in policy.12

Most of the WRs still on active duty in the summer of 1946 were working at Headquarters on the administrative job of demobilization of the wartime Marine Corps. In spite of the general feeling against retention of women in the Marine Corps, individual work supervisors were anxious to keep their women on the job. As the September deadline for the release of all WRs neared, case after case of exception was requested. Few were granted, but this activity not only kept Captain Illich on the job, but also on 30 August gave her an assistant, First Lieutenant Mary Janice Hale.*

* Lieutenant Colonel Hale, who retired in March 1964, is the only woman officer to have served on continuous active duty from World War II until the completion of a 20-year career.

Marine Corps Commandant Gen A. A. Vandegrift (center) is shown with Col Katherine A. Towle (right) and Col Ruth C. Streeter (left) in December 1945. Col Towle has just succeeded Col Streeter as the post-war Director, Marine Corps Women's Reserve.

This appointment followed a major change in policy announced on 7 August 1946 when the Commandant authorized the retention on active duty at HQMC, on a voluntary basis, of 100 WRs for a period of eight months. These women, clerk typists, payroll clerks, and auditors, were to be assigned to a new division of the Personnel Department established to administer the Armed Forces Leave Act of 1946. One officer would be retained to command a company to be activated on 1 September, all of whose members would live off post and be placed on subsistence and quarters allowances. The last of the WR barracks was finally closed. As an inducement to apply, privates first class who were accepted would be automatically promoted to corporal.13

The next day, 8 August, the Commandant authorized the retention of 200 additional WRs until 30 June 1947. It was specified that these women ". . . must have clerical, stenographic or other specific ability (no cooks, truck drivers, hairdressers, etc., unless they have a secondary clerical specification)."14

Company E, 1st Headquarters Battalion, Headquarters, U.S. Marine Corps, commanded by First Lieutenant Regina M. Durant, was activated on 19 August 1946 with a strength of 12 officers and 286 enlisted women, with Master Sergeant Geraldine M. Moran as first sergeant.

A New Director

Major Julia E. Hamblet had served as assistant for the Women's Reserve from December 1945 until she was released from active duty in April 1946. She had never considered the military as a career and was very much in favor of the Marine Corps plan for women in organized and volunteer Reserve units.

While in England visiting her family, Major Hamblet, as other Marine veterans, received numerous letters from Headquarters Marine Corps. The familiar brown envelopes contained words of thanks and appreciation for wartime service, advice regarding veteran's benefits, a request to keep in contact with the Reserve District commander, and information regarding the planning for the postwar Reserve.

In mid-June 1946, rushing to an appointment from her brother's London home, she found yet another message from Headquarters. In a hurry, she put it in her purse and promptly forgot it. Nearly a week later, while at a party, she remembered the letter and opened it to find that it was not the routine form letter she had come to expect. Instead it was a personal letter to her from the Commandant, General Vandegrift.

In the letter he explained the plan to establish women as part of the Organized Reserve and to maintain on active duty a limited number of women Reservists to administer the program. He stated:

Because of your record and experience in the present Marine Corps Women's Reserve, you have been selected to fill the position of Director of the postwar Women's Reserve, and it is hoped that you will be interested in accepting this appointment. If you do accept, it is desired that you be available for duty at Headquarters Marine Corps not later than 1 September 1946. You will understand, of course, that the continuance of a postwar Women's Reserve and the position of Director are contingent upon the enactment of enabling legislation by the Congress which is currently giving it consideration.

A prompt reply will be appreciated.15

Had she not immediately thereafter received letters from both Colonels Streeter and Towle expressing their pleasure at her selection and their concern for the future of the MCWR, Major Hamblet's first inclination would have been to refuse the appointment. Rather, on 25 June, she wrote to the Commandant and accepted.

Due to the difficulty in obtaining transportation from England at the time, she asked to be activated there, so that she could travel on military orders.18 Existing laws did not permit members of the MCWR to be on active duty anywhere outside the United States except Hawaii. Therefore, she was informed that she could not be assigned to duty until her return.17 Major Hamblet reported to the Division of Reserve, Headquarters Marine Corps on 6 September 1946, and became the Director, MCWR.

At this time two distinct women Marine programs existed with the sex of their members as the only common denominator. At Headquarters, the several hundred retained wartime WRs continued to work on administrative matters unrelated to the MCWR. These women were under the cognizance of Captain Illich in the Personnel Division. Then there was Major Hamblet in the Division of Reserve concerned with initiating detailed planning for a postwar, inactive Reserve. Inevitably, some confusion arose. In a study dated 8 October, Major Hamblet wrote:

The relationship of the undersigned to the 286 enlisted women and 5 officers retained on active duty after 1 September 1946 for assignment other than MCWR postwar planning is not at present clear. It would seem evident, however, that the powers assigned to the Director, MCWR, should be exercised in relation to all women reservists, on whatever basis they may be serving.18

Clarification was soon made, in no uncertain terms, in a Headquarters Memorandum of 16 October 1946 which stated the policy for the administration of the Marine Corps Women's Reserve. The wording was precise and unequivocal, and it was the foundation of a policy that was to last for more than 25 years. The Commandant directed:

That all matters of policy and procedure pertaining to the Marine Corps Women's Reserve, which are initiated by any department or division of Headquarters Marine Corps, be referred to the Director, MCWR, for comment and recommendation. In regard to matters of policy, such reference shall be made prior to submission to the Commandant of the Marine Corps for approval; in matters of procedure, such reference shall be made prior to execution.19

The Volunteer Women's Reserve

With a staff of two women, First Lieutenant Mary J. Hale and Technical Sergeant Dolores M. Adam, Major Hamblet began her work. She faced the task totally committed to the urgency of obtaining as soon as possible the nucleus of a postwar women's Reserve. Her visit to England and France during the summer convinced her that the world situation was still unsettled and that greater utilization of womanpower in the U.S. military would be required in the event of another war. As a member of the first officer training class in the wartime MCWR, she saw the difficulties of building up such an organization after an emergency had already occurred. In 1943, the Marine Corps had been forced to rely on civilian facilities and Navy personnel to get its women's program started. Worse, male Marines, needed for combat, were used instead to train women.

Major Hamblet recognized that the unclear status of the women's legislation in 1946 jeopardized the success of a women's Reserve. The long and uncertain delay allowed former women Reservists to become absorbed in their civilian interests and lessened the chance of their enlisting in a future Reserve.

She questioned the necessity of waiting until the legislation was actually passed before taking positive action. There was reasonable doubt about the legality of an Organized Reserve bur she believed that no such obstacle blocked the creation of a Volunteer Reserve. Indeed, the WAVES were, at that time, reenlisting women for full-time active duty in the Volunteer Reserve.

Pending the enactment of permissive legislation, Major Hamblet urged immediate enlistment of as many former members of the MCWR as possible in a volunteer status since, she reasoned:

These women already have had indoctrination and training; and those among them who do desire could later transfer to an "Organized Reserve," if one were activated. Meanwhile, they would at least constitute a roster of trained personnel, available for active duty if the need arose.20

A step in this direction was taken on 23 December with the publication of Marine Corps Letter of Instruction 1391, authorizing the enlistment of former women Reservists in the Marine Corps Reserve. This was part of a purposeful effort to maintain contact with the women who had served so well in World War II. The intention was to keep the women interested and predisposed to join a volunteer or organized unit when legally possible. Furthermore, it supplied the Corps with a pool of ready, trained volunteers. The first enlistment contract received was that of Staff Sergeant Elizabeth Janet Steele, who, a few months later, activated and commanded Volunteer Training Unit 3-I(WR), New York, New York.21

4th Anniversary Celebration, 13 February 1947

Keeping in touch with former WRs became a task of giant proportions for the three women —Major Hamblet, Lieutenant Hale, and Sergeant Adam. They drew the cases of nearly all the 18,000 World War II women Reservists and personally reviewed each one in order to compile an up-to-date roster with current addresses. Ostensibly, this list was to be used in determining the geographic areas best suited for future Organized Reserve units, but it was put to a more immediate use in planning a celebration in honor of the fourth anniversary of the Marine Corps Women's Reserve.22

Selected officers in 25 cities were asked to accept chairmanship of these birthday parties and were provided with the names of officers and capable NCOs in their area. They were told:

In order to afford continuity to the MCWR it is important that we have anniversary parties all over the country this year and bring together again as many as possible of the former WR's, both officers and enlisted personnel. . . . Because there has been such a delay in getting the postwar program underway, it is just that much more important that we do a bang-up job on February 13th. . It is realized what an undertaking this will be, but the dividends in the form of the goodwill of former WR's (which we are most anxious to have!) will be tremendous.23

Since no funds were provided, many of these officers and NCOs used their own money for stationery and postage in order to contact the veterans.

Birthday greetings were sent to individual women Reservists reminding them that this was the time to recall friendship and experiences. "Get out the uniform —dust off the moth balls, let out the seams, roll up the hair and gather round to rehash the Marine Corps days," they were told.24

More than 2,500 WRs attended the parties in 22 cities and at the Marine Corps Air Station at Cherry Point, North Carolina. San Francisco, where 395 women gathered under the chairmanship of First Lieutenant Pearl Martin to hear the guest speaker, Colonel Towle, was the site of the largest celebration. Another coup was scored by Captain Mildred Dupont and the New York WRs when former Colonel Streeter agreed to be the honored guest and to help cut the traditional birthday cake.

The Marine Corps Women's Reserve Post 907, American Legion, in Chicago sponsored a grand event in the Gold Room of the Congress Hotel. The committee was headed by First Lieutenant Dorothy R. Dietz. Captain Emma H. Hendrickson (later Clowers), who was to become one of the first 20 Regular women Marine officers in November 1948, read congratulatory messages from Headquarters and spoke to the group of the plans to utilize women in the Reserves.

The Washington, D.C. area celebration was unique in that it was attended by former WRs, inactive women Reservists, and numbers of women still on active duty.

The fourth anniversary parties accomplished their mission. In addition to being occasions of much fun and recall, they provided Headquarters with a roster of former WRs who were still interested in the Marine Corps and a nucleus of officers and NCOs who were able organizers.

The Women's VTUs

Authorization for the formation of volunteer training units (VTUs) came on 9 January 1947 in Letter of Instruction 1397. The objective of this program was to develop a ". . . pool of efficient general duty, staff and specialist personnel which, on call, can fill needs for individuals or groups in an emergency."25. In order to form a VTU, a group of 10 Reservists, commissioned or enlisted, male or female, was required. Women could, of course, join a unit already established by men.

The appeal was made almost entirely to patriotism and esprit de corps. The Marine Corps Reserve recruiting material offered membership, tradition, and prestige of the Corps, credit toward promotion in rank, social and athletic activities, a lapel pin, and an I.D. card. Attendance and participation were voluntary and members could not be called to active duty without their consent except in the event of war or national emergency. Reservists would retain the rank held on discharge, and only male members would be eligible for periods of active duty.26

There was considerable latitude allowed in planning a VTU training schedule. Units could specialize in one field, such as intelligence, communications, photography, etc., or follow a more general pattern. A general unit might emphasize lectures on current world problems, and a women's unit might spend all its time giving clerical assistance to the male Marine Reservists.

Seattle has the distinction of being the home of the first women's Volunteer Training Unit—VTU 13-12(WR) —established in January 1947 and commanded by Captain Nancy M. Roberts.

In November 1947, Maj Julia E. Hamblet (right) congratulates Capt Constance Risegari-Gai (left), commander of Volunteer Training Unit 1-1, Boston, Massachusetts during ceremonies to present awards earned by Women Reservists during World War II.

From the 1st Marine Corps Reserve District Headquarters, then located in Boston, Captain Constance Risegari-Gai, commanding officer of VTU I-I(WR), wrote:

Dear Ex-Marine,

Do you want to remain an ex-Marine —or would you like to drop the "ex", remove the "homing pigeon", "ruptured duck" or whatever you call it from your uniform, and again be able to write USMCR after your name?

Yes, the Corps wants you back, right now, in the Volunteer Reserve, although later you may have an opportunity to go into the Organized Reserve.27

Boston chose Marine Corps administration as its specialty, scheduled regular lectures, and got "field practice" by assisting the 2d Infantry Battalion, USMCR, with its paperwork. The Boston WRs met every Wednesday night on the fourth deck of the Navy Building-Marine Corps Reserve Armory (formerly the Fargo Building) to type enlistment papers, medical records, and routine correspondence.

Elements of that unit gave similar help on Saturday and Sunday mornings to the three Marine aviation squadrons at nearby Squantum. And, on Tuesday, others went south to Hingham Naval Ammunition Depot to lend a hand to Company B, 2d Infantry Battalion. Frequently, the women were called on for recruiting and public relations activities as well. Lack of work was never a problem.

In the notice for the week of 12 November 1947, Captain Risegari-Gai added, "Major Julia Hamblet expressed much pleasure and satisfaction with the work of VTU 1-1. She stated that we have the largest actually working unit (there is a larger unit in New York which meets for training lectures once a month)."28

The WRs of New York would, no doubt, have taken exception to the captain's assessment of their unit. VTU 3-l(WR), activated in February 1947, and commanded by Staff Sergeant Steele was not only the largest women's volunteer training unit, with a strength at one time of 100 members, but it was the only all enlisted women's VTU and it remained active until 20 August 1957 —a little more than 10 years.29 By 1954, it had logged in a record of over 7,000 voluntary unpaid hours of service to the Marine Corps, doing clerical, recruiting, and typing duty for many Marine Reserve units including Marine Fighter Squadron 132, the 1st Infantry Battalion, the 19th Infantry Battalion, and the l4th Signal Company.30

Among its early members were Helen A. Brusack, who eventually integrated into the Regular Marine Corps and remained until her retirement as a gunnery sergeant in May 1972; Agnes Hirshinger, who commanded the unit from July 1949 until its deactivation; Dorothy T. Hunt (later Stephenson), who integrated and was a member of the staff that established women's recruit training at Parris Island in 1949; Pearl Jackson, the first enlisted woman accepted for officer candidate training after the integration of women into the Regular Marine Corps; and Alice Mclntyre, who later integrated, became a warrant officer, and served 20 years.31

Second Lieutenant Julia M. Hornsby activated the Baltimore VTU(WR). Members of the Woman Marine Organized Reserve platoons of the post-Korea era remembered her as the Reserve liaison officer at Parris Island who was vitally involved with their summer training period.

First Lieutenant Kathyrn E. Snyder established VTU 12-4 (WR) at San Francisco on 10 February 1948. The next year, serving on continuous active duty, she became the first inspector-instructor (I&I) of the women's Reserve platoon in that city and eventually the I&I of the post-Korea Women Reserve Administration Platoon in Detroit.

In Philadelphia, Captain Dorothy M. Knox commanded VTU 4-4 (WR), activated in September 1947. When the Organized Reserve finally became available to women in 1949, Captain Knox and her entire VTU became the nucleus of Philadelphia's WR platoon. They had already lost one member to the Regulars — Captain Elsie Eleanor Hill. In time, Dorothy Knox integrated, served with the major women's commands —to include assignments as commanding officer of the Woman Marine Detachment at Quantico and later of the Woman Recruit Training Battalion at Parris Island —and retired as a colonel in 1970.

San Diego's Volunteer Training Unit, VTU 11-2 (WR) was activated on 26 February 1948 with First Lieutenant Ben Alice Day as commanding officer. Lieutenant Day, among the first 20 Regular women officers, later reverted to the Reserve when, as a major, she married Brigadier General John C. Munn (later Lieutenant General Munn, Assistant Commandant of the Marine Corps). The Munns retired in 1964 in the first husband-wife, Regular-Reserve retirement ceremony in Corps history.32

In 1977, Lieutenant Colonel Ben Alice Munn recalled:

. . . with respect to the interest Colonel W. R. Collins (later Major General, USMC; now retired) had in the group. As the Inspector-Instructor of the Reserve unit in San Diego, he gave most generously of his time and energy to help set up a program, and to keep the meetings interesting. This was very difficult as the question of what to do with Women Reserves, besides sitting them in front of typewriters, was an unanswered question. There was no training program or syllabus. (The question remained for a good 20 years or more! The Marine Corps had bowed under wartime pressure that historic February 1943, and it was my impression that the Corps was glad, or relieved, to see the last of us go off to inactive duty or to civilian life!)

Perhaps Colonel Collins was ahead of his time for I well remember one lecture he gave to VTU 11-2 (WR) in which he described a trip he made to Russia immediately after hostilities ceased. He gave a vivid description of his observation of Russian women being used in every military job, from sweeping snow off runways to driving tanks.33

Women's VTUs were also formed in Indianapolis, Indiana; St. Louis, Missouri; Los Angeles, California; Oakland, California; Chicago, Illinois; Rochester, New York; Milwaukee, Wisconsin; Kansas City, Missouri; Portland, Oregon; New Orleans, Louisiana; Minneapolis, Minnesota; Atlanta, Georgia; and Washington, D.C. The WR volunteer training units were a source of great pride to the Marine Corps. Between March and December 1947, women Reservists worked a total of 5,000 hours of voluntary service.

The immeasurable importance of these units lies primarily in their effectiveness in keeping hundreds of WRs interested in their Marine Corps affiliation during the two years it took to pass legislation allowing Regular and Organized Reserve status for women. Many of the units later transferred 100 percent to the Organized Reserve. Individuals integrated into the Regular Marine Corps when it became possible in late 1948 and early 1949. Others, mobilized for Korea, remained to complete a 20-year career.

Plans for the Organized Reserve

Planning for the Organized Reserve, which was to be the heart of the peacetime women's program, continued based on the expected passage of enabling legislation. The Marine Corps was deeply committed to this concept and Major Hamblet and her staff worked out the details while at the same time they tried to maintain the interest of former women Reservists. At one time there was talk of 30 women's companies throughout the country. But, by 1947 this figure was reduced to 15 companies at 10 officers and 235 enlisted women each, for a total of 150 officers and 3,525 enlisted women.34 Reserve companies were planned for those cities with the greatest concentration of women Reservists and where interest was the most obvious.

During the year and a half before the law was finally passed, it was the intention of the Marine Corps to activate a Women's Reserve company in each of the following cities: Atlanta, Georgia; Boston, Massachusetts; Chicago, Illinois; Dallas, Texas; Detroit, Michigan; Indianapolis, Indiana; Los Angeles, California; New Orleans, Louisiana; New York, New York; Philadelphia, Pennsylvania; San Francisco, California; Seattle, Washington; St. Louis, Missouri; Toledo, Ohio; and Washington, D.C.

The legislative delay was frustrating and costly. In spite of efforts to keep the women interested, they drifted away and company-size units never materialized. (For a more thorough discussion of the women's Organized Reserve Program, see Chapter 3).

Release of the WRs Delayed Again

In February 1947, the first hashmark, the official insignia of a full four years of active duty and the traditional mark of a "salty" Marine, appeared on the uniform of Technical Sergeant Mary F. Wancheck.35 Others would soon sew them on. Just as the women were settling in and beginning to feel quite at home, the plan for their release was again under discussion.

The Assistant Commandant and Chief of Staff, Major General Lemuel C. Shepherd, Jr., seemed reluctant and on 17 April 1947, he sent a short memorandum to General Thomas: "Now that the time has come to discharge our WRs do you still want to go through with it? We will lose many good clerks, a number of whom are processing claims, etc."36 The predictable response was, "I feel that we must carry out these discharges. Only 23 of these WR's are working on claims."37

Careful coordination between work sections and the separation center was necessary to facilitate an orderly demobilization. The women were to be transferred to Quantico in groups of 20 per working day during the period from 13 June to 30 June in order to meet the deadline. Because the medical and administrative processing would take several days, it could not be done at Henderson Hall where WR barracks were no longer available. Work sections were assigned quotas of women to be released on a regular schedule to avoid a last-minute overload.

Hardly had the details been arranged when on 22 April, Colonel John Halla, Acting Chief of the Disbursing Branch, asked to keep 28 women Reservists on active duty until 31 December 1947 to work on a backlog of claims. The Commandant approved the request, bur, added a terse directive, ". . . see to it that they are not deviated to any other work."38

Contrary to the Commandant's published policy that all matters affecting the MCWR be submitted to the Director, MCWR, Major Hamblet was not consulted on the transaction involving the retention of the 28 women. She called this omission to the attention of the Director, Division of Reserve and reiterated:

The undersigned has stated her arguments against the retention of women on active duty either as reservists or as members of the regular Marine Corps. It is believed that all women who are not working on postwar plans for the MCWR should be discharged as expeditiously as possible. It is considered particularly unadvisable to retain a group as small as twenty-eight.39

Major Hamblet was fighting a losing battle. Not only were there more requests to keep women on active duty but some divisions wanted to call back already released women officers with special qualifications.

The case of Captain Edna Loftus Smith put the whole matter of WR retention back into the spotlight. She was recalled for membership on the Marine Corps , Aviation History Board. The Director of Aviation wrote: "This officer is peculiarly well qualified for this duty, more so than any officer in the Marine Corps, due to her wartime duties. . . "40

The legality of her recall opened a Pandora's box of legal considerations. How would she be paid? There was no authorization to use Reserve funds for matters connected to the war already fought and the Commandant had made no mention of women in his statement to Congress relative to the 1948 Reserve appropriations. Beyond the question of money, Brigadier General William T. Clement, Director, Division of Reserve, even doubted the authority to maintain WRs in the Volunteer Reserve under existing laws.

In spite of his uncertainty and due to the critical personnel shortage, he suggested that the Commandant's policy to discharge all WRs by 30 June be reversed. This would eliminate the problem of recalling individual Reservists and take care of the problem of pay since WRs on active duty were being paid from Regular Establishment funds.

Twenty-eight women were already being retained beyond the 30 June 1947 deadline to work on claims. "However," wrote General Clement, "claims cannot be settled until muster rolls are checked which justifies the retention of the WRs in that section, and by the same token, those on duty in the Decorations and Medals Section are working to clean up the war load."41 He believed it was better to keep all WRs on active duty on a voluntary basis until the passage of permanent legislation to resolve the situation. To ease the embarrassment caused by the constant shifting of dates and policy changes it was rationalized that the 30 June 1947 date was originally set with the idea that permanent legislation covering the women would have been enacted by that time.

Following General Clement's suggestion, a week later in early June, General Shepherd recommended the retention of WRs rather than approve a request that several hundred enlisted men be transferred to Headquarters. Since the efficiency of each woman Reservist was considered to be far greater than that of the average enlisted man to be brought in, he feared a marked loss in work output with the proposed changeover.

Thus another last-minute reprieve for the women at Headquarters arrived on 9 June when the final demobilization deadline was changed to read, ". . . for a period of six months after the war is declared over or such shorter time as meets the requirements of the Marine Corps."42

General Thomas once again asked that the previously published policy be strictly adhered to and that only the five officers actually working on the postwar program and the enlisted women kept as a result of the latest change be allowed to remain on active duty. He recommended that the other four women officers still on duty (Smith not included) be released as soon as their work was completed and that no more women officers be recalled except to fill a possible vacancy in the billets designated for the MCWR.* General Vandegrift's approving signature was a bittersweet victory, for next to the word, approved, he wrote "with the addition of one (1) WR officer for duty in the office of the J.A.G. (Judge Advocate General]."43

* At the time of General Thomas' memo, there were 10 women officers on active duty: Major Hamblet and Lieutenant Hale working on MCWR plans; Captain Illich working on matters related to the women kept on active duty, Captain Elizabeth J. Elrod and Captain Durant at the WR company; Major Frances W. Pepper and Second Lieutenant Pauline F. Riley at the Post War Personnel Reorganization Board; First Lieutenant Marie K. Anderson in the Supply Department; and Captain Sarah M. Vardy and Captain Smith in the Division of Aviation.

In the files of the Director of Women Marines was found an undated, unsigned, brief history of the women in the Marine Corps which begins:

It is rumored that when it was announced that women were going to be enlisted in the Marine Corps that the air was colored with profanity in the language of every nation as the members of the old Corps gathered to discuss this earth-shaking calamity. It is entirely probable that the wailing and moaning which went on that day amongst the old Marines was never equalled —never, that is, until it was announced that the women

Marines were going home. Then, with a complete reversal of attitude many of those same Marines declared that the women in their offices were essential military personnel and absolutely could not be spared from the office.'44

Stenographers Recalled A severe shortage of clerk-stenographers brought another demand for the recall of formerly active enlisted women Reservists. Few enlisted men were qualified and Civil Service was unable to fill the needs of Headquarters, so, in October 1947, 1,500 applications were mailed to women Reservists in the Volunteer Reserve. It came as a great surprise and disappointment when only 56 were returned —and of the number only 28 were considered qualified. The fact is that the letter soliciting applications was not very enticing. The maximum tour assured was for six months —the women could not request earlier release and the Marine Corps could not guarantee anything more.45

Among the women recommended for recall were Staff Sergeant Lotus T. Mort, who later became the third woman warrant officer in 1954; Corporal Mildred A. Novotny, who was among the first eight enlisted women to be sworn into the Regular Marine Corps on 10 November 1948; and Technical Sergeant Helen L. Hannah, who retired in 1975 with 32 years' service as a Reservist. Lotus Mort recalled that she was a bit hesitant when her orders arrived on Christmas Eve, but on 5 January 1948, she reported for six months and stayed for 17 years until her retirement in 1965. The poor response to the call for stenographers was the first indication that competent women needed to be assured of more security if they were going to leave their homes and good jobs. Colonel Knighton's prediction of 1946 had come to pass.

Col Katherine A. Towle cuts cake on the 6th anniversary in February 1949 of the Marine Corps Women's Reserve. Mrs. Ruth Cheney Streeter looks on. In the background (from left to right) are TSgt Grace L. Benjamin, Cpl Emilie Pranckevich, TSgt Agnes T. Hirshinger, SSgt May Ann Henritze, MSgt Marie B. Benziger, and Sgt Elsie F. Futterman.

CHAPTER 2

Women's Armed Forces Legislation: Public Law 625

Women's Armed Forces Legislation —Provisions of Public Law 625

Women's Armed Forces Legislation

Nearly three years elapsed from the end of hostilities in August 1945 until legislation giving women regular military status was finally passed and signed into law by President Harry S. Truman on 12 June 1948. The drawn-out process, marked by gains and reverses along the way, was the cause of much of the uncertainty experienced by women Marines on duty at Headquarters. Without the legislation there was no security for those women, and no one knows how many competent WRs, who would have preferred a career in the Marine Corps, asked to be discharged simply because they could not afford to wait.

The proposed law received little support from the Commandant —and for some very good reasons. The Marine Corps had an authorized regular enlisted strength of 100,000 and then as now, operated on a limited budget. Understandably, neither the men nor the women wanted to sacrifice combat billets to make room for the women. General Vandegrift was heartily in favor of women as Regular Marines provided they would not count against his end strength; otherwise, he was unalterably opposed.

A study of the position taken by the other services regarding the women's bill reveals that the Army and the Navy intended to use large numbers of women in occupational fields not required in the Marine Corps. There was a strong case made, for example, for women in the medical field: nurses, Medical Corps WAVES, dental technicians, and laboratory technicians. Furthermore, they contended that these billets which were planned for the WAVES and the WACs would not affect overseas rotation of the men. This was not the situation in the Marine Corps.

* Colonels Streeter and Towle, although no longer on active duty, were frequently consulted on matters relating to the postwar plans for the women in the Marine Corps.

The senior women officers, Colonels Streeter and Towle and Major Hamblet, were aware of the unique problems faced by the Commandant, and they were also conscious of the climate at Headquarters* They recognized exactly how far the Marine Corps would be willing to go and believed that a crusade by the women would have had negative results. The plan for a strong Women's Organized Reserve backed up by a Volunteer Reserve was a compromise that most Marines could accept, and this was the proposal they carried to Capitol Hill.

The Honorable Carl Vinson, on 29 March 1946, introduced H.R. 5919, "To amend the Naval Reserve Act of 1938, as amended, so as to establish the Women's Reserve on a permanent basis . . . ." (79th Congress, 2d session). As the purpose clearly states, the bill was strictly a Reserve measure and in its original form allowed the Marine Corps only 50 officers and 450 enlisted women on active duty during peacetime. It was referred to the Committee on Naval Affairs and hearings were held on 9 and 10 May.

In her book, Lady In The Navy, Captain Joy Hancock notes, "The burden of presentation before that committee was carried largely by the members of the Women's Reserve who were not in a position of sufficient authority to speak with the necessary assurance of Navy plans and policies."1 Colonel Towle, the Commandant's representative, prepared a short statement summarizing the plans for a Reserve organization with an active duty strength of 32 officers and 28 enlisted women —at the most.2

American military women enjoy a relationship of unusual cooperation. Perhaps it stems from the shared experience of being a minority in a previously all-male world. For whatever reasons, they have made it a point of honor to be mutually supportive. Accordingly, when the time came to testify before the committee, Colonel Towle was careful not to undermine the much stronger WAVE position.

After the initial hearings in the House, Admiral Denfeld enlisted the aid of Congresswoman Margaret Chase Smith, who had taken a public stand in favor of Regular status for service women. Mrs. Smith had been cautioned by the chairman, Carl Vinson, that her amendment to include Regular as well as Reserve status would kill the whole bill.3 Mrs. Smith's view was, "The Navy either needs these women or they do not. . . .""

As a result of the efforts of Admiral Denfeld and Mrs. Smith, a new draft was prepared which would extend the scope of existing laws governing the Regular Navy and Marine Corps to include women. For all that, time ran out before further action was taken. When the 79th Congress adjourned, the women's bill died in committee. Consequently, it would be necessary to begin fresh at the next session.

The women in the Army worked on a separate bill until the armed services were combined to become the Department of Defense. At that time, the women joined forces in order to present as strong a case as possible while allowing for the unavoidable differences.

Added to the varied duties assigned to Major Hamblet when she returned to active duty in the fall of

1946 was the task of tracking the pending legislation. Sandwiched between the planning of the postwar Reserve, and the vain attempt to demobilize the wartime WRs, she studied and commented on the women's bill and made occasional appearances before congressional committees. She was asked verbally by Colonel Pate to submit, "arguments against keeping women on active duty in the Marine Corps either as reservists on continuous active duty or as members of the Regular establishment." She did so in a 29 April 1947 memo, ending with the statement:

If it is decided that women shall be on active duty for an indefinite period of time, their rights should be protected by making them members of the Regular establishment of the Marine Corps rather than keeping them on continuous active duty as reservists.5

By the time the Senate subcommittee hearings of the 80th Congress began on 2 July 1947, the Navy bill S. 1529 and the Army bill S. 1103 were combined to form S. 1641. Most observers were certain that women were going to be made part of the Regular Armed Forces. General of the Army Dwight D. Eisenhower opened his testimony saying, "Not only do I heartily support the bill to integrate women into the Regular Army and Organized Reserve Corps, but I personally directed that such legislation be drawn up and submitted to this Congress."6 A critical shortage of infantrymen and the need to stabilize the Women's Army Corps prompted him to stress the urgency of action to the Congress.

General Eisenhower was followed by Fleet Admiral Chester W. Nimitz who said, "The real fact must be acknowledged that in any future war it will be mandatory to have at our command immediately all possible resources. Womenpower is one of them."7 It should be noted that the Allies made good use of women in the armed services in World War II.*

* In an interview in October 1976 in Heidelberg, Germany, Albert Speer, Hitler's weapons production chief said: "How wise you were to bring your women into your military and into your labor force. Had we done that initially, as you did, it could have affected the whole course of the war. Women would have been far superior, for example, to our impressed labor force from occupied countries, which you called 'slave labor.' We would have found out, as you did, that women were equally effective, and for some skills superior to males. We never did, despite our critical manpower shortage in the late years of the war, make use of this great potential." (San Diego Union, 30 Nov 76).

Colonel Knighton followed, reading a brief, two-sentence Marine Corps statement: "The previous witnesses have expressed the views of the Commandant; the Commandant of the Marine Corps is in favor of the bill and trusts that it will be enacted as soon as possible."8

The brevity and the wording of the statement cast some doubt on the Commandant's true feelings. In order to offset its negative effect at Headquarters, Colonel Knighton sent a memorandum to the Assistant Commandant, General Shepherd, along with a file of statements given before the Senate Armed Services Committee which he said:

. . . contain almost unrefutable arguments why: it is vital that women be integrated into the Regular Establishment of all services.

I informed the Senate Committee that the views expressed by these witnesses reflected the views of the Commandant.

As it has been rumored that the Commandant is opposed to having women in the Regular Marine Corps, it might be well to circulate these statements to the heads of all Departments and offices.9

Colonel Knighton was perhaps the strongest voice heard in the Marine Corps in favor of integration of the women. As legal aide to the Commandant, legislation was his responsibility but he seemed to go a step further in an effort to convince others of the need for this particular bill. He went so far as to testify at a

Senate hearing in place of Major Hamblet when he feared that she, due to her own doubts, would not be convincing enough. The bill passed the Senate on 23 July 1947 and was sent to the House committee where it sat until the adjournment of the first session, but this time it would not be necessary to begin anew.

In anticipation of the enactment of the legislation, a board was convened in December 1947 to propose a program for women as Regular Marines. Keeping in mind that every woman in the Regular Marine Corps would be at the expense of a man, careful thought was given to their most efficient utilization. The study, therefore, provided for 65 officers and 728 enlisted women to be assigned to Headquarters Marine Corps, both at Henderson Hall and the Marine Corps Institute; offices of the directors of the Marine Corps Reserve Districts; Headquarters Recruiting Divisions; Department of Pacific and Depot of Supplies at San Francisco; Marine Corps Schools, Quantico; and to the Organized Women's Reserve Program.10

Congresswoman Margaret Chase Smith of Maine.

In February 1948 just before the House Armed Services Committee was scheduled to meet, Captain Ira H. Nunn of the Navy Judge Advocate General's office wrote to the Commandant asking for his help. In view of the considerable opposition to the bill, a strong presentation was deemed necessary, and plans were being made for appearances by the Secretary of Defense, the Chief of Naval Operations, the Chief of Naval Personnel, and the Deputy Surgeon General. The letter read:

Advice is requested as to whether the Commandant can appear in support of the bill It is understood that the Departments of the Army and Air Force will be represented by Generals Eisenhower, Bradley, Spaatz, Devers, Paul, Armstrong, and Strothers."11 *

* General of the Army Dwight D. Eisenhower; General Omar N. Bradley, Chief of Staff of the Army; General Carl T. Spaatz, Commanding General, Army Air Forces; General Jacob L. Devers, Commanding General, Army Ground Forces; Lieutenant General Willard S. Paul, Director of Personnel Administration, General Staff, United States Army; Brigadier General Harry G. Armstrong, U.S. Army Air Forces, Commandant of the School of Aviation Medicine; Brigadier General Dean C. Strothers, U.S. Army Air Forces, Director of Military Personnel under Deputy Chief of Staff, Personnel and Administration.

The Marine Corps was represented at those crucial hearings by Major Hamblet, who was introduced by Colonel Knighton.

The hearings were heated and prolonged, but the outcome seemed assured. To almost everyone's surprise, however, in early April, the committee reported out a measure which would have limited enlistment of women in the armed services to Reserve status only. During the debate, Margaret Chase Smith tried to get House approval of the Senate version, but only 40 members backed her while 66 were opposed. The opponents argued that, "Regular status for women in the military service now might result in a draft for women in another war and West Point would become a coeducational college."12 The solution seemed to be to put women in a Reserve status.

The bill, S. 1641, then went into a joint conference by members of both the Senate and the House to reconsider the differences. Support came from patriotic organizations, professional and business women groups, and most importantly from the ranking military men of the day. Fleet Admiral Nimitz, Chief of Naval Operations, in backing the legislation said:

This legislation has been requested after careful study of the overall requirements of the Navy, now and in the future. It is the considered opinion of the Navy Department and my own personal belief that the services of women are needed. Their skills are as important to the efficient operations of the naval establishment during peacetime as they were during the war years.13

The bill that emerged from the joint conference established a Women's Army Corps in the Regular Army, authorized the enlistment and appointment of women in the Regular Navy and the Regular Marine Corps and the Navy and Marine Corps Reserve, and the Regular and Reserve of the newly created Air Force in which the women would be known as WAFs (Women in the Air Force). Ten days later, 12 June 1948, President Truman signed the long-debated Women's Armed Services Integration Act, Public Law 625.

Provisions of Public Law 625

Generally, P. L. 625 gave equal status to women in uniform, but there were a number of restrictions and special provisions. While the law placed no limit on the number of women who could serve in the Reserves, it did specify that the number of women Regulars could not exceed two percent of the nation's total armed strength in the Regular Army, Navy, Air Force, and Marines. It provided for a gradual build-up which would allow the Marine Corps a strength of 100 officers, 10 warrant officers, and 1,000 enlisted women by June 1950. In fact the Marine Corps did not anticipate or want to fill the allotted quota.

Based upon a strong recommendation from Mrs. Streeter, the new law contained the provision that the Director of Women Marines would be detailed to duty in the office of the Commandant to assist the Commandant in the administration of women's affairs. Originally, she, like the WAVE director, would have been responsible to the Personnel Department. Mrs. Streeter, in response to a letter from General Vandegrift in August 1947, recalled her duty in the Personnel Department and the limitations under which she worked during the war. She gave great credit to the courtesy and cooperation of all the men at Headquarters with whom she worked, but she argued that the Director would be in a better position to deal with all branches, and that her cognizance over all women Marines and all matters affecting them would be recognized if she did not come under one particular branch.17 General Vandegrift agreed and the women's bill was amended before it came to the final vote. For all services, the director was to be selected from among the Regular women officers serving in the grade of major or above (lieutenant commander for the Navy) and would hold the temporary rank of colonel or Navy captain.

Promotion regulations loosely paralleled those of male components, except that women could not hold permanent rank above lieutenant colonel. Additionally, the number of Regular women lieutenant colonels could not exceed 10 percent of the number of Regular women officers on active duty —for majors, the law read 20 percent.* Inasmuch as lieutenant colonel was the senior grade that women officers could then hold (with the exception of the Director), non-promotion to this rank was not considered a passover. Women officers retired from the senior ranks upon reaching a mandatory retirement age which was for majors, 20 years or age 50, whichever came sooner, and for lieutenant colonel, 30 years' service or age 55, whichever was sooner. The law also specified that women could not be assigned to duty in aircraft engaged in combat missions nor to vessels of the Navy other than transport and hospital ships.

* The provision held up a number of promotions to field grade rank. In 1962, Captain Grace "San" Oberholser Fields stayed on active duty longer than she intended after her marriage in order to keep up the strength figures of the Regular active duty women officers, thereby allowing Major Jeannette I. Sustad, a future Director of Women Marines, to be promoted to lieutenant colonel. (Grace Overholser Fields interview with HQMC).

Women were entitled to the same pay, leave, allowances, and benefits as men, but with an important proviso. Husbands would not be considered dependents unless they were in fact dependent on their wives for their chief support, and the children of servicewomen would not be considered dependents unless their fathers were dead or they were really dependent upon their mothers for their chief support. This apparently simple exception was the cause of much frustration and bitterness as the law was interpreted over the years. In effect, it negated many of the service benefits normally considered routine by the men. For example, quarters could not be assigned to a woman married to a civilian, nor could her husband shop at the post exchange or commissary store.*

* For a detailed discussion of marriage, motherhood, and dependent husbands, sett Chapter 13.

The Marines especially appreciated the section of the law dealing with the Reserves for it made possible, at last, the much-discussed Organized Women's Reserve. Nearly two years had passed since Major Hamblet had been called to active duty to frame the postwar women's plans which, by this time, were laid out in great detail and ready for implementation.

Women were now a part of the Regular Marine Corps in spite of earlier opposition to this radical idea. In the spring of 1946, when the legislation was first introduced, no one, least of all the women themselves, ever thought in terms of Regular status. As time went on, however, there was increasing evidence that no really effective and continuing nucleus of trained personnel could be counted on in the Defense Establishment unless some permanency was assured women who volunteered for training and assignment in peacetime.

The passage of the Women's Armed Services Integration Act of 1948 recognized this fact and was a natural sequel to the excellent record of the women who served in World War II.

Col Ruth Cheney Streeter, wartime Director of the Marine Corps Women's Reserve, before leaving her post recommended that the position be strengthened, a proposal which lead ultimately to the Marine Corps amendment to Public Law 625 and placement of the Director in the table of organization of the immediate office of the Commandant.

CHAPTER 3

Going Regular

The Transfer Program — Establishing the Office and Title, Director of Women Marines The First Enlisted Women Marines — The Pioneers — Reindoctrination of the Officers - Reindoctrination of Enlisted WMs — Designation of Women Marines - Recruit Training Established at Parris Island — The First Black Women Marines - Establishing the Women Officers' Training Class at Quantico

The Transfer Program

The integration of women was now a fait accompli, and in Colonel Towle's view, ". . . the Marine Corps had, with varying degrees of enthusiasm but always in good grace, accepted the fact that women as potential 'careerists' in the Marine Corps must be reckoned with and provided for."1 To this end, the first step was to find a suitable Director, but the process of transfer from Reserve to Regular could not wait for her selection, acceptance, and arrival.

Major Hamblet, still the Director of the Marine Corps Women's Reserve, recommended Colonel Towle be named to that post. Although the press had announced that the services would probably retain the current directors, and certainly she was the one most familiar with the plans to be implemented, Major Hamblet recognized that her age and rank would work to her and ultimately to the women's disadvantage. There would be, she was certain, a good deal of opposition to the appointment to colonel —even on a temporary basis —of a 33-year-old woman with only five years of military experience.2 Colonel Towle, on the other hand, was happily ensconced as the Assistant Dean of Women at the Berkeley campus of the University of California, and she felt that Major Hamblet should continue as Director.

General Clifton B. Cates, then Commandant, found himself in the uncomfortable and certainly unusual position of personally having to ask a woman to accept a Regular commission. In the summer of 1948, his aide called Colonel Towle to tell her that the Commandant was planning an official trip to California and wished to meet with her in San Francisco at the Saint Francis Hotel. At the ensuing interview, Colonel Towle was not prepared to make a definite commitment to return, but she and General Cates discussed details of organization and particularly the position of the Director and her access to the Commandant.3 The general agreed to consider her recommendations and to talk them over with his advisors at Headquarters. The outcome was the appointment of Colonel Katherine A. Towle as the first Director of Women Marines.

Admittedly, she was one of the women who originally had grave doubts about the need or even desirability of having women in the military during peacetime, but on thinking it over, she said, "the logic of the whole thing did occur to me: that this was sound. . . ."4 Any uncertainties she entertained were set aside once and for all when she returned to Washington in the fall of 1948, and she undertook her work determined to make the women truly integrated, contributing members of the Corps.

In July, while the matter of a director was still unsettled, letters containing information about the transfer program were sent to women Reservists and former women Reservists. The women were to be selected based upon their qualifications to fill the 65 officer and 728 enlisted billets. Of the 65 officers selected, 21 would receive Regular commissions and 44 would be assigned as Reservists on continuous active duty, presumably with the Organized Reserve companies.5

Since 18,000 enlisted women had served in World War II, it was not anticipated that nonveterans would be accepted for perhaps nine months to a year after the transfer program got underway. A continuing board would be convened at Headquarters to select applicants at the rate of 75 per month until the planned strength was reached. After that, several recruit classes per year would be conducted at Henderson Hall to compensate for losses due to normal attrition. It was estimated that no more than 200 recruits would be needed during the first two years.6

Former enlisted Reservists could enlist for two, three, or four years, and had to meet the following requirements: be 20-31 years old; have two years of high school or business school; be a citizen of the United States or its insular possessions; be married or single; have no children under 18 years of age regardless of legal custody; have no dependents; be able to pass the prescribed physical examination; and possess an honorable or under-honorable-conditions discharge. The deadline for receipt of applications was set at 15 September 1948. 7

In the case of officers, the flow of promotions as well as available billets had to be considered. It was decided that the 21 initial selections for Regular status should be allocated to: majors and above, two; captains, five; first lieutenants, seven; and second lieutenants, seven. All officers and former officers were sent letters similar to the ones used to solicit enlisted candidates. The promise of security in these was a bit vague in that they were told, "Subject to budgetary limitations and satisfactory performance of duty, applicants ate assured at least a 3-year tour of duty. . . ." And following the details of the projected officer candidate class was written, "As these new officers are obtained, the Reserve officers on continuous active duty will be ordered to inactive duty."8

To be considered for transfer to the Regular Marine Corps, women officers had to have completed two years of accredited college work or pass an equivalent examination; be physically qualified; have no children under 18 years of age; and fit into a complicated age-grade structure which would protect them later from mandatory, involuntary retirement.

The enlisted selection board convened on 21 September with Colonel Lester S. Hamel as senior member. The first report, submitted on 4 October, recommended the approval of 142 applicants and the tentative approval of 45 others subject to age and physical waivers.9

It became increasingly apparent and by late September it was conclusive that the number of enlisted applicants was below expectation and the quota would not be reached. The cause of the disappointing response is a matter of speculation. First, there is no evidence that large numbers of women were interested in a military career. During the congressional hearings on the women's armed services legislation, the voice of the woman veteran was not heard. Then, the age group involved was vulnerable to marriage and motherhood, and while marriage itself was not a prohibiting factor to enlistment, it certainly was a deterrent. Finally, the physical standards were quite stringent and the age restrictions for officers were, at the very least, difficult. The women officers of World War II were, by and large, older than average when compared to men of the same rank.

On 4 November 1948, Commandant of the Marine Corps Gen Clifton B. Cates administers the oath to the first three women to be sworn into the Regular Marine Corps, (left to right) LtCol Katherine A. Towle, Maj Julia E. Hamblet, and 1stLt Mary J. Hale.

A Plans and Policy Division study of 24 September 1948 recommended that the grade distribution for officers be revised in light of the applications received; that the deadline for enlisted applications be extended to 1 January; that officer applications be forwarded to the board for consideration regardless of ineligibility for age or physical condition; that applications for new enlistments by nonveterans be authorized; and that recruit classes begin by 1 March 1949. 10

Many of the recommendations were approved. The enlisted transfer program was extended and age and physical waivers were granted, but the problem of opening up the program to nonveterans was set aside. And, indeed, at the time it was a problem. The Marine Corps was not yet racially integrated and to open enlistments meant to face "the Negro question." Furthermore, it required the hasty establishment and staffing of a recruit training command for women.

In spite of the liberalized reenlistment procedures, less than 350 applications were received and about 25 percent of these came from WRs on duty at Headquarters.11 Even as Colonel Towle arrived on 18 October, suggestions, plans, and recommendations for the reenlistment, recruitment, and training of women Marines were being discussed and changed almost daily. The paucity of applicants for the transfer program demanded new thinking.

The officer transfer program, for its part, moved relatively smoothly requiring only a few changes in rank distribution. On 26 October the names of the 21 Regular officers selectees were announced. The list included 1 colonel, 2 majors, 7 captains, and 11 first lieutenants. Not counting Colonel Towle, who had recently reported aboard, only Major Hamblet and Lieutenant Hale were on active duty at the time of selection. The initial list of women recommended for Regular commissions named:

Colonel Katherine A. Towle

Major Julia E. Hamblet

Major Pauline E. Perate

Captain Pauline B. Beckley

Captain Barbara J. Bishop

Captain Margaret M. Henderson

Captain Emma H. Hendrickson

Captain Elsie E. Hill

Captain Helen J. McGraw

Captain Nancy M. Roberts

First Lieutenant Kathleen J. Arney

First Lieutenant Eunyce L. Brink

First Lieutenant Ben Alice Day

First Lieutenant Frances A. Denbo

First Lieutenant Mary J. Fisher

First Lieutenant Jeanne Fleming

First Lieutenant Mary J. Hale

First Lieutenant Margaret S. Ordemann

First Lieutenant Pauline F. Riley

First Lieutenant Margaret L. Stevenson

First Lieutenant Jeanette I. Sustad 12

The Commandant of the Marine Corps, General Cates, administered the oath to the first women to become Regular Marines, Lieutenant Colonel Towle, Major Hamblet, and Lieutenant Hale, in his office on 4 November 1948. On the previous day, Colonel Towle had been discharged as a colonel from the Marine Corps Reserve. Upon accepting a Regular commission, she was appointed a permanent lieutenant colonel, and then, assuming the position of director, she was promoted to the temporary rank of colonel once again.

Establishing the Office and Title, Director of Women Marines

In an analysis of the wartime Marine Corps Women's Reserve written in 1945, the authors, very diplomatically, but very clearly, pointed out the handicap under which Colonel Streeter worked —as an advisor with no real authority of her own. The report explained:

. . . the first real problem confronting the Marine Corps was what to do with the Director, MCWR. There really did not seem to be much place for her. Certainly she could not "direct" anything without cutting squarely across all official channels and chains of command, and creating divided responsibility at all points.

Luckily, Colonel Streeter had great good sense, and a wonderful knack for getting along with people, for it was through the medium of friendly relations with department heads and commanding officers that she eventually gained their confidence so that. . . suggestions could be made to them with some hope of success.13.

Colonel Streeter rightfully concluded that the middle of a war was no time to quibble over administrative and organizational details, but before leaving the Marine Corps, she respectfully made the recommendation that, " . a new study be made by the Division of Plans and Policies embodying the experience of this war as to the best possible use which can be made of a Director, MCWR, in case of another war," and "That her position be strengthened if this can be properly done within the structure of the Marine Corps."14.

Colonel Streeter was ultimately responsible for the Marine Corps amendment to P. L. 625 which placed the Director in the table of organization of the immediate office of the Commandant. While serving as Director of the MCWR between September 1946 and November 1948, Major Hamblet continually strived to maintain some degree of control over all matters that affected the women. When Colonel Towle was asked to return as the first Regular Director, the clarification of this one issue was a factor in her acceptance. Clearly, to the most senior women officers, the position of the Director of Women Marines was a matter of concern. This position was defined in a study of 20 October 1948 which stated:

In establishing the office and title of the senior woman Marine, consideration is given to the following:

(a) An important aspect is the field of public relations, involving contacts outside of the Marine Corps. To insure maximum prestige and effectiveness in these duties, it is necessary that the senior woman Marine hold a title which indicates a position of importance in the Marine Corps.

(b) This officer must have cognizance of all matters pertaining to women Marines, Regular and Reserve, even though such matters are handled by the appropriate Headquarters agency in the same manner as for other Marines. Assigning actual administration and control of women Marines to existing agencies precludes establishment of a separate division or department to carry out such functions. Under these circumstances, the senior woman Marine could best exercise cognizance over matters in her sphere if she were established as an assistant to the Commandant for woman Marine matters. In this capacity she could initiate action on matters affecting women Marines or make recommendations on policies and procedures concerning them but prepared by other agencies.15

The recommendations were approved and the senior woman Marine was called the Director of Women Marines. Due directly to the efforts of Colonels Streeter and Towle and Major Hamblet between 1945 and 1948, the Director of Women Marines enjoyed a somewhat autonomous role, able to attend the Commandant's staff meetings in her own right, and able to bring to the Commandant or to a division head any conflict which she felt merited his attention.

The First Enlisted Women Marines

The enlisted WRs stationed at Headquarters lost no time in applying for Regular status, and, by November, Colonel Towle was most anxious that the 210 already selected women be sworn in as soon as possible in order to generate some favorable publicity and interest. On the 173rd anniversary of the Marine Corps, 10

November 1948, the first eight women, all WRs on duty at Headquarters Marine Corps, were given the oath of enlistment by the Commandant. Seven of those women, Master Sergeant Elsie J. Miller, Technical Sergeants Bertha L. Peters and Mary F. Wancheck, and Staff Sergeants Margaret A. Goings, Anna Peregrim, Betty J. Preston, and Mary E. Roche, had been on continuous active duty since their enlistment for wartime service. The eighth, Sergeant Mildred A. Novotny, had responded to the call for stenographers made in late 1947. The eight new women Marines were enlisted at the same rank that they held in the Reserve.18

On 10 November 1948, the Commandant, Gen Clifton B. Cates, administers the enlistment oath to the first eight women sworn into the Regular Marine Corps, (left to right) MSgt Elsie J. Miller, TSgt Bertha L. Peters, SSgt Betty J. Preston, SSgt Margaret A. Goings, Sgt Mildred A. Novotny, TSgt Mary F. Wancheck, SSgt Anna Peregrim, and SSgt Mary E. Roche. Col Katherine A. Towle, Director of Women Marines, is at far right.

A WR at Headquarters during that period, retired First Sergeant Esther D. Waclawski, remembered that she had already spent two days in Separation Company when the transfer program was announced. She and her friend, Technical Sergeant Petrina "Pete" C. Nigro, rushed to the recruiting station on Pennsylvania Avenue to "join the Marines." Although on active duty, these women had to follow the same procedures as former WRs all over the country.17 Upon acceptance, they were issued the usual travel orders with the senior woman put in charge. Typical of the travel orders of the time was a set dated 17 November 1948 and addressed to Master Sergeant Alice Julia Connolly, which read:

Having been enlisted this date in the USMC-W, you will, when directed, take charge of the below named women and proceed this date to Headquarters Battalion, Headquarters U.S. Marine Corps, Washington, D.C, where upon your arrival you and the women in your charge will report to the Commanding Officer thereat for duty.

Technical Sergeant Marion Olson Barnes

Technical Sergeant Anna Marie Scherman

Staff Sergeant June Virginia Andler

Staff Sergeant Rose Mary Barnes

Staff Sergeant Wilma Greifenstein

Staff Sergeant Jeanette Marie Johnson

Staff Sergeant Vera Eleanor Piippo

Sergeant Ruby Alwilda Evans

Sergeant Bertha Janice Schultz

As no transportation is involved none is furnished.18

Since it is safe to assume that a group of senior NCOs is not likely to get lost on the way to the battalion to which they are already attached, the orders must have been issued because "it is always done that way."

The Pioneers

The original band of women in the Regular Marine Corps, now to be known as WMs, must have been an adventuresome lot. They had little idea of what was in store for them, either in the way of assignments, length of service, or acceptance by the men of the Marine Corps. Colonel Margaret M. Henderson, later to be a Director of Women Marines, recalled that she applied more or less to see if she could make it. Lieutenant Colonel Elsie Eleanor Hill submitted her application with the thought in mind that she would probably be stationed at home, in Philadelphia, where she had spent her entire wartime tour.19 The Inspector-Instructor of the Reserve unit there told her of the plans for an organized platoon in the "City of Brotherly Love."

Lieutenant Colonel Emma Hope Hendrickson Clowers, reminiscing about her feelings when she was sworn into the Regular Marine Corps on 3 December 1948, said:

I think most women officers in the first group who came back as regular officers wondered how we would be received by the career Marines. . . . We knew there had been no lack of enthusiasm on the part of the men for the many thousands of us who enlisted during WW II to lend a hand and "FREE A MAN TO FIGHT"-our WW II motto. But that was quite a different situation from one in which we were returning as career officers and would inevitably be in competition with them in varying degrees. It therefore was with much pleasure and surprise that, through the efforts of a male officer and his men, I was made to feel that they were happy and proud to welcome me back in the Marine Corps as a regular officer. At that time I was completing some studies at the University of Southern California and was ordered to report to the CO, MB, NB, [Commanding Officer, Marine Barracks, Naval Base] Long Beach to be sworn into the Regular Marine Corps. The CO (Lieutenant Colonel Charles T. Hodges] put on a formal parade, with all his men in dress blues and held the swearing in ceremony on the parade grounds, followed by a reception in my honor. Pictures and a write-up appeared in two of the L.A. papers and in the USC paper. I think this first experience as a regular officer not only made me feel that I was again a part of the Marine Corps but also served to erase my doubts as to acceptance as a regular officer.20

Reindoctrination of the Officers

In view of the long period of inactive service for most of the returning women —over two years for some — Colonel Towle planned a short reindoctrination course to be held at Henderson Hall. The onetime class of 17 of the new officers was scheduled for 13 to 17 December under the direction of Captain Illich. Then one of these officers was to be selected to conduct similar training classes for the enlisted women to begin in January.21

Reindoctrination for the officers included classes in administration, naval law, military customs and courtesies, leadership, recruiting, and a discussion of the role of women in the Regular services. There was a myriad of administrative details to attend to and then there was the matter of "close order drill."

In her wisdom, Colonel Towle asked for an indoor hall where the officers could drill unobserved, and so the Post Theater at Henderson Hall became their drill field. But the colonel underestimated the drawing power of the sight of women officers in a military formation trying to recapture the marching precision of their "candidate days." Enlisted men crowded in the doorways and enlisted women filled the projection booth to watch the group in which, retired First Sergeant Betty Schultz remembered, "Each officer had a step of her own."22 To make matters worse, the floor was slippery and the women were self-conscious of their too short, and in some cases too tight uniforms in front of the onlookers and in particular in front of the handsome drill instructor, First Lieutenant William H. Lanagan, Jr., later to be a brigadier general.

Most of those women had never expected to return to the Marine Corps and were lucky if they had even one uniform as a souvenir of their days in the Corps. After the war, skirt lengths dropped drastically with the arrival of the fashion called "The New Look." Lengthening skirts became a major preoccupation. "We were very interested in looking each other over to see how we managed to put together a uniform," recalled Colonel Henderson. Like the other tall women, her only recourse had been to insert a piece of fabric just below the skirt waistband. This meant, of course, that she could never remove her jacket.23

They had the opportunity to order new uniforms from the tailor during the week of reindoctrination, but there was no solution to the problem of the fashionable longer skirts hanging several inches below the short overcoats. Major General William P. T. Hill, the Quartermaster General, insisted upon depleting the wartime supply of uniforms before ordering new ones but later he relented and bought longer skirts which, of course, did not match the five-year-old jackets.24

It is likely, believing that they had seen the last of the women, that the Marines sold WR uniforms to surplus dealers after the war. Although no documents have been found to prove it, the evidence is convincing. When PL. 625 was finally signed by President Truman, a surplus dealer came to Headquarters and offered to sell WR uniforms to Lieutenant Hale. There is a well-known story of a former woman Reservist shopping in a Pittsburgh department store and finding all the elevator operators dressed in Marine uniforms complete with the distinctive buttons. But perhaps the worst incident of all is the one told by Colonel Hamblet. Among the novelties for sale by a concessionaire at the circus was a woman Marine uniform hat. There was but one displayed and she bought it.25

Next to the uniform problem, the officers in that first group were confronted by the postwar Washington housing shortage. Although some expected to be permanently stationed in the area, others knew that their stay was temporary. Tired of paying exorbitant rates in a downtown hotel, about 10 of them rented several unfurnished apartments in Shirlington (Arlington, Virginia), a few miles from Marine Corps Headquarters. Captain Hill, the OIC (Officer in Charge) of the enlisted reindoctrination program, was able to borrow cots, dressers, and mess rabies from Headquarters Battalion, Henderson Hall, and thus allow the women to set up "squadbays" in the empty apartments. A card table and chairs were loaned by newly arrived Senator Hubert H. Humphrey, when his secretary, June Hendrickson, joined the group.26

Reindoctrination of Enlisted WMs

Beginning in January 19^9, Captain Hill supervised a series of enlisted reindoctrination classes and had an office at Henderson Hall. The women had to be issued uniforms, reclassified, and given refresher classes in military subjects. As with the officers, much time was spent on administrative matters such as allotments, savings bond purchases, issuance of new identification cards and tags (dog tags), photographs, and physicals. The WMs attended the five-day class in groups of 15 and were billeted in the former dispensary during the course.

Twenty-seven women Reservists living on the west coast were selected for transfer to Regular status and Captain Illich went to the Headquarters of the Department of Pacific in San Francisco in late January to conduct their training on the spot. In a letter to the commanding general, Major General Leroy P. Hunt, Colonel Towle explained the reindoctrination course and made assurances that Captain Illich could handle it with a minimum of effort on the part of the general's staff. She also told him of her intention to assign First Lieutenant Margaret Stevenson to the Department of Pacific. Tactfully, she wrote:

As you probably know, it was always the policy in the MCWR to have at least one woman officer detailed to duty at a post or station where enlisted women were serving, who in addition to her regular assignment, could have general supervision over their welfare, appearance, etc. and to whom they could go for advice and information if they wanted to. I believe such a policy is sound and highly desirable for many reasons.

Lieutenant Stevenson has had Quartermaster training, but can, I feel certain, do almost any kind of administrative work. She had an excellent record as a Reserve officer, is most conscientious and sincere, and very pleased with her assignment. I am sure you too will be pleased to have such a competent woman officer as our first "regular" representative in your Headquarters. Since she comes from California, she is as amazed as she is pleased that the Marine Corps is sending her back there for duty.

Forgive this long letter, but I thought this information might be of interest and assistance to you in your consideration of plans for the coming invasion of Women Marines.27

While the Director of Women Marines personally selected women officers with specific billets in mind, she was totally aware that assignment is a command prerogative and that she had no authority once the woman reported to her duty station. Colonel Towle, in her gracious way, developed the peacetime women's organization in a spirit of cooperation rather than competition with the male Marines. After the initial doubts and outright opposition to the integration of women, it came as a pleasant surprise when the men not only tolerated the female presence but went out of their way to help them get established.

Designation of Women Marines

A Marine Corps Memorandum, dated 16 November 1948, directed that women entering the Regular Marine Corps be referred to as "Women Marines," with "USMC-W" as the short title or reporting form. The identification of Reservists would be "USMCR-W."28 Colonel Towle took great exception to the "W" and the proper designation of women Marines became one of her first priorities. She suggested an alternative in a memorandum which stated:

It is believed the apparent inconsistencies can be resolved if the "W" as indicator of a woman Marine were used with the service number rather than as a component designator. For example: Second Lieutenant Jane Doe, USMC (W050123) (0105) or for a reservist, Sergeant Jane Doe, USMCR (W755123) (0143). This is clear and concise, and would be used in every instance in official correspondence, orders, records, and publications where the service number is customarily indicated. It would also be evidence, which the Director of Women Marines considers important for the morale and prestige of the women, that women are an integral part of the Marine Corps or the Marine Corps Reserve, and not relegated to a specially constituted women's component as USMC-W and USMCR-W imply.29

Her plan met with some opposition. While one staff comment noted the naval tradition to identify non-combatant components; for example, Captain Joe Doe (MC), another suggested the idea could be carried to the extreme and cooks would be designated Corporal Joe Doe, USMC-C. Written, staffed, and rewritten, the recommendation was finally approved on 17 March 1950 and thereafter the "W" was placed before the serial number of women Marines.30

In the same vein, Colonel Towle preferred the word "women" to "female," and in her comments on a proposed order regarding officer promotion examination, she wrote:

The use of "female" instead of "women" in referring to the distaff side of the Marine Corps was gone into quite thoroughly when the new Marine Corps Manual was written. It was finally agreed upon that "women" would be the accepted terminology even when used as an adjective, e.g., "Women Marines," "women officer," etc. The usage follows that established in Public Law 625, "Women's Armed Services Integration Act of 1948." From a purist's point of view "female" may be correct when used as a counterpart of male, but from a woman's point of view it is very objectionable. I would appreciate, therefore, having reference to "female" deleted and "women" substituted

This sounds a little like "the battle of the sexes." It won't be unless we are called "females"!3'

Recruit Training Established at Parris Island

The idea that only 200 new recruits would require basic training during the first two years was soon abandoned. On 29 November 1948, even before the transfer program was completed, Colonel Towle was investigating the possibility of conducting woman recruit training at Parris Island, South Carolina. Because the majority of women Marines would have to be recruited from among civilians, and because of the numbers involved, Henderson Hall was no longer considered suitable. Not only was it too small, but it was not considered the type of Marine Corps post whose mission and atmosphere would help instill the desired esprit de corps and pride which distinguish Marine recruits. To strengthen her case, Colonel Towle pointed out the convenience of having several appropriate specialist schools at Parris Island since training beyond basic military indoctrination would be essential if the WMs hoped to attain the mobilization objective of being a skilled group ready for expansion in case of war.32 Happily, Major General Alfred H. Noble, Commanding General, Marine Corps Recruit Depot, Parris Island, gave his unqualified support to the idea.

Capt Margaret M. Henderson (right) reads the order activating the 3d Recruit Training Battalion, Marine Corps Recruit Depot, Parris Island, South Carolina, in Feburary 1949.

Captain Margaret M. Henderson was selected to head up recruit training. With no more written guidance than a piece of paper on which was typed the general training plan, she and several members of her staff went to work at a long table outside Colonel Towle's office on the first floor of Marine Corps Headquarters.33 Lieutenant Colonel Mary Hale, who as a lieutenant was assigned as training officer to the embryo command, believed that, "Margaret Henderson was the perfect choice" to establish recruit training. She had had extensive teaching experience in civilian schools and was OIC of the Marine Corps Institute Business School during the war.34

In early January, Captain Henderson accompanied Colonel Towle to Parris Island to inspect the available facilities and to discuss the proposed training schedule. The women were assigned Building 902 in the same area used by World War II WRs. They would share the mess hall, Building 900, and the administration/gymnasium facilities, building 914, with other activities, primarily the Recruit Depot's Instruction Company.

Captain Henderson arrived at Parris Island for duty on 25 January with Lieutenant Arney who was on temporary duty to set up the WM uniform shop. By the end of the month Lieutenants Hale, Fisher, and Sustad reported and by mid-February the enlisted women were on the island, and all were attached to Headquarters Company, H&S Battalion. The roster included:

Captain Margaret M. Henderson, Commanding Officer.

First Lieutenant Jeanette I. Sustad, Executive Officer.

First Lieutenant Mary J. Hale, Training Officer; Security Officer

First Lieutenant Mary J. Fisher, Police & Property Officer; Special Services Officer.

First Lieutenant Kathleen J. Arney, Temporary duty connected with WM uniform matters.

Master Sergeant Elsie J. Miller, Sergeant Major.

Technical Sergeant Bertha L. Peters, Chief Clerk.

Technical Sergeant Barbara A. Ames, Special Services NCO.

Staff Sergeant June V. Andler, Pay Clerk.

Staff Sergeant Dorothy T. Hunt, Instructor.

Staff Sergeant Dorothy E. Sullivan, Platoon Sergeant.

Sergeant Margaret K. Leier, Instructor.

Sergeant Marie A. Proulx, Correspondence Clerk.

Sergeant Ruth Ryan, Police Sergeant.

Sergeant Bertha J. Schultz, Platoon Sergeant.

Sergeant Agnes C. Thomas, Duty NCO.

Sergeant Ardella M. Wheeler, Quartermaster Clerk.

Sergeant Mary E. Zabriskie, Platoon Sergeant.

Corporal Rosa V. Harrington, Instructor.

Corporal Grace M. Karl, Instructor.35

Although set up like a battalion and so designated, the 3d Recruit Training Battalion, the unit in no way resembled a battalion in size. A visiting Army general saw the "battalion" led by a captain and remarked, "Now I've seen everything!" The organizational plan was deliberate, however, and was based on General Noble's desire that the senior woman Marine on the depot, Captain Henderson, have disciplinary control over all women Marines at Parris Island. Captain Henderson was designated his advisor on matters concerning WMs and as such was a member of his special staff.36

The six-week training schedule for women recruits was organized into eight periods daily Monday through Friday and four periods on Saturday for a total of 264 hours. The objectives were stated as:

1) To give basic Marine Corps indoctrination to women who have no previous experience.

2) To give the women information on the part the Marine Corps played in our national history and its place in the current National Military Establishment.

3) To classify each individual to fill an available billet according to her abilities.

4) To develop in each individual a sense of responsibility, an understanding of the importance of teamwork, and a desire for self-improvement and advancement in the Marine Corps.37

With those objectives in mind, the 20 women went to work preparing the barracks and classroom; writing lesson plans, recruit regulations, and battalion orders; making out training schedules and coordinating their plans with all the depot facilities that supported recruit training. The barracks needed little renovation, but they had to be scrubbed and shined to meet the standards of distaff Marines. Sergeant Ryan ordered bunks, locker boxes, linen, and supplies and her job was made easier by the depot supply people who saved their best for the 3d Battalion. Sergeants Schultz and Sullivan arranged squadbays. Several of the enlisted women had some college background, and they went to work writing lesson plans. Lieutenant Hale, a self-described "pack rat," made good use of orders and schedules she had saved from her wartime tour at the WR school at Camp Lejeune, and the Marines of Instruction Company under the command of Major Gerald T. Armitage helped in all facets of the preparation.38

Future Director of Women Marines, 1stLt Jeanette I. Sustad (standing second from left), is photographed with the original staff of the 3d Recruit Training Battalion, Parris Island.

Platoon sergeants SSgt Dorothy E. Sullivan (left) and Sgt Betty J. Schultz (right) with the first platoon to undergo training at the 3d Recruit Training Battalion, Parris Island.

The enlisted staff—all ranks from master sergeant to corporal—was billeted on the lower deck of Building 902. Recruits would eventually occupy an upper squadbay. In addition to everything else, the women prepared themselves for this important assignment by practicing close order drill in an empty upper squad-bay. They had no other training, and they were as apprehensive about meeting the recruits as the recruits were about meeting them.39

The drill instructors were selected from among male Marines with experience on the drill field. Staff Sergeant Jack W. Draughon had been a D.I. for two years when Lieutenant Colonel Herman Nickerson, Jr., asked him if he would be interested in the job with the 3d Battalion. After a careful screening by Captain Henderson, Staff Sergeant Draughon, Sergeant Payton L. Lee, and Corporal Paul D. Lute were assigned as the drill instructors. Sergeant Draughon remembered very clearly his first interview with Captain Henderson. It was strange in those days to sit across from a Marine captain answering, "Yes, ma'am" and "No, ma'am." Leaving her office, he met Lieutenant Colonel Nickerson and Colonel Russell N. Jordahl in the passageway and Colonel Jordahl said, "So you're going to be the D. I. for the women Marines?" to which Draughon answered "Yes, ma'am." The story quickly made the rounds and Marine artist Norval E. Pack-wood immortalized the incident in a "Leatherneck" carroon.40

The male drill instructors taught close order drill, first aid, chemical warfare, and classes on general orders. At first they had to endure some good-natured harassment when they took the recruits outside the battalion area, and Marines taunted them with, "Hey Sarge, your slip is showing." To avoid snickers and kidding, Sergeant Draughon often got the platoon going and then stepped up on the sidewalk and walked as if alone, but with one eye on his recruits.41

While the staff was still readying itself at Parris Island, the Marine Corps formally announced on 13 January 1949 that enlistment was open to nonveterans. General requirements were somewhat stricter than those for WRs who transferred from Reserve to Regular in that recruits had to be single, had to be high school graduates, and had to be approved by a board, convened quarterly, at Headquarters Marine Corps. Private Connie J. Lovil of Locksburg, Arkansas, was the first woman Marine recruit to arrive —reporting in on the day the battalion was formed, 23 February.42 Retired First Sergeant Betty Schultz remembers being "scared as all heck," when going to Port Royal to meet the first contingent of recruits. She and Sergeant Dot-tie Sullivan were the platoon sergeants of Platoon 1A which began training on 2 March, donned its uniforms for the first time on the 11th, and graduated on Tuesday, 12 April.43

Colonel Towle came down from Headquarters as the guest of General Noble and together they attended the ceremonies which included an outdoor inspection, marching to the accompaniment of the Parris Island Drum and Bugle Corps, and the traditional speeches in the classroom. Of the 30 graduating recruits, 15 remained to attend Personnel Administration School and the rest were sent directly to Headquarters for duty.44

The First Black Women Marines It is rumored that several black women "passed" as white and served in the MCWR, but, officially, the first black women Marines enlisted during the summer of 1949 and joined the 3d Recruit Training Battalion on 10 September. Platoon 7 therefore is believed to be one of the first racially integrated Marine Corps units since, at the time, black male Marines were segregated and trained separately.45

The press had often questioned Colonel Towle on the Marine Corps policy regarding black women, and she answered that they would be recruited the same as whites. During the congressional hearings, after the war, Representative Adam Clayton Powell of New York had made quite an issue of the fact that no black women had served in the MCWR. It was a serious matter complicated by the southern tradition of segregation. The number of black women Marines was sure to be too few to allow for any type of separate facilities and no one was quite certain how white women, unaccustomed to mixing with blacks, would react to an integrated barracks situation.

Colonel Towle called Captain Henderson and told her that she would not send one black woman, by herself, to Parris Island —this out of consideration for the woman. Captain Henderson and Lieutenants Sustad and Hale discussed what they foresaw as potential problems, and they decided to assign bunks to the incoming platoon geographically rather than alphabetically—northern recruits at one end of the squadbay and southern recruits at the other. They told no one of the plan, including the platoon sergeants, and according to First Sergeant Schultz, they were completely unaware that the precaution had been taken.46

A more frivolous concern was the beauty shop. The white hairdressers from Beaufort did not know how to do the black women's hair, and it is doubtful that they would have been willing to do it in any case. Both Captain Henderson from Texas and Lieutenant Hale from Georgia knew that the recruits would need special preparations and equipment but neither was quite certain what they were. They enlisted the help of the black maid who worked in the Women Officers' Quarters to buy the necessary supplies.47 When she had completed all arrangements, Captain Henderson called in the staff and gave a stern warning that if anyone treated these recruits differently from the others, they would answer to her.

Ann Estelle Lamb of New York City, whose enlistment contract was signed by Major Louis H. Wilson, Jr., a future Commandant of the Marine Corps, and Annie E. Graham of Detroit arrived on the same day, and from all accounts their boot training was uneventful.48 Although both women were from northern cities they undoubtedly understood the time and the place, and they did not complain, for example, about fixing their own hair, after hours in Lieutenant Hale's office.

No one connected with recruit training at the time remembers any unpleasantness and, in fact, Colonel Henderson now believes that the separation of the southerners from the blacks was unnecessary. She does recall, however, that the curiosity of the entire depot was piqued and that all eyes were on Platoon 7. Wherever they went, Marines, including the commanding general, were at the window to stare.49

Occasionally, recruits attended football games in Savannah, drawing lots for tickets. As chance would have it, Privates Lamb and Graham were among the lucky recruits one weekend and everyone took a deep breath as blacks and whites left together on their way to the segregated stadium. Again all went well.50*

* See Henry I. Shaw, Jr., and Ralph W. Donnelly, Blacks in the Marine Corps (Washington: History and Museums Division, HQMC, 1975), p. 56 for a discussion of General Noble's attitude towards integration while he was the Commanding General, Marine Corps Recruit Depot, Parris Island, S.C

Private Lamb remained at Parris Island to attend the Personnel Administration School where she finished first in a class of 61. Now a student rather than a recruit, she went on liberty, but it was somewhat inconvenient outside of the depot. Many years later, Colonel Henderson met a women who had been in charge of the USO at Beaufort during the period, and the woman told her of an incident concerning a WM who called to make reservations for roller skating, but she said that there would be a Negro with the group and if she was not welcome, none of them would come.51

The third black woman Marine, enlisted in Chicago in 1950, was Annie L. Grimes, destined to become a warrant officer in 1968 and the first black woman officer to retire after a full 20-year career.52 From the beginning, black and white women Marines trained and lived together. Accounts differ as to whether the blacks were subjected to discrimination, but there is general agreement among active duty and former WMs that any discrimination or harassment directed at the black women was always a case of individual personalities and never a case of organizational bias.*

* "I find it hard, in 1980, to look back on those days. But it was a fact of life during the years 1949 and 1950. My friends today are just friends, whether white or black. But I was just as guilty as anyone in the change process. I can recall that at MCAS, Cherry Point, I was very much concerned about the acceptance and/or treatment of my Negro enlisted women, who arrived in 1950 to become a part of WMD-2. It all worked out — thanks to the wisdom of Sgt Major Alice J. Connolly and T. Sgt Katherine O'Keefe —two superb human beings.

When I learned that two Negro women would be reporting to my command, I was concerned. But I consulted my trusty Sgt Major Alice J. Connolly, and together we decided on a course of action. They would be billeted in an area with T. Sgt O'Keefe, a devout Christian woman, and if there were any problems, they would be referred to the Commanding Officer. How antiquated this decision now seems to be! But in retrospect, it was important that we placed the two Negro women in areas where there would be minimal or no rejection — and, of course it worked. We had no problems." Col Helen A. Wilson comments on draft manuscript, dtd 1 Jan 80.

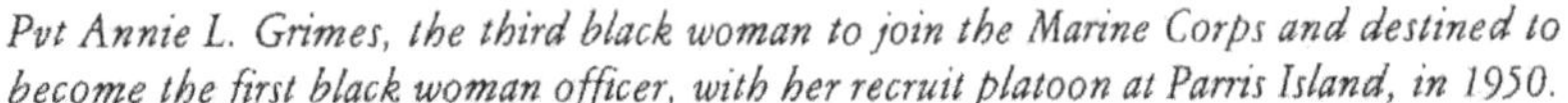

Pvt Annie L. Grimes, the third black woman to join the Marine Corps and destined to become the first black woman officer, with her recruit platoon at Parris Island, in 1950.

Establishing the Women Officers' Training Class at Quantico

After the initial selection under the so-called transfer program, the only source of women officers was through the commissioning of second lieutenants who successfully completed the Women Officers' Training Class. The class, which vaguely resembled the male Platoon Leaders Course, was conducted at the Marine Corps Schools at Quantico. WOTC, as it was known, was the responsibility of the Commandant of the Marine Corps Schools and fell under the operational control of the Education Center and the administrative control of Headquarters Battalion.

The class, held only in the summer, was divided into two six-week periods: the first a junior course; and the second a senior course. College graduates and seniors would attend both sessions, juniors would attend only the junior course, and qualified enlisted women were scheduled only for the senior course. Successful candidates who held a bachelor's degree and who were at least 21 years old would be commissioned second lieutenants in the Marine Corps Reserve. Only seven honor graduates would be offered Regular commissions and these would then attend an additional eight-week Women Officers' Basic Indoctrination Course (WOIC) to be held at the Basic School. The Reservists could request assignment to continuous active duty, but most would return home in an inactive status.

Each session was limited to about 50 candidates who were at least 18 years old; single; citizens of the United States; and college graduates, or in the case of undergraduates, regularly enrolled in an accredited school and pursuing a course leading to a degree. Enlisted women and former WRs who were college graduates or who could pass a college educational equivalency examination were encouraged to apply.53

Publicity for the program began in April 1949 but there were no pamphlets, posters, mailing lists, or other procurement aids. The recruiters' teams for the Platoon Leaders Course brought mimeographed information sheets to the coeducational schools they visited, but it was very late in the season for a class beginning in June. The first woman officer procurement officer was, in effect, Colonel Towle herself, who made a three-week tour in May of women's colleges in the northeast and southeast to acquaint the colleges and the students with the program.54

Captain Hill was selected to head the WOTC staff of four officers and six enlisted women, all temporarily assigned to Quantico and attached to the Schools Company, Headquarters Battalion. Captain Hill and Lieutenant Eunyce L. Brink left Headquarters on 20 April for the five-month tour. Colonel Towle wrote long, explanatory letters to Captain Nita Bob Warner and Lieutenant Doris V. Kleberger, both Reservists, and asked them to join the staff. In her letter to Lieutenant Kleberger she wrote:

While on active duty your base pay would be that of a first lieutenant. In case you have forgotten, $200.00 is a first lieutenant's pay. You would also, of course, be entitled to any longevity which you have earned. For every three years this is a 5 per cent increase. By this time, you must be very close to the second pay period, or 6 years. You would also draw the customary $21.00 a month subsistence. As you would be in Government quarters at Quantico you would not draw quarters allowance.

Naturally, I have no way of knowing whether you are in a position to consider this proposition, or even whether you are interested. I can only hope for both, as I know you would help immeasurably in this important venture. I also think it could give you not only satisfaction in a job well done but afford you a rather pleasant and profitable occupation for the next few months. I would not, however, want to interfere with any future plans you may have made, or to have you sacrifice the permanency of a civilian occupation for temporary duty with the Marine Corps. Whether there would be opportunity for you to continue in a Reserve billet after this summer job is finished is something I cannot predict right now. For a limited time there might be, but I don't want to hold that out as an inducement.55

At the time, both Captain Watner and Lieutenant Klebeiger were graduate students at the University of California, Berkeley, and were personally known to Colonel Towle. Luckily for the woman Marine program, a number of competent WRs and former WRs were in school during that period and could afford to take a chance on a temporary assignment. Lieutenant Brink, a Regular officer, was temporarily detached from her duties as administrative assistant to the Director of Women Marines in order to be platoon leader. The staff was completed by Technical Sergeant Janet R. Paterson, Technical Sergeant "A" Fern Schirmer, Staff Sergeant Mary S. Cookson, Sergeant Rosalie C. Evans, Corporal Helen C. Cathcart, and Corporal Anna M. Delaney.56 Most of the instruction was done by male officers from the staffs of the Basic School, Junior School (later Amphibious Warfare School), and Senior School (later Command and Staff College). Colonel

James T. Wilbur and his staff at the Education Center worked very closely with Captain Hill in developing a syllabus, schedules, and lesson plans.57

The women were quartered in the old WR area overlooking the Potomac. The candidates and the enlisted staff were assigned to Barracks 3076 which was used as a dependents' school during the winter. The NCOs, on the lower deck, had a lounge and private rooms — the candidates were billeted in squad rooms on the second deck. The four women officers lived nearby in Married Officers' Quarters, Building 3078, which was an apartment building convened from a barracks. It was unheard of at the time for women officers to live in bachelor officers' quarters, so they were given a three-bedroom apartment in the quarters reserved for married lieutenant colonels and colonels. Few colonels wanted to live in the building, yet there was some healthy grumbling about giving junior women Marines a field grade apartment.58

Capt Elsie E. Hill, officer-in-charge, conducts Saturday morning personnel inspection of the first Woman Officer Training Class, Quantico, Virginia in 1949.

Col Joseph C. Burger, commander of The Basic School, awards regular commissions to members of the first Woman Officer Training Class, 1949: Virginia M. Johnson, Essie M. Lucas, Anna F. Champlin, Eleanor M. Bach, Doris V. Kleberger, Betty J. Preston.

In spite of the late start and the lack of recruiting material, 180 completed applications were received, and 67 candidates from 35 colleges began the junior course on 10 June 1949- They were welcomed by the Commandant of the Marine Corps Schools, Major General Shepherd, who told them he personally felt there was a "definite place for women Marines during peace, as there was during war," and he encouraged them to try for the Regular commissions.59 General Shepherd had already given convincing evidence of his positive view toward women in the Marine Corps with his efforts to keep WRs on duty after World War II. In recalling the period, Lieutenant Colonel Hill stated emphatically that the women could not have managed the officer training on such short notice without the "marvelous support" of the male Marines at Quantico, especially General Shepherd. He took an active interest in their training, often appearing during a drill period, where as a perfect southern gentleman he always removed his hat when speaking to a woman Marine —no matter what het rank.60

The first WOTC graduation exercises were held on 9 September 1949 in the auditorium of the Amphibious Warfare School, Junior Course. Thirty-four candidates were recommended for commissions: 18 immediately and 16 pending the receipt of a bachelors' degree. A quota of seven Regular commissions was allowed. Those to be appointed Regular officers were:

Eleanor M. Bach

Essie M. Lucas (former WR; later Dowler)

Joan Morrissey

Betty J. Preston (among the first enlisted WRs sworn into the Regular Marine Corps on 10 November 1948)

Anna F. Champlin

Virginia M. Johnson (later Sherman) 61

The seventh and last one was given to Lieutenant Kleberger, who was in competition with the candidates in her platoon. In a 1977 letter to the History and Museums Division, Lieutenant Colonel Kleberger wrote:

While serving on the staff, my interest in remaining in the Marine Corps became very intense. 1 discovered that 1 met all "requirements for commissioning" (including age . . . less than 27 on 1 July of the year of commissioning) with the exception of the requirement that 1 be a graduate of WOTC. 1 requested commissioning in accordance with existing regulations, requesting that "graduation from WOTC" be waived in that 1 was a platoon leader and certainly possessed the required training. Additionally, in view of my six years in the Marine Corps Reserve, 1 requested appointment to the rank of first lieutenant (a request that was not granted).92

This case was repeated in 1950 when Lieutenant Elaine T. Carville, then on continuous active duty, asked to be transferred to the Regular Marine Corps. Since there were so few vacancies and they were viewed as recruiting incentives, the Procurement Branch opposed the idea of giving Regular appointments to former WR officers. Having approved Lieutenant Kleberger's case just a year earlier, Colonel Towle felt that Lieutenant Carville should have the same opportunity to compete for a regular commission. Her comments included:

Unfortunately, there is nothing that 1 can find to prevent former WR officers from applying for regular commissions providing they meet all requirements, including that of age. When the directive concerning the "transfer" program was written this loophole was apparently not considered. Actually because of the age requirement 1 doubt if we will have many, if any, more such requests; most of the MCWR officers are already too old even with service adjusted age. Carville herself just got under the wire.

Since the WOTC had been set up as the sole means of procuring regular women officers, 1 would not approve of Carville not being required to take some training. It might be possible to assign her as a platoon commander as we did Kleberger last summer, which could excuse her from attending the WOTC, or her present duties as Assistant Inspector-Instructor of an organized reserve platoon might be considered equivalent training. Certainly, however, she should be required to attend the two months of additional indoctrination if selected for a regular commission as second lieutenant. . . .

Fortunately, Lieutenant Carville is, 1 understand from various sources, a capable officer, and if selected would probably be a credit to the Marine Corps. But if her request is approved she should be given to understand:

(1) That she will compete with WOTC graduates on an equal basis, with no prior assurance of selection.

(2) That she can in no event receive a regular commission higher than second lieutenant.

(3) That she would have to complete such basic indoctrination as the Marine Corps prescribes."3

These women, Doris Kleberger and Elaine Carville, both retired lieutenant colonels, were the only former WRs who had to take a demotion upon transfer to the Regular Marine Corps. Captain Warner, the assistant OIC that summer at Quantico, did not meet the age requirements for transfer and remained a Reservist. During the Korean War, another integration program opened, and she was able to integrate without losing any tank.

A problem surfaced in 1953 when Lieutenants Kleberger and Carville found:

. . . that we were subject to separation from the Marine Corps under P.L. 625 because of the loophole in the law that neither the Marine Corps nor either of us considered when accepting commissions as second lieutenants with date of rank of 1949 and 1950, respectively. Basically, this provided for the separation of officers who had completed seven years of active commissioned service, regular and reserve, and who had not been selected for the rank of Captain. JAG ruled that we could not eliminate our reserve active time and there was no way we could become eligible for Captain before reaching that seven years of active commissioned service. This eventually required seeking relief from the Board of Correction of Naval Records and subsequent reassignment of date of rank to provide eligibility for the rank of Captain before mandatory separation.94

In addition to the Regular commissions awarded to members of the first class, Reserve commissions were given to: Sara J. Anderson, Nedra C. Calender, Catherine L. Frazier, Pearl A. Jackson, Mildred D. Morrow, Mary E. O'Donnel, Emily C. Ogburn, Shirley A. Pritzker, Margaret C. Roberts, Barbara J. Stephenson, Phyllis L. Jones, and Marie L. Henry.65 Among the 16 undergraduates who returned to school, but later served on active duty were Barbara B. Kasdorf, Joan P. O'Neil, Natalie Noble, and Mary Sue Mock.

The seven "Regulars" were assigned to the Basic School and began the Woman Officers' Indoctrination Course on 23 September, but an administrative detail delayed their commissioning until the end of the month. During the intervening week, WOIC consisted of one Reserve first lieutenant and six Reserve sergeants —one of whom, Joan Morrissey, was underage and had to complete the entire course as an enlisted woman.88

Capt Elsie E. Hill, officer-in-charge, leads candidates of the first Woman Officer Candidate Class as they parade on Barnett Avenue, Quantico, Virginia, summer 1949.

Captain Hill, assigned to the S-3 of the Basic School, and now the only woman staff officer left at Quantico, accompanied the students on a trip to Parris Island which was planned to acquaint the new officers with recruit training and to give them the opportunity to drill enlisted troops. In the fall of 1949, there were no enlisted women —except Sergeant Morrissey— stationed at Quantico, and it was awkward, if not impossible, to conduct any type of close order drill with a formation of seven women.87

Upon graduation, 18 November, the lieutenants were transferred and Captain Hill was reassigned to the Testing and Educational Unit, thereby becoming the first postwar woman Marine to be permanently stationed at Quantico.88

CHAPTER 4

The Korean War Years

Organized Reserve Gets Underway - Mission and Administration - The First Seven WR Platoons Add Six More Platoons - Mobilization of Organized Reserve Units, Korea Volunteer Reservists Answer The Call - Women Marines Return to Posts and Stations Korean War Brings Changes to Recruit Training - A Few Changes at Officer Candidate School - The Korean Years, Reprise

Organized Reserve Gets Underway

Of equal importance to the integration of women into the regular service was the development of a strong women's Reserve. During the early phases of planning, in 1946-47, Colonel Pate, Director, Division of Reserve, was a strong advocate of Organized Reserve units for women. He frequently found himself defending this relatively unpopular idea —an idea unique to the Marine Corps.1 Senior Marines at Headquarters recognized the need for a women's Reserve, but Marines, by and large, shuddered at the thought of this female intrusion. Little by little, the concept gained wider acceptance especially when it was considered as an alternative to women Regulars. It effectively solved the problem of maintaining the affiliation of the WRs and of training a group who would eventually take their place.

Until February 1949, the Division of Reserve still thought in terms of 30 women's companies with a total strength of 60 officers and 1,500 enlisted women, but in reviewing the Marine Corps budget for fiscal year 1950, the Bureau of the Budget reduced the estimate and eliminated the provisions for drill pay for organized women's companies. The Division of Plans and Policies reexamined the location of existing organized units with the purpose of determining those in which women's detachments could readily be justified. Based upon the premise that any locality in which 500 or more enlisted personnel were administered would justify a women's Reserve detachment, the study recommended the activation of 30 women's platoons.2 By March, the plans were finally approved for 15 platoons of two officers and 50 enlisted women each. Major Hamblet and Lieutenant Hale studied the case files of former WRs and made projected plans based on the size of existing male Reserve units, the geographic concentration of WR veterans, and upon available training facilities. In the end, they settled on the seven most promising locations in which to begin: Kansas City; Boston; Los Angeles; New York; Philadelphia; San Francisco; and Seattle.3

A mix of Regular and Reserve officers on continuous active duty would administer the program. Women were needed to serve as Inspector-Instructor for each planned unit and for duty in the various Reserve District offices to give overall supervision to women's matters. Accordingly, a board was convened in March and the following selections were made for Inspector-Instructors: Captain Shirley J. Fuetsch, Los Angeles; Captain Helen A. Wilson, Philadelphia; First Lieutenant Frances M. Exum, Seattle; First Lieutenant Mary C. MacDonald, New York; and First Lieutenant Kathryn E. Snyder, San Francisco. For duty in Reserve District offices, the following officers: Captain Constance Risegari-Gai, Boston; Captain Barbara Somers, New York; First Lieutenant Dolores L. Dubinsky, Philadelphia; First Lieutenant Lucille M. Olsen, Washington, D.C.; First Lieutenant Annie V. Bean, New Orleans; First Lieutenant Mary E. Roddy, Chicago; First Lieutenant Elva B. Chaffer, Los Angeles; First Lieutenant Beatrice R. Strong, San Francisco; First Lieutenant Mildred N. Cooke, Seattle; and First Lieutenant Mary W. Frazer, Atlanta.4

Mission and Administration

Reserve Memorandum 15-49 of 14 March 1949 published the specifics of administration and training of the women's portion of the Organized Reserve.5 The mission of these units was to provide individual women trained to meet mobilization needs of the Marine Corps. They were not classified by specialty as the male Reserve units were or as post-Korea women Reserve platoons would be. Designated women's Reserve platoons (WR platoons), they were attached directly to the major parent male unit as an organic element (e.g., WR Platoon, 11th Infantry Battalion) and not to any subunit. Inasmuch as the women were neither assigned to, nor trained for, combat duties, they were grouped into five subdivisions under Reserve Class VI in order to permit immediate distinction between men and women in case of mobilization.8

The male Inspector-Instructor staff was augmented by one woman officer, designated an assistant I&I, and one or two enlisted women who administered the WR platoon. The platoon was under the direct command of the commanding officer, a platoon leader, and a platoon officer. In many ways the platoon was autonomous since the platoon leader was responsible for recruiting, administration, training, rank distribution, and the mobilization state of readiness of her platoon. Furthermore, she was directed to render administrative assistance to the male unit to compensate for the increased workload caused by the existence of the WR platoon. Very often, however, the women actually took over much of the parent unit's administration.

The WR platoons held weekly two-hour training periods during which their time was divided between formal classes, basic military indoctrination courses for the nonveterans, and specialist training classes in subjects like administration, disbursing, or training aids depending upon the background of the members, and giving clerical assistance to the male unit. It was expected that the basic course, closely resembling recruit training, and consisting of classes in drill, military customs and courtesies, history of the Marine Corps, naval law, interior guard duty, first aid, defense against chemical attack, uniform regulations, and current events would take about two years to complete.

Officers were procured only from among former WR officers and successful graduates of the WOTC at Quantico. Enlisted members were recruited from among WRs, women veterans of the Armed Forces, and nonveterans who met the qualifications. For veterans, the age limits specified that all previous active military service plus all inactive service in the Reserve must, when deducted from their actual age, equal 32 or less. Aspiring Reservists with no prior service had somewhat less stringent requirements than women being recruited for active duty: age, 18-31; and education, high school graduate, or high school student and pass the equivalency test. Regular recruits, on the other hand, had to be 20 years old and high school graduates.

To complete the organization, the Division of Reserve requested that WAVE pharmacist mates be included in the naval personnel allowance for those units which had a WR platoon. The decision was approved in the interest of public opinion, as well as health and accident security.7

The First Seven WR Platoons

The first WR platoon was activated on 14 April 1949 at Kansas City, Missouri. A Regular officer, First Lieutenant Ben Alice Day, was appointed Assistant I&I of the 5th 105mm Howitzer Battalion, USMCR, and Major Helen T. Chambers was assigned platoon leader. In a very short time the platoon was up to its authorized strength.8

First Lieutenant Pauline "Polly" F. Riley, Irish and from Maine, was sent to Boston to activate the second WR platoon. Lieutenant Riley, formerly enlisted, was a member of the last WR officer candidate class in 1945- The class was made up entirely of enlisted WRs, and when World War II was declared over about a week before commissioning, the students were given three options: return to enlisted status, take a discharge if they had the required points, or accept the commission and remain on active duty for one year. Most of the candidates took the discharge or returned to enlisted status, but Lieutenant Riley was commissioned in August 1945 and served at Headquarters until 1947 on the Postwar Personnel Reorganization Board. She was released to inactive duty when the board was terminated and later was among the first 20 Regular women officers.9

With her New England background, it was logical to send Lieutenant Riley to Boston, where the WR Platoon, 2d Infantry Battalion, USMCR, was established on 22 April 1949 under the command of Lieutenant Colonel James Dugan and with Lieutenant Carolyn Tenteris as the platoon officer.10

Former WRs Staff Sergeant Frances A. Curwen, Staff Sergeant Katherine Keefe, Corporal Hazel A. Lindahl, and Corporal Dorothy M. Munroe were early members of the Boston unit. Among the nonveterans was Private Eleanor L. Judge, who originally enlisted in the Reserve because she happened to be free on Wednesday evenings, the women's scheduled drill night. But that was only the beginning; in 1977 with 27 years active service as a Regular, she reenlisted for three more years.11

Sergeant Major Judge remembered that the women were "put through a pace." There were classes to attend as well as battalion administrative work to be done. The non-veterans were not issued regulation shoes and they drilled in their own civilian shoes which proved impractical and uncomfortable. The classes in naval law, taught by Sergeant Mary L. Attaya, a lawyer, were complete with mock trials in which the women played active roles, and there were Hollywood-made movies featuring the Marine Corps.12 For all of this, a private was paid $2.50 per drill and a captain received $7.67. 13

Captain Risegari-Gai, formerly the commanding officer of VTU I-I(WR), Boston, was not a member since she had been selected for a continuous active duty billet in the office of the First Reserve District, which in those days was located in the Fargo Building in Boston. When Captain Risegari-Gai reported for duty, Colonel George O. Van Orden, District Director, and a Virginia gentleman, was quoted in the Boston newspaper as saying that his first sergeant needed a week off to recuperate because he was, ". . . the finest cussin gent yo'all ever did hear. Had to pretty up his language, though, with all these lady Marines around. He's a beaten man." The colonel, himself, had never seen a woman Marine until he arrived in Boston, saw Captain Risegari-Gai, and described himself as "thunderstruck."14

Capt Rosalie B. Johnson, assistant inspector-instructor of the 5th Infantry Battalion, Washington, D.C., discusses the formation of the local Organized Women's Reserve Platoon with Rachel Freeman, Charlotte De Garmo, and Sgt Theresa "Sue" M. Sousa.

The next five platoons were organized by Reserve officers on continuous active duty, and it was necessary for them to go to Washington for a briefing before taking up their new duties. Captain Helen A.

Wilson was then sent to Philadelphia where recruiting was simplified when the entire VTU under the command of Captain Dorothy M. Knox transferred to the Organized Reserve. The unit became the WR platoon, 6th Infantry Battalion, USMCR, with Captain Knox as platoon leader and First Lieutenant Emily Horner as platoon officer.

From Philadelphia, Captain Wilson kept Colonel Towle informed of the platoon's progress and activities. By Christmas of 1949, recruiting was so successful that the unit was permitted to exceed its authorized strength by 10 percent. When the male commanding officers of other battalions heard of this, they were very much interested in receiving a similar authorization. The women in Philadelphia formed a rifle team, and a bowling team, and even fielded a team for a swim meet.

In response to one of Captain Wilson's informal reports, Colonel Towle, always conscious of the service woman's image, wrote:

I think you were wise to put a stop to post drill activities such as drinking in bars while in uniform. There is nothing intrinsically wrong, of course, but the very fact that a woman is in uniform makes her liable to criticism even though she is behaving herself in every respect. As you say, Women Marines have established a fine reputation and it would be most unfortunate to have any criticism leveled at them, especially when we ourselves can do much to prevent it. I think you have shown excellent judgement in your decision.15

First Lieutenant Kathryn E. Snyder, who had served at the Department of the Pacific during World War II, was assigned as Assistant I&I, 12th Infantry Battalion, Treasure Island, and together with the Reserve officers Lieutenants Katherine W. Love and Marjorie J. Woolman, started San Francisco's WR platoon, whose roster included Sergeant Alameda Blessing; Corporal Rosita A. Martinez, who eventually integrated and retired as a master gunnery sergeant; and Corporal Ouida Craddock, who also went Regular, and later became the Sergeant Major of the Women Marines.16

Captain Shirley J. Fuetsch and First Lieutenant Frances M. Exum drove west together and parted at Denver —Fuetsch to go to the 13th Infantry Battalion, USMCR, in Los Angeles and Exum to go to the 11th Infantry Battalion, USMCR, at Seattle. In Los Angeles, two Reserve First Lieutenants, Esther N. Gaffney and Christine S. Strain, took the reins of the WR platoon while the Seattle unit was headed by Captain Nancy M. Roberts and First Lieutenant Fern D. Anderson.17

First Lieutenant Mary C. MacDonald, who before the war had been personal secretary to Laurence Olivier and Vivien Leigh, was sent to New York to activate the WR platoon, 1st Infantry Battalion, USMCR, at Fort Schuyler. Captain Mildred Gannon and First Lieutenant Elizabeth Noble filled the two Reserve officer billets. Like Philadelphia, the Fort Schuyler platoon also increased its strength to 55, but eventually the authorization was rescinded, and the women had to "keep on their toes" to stay in. Those with poor attendance records were transferred involuntarily to the Inactive Reserve, and the platoon maintained a waiting list of potential recruits.18

Add Six More Platoons

After the original seven platoons were well established, plans were announced for an additional four. On 15 October 1949, WR platoons were activated as elements of the 4th Infantry Battalion, Minneapolis; the 5th Infantry Battalion, Washington, D.C.; and the 9th Infantry Battalion at Chicago. On 1 November, the fourth WR Platoon was activated at St. Louis as part of the 3d Infantry Battalion.

Chicago's WRs were led by First Lieutenant Genevieve M. Dooner who had compiled quite a record as a volunteer recruiting officer in the postwar years. She was assisted by platoon officer Lieutenant Isabel F. Vosler and I&I Lieutenant Dorothy Holmberg.

First Lieutenant Elaine T. Carville, although of French background and from Louisiana, was ordered to Minneapolis because "she looked like a Swede." A Reserve officer on extended active duty, she activated the WR Platoon, 4th Infantry Battalion, USMCR, which came under the leadership of First Lieutenant Ardath Bierlein and Second Lieutenant Phyllis Davis. Well known for her enthusiasm and esprit de corps, Lieutenant Carville soon had a unit made up of 10 former WRs, 37 nonveterans, 2 ex-WAVES, and 1 ex-SPAR. Minneapolis-St. Paul had been chosen for a WR platoon from among a number of cities which had asked for one. The large number of wartime WRs from Minnesota plus the personal interest in the project displayed by Lieutenant Colonel Emmet O. Swanson, commanding officer of the 4th Battalion, combined to bring the unit to the "Twin Cities."

When plans for the platoon were first announced, 250 inquiries flooded the Reserve office at Wold-Chamberlain Naval Air Station. Lieutenant Carville personally interviewed 150 applicants. The first group of 45 selectees was sworn in on 2 November 1949 by Brigadier General Elmer H. Salzman in a ceremony at the airfield. Wartime WRs included Master Sergeant Cecilia Nadeau, Staff Sergeant Lucille Almon, Staff Sergeant Leona Dickey, Staff Sergeant Betty Guenther, Sergeant Gladyce Pederson, Sergeant Anna

Homza, Private First Class Betty Lemnke, Private First Class Grace Moak, Private First Class Ruth Mortenson, and Private First Class Kathleen Schoenecker. Among the nonveterans was Private Julia L. Bennke, who later went on to a full active duty career and retired in 1970 as a master sergeant.

Despite the commanding officer's enthusiasm for a WR platoon some members of his staff were concerned at the changes it would bring. Reportedly, Sergeant Major Thomas Polvogt said that on occasion he would issue rifles to the women Marines so they would know what they were dealing in when they handled records for M-1s issued to guards, but he was not going to be responsible for powder puffs "or them other things they are going to issue." Lieutenant Carville assured him that the women would be issued full Marine Corps uniforms "from the skin out" and Sergeant Major Polvogt would not have to worry about "them other things."19

Captain Jeanette Pearson, Assistant I&I of the 5th Infantry Battalion, USMCR, Washington, D.C., activated that WR platoon with Major Mary L. Condon as platoon leader and First Lieutenant Ethel D. Fritts as platoon officer. Theresa "Sue" M. Sousa, later president of the Women Marines Association, was an early member of that very active unit which met at 230 C Street, N.W.20

After the first WOTC, Captain Nita Bob Warner, selected for a three-year active duty contract, left Quantico for a Headquarters Marine Corps briefing before setting out for St. Louis to form the WR Platoon, 3d Infantry Battalion, USMCR. Officially activated on 1 November 1949, the unit received a great deal of publicity. On the night that enlistments opened, more than 100 applicants —one of whom was former WR Peggy Musselman, later assigned as the platoon leader—came to the Navy-Marine Corps Reserve Training Center at the foot of Ferry Street. According to retired Lieutenant Colonel Warner, this unit was supposed to be self-contained. That meant they were to recruit or train women to handle all matters of administration, supply, recruiting, disbursing, or whatever else it took to run an efficient organization.

Like the rest of the women Marine Reservists, those in St. Louis were shod in civilian shoes of various shades of brown and tan —an intolerable situation to Captain Warner. She enlisted the help of Staff Sergeant Mabel Otten, stationed at Headquarters Marine Corps, who sent a full case of cordovan brown shoe dye to the WR platoon. All 50 Reservists spent one drill period outside the armory ". . . wielding a bottle of cordovan brown shoe dye and shoe polish, dying their shoes dark brown and then learning how to give them a Marine Corps spit shine." When St. Louis saw its first women Marines, a proud group, on 20 May 1950 in an Armed Forces Day parade, they were stepping out in regulation cordovan brown shoes.

As it turned out, the shoe color problem was more easily solved than that of providing the Reservists with summer uniforms. There were none! In the summer of 1950, Headquarters allowed the platoon two weeks of active duty for training at the armory, which they performed wearing the utility uniform — bib overalls and white T-shirts—which Lieutenant Colonel Warner laughingly recalls, ". . . made really quite a handsome outfit."21

February 1950 saw the formation of the last two WR platoons. Second Lieutenant Doris Kleberger left Quantico to become the Assistant I&I, 17th Infantry Battalion, USMCR, Detroit, with Captain Cecelia Van-den Bossche as the platoon leader.22

Captain Mary J. Hale went from Parris Island to Dallas where she served as Assistant I&I, 23d 155mm Howitzer Battalion, USMCR. She remembers that the Marines, Regular and Reserve, were very proud of the preparations they had made to welcome the WR platoon. On the night of the open house, planned to kick off the recruiting effort, Dallas was the scene of a "terrible ice storm," but the Texans were undaunted and the unit was off to a good start. Captain Hazel C. Tyler was platoon leader and First Lieutenant Grace E. Kathan was platoon officer. Captain Hale, scrupulous in her explanation to recruits of a Reserve unit's mobilization potential, was asked by the I&I if she really had to emphasize the point so strongly. Fortunately she continued to make an issue of it because within six months mobilization became a fact.23

Inspector-Instructor 1stLt Doris V. Kleberger (standing second from right) attends an Open House for the Women Reserve Platoon, 17th Infantry Battalion, U.S. Marine Corps Reserve, in Detroit, 1950.

Capt Cecelia Vanden Bossche, Commanding Officer, WR Platoon, 17th Infantry Battalion, Detroit, reads mobilization orders resulting from the Korean crisis in August 1950.

Mobilization of Organized Reserve Units - Korea

Within 15 months of the initiation of women into the Organized Reserve, the value of the program was realized with the mobilization of all 13 WR platoons. Women, as a result of the Korean crisis, and for the first time in American history, were called involuntarily to military service along with men. Mobilization of Reserves, including women veterans, was announced in June 1950.

Since a number of women Reservists had belonged to organized platoons for only a few months, the term "veteran" was defined as women who had:

a) served 90 days or more on active duty with the Marine Corps, Marine Corps Reserve: or

b) attended 36 drills as members of an organized platoon; or

c) attended 30 drills and 10 days active duty for training.

Those women who did not meet the criteria were classified as nonveterans, transferred to the Volunteer Marine Corps Reserve, Class III, and directed to await orders to recruit training at Parris Island.24

Unfortunately, the 3d Recruit Training Battalion had closed down for the summer. Recruiting was something of a disappointment and thus far, no women recruit platoon had reached its authorized strength of 50. That fact coupled with the manner in which WOTC was organized —as a temporary unit established anew each summer—led to the decision to terminate training at Parris Island and to assign the staff to Quantico temporarily to conduct officer training. Platoon 2A, graduating in May, was the last scheduled class until 18 September Three officers and seven enlisted women from the permanent staff of 3d Recruit Training Battalion were temporarily reassigned to a subunit activated at Quantico on 2 June. The first group to leave Parris Island included Captain Jeanette I. Sustad, Second Lieutenants Joan Morrissey and Betty Preston, Technical Sergeant "A" Fern Schirmer, Staff Sergeant Bertha Schultz, and Sergeants Rosa V. Harrington and Ruth Ryan. Sergeants Grace M. Karl and Agnes C. Thomas and Private First Class Allis V. Wall soon followed.25 They were barely established in Virginia when the news of mobilization broke and the urgent need for recruit training was realized, but it was too late to change plans as WOTC would be without a staff. So, when the WR platoons left for military duty, the nonveterans stayed behind expecting orders to Parris

Island in early September. The women Reserve officers were not mobilized in order to maintain a sufficient number of stateside billets to allow the rotation of male officers. Before the plan was published, several officers gave notice to their employers and prepared to leave for duty. The decision to exclude WM officers caused a morale problem at several levels of the women's Reserve program. According to retired Lieutenant Colonel Carville, Assistant I&I at Minneapolis at the time of • mobilization, "It was a terrible, terrible, terrible mistake!" The I&I hated to tell Reserve officers, who, in turn were embarrassed in front of their troops. The enlisted women were at first apprehensive at the thought of leaving without their own, familiar officers. Later, some were even angrily asking, "Why us, and not them?"26

The mobilization of the women caused by the conflict in Korea brought two significant changes to the women Marine program: it enabled women Marines to return to several duty stations, from which they had been absent during the postwar years, and it enabled them to break out of the strictly administrative mold into which they were cast after World War II. An analysis of tables of organization indicated that 1,183 women Marines could be assigned immediately, releasing an equal number of men according to the following distribution:27

Hq, Department of Pacific and Depot of Supplies, San Francisco / 172

Marine Barracks and Marine Corps Supply Depot, Camp Pendleton / 189

Marine Barracks and Marine Corps Supply Depot, Camp Lejeune / 190

Marine Corps Air Station, El Toro / 95

Marine Corps Recruit Depot, Parris Island / 133

Marine Corps Air Station, Cherry Point / 195

Marine Corps Recruit Depot, San Diego / 68

Marine Corps Schools, Quantico / 141

Total / 1,183

The WR platoons with 25 officers and 594 enlisted women were up to 88.6 percent of their authorized strength.28 To make up the difference and to fill vacancies in critical specialties, an immediate call was made for veteran volunteers in the following occupational fields:

01 Personnel Administration

15 Printing and Reproduction

22 Fire Control Instrument Repair

25 Operational Communications

30 Supply Administration, Accounting and Stock Control

31 Supply Procurement, Warehousing, Shipping, and Receiving

34 Disbursing

35 Motor Transport

40 Machine Accounting

41 Post Exchange

43 Public Information

46 Photography

49 Training and Training Aids

MSgt Petrina C. Nigro leads the platoon of the first post-World War II women Marines assigned to Headquarters, Department of the Pacific, San Francisco, California in 1950.

52 Special Services

67 Air Control

70 Aviation Operations and Intelligence 29

Volunteer Reservists Answer The Call

An intensive short-term recruiting drive attracted former WRs like Corporal Anne Revak who volunteered at the start of the war, but could not be recalled from her home in Fairbanks, Alaska. She drove to Seattle in order to report within the continental United States, was accepted, and sent to Camp Pendleton.30

Sergeant Ethyl Wilcox was recalled in August 1950 and ordered to recruiting duty, a billet she filled all through World War II. She was on the job, in civilian clothes, for several months before she had rime to go to Chicago for a physical examination and uniforms. On duty in Minnesota, she spent her time processing Reservists and later recruiting women.31

Sergeant Mary S. Mock completed officer candidate training in 1949, and returned home to finish college. Too young to be commissioned, she accepted a teaching position but on 12 September, two days before school was scheduled to begin, she received a collect telegram ordering her to report to Quantico on 14 September. She attended Basic School, which was shortened from eight to four weeks because of the emergency, as an officer candidate, the only enlisted WM on the base. As such, she could not eat in the officers' mess with her classmates, and the commanding general thought it inappropriate for her to eat by herself in the general mess hall, so, in time, she was given an allowance to eat in civilian restaurants in the town of Quantico.32

There were a number of women serving in district offices on continuous active duty contracts which stipulated that they could not be transferred against their wishes. One of these was First Lieutenant Mary E. Roddy, who had been the last WR to leave Cherry Point in 1946. When the transfer program was announced in 1948, she found that she did not meet the age criteria for integration, bur that she was eligible for continuous active duty. She was selected and assigned to the 9th Reserve District Headquarters in the

Federal Court Building on Lake Shore Drive in Chicago. She was the woman Marine liaison officer and handled all WM matters, Reserve and Regular.

During this time, the Korean situation "was heating up" and the district director asked if she could find women Reservists to help with the administrative work. She successfully recruited some 15-20 former WRs for continuous active duty. At the time that they were recruited, Lieutenant Roddy explained that the contracts did not offer too much —a minimum of one year's duty and a clause that protected them from an involuntary transfer. But, she added that they had all left the Corps with good records, and if an emergency arose, she expected that they would fulfill the spirit of their contract as a Marine. Not long after, a mobilization roster, not entirely unexpected, arrived and the lieutenant called a meeting in the only available private spot, the ladies room. The women knew what was coming and although not legally obligated, they accepted the fate of mobilization "with good grace" and all, including Lieutenant Roddy, were soon sent to Washington, D.C.33

At the time of mobilization, only 12 women were deferred or rejected which resulted in a mobilization of 98 percent of the women in the Organized Reserve.34 Two hundred eighty-seven veterans were ordered to extended active duty and 298 nonveterans were ordered to Parris Island. All had been trained and assigned by January 1951. Together with the volunteer Reservists, a total of approximately 1,000 women were assigned to extended active duty. They worked in clerical fields, recruiting, public information, communications, photography, cartographic drafting, disbursing, and motor transport.35

Women Marines Return to Posts and Stations

In June 1950 the only woman Marine company was Company E at Headquarters Battalion, Henderson Hall. The battalion at Parris Island was strictly a recruit command and no regular WMs worked outside of it. Women Marines were assigned to the Department of the Pacific at San Francisco, but they had no government quarters. All other WMs were working with the Reserve districts, Reserve platoons, or as recruiters.

The first priority then was to prepare billeting space at the posts and stations for the incoming women Marines. Major Pauline B. Beckley, Commanding Officer, Company E, was Transferred to Parris Island to assume command of the recruit Training battalion, with a temporary assignment en route. She, Technical Sergeant Schirmer, and Corporal Leona M. Fox reported to Camp Lejeune on 24 July 1950 to open and ready a barracks for occupancy by the women Reservists being ordered to active duty. The building had been vacated by men and, of course, did not pass the women's inspection. Lieutenant Colonel Beckley, looking back, wrote in 1977, "Don't think any three WMs worked harder — manually — than we did." With the exception of a battle with the G-4 for supplies, the women received fine cooperation from the Marines at Camp Lejeune, especially the commanding general, Major General Franklin A. Hart, and his staff.36 Major Beck-ley was no stranger to Camp Lejeune, having served there as the postal officer of the schools and the executive officer of the WR battalion during World War II.

With Camp Lejeune prepared on the east coast, and San Francisco ready to process WMs on the west coast, it was at last possible to ship the Reserves. Many of the WR platoons left home on the same troop trains as the men. When the 5th Infantry Battalion of

Washington, D.C. entrained for Camp Lejeune, on 31 July 1950, the Marine Band gave them a sendoff befitting the country's first mobilized Marine Corps Reserve unit. Along with wives and children at Union Station to say goodbye were two husbands, W. G. Kegel and Edmund A. Gibson, there to bid farewell to Corporal Virginia S. Kegel and Technical Sergeant Josephine R. Gibson.37

The WR platoon in Boston was mobilized on 7 August, one week before actual departure, and the women reported to the armory where they lived while performing the administrative tasks essential to the mobilization of an infantry battalion. When the day came to leave, 15 August 1950, marching to the music of the 2d Infantry Battalion band, 700 male Marines and 32 women Marines boarded the train for North Carolina. Billeting was carefully arranged so that the men occupied the forward cars, followed by the dining car, then the male officers' car, and finally the women's car, guarded by MPs.38

In August 1950, Base Commander MajGen Oliver P. Smith greets (from left to right) TSgt Catherine G. Murray, Capt Jeanette I. Sustad, and Sgt Beatrice M. Kent, the first women Marines to be stationed at Camp Pendleton since the end of World War II

The first three Reserve platoons to arrive at Camp Lejeune were those from Washington, Philadelphia, and Boston. Three Regular staff NCOs, Staff Sergeants Esther Waclawski, Ruth Ryan, and Virginia L. Moore, students at Supply School, were already living in the barracks. In 1977, First Sergeant Waclawski could still hear the "click . . . click . . . click" of the high heels of the Reservists trooping off the buses and into the barracks. Customarily, women Marines wore oxfords for such formations and so the Regulars were undecided as to whether they should laugh at the Reservists in their more attractive shoes or envy them.39

As soon as they arrived, and before they had time to settle, the women were processed and put to work to alleviate the personnel shortage caused by troop drafts for Korea. After the Camp Lejeune quota of 190 women was reached, Reservists were sent for duty to other east coast duty stations —Cherry Point, Parris Island, and Quantico. To avoid the establishment of additional administrative units, the women were attached to existing male units, and unlike World War II, they ate in existing male mess halls.40

Those first few months were hectic. Many of the so-called "veterans" had never seen a Marine Corps base before. In addition to working long hours, an improvised boot camp was held evenings by the handful of experienced NCOs. Typically, a WM worked five days, had one-half day of military subjects training, and attended close order drill classes after evening chow, and according to Sergeant Major Judge, excuses from training were unheard of. The barracks routine, which included outside morning muster and chow formations (to make the formation and march up to the mess hall was mandatory; to enter and to eat was optional) was a culture shock to many of the women.41

The WM Company, Marine Barracks, Camp Lejeune, the first postwar women's company was formally activated on 13 October 1950, with Captain Mary J. Fisher commanding, and with Technical Sergeant

Schirmer, first sergeant.42 The women were housed in Barracks 60 and 63 with the main area service club between. At the height of the Korean War, the WM company numbered approximately 400 women: 270 on duty with the base; 75 attached to the depot quartermaster; and 155 attending supply school and disbursing school.43

At the same time that Camp Lejeune was being readied for the arrival of the WMs, women Reservists from cities west of the Mississippi were reporting to San Francisco for processing and classification. Captain Sustad, Technical Sergeant Catherine G. Murray, and Sergeant Beatice M. Kent reported to Camp Pendleton on 8 August to "make advance preparations for the billeting of women Marines who would arrive as soon as the Department of the Pacific's and Depot of Supplies' quotas were filled.

The Pendleton WMs were assigned the same barracks in the "24" area occupied by their predecessors during World War II. Just before the Reservists arrived a fire destroyed all the mattresses, chests of drawers, and other supplies set aside to furnish their quarters.44 A lesser crisis arose with the news that Headquarters required a guard from 1800 to 0600 posted around the WM barracks. To save personnel, the Marines at Camp Pendleton fenced in the WM area, and the gate was locked each night when liberty expired. In First Sergeant Waclawski's view, it looked like a prisoner-of-war compound, and she was pleased to see the fence come down after a visit by Colonel Hamblet in the mid-Fifties.45

In addition to her regularly assigned duty as the custodian of registered publications, Captain Sustad was the "Supervisor of Women Marines," all of whom were attached to Headquarters Company, Headquarters Battalion, Marine Barracks, Camp Pendleton. The WM company, under the command of Captain Sustad, was eventually activated as an element of Service Battalion on 1 June 1951.

One month after the WMs landed at Camp Pendleton, the Marine Corps Recruit Depot, San Diego saw its first postwar woman Marine, First Lieutenant Kathyrn E. Snyder, who had been on I&I duty in San Francisco until the WR platoon there was mobilized. In November, she was joined by Second Lieutenant Dorothy Dawson. Both women were assigned primary duties in the depot G-l office, and additional duties, respectively, as WM platoon commander and platoon officer. The enlisted women arrived in December 1950 and were attached to Headquarters Company, Headquarters and Service Battalion. Private First Class Dawn Zimmerman was first to report. By 8 December she had been joined by 15 others: Master Sergeant Cecilia Nadeau, Staff Sergeant Annette Burkhead, Sergeant Dorothy Walker, Privates First Class Inga Boberg, Margaret Cooper, Patricia Pfeiffer, and Frances Quinlan, and Privates Norma Adams, Jo Carrera, Phyllis Curtiss, Nita L. Fagan, Joy Hardy, and Rebecca Rarrick. The balance of the WM platoons came directly from recruit training.48

Major Emma Hope Clowers (nee Hendrickson) reported to San Diego in December of 1951 and in 1977 gave the following account of the activation of the WM company and of the problems encountered by the women officers assigned as supervisors rather than as commanding officers:

When I reported to MCRD in Dec 1951, the women were housed in two two-story barracks near the main gate and were carried on the rolls of HqCo, H&S Bn. Both barracks had open squadbays, with double-deck bunks for most of the women. (I believe the NCOs and SNCOs had single deck bunks, but that there were no separate areas set aside for them.) As I recall, even SNCOs were scattered at random through both barracks, alongside PFCs, in some cases. There was only one woman officer and myself, and there were no quarters on the base for either of us. Therefore, supervision of the women Marines after working hours and during weekends and holidays was almost entirely in the hands of the NCOs, even though I was on call much of the time at the home I had in Ocean Beach. It seemed as though a night rarely passed when I wasn't called at least once by the Post Duty Officer or by our Barracks NCO and I made many a trip to the base during the night. My position was strictly that of a barracks officer (such as WAVE officers at that time frequently held as additional duty). I had no authority over the women in administrative or disciplinary matters, or in fact any area, and the women were aware of that fact. At one time the women's CO was the Post Communications Officer, who had command of the company as additional duty. It was an impossible situation as I soon found out when I reassigned the women within the two barracks to break up the little cliques that had developed and to have the Staff NCOs in a separate area. I recall that some of the women staged what was probably one of the first of the "sit-ins" when I rearranged the barracks and reassigned them. It is amusing now but wasn't then. My "CP." was a tiny converted stock room in the barracks with scarcely enough room for a desk. I was receiving urgent calls from Colonel Towle at HQMC about the formation of a women's company, but could never clear the hurdle set up by the base —a magic number which we had to meet before they would give us a company. Each time our strength was about to reach that number, we would have an unexpected discharge or transfer. But eventually we were given company status, and by the time I was transferred back to HQMC in May 53 I felt we had accomplished much in organization of the company, improvements in the barracks, reduction in disciplinary problems, and improvement in morale of the women.47

The WM Company, Headquarters and Service Battalion, Marine Corps Recruit Depot was activated on 1 July 1952, Captain Clowers, commanding; Second Lieutenant Joyce M. Hamman, executive officer; and Master Sergeant Vera E. Piippo, first sergeant.

El Toro was originally programmed to receive 90 WMs, but later the commanding general actually identified 235 positions which could be filled by women. Plans were made at once to receive and quarter the women Marines —even before the usual advance group arrived. The large, eight-wing barracks behind the station administration building which had been occupied by the WRs during the war was vacated by the male Marines, then repainted and renovated.

Captain Warner left St. Louis shortly after her platoon was mobilized and during the first week of October became the first woman Marine to report to the Marine Corps Air Station, El Toro since 1946. Until the company was activated, she was assigned as the station assistant personnel officer and administrative assistant for WMs.

Seven NCOs from Headquarters Marine Corps (Master Sergeant Bette A. Kohen; Staff Sergeants Margaret H. Crowell, Doris M. Plowman, and Martha J. Clark; Sergeants Chadeane A. Rhindress and Rita M. Walsh; and Corporal Maxine H. Carlson) who arrived in early November 195-0 were the vanguard of the unit which would be known as the Woman Marine Detachment 1 (WMD 1) Waiting for more women to report in, the seven lived in the station hostess house.

Public Works had scrubbed and polished the barracks, and the NCOs settled in and made up the bunks for the incoming women, newly graduated recruits from Parris Island. Just one week before the barracks was to be occupied, a Santa Ana windstorm blew in from the desert and dumped an inch of red sand throughout all the squadbays in the women's building. Lieutenant Colonel Warner remembers that it was "an awful mess." There was sand everywhere and in everything—sheets, blankets, pillow cases. She and the NCOs literally shoveled out the barracks, got two wings ready, and closed off the others. A squared away living area awaited each new group of privates. Settled in, they, in turn cleaned a wing for the next contingent.

WMD 1 grew to a strength of approximately 250; almost all were recent graduates. The officers and the NCOs felt a great sense of responsibility and were like "mother hens" to the 18-year-old WMs —a new phenomenon in the Marine Corps. An NCO advisor was assigned to each squadbay and was always ready to listen and to help the young Marines make whatever adjustment was necessary. WMD 1 was a closely knit unit which Lieutenant Colonel Warner remembers as a "fine group of women."48

Hard pressed for personnel, the Marines at El Toro made the women feel welcome and needed. The various squadron and station offices vied for WMs who were assigned to all except combat units. Interest ran so high that the Flight Jacket, the station newspaper, regularly published the number of women Marines expected along with their occupational specialty. On 20 October 1950 one article read:

Out of El Toro's first draft will be 11 basic personnel and administration women, seven basic communication girls and four basic supply people. There will be two basic shipping and receiving WRs, five basic post exchange stewards, two basic air control women, and one basic flight equipment woman.49

The return of the WMs made a similar impact on East Coast posts and stations, Matters of housing, uniforming, administration, and assignment had to be resolved quickly. At two of the bases, Quantico and Parris Island, training sites for WM officers and recruits, the adjustment was minimal.

The 3d Recruit Training Battalion underwent a minor organizational change on 20 November 1950, and WMs not involved in training but rather assigned to the depot offices were made members of Post Troops Section under the section commander, Second Lieutenant Mary S. Mock. On 16 November 1951, the Post Personnel Company under the command of Captain Emily Schultz was officially activated as an element of the 3d Recruit Training Battalion.

The influx of women Marines to the Marine Corps Schools at Quantico was made less traumatic by virtue of the presence of a senior woman officer involved in officer training, a barracks already occupied by WMs, and a male unit, Headquarters Battalion, accustomed to having women on its rolls. Lieutenant Carville, having seen the Minneapolis WR platoon off to duty in San Francisco, was transferred to Quantico, where in addition to her assignment as administrative officer for the Marine Corps Landing Force Tactics and Techniques Board, she became the barracks officer for the permanently assigned WMs, the first of whom included Technical Sergeant Mary C. Quinn; Staff Sergeants Dorothea E. Hard, Mary K. Arcure, and Martha E. Kirchman; Sergeant Muriel V. Artz; Corporals Alma Noffke, R. F. Black, and Jane L. Reynolds; and Private M. L. Williamson.50 In spite of the nontraditional command and administrative relationship where the women Marines were attached to one unit, worked in another, and were under the supervision of a woman officer with no real authority, the first arrived WMs at Quantico were a cohesive group, and evidently, a well-disciplined one. For a period of a year, there was not a single case of nonjudicial punishment involving a WM. Maintaining the record became a matter of great pride. But bad luck was their undoing when a private first class' auto broke down in the town of Triangle and after walking the three miles to the barracks in her high heels, she reported in from liberty 10 minutes late. On this and other occasions when a WM appeared before the battalion commander for office hours, it was Lieutenant Carville's habit to stand behind him and squeeze his shoulder when it appeared that he was weakening and unduly moved by a tearful story.51

The first post-World War II women Marines arrived at Quantico, Virginia, in 1951 and were assigned to the Administrative Section of the Landing Force Development Center.

The Commanding Officer of Woman Marine Detachment 2, Cherry Point, North Carolina, Maj Helen A. Wilson (center), pictured in 1953 with (from left to right) MSgt Elizabeth Tarte, SSgt Muriel Artz, MSgt Alice Connolly, and MSgt Jessie Van Dyke.

For about 18 months, the WMs at Quantico were customarily attached to Headquarters or Service Battalion. A WM company was eventually formed under the command of Captain Bernice M. Pittman on 1 May 1953 as an element of Service Battalion.

Captain Helen A. Wilson, on 7 September 1950, was the first of the WMs to return to the Marine Corps Air Station, Cherry Point, North Carolina. She easily moved into the Navy nurses quarters, but housing the newly arrived enlisted women was more of a problem. When Staff Sergeant Katherine Keefe, a Boston Reservist, was transferred to Cherry Point after spending only a very short time at Camp Lejeune, she was temporarily quartered in the maternity ward of the naval hospital.52 The station WMs were attached to Headquarters Squadron until WMD 2 was officially activated on 1 March 1951 with Captain Wilson commanding, Second Lieutenant Natalie Noble, executive officer, and Master Sergeant Alice J. Connolly, sergeant major. In November 1951, ground was broken for the Jet Hangar, a new WM service club, and when it opened the next spring, complete with juke box and patio, it was a popular spot for snacks, beer, soft drinks, and milk shakes.53*

Headquarters, Fleet Marine Force, Atlantic (FMFLant), located at Norfolk, Virginia, asked for and received a total of 10 WMs; all were administrative clerks, and all were privates first class. It was Colonel Towle's policy to assign a woman officer to any base where enlisted women served and so Lieutenant Kleberger was assigned to Norfolk as the assistant force adjutant and additionally as the "Supervisor of Women Marines."54

The original 10, Privates First Class Henrietta L. Belcher, Dorothy P. Eastman, Naomi M. Hallaway, Beatrice I. Harper, Theresa S. Kovar, Martha M. Ludwig, Margaret M. Martin, Mary A. Seman, Earlene Slaton, and

Mary H. Clements were attached to Headquarters Company, Headquarters and Service Battalion, FMFLant and quartered with the WAVES at the Norfolk Naval Base. Eventually on 1 April 1952, a WM Company was activated with Second Lieutenant Mary E. Sullivan commanding.

* "Being the first Woman Marine on a major Marine Corps Air Station (MCAS - Cherry Point) in five years (1945 -1950) posed its problems. Upon my arrival, I was directed to report to the Commanding General. During this meeting, he pointed out that the five-year interim that had elapsed since women (other than Navy nurses) had been aboard made it evident that male Marines were unaccustomed to having female Marines as an integral part of their daily lives. Therefore, I was stunned when he said he'd hold me personally responsible if 'anything happened' to any of the women! He further suggested that no women should leave the base except in pairs (like Nuns, as I later expressed it). I wanted to remonstrate, but all I could say was Aye, Aye, Sir!'—knowing full well that I couldn't go on liberty with the women. They arrived shortly after my meeting with the General, in increments of 100 to 200. Nothing untoward happened. The men seemed happy to have them aboard, and I think they really were!" Col Helen A. Wilson comments on draft manuscript, dtd 1 Jan 80.

During the Korean War years, women Marines returned to Hawaii, in 1951 to FMFPac at Pearl Harbor and in 1953 to the Marine Corps Air Station at Kaneohe Bay. On 31 July 1951 Lieutenant Colonel Hamblet became the first WM to be assigned to Headquarters, FMFPac. It was three months before Second Lieutenant Essie M. Lucas, graduate of the first WR recruit class in 1943 and the first officer candidate class in 1949, left San Francisco with 17 enlisted WMs on 5 October 1951. On board the military transport were Technical Sergeant Mary E. Roche; Sergeant Julia M. Pierce; Corporals Doris Allgood, Shirley Anderson, Lillian Brown, Olive G. Chapman, Anita F. Dale, Joyce R. Dupuy, Evangeline I. Lyon, Audrey E. Kleberger, Mary E. Scudder, Naomi J. Sexton, Ruth V. Tate, and Joan V. Walsh; and Privates First Class Nita M. Oliver, Vivia Smith, and Adoree R. Troche.55

Upon arrival, the women were attached to Headquarters Company, Headquarters and Service Battalion, FMFPac, and were assigned a small, but very attractive two-storied wooden barracks overlooking the parade deck. Mrs. Victory, wife of Brigadier General Randall M. Victory, had supervised the decoration and when dignitaries visited the command, receptions were often held in the WM lounge.58 Within six months the WMs had their own command, Company A, Headquarters and Service Battalion, FMFPac, under Second Lieutenant Margaret M. Schaffer. Unlike the male companies in the same battalion, the commanding officer of the woman Marine company was not empowered to sign record books or to issue company regulations. Only through the intervention of Colonel Towle several years later did the company commander gain the control usually associated with that position.57 Early members of the command included: Master Sergeant Mary E. Roche, Technical Sergeants Mary E. Grande and Ann M. Kopp, Staff Sergeant Margaret E. Boerner, and Sergeants Barbara Jean Dulinsky (who later was to be the first WM to serve in Vietnam) and Emma G. Ramsey (who retired as a captain in May 1971).

Capt Helen Wilson, the senior woman officer at Cherry Point, and Col Katherine A. Towle, Director of Women Marines, check clothing display in 1952.

In January 1956, Headquarters, FMFPac, moved from the Naval Base at Pearl Harbor to the old naval hospital at Aiea, which was designated Camp H. M. Smith. The women's company, commanded by Captain Kleberger, moved into former Navy nurses' quarters. The newly renovated barracks afforded suites for the senior SNCOs, private rooms for some, and rooms of two-to-four persons for sergeants and below. "The building abounded in lounges, exercise rooms, study rooms, and other fantastic facilities," recalled Lieutenant Colonel Kleberger.58

WMD 3, a group of 56 WMs led by First Lieutenant Phyllis J. Young, stationed at Kaneohe Bay, on the opposite side of the island from Pearl Harbor, was the last woman Marine command to be activated in the 1950s. In an interview published in the San Diego Chevron, First Sergeant Doris P. Milholen recounted her trip to the island:

There were four of us from the detachment that were to leave by seaplane [the MARs] to arrive in Kaneohe ahead of the rest of the women Marines. But for about four days before takeoff the plane had engine trouble and the flight was delayed. The main detachment almost made it to the islands by ship before we finally got off the ground.59

The women were quartered in one of the Marine Corps' newest and most modern barracks, sometimes referred to as "The Waldorf." The living areas were painted in pastel colors, and the amenities included a complete kitchen and adjoining dining room. The staff noncommissioned officers, living in single rooms, had private showers and their own lounge.60

WMD 3 was a short-lived unit. It closed on 1 September 1956 due to personnel replacement problems, but was reactivated during the Vietnam War.

Korean War Brings Changes To Recruit Training

The year 1950 marked significant changes to the woman Marine program and consequently to the 3d Recruit Training Battalion at Parris Island. Until May 1950, classes with a quota of 50 recruits each were convened consecutively. Beginning with the class of 18 September each class was composed of three platoons with a total strength of 150 women, and for the first time since World War II classes overlapped each other.

The Division of Plans and Policies indicated a need for 2,257 women Marines at posts and stations during fiscal year 1950 in addition to the 492 regular enlisted women on active duty. Based upon an estimate of 1,000 Reservists —organized and volunteer —on extended active duty, 1,257 women had to be provided for regular recruits. Added to this figure were the 300 nonveterans of the WR platoons who required basic training. The plans necessitated an increase in the table of organization of the recruit battalion and the assignment of another barracks, Building 901.61

Most of the staff members returned from Quantico where they had been assigned to WOTC and were supplemented by the I&Is of mobilized platoons. Captain Hale, away only six months, returned to Parris Island on 29 August as the interim commanding officer with First Lieutenant Dorothy A. Holmberg, the executive officer. Major Beckley, her work at Camp Lejeune completed, assumed command of the 3d Recruit Training Battalion on 18 September 1950 and Captain Hale became the executive officer.

With the increased need for Marines, the recruiting requirements were eased, allowing for the first time the enlistment of 18 year olds and also women who were not high school graduates but who could pass a high school equivalency examination. Colonel Towle was much opposed to the lowered educational standards, but was pressured by the other services and the Department of Defense. During this period the Veterans Administration, working on behalf of veterans desiring a college education, asked the colleges and universities to accept the equivalent examinations as evidence of successful completion of high school. The academic community was quick to point out the anomaly of asking an educational institution to recognize the examination when the military services did not.62

It was a different woman recruit who reported to Parris Island in September 1950: many were younger and less skilled; others, with a smattering of Reserve experience, arrived wearing PFC stripes. In the class that convened on 18 September, 33 of the 144 were nonveterans from WR platoons.63 Reluctantly, they moved the stripes from their uniforms. First Sergeant Schultz spoke of her duty as platoon sergeant and of her last recruit platoon —an honor platoon—which consisted mainly of Seattle Reservists. She said, "They must have had very good training. They were an outstanding platoon and my job was really alleviated as far as basic training was concerned."64

A Few Changes at Officer Candidate School

The changes at the Woman Officer Candidates Course marked a significant shift in policy regarding the entire woman Marine program. Until the Korean situation arose, only a few women were offered commissions in the Regular service and allowed to remain on active duty. In contrast, the entire graduating class of 1951 was ordered to duty for 24 months.65 Although this was intended as a temporary, emergency measure, it continued thereafter, changing only to lengthen the required service. The emphasis had changed from a strictly Reserve force on inactive duty to a nucleus of trained women Marines with at least a minimum of active duty experience.

The candidates who arrived in the summer of 1951 were uncertain of their status through much of the training, and those who were not college graduates feared that the Marine Corps would retain them on active duty as enlisted personnel rather than releasing them to finish their college education. Candidate Margaret A. Brewer, the last Director of Women Marines, and destined to be appointed the first woman general in 1978 was in this category, and she remembers the daily, changing rumors. The final result was that the women who accepted commissions were retained, those who refused commissions were discharged, and undergraduates returned home in a Reserve status. Colonel Brewer recalled that with one semester remaining she returned to school, finished in January, and expected to attend the officer's basic class convening in the fall. Instead, she was ordered to active duty in May and assigned to El Toro as a communications watch officer, one of only a few woman Marine officers never to have attended the Basic School.66

During the same period the Woman Officer Indoctrination Course underwent only a modest revision—shortening its training for the new lieutenants from eight to four weeks. For the graduates of the Woman Officer Candidate Course of 1952, however, the basic indoctrination class was lengthened to six weeks.

The Korean Years - Reprise

During the Korean years, the relatively few experienced women Marines were spread thinly and transferred often —Lieutenant Kleberger, for example, had four assignments, Quantico, Detroit, Norfolk, and Washington, D.C. in just two years. The officers and NCOs worked together scrubbing and polishing barracks, setting up the new companies, training Reservists and Regulars, guiding young lieutenants and privates, and holding together a group consisting of a disproportionate number of inexperienced Marines. In March 1950, at the beginning of the Korean war, there were only 28 Regular officers and 496 Regular enlisted WMs and 18 Reserve officers and 41 Reserve enlisted women on continuous active duty. Their common purpose and special pride in being a woman Marine served to override any personal differences which, if aired, would have undermined the group. They worked as one to bring the WMs back into the mainstream of the Marine Corps. Until one by one, the members of this pioneer group began to retire in 1963, they served as role models for the WMs who followed.

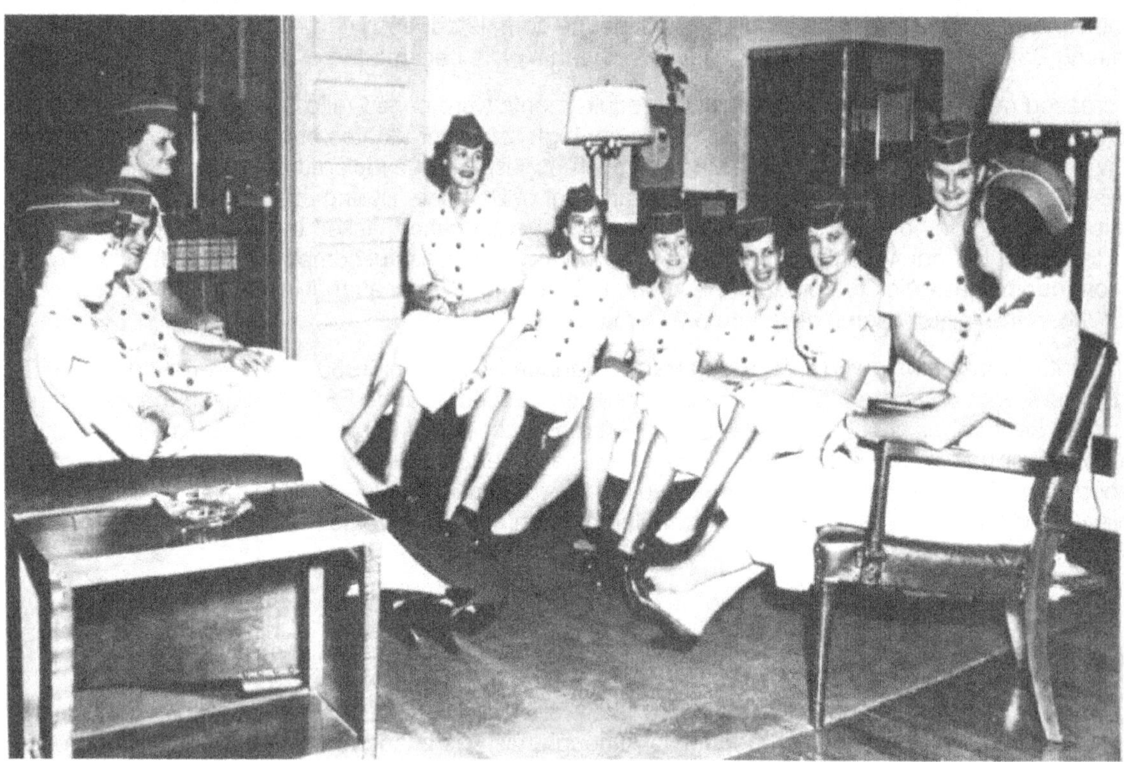

In the summer of 1951, Officer-in-Charge 1stLt Doris V. Kleberger (seated at far right) meets in barracks lounge with the first women Marines assigned to FMFLant, Norfolk.

Congratulations are extended to 2dLt Nancy Flint (right) by Col Katherine A. Towle, Director of Women Marines (left), and LtCol Julia E. Hamblet, Commanding Officer, Women Officer Training Detachment, upon Lt Flint's graduation from the 4th Woman Officer Indoctrination Course, Marine Corps Schools, Quantico, on 1 November 1952.

CHAPTER 5

Utilization and Numbers, 1951-1963

Utilization of Women Marines, Evolution of a Policy - Report of Procedures Analysis Office, 1951 - Women Officers' MOSs, 1948-1953 - 1950-1953 Summary - 1954-1964 Numbers - Utilization, 1954-1964 - Rank Does Not Have Its Privileges, Officers - Rank Does Not Have Its Privileges, Staff Noncommissioned Officers - Noncommissioned Officer Leadership School - A Woman in the Fleet Marine Force - 1954-1964 Summary

Utilization of Women Marines—Evolution of a Policy

The war in Korea marked the first of three turning points, each one opening new career fields to women Marines. The second turning point was the Woman Marine Program Study Group (Pepper Board) meeting in

1964. The third was the Ad-Hoc Committee on Increased Effectiveness in the Utilization of Women in the Marine Corps (Snell Committee) of 1973.

After World War II nearly all women Marines worked in the areas of administration and supply. WR veterans who had served in technical fields in World War II, especially in aviation specialties, were disappointed when they found themselves reclassified as typists and stenographers upon integration in 1948 and 1949. It is probable that many skilled WRs, trained during the war, when faced with the prospect of a change in occupational field, did not apply for Regular status.

Pre-Korea recruits, in spite of the detailed classification procedures followed at Parris Island, were invariably earmarked for administrative work. Ninety-five percent of them were assigned directly to a job; the remainder, however, were given formal training at the Personnel Administration School at Parris Island or the Yeoman Course at San Diego.1 In the spring of 1950, just before the war, two recruits, Privates Nancy L. Bennett and Cynthia L. Thies, slated to be photographers, became the first WMs to complete boot camp and to be assigned to an occupational field other than administration. Both Marines had had experience in photography.2

The shortsightedness of these restrictive measures limiting the occupational opportunities and training of women to clerical duties was evident as soon as the North Koreans invaded South Korea in June 1950. Then, expediency dictated a more diverse classification of women. Manpower was in critically short supply. Each Marine Corps base was polled on the number of billets that could be filled by women, and on the billeting space available for distaff Marines. Unfortunately, the available women Marines had not been trained to fill many of the needs identified by this survey.

Report of Procedures Analysis Office, 1951

On 12 December 1950, four months after the mobilization, an internal memorandum in the Division of Plans and Policies on the subject of requirements for women Marines revealed that there were 76 military billets at Headquarters Marine Corps which by their nature could be filled by WMs but to which women were not assigned. Lack of training was cited as the cause. Furthermore, women were assigned to billets in accordance with ability, regardless of rank deficiency. At the time of the memorandum, 70 women privates first class were assigned to billets designated for higher ranks: 27 filling corporals billets; 32 filling sergeants billets; 9 in staff sergeant billets; 1 in a technical sergeant slot; and 1 in a master sergeant billet. It was noted, as well, that of a total of 438 military jobs at Headquarters, 230 were coded as requiring male Marines and of these "must be male" billets, 12 were filled by WMs. The recommendations made in view of the situation was that the table of organization be reviewed with an eye towards decreasing 'requirements for male Marines and that WMs, Regular and Reserve, with adequate work qualifications and rank be ordered to Headquarters. A like number of WMs from Headquarters, the least qualified clerically, would be transferred to posts and stations.3

Colonel Towle found the memorandum useful in pointing out what she saw as, "The difficulty of attempting to utilize untrained personnel in skilled military billets" and "the need of remedial measures."4 She reiterated her position that specialist training beyond recruit indoctrination was essential to meet the needs of both the Marine Corps and the individual Marine. Her conclusion was:

A policy which relies upon an ever-diminishing supply of World War II women reservists to continue to provide the skills presently needed by the Marine Corps as well as those which would be required in all-out mobilization, rather than establish systematic long range training beyond recruit indoctrination for younger women enlistees of the regular Marine Corps is considered unrealistic and shortsighted, as well as uneconomical.5

Subsequently, in May 1951, Plans and Policies Division asked that a study be made to determine the military occupational specialties (MOS) in which women could be utilized and the proportion of the total number which could be profitably employed. The ensuing study conducted by the Procedures Analysis Office, evaluated MOSs on the basis of utilization of women in the past, legal restrictions, physical requirements, job environment, availability of training facilities, and the existence of promotional outlets. They noted that while women Marines were assigned MOSs in 25 different occupational fields, actually about 95 percent of the WMs were concentrated in only six fields. The lessons learned in the emergency brought on by the war in Korea were apparent in the conclusions drawn by the committee that:

a. Women can be used in 27 of the 43 occupational fields.

b. For maximum effectiveness, women should be employed (as a general rule) in a limited number of major activities.

c. Under the present tables of organization, a maximum of approximately 6,500 women can be employed.

d. Full utilization of women Marines requires an evaluation of the combined influence of all "restricted assignment" groups upon rotation policies.

e. Immediate steps should be taken to utilize women in all appropriate MOSs so that under full mobilization, expansion can be readily accomplished.

f. Service schools must be opened to women to train them for the appropriate MOS.

g. Billets that can be filled by women must be identified on tables of organization.

The 27 occupational fields considered appropriate were:

01 Personnel and Administration

02 Intelligence

04 Logistics

14 Mapping and Surveying

15 Printing

22 Fire Control Instrument Repair

25 Operational Communications

26 Communication Material

27 Electronics

30 Supply

31 Warehousing, Shipping, and Receiving

33 Food

34 Disbursing

35 Motor Transport

40 Machine Accounting

41 Post Exchange

43 Public Information

Attending the Conference of Women Marine Commanding Officers and Women Representatives of Marine Corps Reserve and Recruitment Districts in June 1955, were (from left, seated): Maj Dorothy M. Knox; LtCol Pauline B. Beckley; Col Julia E. Hamblet; LtCol Elsie E. Hill; LtCol Barbara J. Bishop; and Maj Helen M. Tatum. Also (from left, standing): 1stLt Rita A. Ciotti; Capt Mary S. Mock; 1stLt Ruth J. O'Holleran; Capt Dolores A. Thorning; Maj Emily Horner; 1stLt Anne S. Ritter; Capt Valeria F. Hilgart; Capt Jeanne Fleming; Maj Nita B. Warner; Maj Shirley J. Fuetsch; 1stLt Nancy L. Doser; Capt Margaret E. Dougherty; Capt Elena D. Brigotti; and Capt Rosalie Crites.

46 Photography

49 Training and Training Aids

52 Special Services

55 Band

66 Aviation Electronics

67 Air Control

68 Aerology

69 Aviation Synthetic Training Devices

70 Aviation Operations and Intelligence

71 Flight Equipment 6

Colonel Towle endorsed the study calling it, "thorough, thoughtful, and essentially a realistic presentation of facts pertinent to the utilization of women within the Marine Corps." She did, however, take exception to the stated position that while women could perform the duties of the 27 recommended occupational fields, they could not be placed in all of the billets falling under each major heading since the "most effective utilization occurs when women supervise only women and when situations in which women supervise men or mixed groups are minimized."7 She submitted that:

the most effective utilization of women does not necessarily depend upon women supervising women, unless credence is also given to the corollary of this statement that men should supervise only men. The situation at Headquarters Marine Corps is an excellent example of the invalidity of this contention. During World War II there were many instances at many posts and stations where women supervised both men and women with notable success. In this connection, it should be remembered that women officers' commissions are identical in wording to those of their male counterparts charging them not only with the duties and responsibilities of their grade and positions, but also assuring them of comparable military authority.8*

* In fact, during the Korean War, women Marines made a few tentative steps toward taking over supervision of several all-male groups. In 1952, Staff Sergeant Hazel A. Lindahl, a Reservist from Boston, held the top enlisted post at Camp Lejeune as Camp Sergeant Major of more than 40,000 Marines. During the same period, Master Sergeant Margaret A. Goings was the First Sergeant, Headquarters and Service Battalion, Marine Corps Base, Camp Lejeune. (Div WMs Scrapbook, box 4, WMs HQMC Records)

The final report of the Procedures Analysis Office was submitted in November 1951 and generated a letter the following January to all interested divisions and sections for comment. For the most part there was general agreement with the theory that wider utilization of women Marines would increase their potential effectiveness upon all-out mobilization. The Division of Aviation suggested a greater percentage of WMs could be properly assigned aviation specialties and recommended the addition of Occupational Field 64, Aircraft Maintenance and Repair, to the list of appropriate MOSs, but was overruled. The agency managing the 35 field, motor transport, commented that women were qualified to drive the cars, trucks, and jeeps, but the requirement that the driver load and unload the vehicle restricted their use. In the area of communications, it was recommended that a new field, administrative communications, be created and that women be used as switchboard operators. Women as instructors at the Communications-Electronic School was specifically ruled out due to their lack of combat experience and because they would have to supervise men.9 *

* In 1961, 10 years later, Lance Corporal Priscilla Carlson became the first woman Marine to instruct at Communications-Electronic School at San Diego. She was a graduate of 36 weeks training at the Basic Electronic Course, Radar Fundamentals Course, and Aviation Radar Repair Course, and she instructed the Radar Fundamentals Course. (San Diego Chevron, 28 Jul 61).

All comments and recommendations were incorporated and the list of appropriate MOSs for enlisted women Marines was promulgated in April 1952, about a year before the end of the Korean conflict.10

The same memorandum identified the following 16 occupational fields as unsuitable for women Marines.

03 Infantry

07 Antiaircraft Artillery

08 Field Artillery

11 Utilities

13 Construction and Equipment

18 Tank and Amphibian Tractor

21 Weapons Repair

23 Ammunition and Explosive Ordnance Disposal

32 Supply Services

36 Steward

56 Guided Missile

57 Chemical Warfare and Radiological Defense

58 Security and Guard

64 Aircraft Maintenance and Repair

65 Aviation Ordnance

73 Pilot

In spite of the above exclusions, during the Korean War at least a few women served in the utilities, weapons repair, supply services, and security guard field.11 It is probable that they were Reservists already knowledgeable in these occupations.

At the time of the study, only six WMs were in the motor transport field. One of these, Sergeant Theresa "Sue" Sousa, mobilized with the Washington, D.C. Reserve platoon and on duty at Camp Pendleton, became a driver through determination, persistence, and because she proved she could handle a truck and jeep.12 Then, in the fall of 1952, women were assigned to motor transport school for the intensive five-week course. The first WMs to receive such training since 1945 were Privates First Class Hazel E. Robbins, Christin Villanueva, Jessie Chance, Elizabeth Drew, and Ann Oberfell. By 1954, the number of women in motor transport jumped to 111.13 Colonel Valeria F. Hilgart, who was Commanding Officer, Company A, Pearl Harbor that year, remembered that she had 22 women Marine drivers and a woman Marine dispatcher, Sergeant Barbara Jean Dulinsky.14 This career field has been volatile for WMs as the number dwindled to seven in 1964 and rose to 186 in 1977.15

Now retired Gunnery Sergeant Helen A. Brusack and one other former WM worked in radio repairman assignments in 1950 but formal training in this field was not reopened to women until March 1953 when four WMs (Technical Sergeants Rosita A. Martinez and Katherine F. Tanalski and Sergeants Norine Anderson and Mary Williams) received orders to the 16-week course at the crystal grinding shop at the Baltimore Signal Depot in Fort Holabird, Baltimore. The highly technical course covered the manufacture of precisely cut crystals which controlled the frequency in radios.19 Like the motor transport field, this also proved to be a volatile field as the number of WMs assigned to it dropped to two in 1961 and then grew to 166 in 1977.17

Women Officers' MOSs, 1948-1953

After World War II, all officer MOSs were grouped into categories.18 For example, Category I included MOSs suitable for Regular unrestricted officers; Category II MOSs were suitable for Regular limited duty officers of company grade; and with the passage of the Women's Armed Services Integration Act of 1948, Category V MOSs were deemed suitable for Regular women officers. Only the following nine MOSs in four occupational fields, plus the designation for basic officers (unassigned second lieutenants) and one ground colonel were considered to be appropriate for women:

0101 Basic Personnel and Administration Officer

0105 Administrative Officer

0110 Personnel Classification and Assignment Officer

0130 Adjutant

0190 Personnel Research Officer

3001 Basic Supply Administrative Officer

4001 Basic Machine Accounting Officer

4010 Machine Accounting Officer

4301 Basic Public Information Officer

9901 Basic Officer

9906 Colonel, Ground

For most of the fields, women officers were limited to the basic position and therefore not allowed to move up the ladder in that specialty as they were promoted. The war in Korea caused some of the restrictions to be lifted in 1950, but women officers continued to serve in a relatively minute number of fields.

This untenable situation was noted by the Classifications Section on 1 November 1952 when it was found that the large majority of the older, more experienced women officers were assigned MOS 0105 (Administrative Officer); few women held an additional MOS; and no woman at the time had two additional MOSs. In all, over 60 percent of all women officers in the Marine Corps were assigned a basic MOS or MOS 0105. The discovery led to a study involving a review of the cases of all women officers on active duty and letters to all sections interested in MOS assignments. In view of the antipathy displayed in 1947 and 1948 toward the use of women in the Marine Corps, the comments emanating from this study were gratifying to the women officers. The Assistant Chief of Staff G-l wrote:

During the congressional discussion prior to the passage of the "Women's Armed Services Integration Act of 1948" it was emphasized that the primary reason for establishing women in Regular services was to provide a nucleus of trained women for rapid expansion in event of an emergency. If the Marine Corps assigns women officers only to the MOSs listed . . . there will not be a group of well trained, experienced women officers who could provide the necessary leadership in the many fields where large numbers of women will be utilized in the event of a national emergency.19

From the Classification Branch came the comment, "In fact in the final analysis it became apparent that a woman officer should be assigned any MOS for which she had become qualified by actual performance of duty in a satisfactory manner."20 And following the list of recommended MOSs submitted by the Personnel Control Branch was the statement, "It is further suggested that women officers not be precluded from assignment of other MOSs for which an individual may be qualified."21

In the second phase of the study each woman officer's qualifications were considered as well as the description of each MOS. Decisions were based on legal restrictions, physical restrictions, rotation constraints, technical schools open to women, billets held by WRs in World War II, and "American mores." As a result, the variety of MOSs assigned to women officers increased somewhat, mainly in the area of additional MOSs, that is, in secondary jobs for which they were considered qualified. On 1 March 1953, the allocation of primary MOSs to women officers was as follows:

01 Administration / 87

02 Intelligence / 1

25 Communications / 7

30 Supply / 25

31 Transportation/ 1

34 Disbursing / 10

41 Post Exchange / 4

43 Public Information / 7

49 Training / 2

52 Special Services / 7

9906 Ground Colonel / 1

Women Marine Officers on active duty 22 / 152

The Division of Aviation had identified the seven fields of aircraft maintenance, aviation electronics, air control, aerology, aviation synthetic training devices, aviation operations and intelligence, and flight equipment as suitable for assignment to women Marine officers, but only three, aerology, training devices, and flight equipment appeared on the final approved list. As it turned out, women officers were not assigned to aviation specialties of any nature until about l960.

Subsequent to the study, in March 1953, the Director, Division of Personnel, Brigadier General Reginald H. Ridgely, Jr., recommended that category restrictions on the assignment of MOSs to women officers be permanently removed and that a policy be established which would be consistent with the intent of the Women's Armed Services Integration Act of 1948.23

Col Julia E. Hamblet (left), Director of Women Marines, and her assistant, 1stLt Doris V. Kleberger, confer with Maj Wesley C. Noren, monitor of woman officer assignments.

1950-1953 Summary

The Korean War brought permanent changes to the women Marine program, the most obvious being the return of WMs to major posts and stations. When the armistice was signed on 27 July 1953, women were serving at Headquarters Marine Corps; at the Marine Corps Air Stations at Cherry Point, El Toro, and Kaneohe; at the Recruit Depots at San Diego and Parris Island; at Marine Corps Bases at Camp Lejeune and Camp Pendleton, Quantico, Norfolk, and Pearl Harbor; at both the Depot of Supplies and the Department of the Pacific in San Francisco; at the various Reserve districts; and in Stuttgart, Germany.*

1954-1964

As the pressures of war subsided, so did the urgency to revitalize the women Marine program. The Personnel Department stated that "The Marine Corps' long range plan for the utilization of women Marines is to utilize them in sufficient numbers and appropriate military occupational specialties to provide a nucleus of trained women for rapid expansion in the event of full mobilization."24 The wording was sufficiently vague to allow commanders to vacillate, to balk at the idea of women placed in key positions, and to deny formal schools to WMs.

Numbers

Numerically, women were limited by law to a ceiling of two percent of the authorized strength of the Corps, and the women officers were limited to 10 percent of the number of enlisted women. The Marine Corps set a goal of one percent rather than the allowable two, but never reached even that figure during the period

1954-1964. The one percent was not just an arbitrary, anti-woman measure but was arrived at in recognition of the Corps' mission and organization. Traditionally, the Marine Corps is a compact fighting unit with much of its logistics and some of its supporting personnel furnished by the Navy. Women Marines were prohibited, by law, from ". . . duty in aircraft while such aircraft are engaged in combat missions and duty on vessels of the Navy except hospital ships and naval transports."25 They were prohibited, by tradition, from Fleet Marine Force units, security forces at shore activities, and any unit whose mission it was to develop tactics or combat equipment.

* In September 1952, for the first time, women Marines were assigned to duty in Europe. Arriving to serve on the staff of the Commander in Chief of U. S. Forces in Europe was Second Lieutenant Sara Frances McLamore, followed a week later by Captain Jeanette I. Sustad. Captain Sustad was assigned to message control and Second Lieutenant McLamore became the commanding officer of the joint detachment of enlisted women. They were soon joined by 11 enlisted women Marines. (Colonel Jeanette I. Sustad interview with Hist & Mus Div, HQMC, dtd 20 Jun 77 [Oral Hist Collection, Hist&MusDiv, HQMC]).

To accomplish its mission, the Marine Corps is divided generally into 60 percent operating forces and 40 percent supporting units. Of the latter, during wartime and based on Korean War figures, eight percent could be patients, prisoners, and transients, leaving only 32 percent of the billets available to women. Even within the supporting establishment, certain factors restricted the utilization of women: legal prohibitions, Marine Corps rotation policy, and the necessity for in-service training for men in preparation for assignment to combat jobs or to the fleet. To further complicate the matter, women are only one in a list of restricted assignment groups which include sole-surviving sons, and twice-wounded Marines.26 Added to the above constraints was the fact that all services planned a cut in women's strength in 1954. During the years between Korea and Vietnam the strength of the women Marines went from a peak of 2,787 in September 1953 to a low of 1,448 on 30 June 1964.

Utilization, 1954-1964

While women were assigned at various times to as many as 27 occupational fields, for the most part they remained concentrated in the same six or seven specialties, with 45-55 percent in personnel administration, followed by supply, communications (telephone operators), disbursing, data processing, post exchange, and public information. It took nearly 100 women officers to fill the strictly women's billets (WM companies, WM recruit and officer training, recruiting, officer selection duty, I&Is of WR platoons). Since the women officer strength averaged 125 for the years 1954-1964, the incidence of their assignment outside the woman Marine program was minimal.

Colonel Hamblet, Director of Women Marines 1953-1959, devoted much time on her annual inspection trips trying to convince the personnel people to assign senior women Marines to jobs other than those within the women's program. She found a reluctance to place women in positions where they had not served before, at least in the memory of the current base population. Most activities, on the other hand, welcomed the presence of young, attractive women Marines in window dressing type jobs, as receptionists, for example, as long as they did not count against their allotted strength. Having succeeded in placing WMs in suitable billets, the director then met just as strong resistance in getting them released for a tour as a recruiter, drill instructor, or company commander.27

A number of factors combined to bring on this ambivalence in the utilization of women Marines, only a portion of which could be attributed to sex discrimination. The average woman Marine was in the marriageable and child bearing age group and the forced separation brought on by prevailing regulations in this regard caused a proportionately high attrition rate for WMs compared to male Marines. A married woman could ask to be discharged after serving only one year of her enlistment. * There was, therefore, some instability and an unsatisfactory rate of personnel turnover that could not be stemmed without a drastic change in policy.

* See Chapter 7 for a detailed discussion of marriage and motherhood regulations.

A second factor working to the detriment of the women was the insufficiency of their training coupled with the male Marines' expectation that women are naturally good typists, stenographers, and clerks. As late as 1955, only five percent of the WMs received formal training of any kind 28 The majority of the enlisted women reported to their first duty assignment after a mere eight weeks of recruit training whereas the male private spent 12 weeks in boot camp followed by advanced training, and usually a tour in the Fleet Marine

Force, thereby arriving at a post with some service behind him. The woman private suffered in comparison from both a military and a professional point of view, unless her supervisor understood the situation and took extra time not only to correct her work but to help her with the basics of military life like uniform regulations and saluting. Lieutenant Colonel Gail M. Reals, recalling her first job out of boot camp, relates that she reported to one office in the Education Center at Quantico in 1955 and was transferred to another almost immediately because she did not have a firm grasp of naval correspondence procedures, although she was an above average typist.** 29

** In 1985, while serving as the chief of staff of the Marine Corps Development and Education Command, Colonel Reals became the first woman to be selected by a promotion board, in competition with her male Marine peers, to the rank of brigadier general.

There is a feeling among women veterans of the time, almost impossible to prove, that women had to perform better than men to be considered acceptable. Then, once a women was found unsatisfactory, the office would not want another woman, no matter how many men had done poorly in the same billet.'

Women officers were in an even less favorable position since their training after officer candidate school was limited to the six-week Woman Officer Indoctrination Course compared to the male lieutenants' nine-month Basic School. Furthermore, technical training was extremely rare and, for women, professional military schools were unheard of.

During these years, 1954-1964, very few new fields became available to women Marines. Generally, they were assigned to the same 27 occupational fields that were opened to them as a result of the Korean War. Most of the time, they served in no more than 21 of these at one given moment, and they maintained the usual 50 percent in administration, followed by supply, operational communications, and disbursing.

Rank Does Not Have Its Privileges - Officers

In this post-Korean era, senior women officers and senior staff noncommissioned officers faced similar problems, since by this time there was a sizable number of each and only a limited number of women's program billets requiring so much rank. Women lieutenant colonels exchanged a few jobs as if on a circuit: Commanding Officer, Woman Recruit Training Battalion; Commanding Officer, Woman Marine Training Detachment; and an occasional assistant G-l billet at a base that had been asked if it would accept a woman. It was the rule rather than the exception to serve in the same billet a second time. Typical of the pattern was the career of Lieutenant Colonel Elsie E. Hill, who commanded the officer candidate school 1949-1951 and again 1965-1966. She commanded the recruit battalion 1954-1956, exchanged positions with Lieutenant Colonel Barbara J. Bishop as Head, Women's Branch, Division of Reserve, Headquarters Marine Corps and in 1959 returned to the recruit battalion at Parris Island. In contrast to the Regular women officers, the two Reserve lieutenant colonels on active duty, Hazel E. Benn in educational services, and Lily H. Gridley, a lawyer, served a full 20 years in specialized jobs.

LtCol Lily H. Gridley, U.S. Marine Corps Reserve, first woman to serve as a legal assistance officer, is photographed at Marine Corps Headquarters in 1955.

LtCol Emma H. Clowers discusses the assignment of women Marines with a fellow officer in the G-1 Division at Headquarters, U.S. Marine Corps in 1955.

Perhaps the most remarkable senior woman officer assignment during this period was that of Lieutenant Colonel Emma H. Clowers as Head, Personal Affairs Branch, Personnel Department, Headquarters Marine Corps.30 She was originally ordered in as the assistant branch head on 28 April 1959 but became branch head when a male colonel's orders to that department were rescinded. No record can be found of a woman Marine branch head on that level either before or for many years after her tour. She served in that capacity for seven years, during which she received strong and loyal support from the director of the Personnel

Department and from the 15-20 male officers serving as heads of the various sections and as assistant branch head. Lieutenant Colonel Clowers found only one difficulty in her position which was directly related to her being a woman, and that was her lack of rank during some of the interbranch negotiations. The law at the time barred women officers, other than the director, from promotion to colonel, resulting in a woman officer (Clowers) performing duties for many years in a billet which before and after her assignment were performed by male colonels. Upon completion of that tour, Lieutenant Colonel Clowers was awarded her second Navy Commendation Medal, having received the first during World War II. The citation that accompanied her award noted that the duties were normally assigned to an officer of greater rank and that the hostilities in Vietnam demanded a rapid expansion of the branch. The scope of her responsibilities are underscored in that citation which read in part:

Extremely competent and resourceful, Colonel Clowers performed duties, which are normally assigned to an officer of greater rank, in a highly professional manner during a time when hostilities in Vietnam demanded rapid expansion of the Personal Affairs Branch to meet the added responsibilities. Through infinite foresight and judicious planning she accomplished organizational reforms which enhanced the effectiveness of the Personal Affairs Branch. In addition to establishing and maintaining excellent liaison and cooperation with agencies in both the military and civilian communities through which Marines and their dependents receive counselling, financial help, and other needed assistance, she substantially improved and expedited methods of informing concerned and anxious families of the condition of wounded or seriously ill Marines. She brought the needs of Marines and their families to the attention of those who draft and present proposed legislation to the Congress, thereby improving the scope and applicability of laws directed toward the necessities of military servicemen. With immeasurable personal concern and a keen sense of responsibility for the welfare and interests of Marines, she formulated a program for personal notification of the next of kin of casualties in Vietnam; developed and coordinated a system by which Marine Retired and Reserve General Officers visit evacuees in twenty-three naval hospitals; contributed materially to the formation of the Family Assistance Program, and directed expansion of job counselling facilities to assist retiring and retired personnel in finding suitable employment. Throughout her seven years in this capacity she skillfully directed her attention to the most minute details of each facet of her responsibilities in a manner which exemplifies more than could possibly be expected from any officer. Colonel Clowers' outstanding service, judgment and devotion to duty reflected great credit upon herself and the Marine Corps and upheld the highest traditions of the United States Naval Service.31

Rank Does Not Have Its Privileges - Staff Noncommissioned Officers

The staff noncommissioned officers were in a slightly different position in that they generally had a specialty and some training, whereas nearly all of the field grade officers at the time were classified as either women's unit officer or personnel administrator. Nevertheless, the staff noncommissioned officer found that 1) she was moved out of her field too often to serve in women's recruiting or training billets, and 2) as she became more senior, she was less welcome since she would be in the position to supervise male Marines. Then, once she proved herself, she was often considered indispensable. Inevitably, a controversy erupted when she was needed to fill a slot in the women's program, and more often than not, the Director of Women Marines was blamed by the woman for sending her on a third recruiting tour, and accused by the assignment branch of meddling in their business.

The staff noncommissioned officers of this period were, for the most part, former WRs who had served in responsible positions during World War II and had seen women perform all manner of duties to include supervision of male Marines. This only made them more incredulous at the narrow attitude taken by many male Marines. Master Sergeant Ruth Ryan, in 1960, for example, was on orders to the Reserve district in Atlanta as the Logistics Chief until it was discovered that she was a woman. Eventually she went as planned, but only after being interviewed by her prospective officer in charge, an unusual procedure, and then not as the Logistics Chief, but as the Fiscal Chief, since that was deemed more appropriate.32

Retired First Sergeant Frances A. Curwen Bilski represents a similar case. She had been a mail clerk from August 1943 until September 1946 at the fleet post office in San Francisco. Following the war, she was a member of the VTU and later the WR platoon in Boston. Mobilized for the Korean War, she served as postmaster at the Montford Point branch of the Camp Lejeune post office, and as an instructor at the Marine Corps East Coast Postal School in 1952. In the early 1960s, after having served as postmaster at Parris Island, she was ordered to similar duty in Hawaii, but the command absolutely refused to have a woman in the job, saying that the mail bags were too heavy for a female.33

Noncommissioned Officer Leadership School

With a memorandum to the Assistant Chief of Staff, G-3, written by 12 May 1952, Colonel Towle initiated a stream of correspondence that culminated with the creation of an NCO Leadership School for women Marines.34 She cited the prevailing accelerated promotions of enlisted Marines with short periods of service and the loss of older, qualified NCOs as evidence of the need for such a course. Colonel Towle recommended that the school be located at Quantico in the same barracks used by officer candidates and basic second lieutenants from June through November.

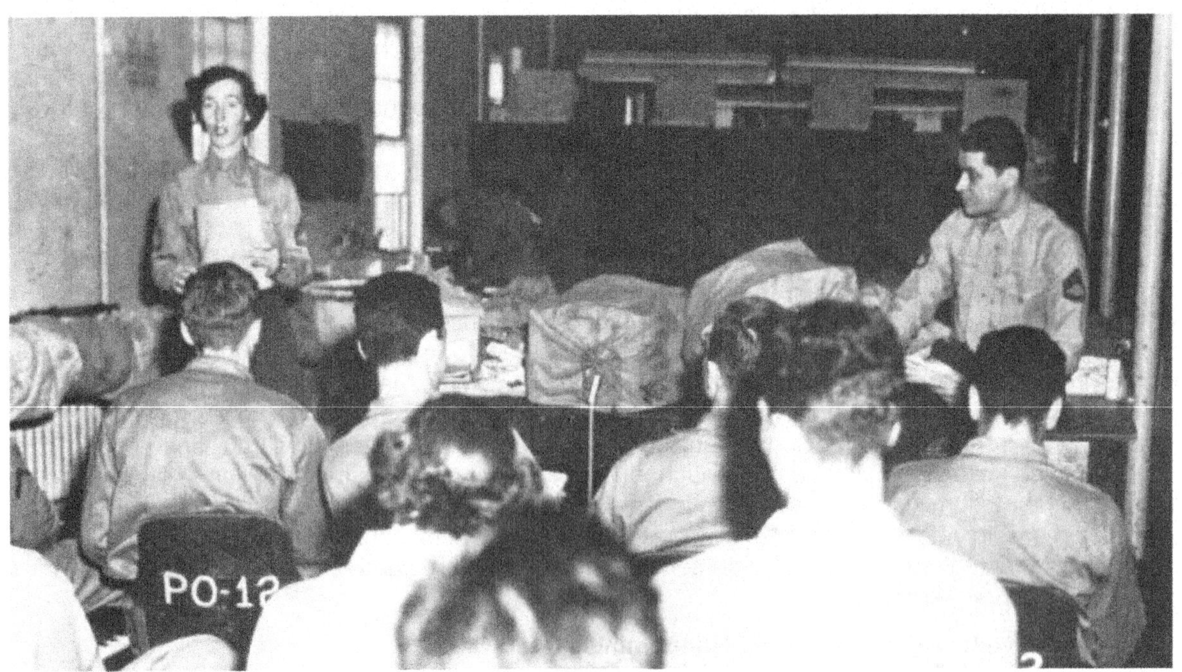

A World War II mail clerk, TSgt Frances A. Curwen, the Marine Corps' only female postmaster in 1952, supervised the Montford Point Branch, Camp Lejeune Post Office.

Instructors of the Woman Marine Staff NCO Leadership School, Camp Lejeune, congratulate Officer-in-Charge Elaine T. Carville on her promotion to captain in July 1953.

The Commandant, Marine Corps Schools, and Commanding General, Marine Corps Base, Camp Lejeune, were both queried on the matter and in the meantime, the Director was asked to furnish guidance concerning the mission of the proposed school, subject matter to be covered, course length, and appropriate rank of the students. In answer, Colonel Towle recommended a four-week course whose mission would be ". . . to train an efficient and continuing staff of women noncommissioned officers for the duties and responsibilities commonly associated with 'troop' leadership,"35 and to provide a source of potential officer candidates. She emphasized classes in leadership, personnel management, technique of instruction, use of training aids, Uniform Code of Military Justice, and military customs and courtesies for students ranking from staff sergeant through master sergeant.

Camp Lejeune was selected as the site and First Lieutenant Mary Jane Connell was named officer in charge. On 19 January 1953, for the first time since 1945 a Staff NCO Leadership School for women was convened. Major General Henry D. Linscott, the commanding general, gave the opening address to the 25 members of the new class.36 Classes were held in a wing of Barracks 65 at the Navy Field Medical Research Laboratory five and a half days a week. In preparation, all the hand-selected instructors, Technical Sergeant Alice McIntyre, Technical Sergeant Frances A. Curwen (later Bilski), Master Sergeant Lillian V. Dolence, and Technical Sergeant Josephine R. Milburn attended a month-long session at the Navy Instructors School at Norfolk, Virginia.37 Members of the first class included:

Master Sergeant Margaret A. Goings

Master Sergeant Alice M. Reny

Master Sergeant Margery R. Wilkie

Technical Sergeant Loraine G. Bruso

Technical Sergeant Eleanor L. Childers

Technical Sergeant Margaret L. Harwell

Technical Sergeant Beatrice J. Jackson

Technical Sergeant Dorothy L. Kearns

Technical Sergeant Blossom J. McCall

Technical Sergeant Sarah N. Thornton

Technical Sergeant Laura H. Woolger\

Staff Sergeant May S. Belletto

Staff Sergeant Phyllis J. Curtiss

Staff Sergeant Anna M. Finnigan

Staff Sergeant Nellie C George

Staff Sergeant Naomi Hutchinson

Staff Sergeant Inez E. Smith

Staff Sergeant Dorothy L. Vollmer

Sergeant Carolyn J. Freeman

Sergeant Sonya A. Green

Sergeant Mary E. King

Sergeant Dorothy L. Ley

Sergeant Carol J. Homan

Sergeant Margaret A. Shaffer 38

Colonel Towle gave the graduation speech and distributed the diplomas at ceremonies held on 13 February 1953, 10th anniversary of the Women Marines. The honor student for this first woman Marine NCO Leadership Class was Master Sergeant Reny, with Technical Sergeant Childers in second place, and Staff Sergeant Vollmer in third. Classes continued at Camp Lejeune for a little more than a year on a five-week cycle, four weeks of training and one week off. Staff changes brought Captain Elaine T. Carville as the officer in charge with First Lieutenant Connell as her assistant and Technical Sergeants Lillian J. West and June V. Doberstein as instructors.39

Colonel Hamblet, successor to Colonel Towle, reevaluated the situation and while convinced of the real need for the school, found the basis on which it was being run to be inefficient. Only 129 students rather than the authorized 225 had completed the training. The table of organization called for one officer, four enlisted instructors, and one clerk typist and the physical facilities used by the women included an office, a classroom, and a wing of a barracks. She proposed a move to Quantico since the staff required to train officer candidates from June through November could handle the NCO School during the winter months with only two additional enlisted women instructors. In turn, these enlisted women could be profitably used as platoon sergeants in the officer candidate program. There was at the time an unsuccessful (in terms of numbers) winter officer candidate class which would have to be cancelled, thereby making the barracks, classroom, and staff available.40

The plan, promising a personnel and financial savings, was enthusiastically endorsed at Headquarters and by September 1954 the change were made. Technical Sergeants West and Doberstein was transferred to Quantico where they worked with NCOs during the winter and officer candidates in the summer. Captain Carville was sent to Parris Island, and the remainder of the staff was dispersed.

Capt E. T. Carville, officer-in-charge, NCO Leadership School, is pictured (front row center) with Class 9 in 1953. MSgt P. C. Nigro (second row left) was the honor graduate.

The majority of women noncommissioned officers received leadership training during these years, 1954-1964, at the course conducted by the Women Marines Detachment, Quantico. Several commands assigned women to local, predominantly male, NCO schools. In fact, as early as 1951, Staff Sergeant Laura H. Woolger attended the 2d Wing NCO leadership school, graduating on 10 August of that year. A different tactic was tried at San Diego, California, where in 1959, the depot NCO school conducted two one-week accelerated courses for women Marines.

A Woman in the Fleet Marine Force

In this decade of status quo, it is surprising to find the first reported WM working in an FMF headquarters, admittedly in a traditional job. On 13 January 1954, Private First Class Betty Sue Murray was assigned as the secretary to the Commanding General, 2d Marine Division, Major General George F. Good, Jr.41 The general had called Captain Elaine T. Carville, Commanding Officer, Woman Marine Company, Camp Lejeune, and told her that his office was in a mess, that he could not find anything, and that he wanted a woman Marine immediately. She explained that women Marines could not be assigned to an FMF unit, but the general only answered that he trusted her to work out the administrative details. Private First Class Murray was officially attached to the office of the Commanding Officer, Headquarters Battalion, Marine Corps Base (Colonel John H. Cook), billeted in the WM barracks, and worked for Major General Good. She stayed at the job long enough to serve his successors, Major General Lewis B. Puller and Brigadier General Edward W. Snedeker.42 Not until 1975, 20 years in the future, would WMs be assigned legitimately to any FMF unit.

1954-1964 Summary

The WM situation then, on 30 June 1964, was a strength of 129 officers and 1,320 enlisted women serving in 20 occupational fields. Women received little formal technical MOS training and were assigned to only one professional development course, the NCO Leadership School.

CHAPTER 6

Utilization and Numbers: Pepper Board, 1964-1972

The Pepper Board - Women Marine Program Revitalized, 1965-1973 - Strength Increases - Women Officers Specialist Training, 1965-1973 - Women Lawyers and Judges, A Beginning - Professional Training - Amphibious Warfare School - Post-Graduate Schooling - Command and Staff College— The Armed Forces Staff College - Advanced Training and Assignment of Enlisted Women Marines, 1965-1973 - New Woman Marine Units, Stateside - Women Marines Overseas - Women Marines in Vietnam - Women Marines in Marine Security Guard Battalion - Women Marines Overseas, Summary

Rapidly waning strength, unsatisfactory recruitment and retention results, and a need to improve the status and acceptance of women in the Marine Corps were the basis of Marine Corps Bulletin 5312, dated 27 February 1963, asking commands for recommendations on more efficient utilization of WMs. The results were collated and sent to the Director, Colonel Margaret M. Henderson, for comment. She categorized the recommendations into:

1. those which could not be implemented by the commands themselves.

2. those which were presumably already in effect.

3. those relating to more formal training for women Marines.

4. those which had possibilities, but required more study.

5. those in which she nonconcurred.

Taken as a whole, the recommendations made by the commands demonstrated a general lack of understanding of the status of women in the Marine Corps. It was readily apparent that the women were not thought of as personnel assets to be managed as all Marines. Statements that WMs should be assigned to billets appropriate to their grade and MOS, that women should be encouraged to participate in correspondence courses relating to their occupational specialty, and that the same performance standards be demanded of them as for male Marines, indicated a flaw in the system at the command level rather than in Headquarters policy since all of these matters came under local purview.1

On one subject, the need for more formal training for women Marines, there was unanimity. Colonel Henderson strongly concurred, pointing out the fallacy of assigning WMs with eight weeks of recruit training directly to support establishment billets, and expecting the degree of knowledge and skill shown by male Marines who, after 11 weeks of recruit training, and four weeks of infantry training, had more than likely served 13 months in the Fleet Marine Force. She supported her stand with the statement:

Seventy percent of our Women Marine recruit graduates are between the ages of 18 and 20 and, in most instances, have come directly from high school into the Marine Corps with little or no work experience. These young women are bright, capable trainees, but we are actually expecting them to be proficient in a specific MOS with only eight weeks of basic training. During calendar year 1963, 771 women Marines completed recruit training and only five were ordered directly from recruit training to a service school. In comparison, the women basic graduates from the Army, Navy and Air Force were ordered directly to service school as follows:

(a) Army, approximately 90 percent

(b) Navy, approximately 50 percent

(c) Air Force, approximately 60 percent2

Colonel Henderson reasoned that specialty training in administration, supply, and communications would greatly improve the performance of WM recruit graduates since 77 percent of the 1963 graduates were concentrated in those three fields.

One week following the submission of her comments, Colonel Henderson completed her tour, and on 3 January 1964, she was relieved as Director of Women Marines by Colonel Barbara J. Bishop. Just three days earlier on the 1st of January, General Wallace M. Greene, Jr., took the helm as the 23d Commandant of the Marine Corps, a timely occurrence for the women Marines. Writing about him later, Colonel Bishop said, "General Greene was light years ahead of his time in his support of increased opportunities for women Marines."3

Shortly after assuming command of the Corps, he directed Colonel Bishop to submit recommendations to effect improvement in the selection, training, and utilization of women Marines. Taking each identifiable problem in order: a strength decline to 1,333 WMs on 30 April 1964; conflicts over the assignments of noncommissioned officers and officers; unsatisfactory recruiting results for officers and enlisted women; inadequate training; inefficient utilization; low retention; and poor living conditions for enlisted women, Colonel Bishop expressed a number of highly controversial facts, observations, and recommendations.4

A discussion of the strength and general utilization of women Marines centered on the traditionally accepted goal of one percent of total enlisted strength, 1,750 enlisted women and 175 officers, which was considered workable based upon billeting conditions at the time. Women were assigned to all bases having mobilization requirements for WMs except the Marine Corps Supply Centers at Barstow and Albany, a factor which would cause a delay in time of emergency. Accordingly, Colonel Bishop recommended that woman Marine units be established at those two activities. And finally, in connection with general utilization of women, Colonel Bishop noted that in filling certain command, training, and recruiting billets there was a conflict between the authority of the Personnel Department and the Director of Women Marines, she asked that all changes of station orders for WM officers and enlisted women be routed to her office for information and concurrence.

Turning to officer training, policy at the time allowed officer candidates to disenroll at any rime during the training cycle, and many did so before giving themselves a chance to adjust to military life. The colonel recommended a change that would require all candidates to complete the course before making such a decision.

As for the career officer, she said:

There is a definite need to provide women majors and lieutenant colonels with professional education in command and staff duties. The value of advanced military education is recognized for male officers and the need is met by assignment to the Senior Course [later Command and Staff College]. Women officers of field grade would benefit equally from broadened knowledge of policies, programs and problems at all levels of the military establishment and of staff functioning at Headquarters Marine Corps, in the Department of Defense, and on joint staffs.5

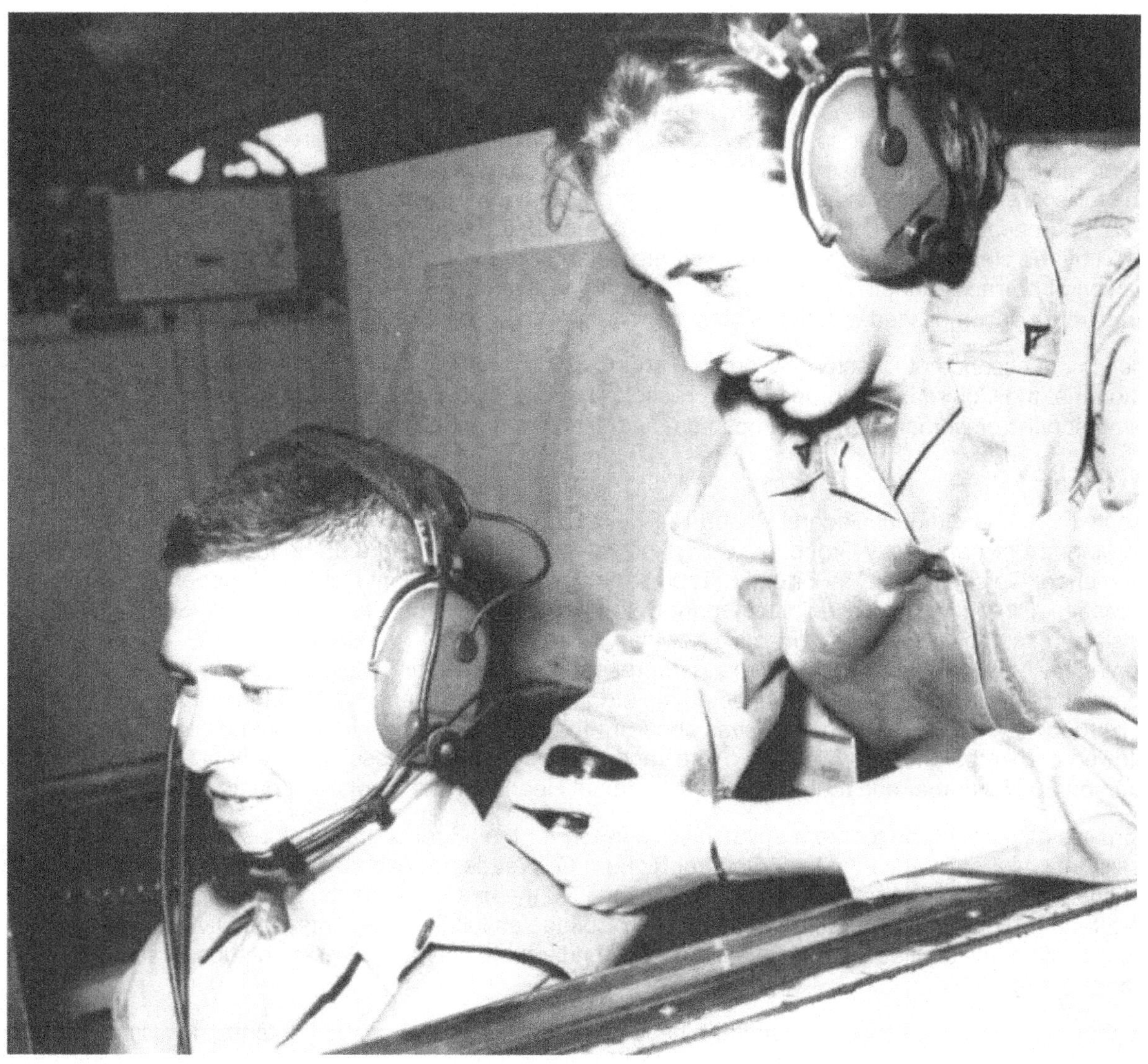

LCpl A. Digman Atau, one of two women at El Toro in 1965 to give pilots training in the aviation trainer field, instructs Cpl J. Harris in the operation of an F8 link trainer.

To that end, Colonel Bishop reviewed the 1964-1965 syllabus for the Senior Course, held at Quantico, and determined that at least 432 hours of instruction would be extremely valuable for women. She specifically identified the following courses: Executive Leadership, Management Techniques and Procedures, Geopolitical and Current World Situation, Organization and Functioning for National Security, and Foreign Language.

In respect to senior WM officers' utilization, she discussed the hesitancy to assign them on the basis of their professional qualifications. She wrote:

When a woman major or lieutenant colonel becomes eligible for transfer and one of the billets requiring a woman is not available, there is a tendency prior to issuance of orders to query commands on their willingness to accept a woman. Acceptance is not based on ability since certainly the Personnel Monitors would not recommend the assignment of a woman to a billet inappropriate to her rank and professional qualifications.6

Then, as each Director of Women Marines before had done, Colonel Bishop pointed out the need for advanced specialist training for enlisted women. And, she ended her report with recommendations designed to improve the retention rate of WMs. These included a stricter policy on separations due to marriage balanced by increased efforts to station husbands and wives together, abolishment of the two-year enlistment contract in favor of a three- or four-year commitment, a guarantee similar to the one made to male enlistees of a change of station during the first enlistment, and improved living conditions. On the latter subject she was emphatic. It was not just that the women needed more privacy, she argued, but they spend more time in the barracks than men; the women staff NCOs who remain in the service are more likely to be single than male Marines who marry and live in their family homes; the majority of career women Marines would never share in the large expenditures made on married quarters and in the support of dependents' programs; and because the women took such good care of their barracks, inspecting officers were duly impressed by the cleanliness and attempts to create a homelike atmosphere. She recommended new construction of barracks adapted to the needs of women or at least the complete rehabilitation of existing structures, to be accomplished with the aid of a nationally known interior decorator.

That then is the essence of Director of Women Marines Study No. 1-64, a report that precipitated so much opposition that the Commandant ordered the creation of a study group to "propose a program to render the peacetime service of women Marines of optimum benefit to the Marine Corps."7

The Pepper Board

On 3 August 1964, Lieutenant General Robert H. Pepper, USMC (Retired), was designated chairman of the Woman Marine Program Study Group, popularly known as the Pepper Board.8 The members included Colonel Bishop; Colonel Frank R. Porter, Jr., representative, G-l; Lieutenant Colonel Eugenous E. Hovatter, representative, Director of Personnel; Lieutenant Colonel Alfred I. Thomas, representative, G-3; Major Paul R. Fields, representative, G-4; Major Parncia A. Maas, representative, WM; Major Charles E. Baker, representative, Aviation; Major Paul P. Pirhalla, representative, Fiscal; and Major Jenny Wrenn, recorder. The Commandant's letter of instruction directed the study group to convene on 11 August 1964 and to submit its report by 1 October. Early on it was apparent that a detailed study could not be completed in the time allowed and verbal authority was given to extend the deadline as necessary. The final report was submitted on 30 November and routed to staff sections at Headquarters Marine Corps for comment.

Reaction was mixed and ranged from enthusiastic support for the 83 recommendations to bitter opposition. The Assistant Chief of Staff, G-3, Major General Richard G. Weede, for example, concurred with all but one recommendation under his purview. The one exception was the recommendation that selected field grade officers attend the Marine Corps Command and Staff College as full-time students. G-3 Division preferred courses in civilian universities for women officers or attendance at only a few selected subcourses of the Command and Staff College.

On the other hand, the Personnel Department, headed by Major General Lewis J. Fields, took issue with the thrust of the report and the philosophy that costly improvement would, in his words, ". . . attract more young ladies into the Marine Corps and induce them to stay longer and be more productive during their stay."9 He continued, "We should . . . tailor our whole women's program to attract not young, untrained small-town high school graduates, but young women of professional skills and training who truly want to make their mark in a man's (which the military is unarguably) world."10 General Fields recommended recruitment of women already trained for a skilled trade, advanced rank, personal freedom comparable with Civil Service, and "a modified training program designed to teach about the Corps and not how to be a male Marine in skirts."11 And lastly, since the Personnel Department reasoned that the greatest problem in WM housing in most places was caused by overcrowding, it was submitted that, "the best and quickest means of improving current housing would be to reduce the WM strength. . . "12

In light of staff comments, some recommendations were changed or modified and on 13 April 1965 a Marine Corps Bulletin directed the staff agencies to take action on 75 of the recommendations already approved by the Commandant, and a reporting schedule was set up to keep General Greene informed of the progress being made. Although the program was considered long-range, not to be fully realized for two years, more than half of the proposals were at least a matter of policy by mid-1965. As a result, Lieutenant Colonel Jeanette I. Sustad was named to the new post of Deputy Director of Women Marines. In the past, the next senior woman officer at Headquarters filled that billet as an additional duty.

Women were to be assigned to and get training in a broader range of occupational fields, to include drafting, lithography, operational communications, communications maintenance, auditing, finance, accounting, informational services, aerology, air control, and flight equipment. The Basic Supply School and Teletype

Operator School were made available almost immediately. The Pepper Board recommendation that senior officers attend Command and Staff College was unacceptable to most staff officers and post-graduate training in civilian or military schools was approved as a substitute.

An impressive list of new duty stations for WMs was published to include: Fleet Home Town News Center at Great Lakes; Marine Corps Reserve Data Services Center, Kansas City; Marine Corps Base, Twentynine Palms, California; Marine Air Reserve Training Center, Glenview, Illinois; the Supply Centers at Albany and Barstow; and Marine Corps Air Stations at Beaufort, New River, Kaneohe, Santa Ana, and Yuma. The absence of a WM Company or barracks no longer precluded the assignment of women Marines to any post or station as long as suitable off-station housing was available. Additionally, women would be afforded more overseas billets.

Changes in basic training included a greater use of male instructors; increased instruction in personal development and grooming;* integration of some classes at the Woman Officer Basic Course and the Woman Officer Candidate Class; and a new requirement that candidates complete four weeks of training before being allowed to disenroll. At Parris Island, a two-platoon system or series system was created to inspire competition, and on-base liberty for recruits was to be in effect by January 1966.

* Strangely (?) this became the most controversial change in WM training and was fiercely and almost entirely opposed by the senior WM officers and senior WM NCOs! I was determined to institute this program for a number of very valid (as they later proved) reasons:

(1) to give polish and new confidence to the individual woman.

(2) to improve WM recruiting by sending the girl back home where her improved and smart appearance invariably brought compliments and new recruits.

(3) to emphasize femininity as an asset to a woman's role in the military—to be coupled with proper assignment.

I enlisted and received the enthusiastic assistance of airlines which conducted aircraft hostess training schools (e.g. Pan Am) to which I assigned selected WM instructors for training and return to P.I. where we established a good grooming school. Beauty aids were provided free of charge by national cosmetic firms." (Gen Wallace M. Greene, Jr., comments on draft manuscript, dtd 26 Dec 79)

Enlistment incentives that guaranteed preferred area, school, and occupational assignments to qualified enlisted women were planned, for the new officers who requested it, there was the promise of two duty stations during the initial three-year period of active duty.

To settle the difficulties of assignment arising from varying interests of the Director of Women Marines and the Personnel Department, a woman officer was assigned to the Classification and Assignment Branch at Headquarters as an occupational field monitor. Major Valeria F. Hilgart was the first to fill that position, arriving in Washington in November 1966.

An aggressive enforcement of the recommendations covering better living conditions for the women awaited the result of a Department of Defense study on the subject. Meanwhile, the Marine Corps reevaluated all WM barracks, SNCO quarters, and the furnishings. At Parris Island, lockers and dressers were installed in the recruit barracks to make their quarters less austere.* At Camp Pendleton, plans were made for a newly constructed WM barracks.

* A new clothing layout inspection requiring certain items to be displayed hanging in a locker hastened the addition of lockers to recruit barracks.

These are but a fraction of the changes in effect or on the drawing board in 1965. Some were implemented quickly; others came only with firm prodding from General Greene. In November of 1965 the Commandant was given a resume of actions completed on the Pepper Board recommendations which indicated considerable progress had been made. Not fully satisfied, he sent it to Colonel Bishop for her views. She began her remarks by noting the strength increase from 128 officers and 1,320 enlisted women on 30 June 1964 to 145 officers and 1,718 enlisted women on board on 31 October 1965 and the increased satisfaction expressed by commands with the performance and appearance of women Marines.13

She then commented in depth on the more disappointing progress shown in some areas. Of particular concern was the question of advanced training for senior officers. The original recommendation to send WM officers to Command and Staff College had been diluted to a statement about providing postgraduate training in civilian or military schools and the notation that WM officers were eligible to compete with male applicants for post-graduate training. No other action was considered necessary on this recommendation. Colonel Bishop wrote:

This has always been the case, with the result that one woman in 1950 managed to obtain a year in Personnel Administration at Ohio State. No gain has been made here as post-graduate training for senior women was to be a substitute for advanced professional training available to career Marines in AWS (Amphibious Warfare School) and Command and Staff College.'4

After comparing Colonel Bishop's separate assessment of the progress made with that provided by the G-I, the Commandant pencilled in on the latter:

1. I want this type of report coordinated with the DIRWM prior to submission to CMC.

2. I have approved this particular report, but I am definitely not satisfied with action reported. See attached comments DIRWMs which deserve consideration and action.15

Women Marine Program Revitalized, 1965-1973

Three unrelated factors of disparate importance all joined to alter the future course of the woman Marine program at this point: a stricter policy on discharge based on marriage effective 15 July 1964; the Pepper Board report of 30 November 1964; and increased involvement of Marines in the war in Vietnam in 1965. Dramatic progress was made in strength, availability of formal training, opening of new occupational fields, and in assignment possibilities in the United States and overseas.

Strength Increases

The Pepper Board reaffirmed the policy stated in 1948 of maintaining a woman Marine strength of one percent of total Marine Corps enlisted strength. Actually the number of WMs had been steadily declining since 1953, leveling off at the one percent goal, approximately 1,700 from 1956 to 1959 and reaching a nadir of 1,281 in December 1964, when the Pepper Board reported its findings. In August 1965, due to Vietnam commitments, a 30,000-man increase was approved for the Marine Corps and higher objectives were concurrently set for WMs. By 31 May 1967, enlisted strength was 2,082 and officer strength reached 190. A peak of about 2,700 WMs was reached during the Vietnam era of 1968 and 1969 and then tapered to 2,288 on 30 June 1973.18

Higher recruiting goals accounted for some of the success, but more impact was made by better retention due to tighter control of discharges solely for reason of marriage. On 15 July 1964, a joint household policy became effective which denied discharge to women Marines who were located in the same area as their husbands. All discharges of this type were then suspended on 20 August 1965 in conjunction with a four-month involuntary extension for all Marines. By 1966 new regulations virtually eliminated marriage as a condition for discharge for WMs resulting in a reduction of that type of separation from 18.6 percent of woman Marine losses in 1964 to 2.3 percent in 1966 and finally 0 percent in 1969.17

Recruiting incentives guaranteeing geographic choices of duty and formal training combined with other enhancements resulting from the implementation of Pepper Board recommendations raised enlisted recruiting from about 60 percent attainment of quota in 1963 to 105.7 percent in 1966. Officer selection not only improved numerically, but a larger proportion of candidates were seniors or graduates than in previous years, a factor which cut down on the drop-out rate of younger students and ultimately led to an increase in commissions accepted. In 1966, officer selection attained 103.3 percent of senior-graduates quota and 152.5 percent of junior quota. Sophomores were no longer eligible.18 At the same time, the percent of women recruited as Regulars to serve a three- or four-year contract as opposed to Reserves with a two-year obligation rose from 48 percent in June to 77 percent on 31 March 1968.19

All told, efforts in the mid-1960s to stabilize the woman Marine program, to encourage women Marines to complete their initial enlistment, to lengthen the average tour of women Marines, and to make the Marine Corps an attractive choice for potential enlistees achieved demonstrable success.

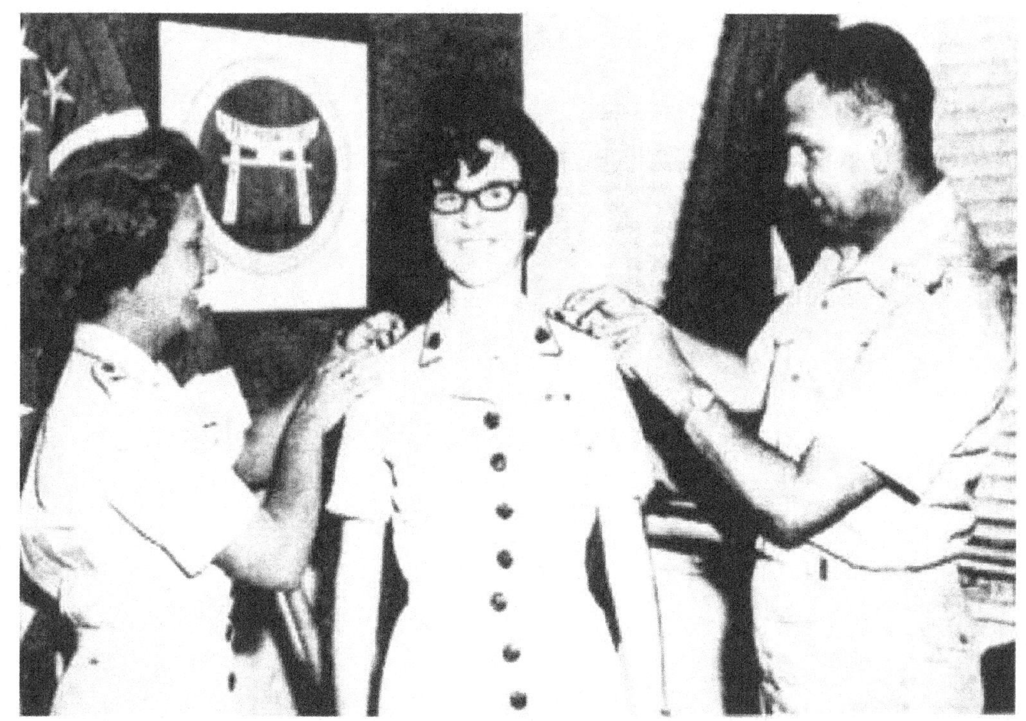

At the time the Marine Corps' only woman Marine lawyer on active duty, future military judge Capt Patricia A. Murphy, is promoted by Maj Jane Wallis, Commanding Officer, WM Company, and LtCol Frederick D. Clements, at Camp Butler in 1967.

Capt Carol A. Vertalino, first woman Marine officer to attend Amphibious Warfare School, is shown with LtGen Carson A. Roberts, Commanding General, Fleet Marine Force, Pacific, at Quantico in 1963.

Women Officers' Specialist Training, 1965-1973

In 1964, women officers were serving in only eight occupational fields with about 70 percent in administrative billets, and no deliberate attempt was made to achieve a wider distribution. Only 30.6 percent of the second lieutenants commissioned in the three-year period ending in 1964 had received formal specialist training. No training was available in personnel administration although the majority of women officers served in this field. In contrast, members of the 20th Woman Officers Basic Course which graduated in October 1966 were assigned in 14 occupational fields to include intelligence, operational communications, transportation, legal, avionics, aerology, and aviation operations, specialties in which women officers had been a rarity since World War II. Other fields to which the graduates were assigned were personnel and administration; supply administration and operations; auditing, finance, and accounting; data processing; Marine Corps exchange; information services; photography; training and training aids; and air control-anti-air warfare. Seventy-two percent of these newly commissioned women officers received formal training at eight schools.20 Earlier in the year, First Lieutenant Alice K. Kutashige, the first woman Marine officer since World War II to be assigned a primary MOS in food service, completed a 12-week course in food services supervision at Fort Lee, Virginia.

The following spring, 1967, Colonel Bishop reported in the Woman Marine Newsletter on the status of this officer training. The first WM officers to attend the Communication Officers Orientation Course at Quantico had made an impressive showing. In a class of three women and 23 men, Second Lieutenant Margaret B. Read finished second; Second Lieutenant Patricia A. Allegree fourth; and Second Lieutenant Lyn A. Liddle sixth. Second Lieutenant Janice C. Scott had completed the Military Intelligence Orientation Course at Fort Holabird, Maryland, in January and continued on to attend the 18-week Aerial Surveillance Officer Course. Second Lieutenant Tommy L. Treasure, also a graduate of Fort Holabird's Military Intelligence Officer Course, was ordered to a subsequent Aerial Surveillance Officers Course. CWO Elaine G. Freeman was to begin a four-week course in automatic data processing analysis in April and Captain Sara R. Beauchamp and Second Lieutenant JoAnn Deberry would follow in June. Four WM officers, Second Lieutenants Alpha R. Noguera, Donna J. Sherwood, Norma L. Tomlinson, and Harriet T. Wendel were scheduled to attend the 10-week Air Traffic Control Officers Course at the Naval Air Station, Glynco, Georgia.21

Women lawyers and Judges—A Beginning

On 1 May 1944, Captain Lily S. Hutcheon, a lawyer stationed at Camp Lejeune, became the first woman judge advocate in the history of the Marine Corps. Captain Hutcheon had originally joined the Navy, but upon completion of Midshipman's School at Northhampton, Massachusetts, was commissioned a first lieutenant in the United States Marine Corps Reserve. She was released to inactive duty in 1946 but returned to continuous active duty in 1949- Under her married name, Gridley, she became a well-known Marine, highly respected for her work in legal assistance at

Headquarters Marine Corps where she served until her retirement in 1965. Lieutenant Colonel Gridley, for all those years, was the only woman Marine lawyer.22

Then, as a direct result of the Pepper Board study, a woman was permitted to complete officer candidate training, accept a commission, and delay her active duty service while attending law school. In 1966-1967, First Lieutenant Patricia A. Murphy received her bachelor of laws degree from Catholic University in Washington, D.C., graduated from the Woman Officer Basic Course, passed the District of Columbia Bar examination, graduated from the Lawyer's Course at Naval Justice School, was selected for promotion to captain, and was certified by the Judge Advocate General to perform as a trial or defense counsel of a general court martial.23 Two years later, she became the first woman Marine officer ever to argue a case before the Court of Military Appeals, and in 1970 while stationed at Treasure Island, California, and by then Captain Patricia Murphy Gormley, she became the first woman Marine lawyer in 26 years to be certified as a military judge.24

Professional Training

The Woman Marine Program Study Group (Pepper Board) identified the lack of career-type formal school training as the most notable deficiency in the woman Marine officer program. There was almost total opposition to the inclusion of women students at the Marine Corps' Command and Staff College since it would deprive a male Marine of the opportunity to attend this career-enhancing school. Less was said of the junior level course conducted for captains and majors at the Amphibious Warfare School and there was no opposition to sending women to Army or Navy schools provided these services would not ask for a reciprocal space in a Marine school for a WAC or WAVE officer.

Through unofficial conversation with the Director, Women's Army Corps, Colonel Bishop was able to lay the groundwork for women Marines to participate in the five-month WAC Career Officers Course at Fort McClellan, Alabama. Captain Barbara J. Lee, the first Marine to attend, graduated in May 196525 She was followed by seven others. Captains Elaine E. Filkins (later Davies), Gail M. Reals, Jeanne Botwright (later Humphrey), and Joan M. Collins, who distinguished herself as an honor graduate by finishing second in the class, comprised an early group. The last three women to attend this school before it was disestablished in 1972 were Captains Karen G. Grant, Judybeth D. Barnett, and Ellen T. Laws.28

SSgts Mary L. McLain (left) and Carmen Adams (right), the first enlisted women to arrive for duty at Marine Corps Air Station, Iwakuni, Japan, are greeted by Col William M. Lundin, commanding officer; SgtMaj J. F. Moore; and 1stSgt K. L. Ford in 1967.

Amphibious Warfare School

Given the climate of the period following the Pepper Board, the intense interest of Colonel Bishop in woman officer schooling, and the vigorous support of General Greene, it was but a matter of time before a woman officer was enrolled in the Marine Corps' Amphibious Warfare Course. Captain Carol A. Vertalino (later Diliberto) was assigned to a modified version of AWS 1-67, on a trial basis, beginning on 23 August 1966. Aware of the limits of her formal military education, and knowing that the future assignment of WMs to the school was contingent upon her performance, Captain Vertalino spoke of her apprehension to Colonel Bishop. The director assured her that her selection was based on her professional reputation and her ability to get along with people. She was not expected to finish first in the class, indeed that might antagonize her fellow students. With five months to prepare herself, Captain Vertalino, on her own time, completed the Basic Officer and the AWS correspondence courses, each one designed to take the better part of a year.

The normal syllabus was altered to allow the lone woman student to visit base staff offices for briefings and informal training while the class was working on combat-related matters. It proved awkward for all concerned, the academic staff making suitable arrangements, the staff sections assigned to brief her, and, most of all, for Captain Vertalino. After her successful completion of the course in May 1967, it was decided that woman officers would attend subsequent, unmodified classes at AWS.27

Post-Graduate Schooling

For the first time in more than 15 years, a woman officer was selected for postgraduate training in the Special Education Program.* In July 1967, First Lieutenant Judith Davenport reported to the Naval Post Graduate School at Monterey, California, to pursue a two-year course in applied mathematics.28

In 1950, Major Julia E. Hamblet attended Ohio State.

Command and Staff College

The question of women officer students at the Marine Corps Command and Staff College remained unresolved for more than three years after the recommendation was made by the Pepper Board. Encouraged by the passage of Public Law 90-130 in 1967 which made women eligible for selection to the permanent grade of colonel, Colonel Bishop sent a memorandum to the Assistant Chief of Staff, G-3, in which she stated:

. . . women officers will be expected to fill established billets appropriate for the grade of colonel in various Marine Corps commands. . . . Women Marines who are now lieutenant colonels have had little or no formal professional education during their service careers. Efforts should be directed toward providing the younger group of these lieutenant colonels with career training which will enable them to serve beneficially in higher grades.29

She asked that Lieutenant Colonel Jenny Wrenn be assigned, on a trial basis, to the class convening in August 1968. Lieutenant Colonel Wrenn had previously asked for such an assignment and the colonel for whom she worked, Chief, Plans and Operations Branch, Marine Corps Education Center, indicated to Colonel Bishop that he considered her to be, "an outstanding candidate should women officers be assigned to Command and Staff College."30 Approval came on 9 February 1968 and included the words:

It is recognized that the restricted nature of assignments for Women Marine officers will preclude the full application of all instruction received from the college. However, participation in the full syllabus will provide valuable professional knowledge to enhance the growth of this selected Woman Marine officer and correspondingly increase her value to the U.S. Marine Corps.31

Women officers at the time reasoned that all Marine officers are limited to some degree by their classification as infantry officer, aviator, supply officer, etc., and none of them could expect to use fully all the instructional material. Since Lieutenant Colonel Wrenn successfully completed the Command and Staff College, women officers have been regularly included as class members.

The Armed Forces Staff College

The Armed Forces Staff College in Norfolk, Virginia, opened its doors to women officers in 1970. Provision was made for a quota of one woman officer of each service for the class which convened in February. Competition for selection between men and women was thereby eliminated and apparently there was no Marine Corps opposition to the plan to send a woman officer to this high-level school. Lieutenant Colonel Mary Evelyn Bane was selected to attend this course, graduated, and was then assigned to the G-l Division at Headquarters Marine Corps.32

Completion of such a prestigious military school did not dispel the notion that women colonels were not to be assigned in the normal fashion. When Lieutenant Colonel Bane was selected for promotion, the personnel monitor responsible for colonel assignments called her in and asked her where she thought she should be transferred since in her words, "The thought of disposing of a woman colonel was turning him pale."33 Based upon her past experience, and her training, she offered the opinion that the most logical place might be Headquarters. He did not agree and said, "That would never do. You would have to be a branch head."34 And so Colonel Bane was ordered to Camp Pendleton where she filled an assistant chief of staff billet.*

* In 1975 Colonel Bane returned to Headquarters as the Head of the Separation and Retirement Branch where she served until her retirement in 1977.

Advanced Training and Assignment of Enlisted Women Marines, 1963-1973

Little time was lost between the Commandant's approval in mid-1965 and the implementation of the Pepper Board's recommendations regarding advanced training for enlisted women Marines. On 1 January 1966 a program emphasizing advanced technical training for women recruit graduates was published. Its purpose was to bring the woman Marine to an effective level of proficiency in her MOS as soon as possible. During the first six months of 1966, 75 percent of the women recruit graduates went on to advanced formal schools in 17 different fields, a sharp contrast to the five recruits who received post-recruit training in 196 3.35 In the Winter 1967 Woman Marine Newsletter, Colonel Bishop reported that women Marines attended a variety of military schools at Army, Navy, and Marine Corps bases and received basic-level instruction in such areas as administration, supply, telecommunications, electronics, disbursing, photography, aviation operations, aerology, air control, aviation training devices, optical instrument repair, transportation, cooking and baking, and journalism. Others attended advanced courses such as NCO leadership, administration chief, recruiting, air control, legal clerk and court reporter, supply, process photography, Marine security guard, instructor orientation, and data processing.36

During the period 1965-1973, opportunities for women Marines were greatly expanded. The gains were evident but not to be taken for granted. Many long-held assignment prejudices persisted. Women Marines sent to the Naval Air Station, Memphis, for advanced training in aviation specialties, for example, were nearly all channeled into aviation supply and aviation operations, crowding these two specialties while others were far short of the planned WM quotas. Others, upon arrival at Memphis were reclassified into fields such as administration, which Colonel Bishop noted as ". . . unfortunate since they are denied advanced training and, having qualified for aviation school, they are among the better qualified WMs. . . "37 The Commandant reacted quickly with a letter to the commanding officer of the Marine Aviation Detachment at Memphis stating:

It is the Commandant's desire that Women Marines be assigned to a greater range of military occupational specialties to form a more efficient mobilization base. In consequence, it is requested that Women Marines assigned to your command for aviation training be assigned in the percentages indicated. . . 38

A second example of strictly "sexist" assignments was the practice of using attractive, intelligent women Marines in jobs that were more show than substance. A number of WMs served in highly visible positions as receptionists in the Pentagon and it often happened that the most capable were retained there for inordinate periods of time. This worked to the disadvantage of the individual woman Marine who, when eventually transferred, found herself on a Marine Corps base as a staff noncommissioned officer without adequate experience to supervise, instruct, and counsel, let alone to drill a platoon or stand a duty watch. In the latter part of 1966, the Marine Corps was queried on the prospect of establishing a new billet in the office of a Deputy Assistant Secretary of the Navy. Colonel Bishop's comment was:

As desirable as these billets may be as "window dressing" for the Marine Corps, they have long been wasteful of the most capable and best appearing Women Marines. The work entailed in receptionists' billets offer no challenge to the caliber of women assigned to them. Each time a replacement is needed unreasonable selectivity requires a long parade of nominees to be submitted for the personal inspection of the office concerned. It is considered that the Marine Corps already had an undesirable monopoly on receptionist billets in the various Navy Secretary's Offices. It is recommended that the invitation to establish yet another billet be declined.39

Overall, the plusses outweighed the minuses in the training and assignment of enlisted women in the years following the Pepper Board. In 1972, Colonel Sustad, as Director of Women Marines, reported to Congress that women could serve in 23 occupational fields; service in two of them, motor transport and band, was restricted to time of war. Women Marines were, in 1972, as a matter of law and of Marine Corps policy, prohibited from the following 12 fields: infantry; field artillery; utilities; construction equipment and shore party; tank and amphibian tractor; ammunition and explosive ordnance disposal; supply services; nuclear, biological, and chemical warfare; military police and corrections; electronics maintenance; aviation ordnance; and air delivery. Colonel Sustad went on to explain that:

Marine Corps policy on the utilization of women permits wide flexibility and interchangeability with male Marines. While 100 percent workability of this policy cannot be attained because of such factors as billeting, physical limitations, rotation base, or combat capability, it is recognized that basically a Woman Marine is qualified to serve in any location or in any billet if she possesses an appropriate and required skill.40

At the time of her statement before Congress, enlisted women were actually assigned in 21 occupational fields with 34 percent in administration, 12 percent in supply, and 5 percent in operational communications, the three fields of greatest WM concentration.

New Woman Marine Units, Stateside

Coupled with new job opportunities came new geographic assignments. In Director of Women Marines Study 1-64, Colonel Bishop recommended the opening of woman Marine companies at bases with a mobilization requirement for women Marines, specifically, the Marine Corps Supply Centers at Barstow and Albany. The Pepper Board reaffirmed the idea and expanded it to include the Air Station at Kaneohe, Hawaii. Additionally, it recommended that women staff noncommissioned officers be assigned to Marine Corps Base, Twentynine Palms; Marine Corps Air Stations at Yuma and Beaufort; the Marine Corps Air Facilities at New River and Santa Ana; and, finally, it proposed that WM sergeants and above, be assigned to appropriate billets with the support and administrative sections of the various Marine barracks overseas.41

Marine Corps Supply Center, Barstow

On 13 January 1966, Prospector, the Barstow post newspaper, announced the arrival of the first woman Marine to report for duty at the Supply Center since 1946. Captain Vea J. Smith was named supply operations officer in Services Division. She became the expert in residence in the planning for a company of 100 women Marines due to be established when billeting arrangements were completed. The following month, First Lieutenant Wanda Raye Silvey assumed duties as disbursing officer in the Comptroller Division42

Gunnery Sergeants Virginia Almonte and Lea E. Woodworth arrived in June 1966, both assigned to the Center's Adjutant office.43 First Lieutenant Rebecca M. Kraft, slated to be the first WM company commander at Barstow, joined them a year later on 25 June 1967. 44

And so, the first WM Company in the 2 5-year history of the Supply Center was activated on 1 July 1967. It was also the first new WM unit to be established in 13 years and brought to 11 the number of major Marine Corps commands with women's organizations. The first contingent of WMs, Lance Corporals Suzanne Bryant, Sheryl L. Moore, and Christina M. Christopher, arrived on 17 July and were greeted by First Lieutenant Kraft and the company first sergeant, Gunnery Sergeant Woodworth. Building 182 had been completely renovated and outfitted with new furniture.45

The company at Barstow was short-lived, being deactivated in August 1971 and designated as a platoon of Headquarters Company, Headquarters and Service Battalion. The senior WM on board was thereafter assigned additional duty as woman Marine advisor on the commanding general's special staff. From 1967 to 1971, seven officers served as WM company commanders at Barstow: First Lieutenant Rebecca M. Kraft, Captain Joan M. Hammond, First Lieutenant Diane L. Hamel, Captain Alice K. Kurashige, First Lieutenant Geraldine E. Peeler, Captain Vanda K. Brame* and First Lieutenant Linda J. Lenhart.48

* Captain Brame was one of four women Marines to receive the Navy and Marine Corps Medal for heroism. See Chapter 15 for details.

Marine Corps Supply Center, Albany

Similar activity was taking place at Albany, Georgia. Private First Class Donna L. Albert, on 4 February 1966, was the first WM to report to that post for duty. Her assignment, making a departure from the custom of only stationing lower ranked women at locations with a WM unit was permitted because she was able to maintain a household with her husband, Private First Class Dennis M. Albert.47

Second Lieutenant Emma G. Ramsey, formerly enlisted, arrived on 29 July 1966, the first WM officer to serve at the center. She was followed shortly thereafter by Master Sergeant Rita M. Walsh, making a total of three.

Second Lieutenant Ramsey, officer in charge of the manpower utilization unit, found herself undertaking the additional duty of commanding officer of the WM company then being formed. Working with Master Sergeant Walsh, she began the task of planning and preparing for a full-strength company. Barracks were remodeled, administrative support was arranged, and directives were drafted.48

Apart from Second Lieutenant Ramsey and Master Sergeant Walsh, the initial company members arriving in August 1967 were: Master Sergeant Bernice P. Querry, the new first sergeant; Corporals Margaret G. Wegener and Barbara A. Zimmer; Lance Corporals Doris H. Pallant, Carrie M. Saxon, Marjorie W. Groht, Donna L. Correll, Cheryl L. Larison, Robin M. Holloway, Virginia Gonzales, Cathy L. Pierce, Barbara L. Bradek, and Rosemary Lamont; Privates First Class Kathleen A. Kisczik, Daryl R. Cessna, Linda A. Dewaele, and Gertrude Martin. Captain Sara R. Beauchamp arrived in September and was named the new commanding officer.49

At the formal activation ceremonies on 13 September 1967, Sergeant Major of the Woman Marines Ouida W. Craddock unveiled a cornerstone plaque on the Woman Marine Barracks. Colonel Bishop and Captain Beauchamp assisted Albany's mayor, the Honorable James V. Davis, with the ribbon-cutting at Barracks 7103.50 But, like the company at Barstow, the WM Company, Albany, enjoyed but a brief existence. It was deactivated on 1 November 1972 and the women became a platoon of Service Company, Headquarters and Service Battalion.51

Marine Corps Air Station, Kaneohe

The Pepper Board had recommended reactivation of a WM unit at the Marine Corps Air Station at Kaneohe Bay, Hawaii. Approval was initially deferred mainly because WM strength could not support establishment of this unit as well as new units at Barstow and Albany. Under the new policy permitting the assignment of women on an individual basis to commands where no WM unit or housing existed, two officers, Captain Manuela Hernandez and First Lieutenant Diane Leppaluoto were ordered to Kaneohe early in 1966. By the end of the year, the decision was made to activate a company of 100 enlisted women and two officers. Alterations began on a barracks and the company was formed in December 1967.52

Women Marines Overseas

In July 1966 a decision was made to assign women Marines to the western Pacific area. The purpose was twofold: to free as many male Marines as possible for duty with committed Fleet Marine Force units and to provide WMs with additional career incentives. Plans were made to send women to Camp Butler on Okinawa; the Marine Corps Air Station at Iwakuni, Japan; and Headquarters, United States Military Assistance Command at Saigon, Vietnam. Each command was queried on the number of billets suitable for WMs and billeting space available.

Women were asked to volunteer for the 13-month tour and had to be recommended by their commanding officers. Those with less than 13 months to serve were required to extend or reenlist to cover the tour length. Opportunities for enlisted women, private through gunnery sergeant, were greatest for those in administration, logistics, operational communications, telecommunications maintenance, supply, disbursing, data processing, informational services, photography, weather service, air traffic control, and aviation operations. Officers, warrant through major, were eligible for assignment to the Far East and were especially needed in administration, communications, supply, disbursing, and legal services. WMs were ordered to the Pacific area in increments to avoid a 100 percent turnover at the end of 13 months.53

Marine Corps Air Station, Iwakuni

There was very little resistance to the idea of assigning WMs to Vietnam. The enthusiasm on Okinawa was somewhat less. There was outright opposition to the proposal at the Marine Corps Air Station at Iwakuni, Japan. The Commanding General, Fleet Marine Force, Pacific, Lieutenant General Victor H. Krulak, had doubts about the plan based on the inadequacy of appropriate on-base recreational facilities and a lack of suitable off-base liberty areas. Colonel Bishop, when asked by the Chief of Staff, Lieutenant General Leonard F. Chapman, Jr., to comment on the subject, wrote:

Verbal and written objections expressed to date concerning the assignment of enlisted women to Iwakuni imply either that the prime consideration is the women's enjoyment of their tour or that their presence constitutes a serious threat to the good order and discipline of their masculine associates.54

She advocated the weighing of adequate liberty facilities against the chance for the women to make meaningful contributions to Marine Corps personnel needs under conditions of minor personal hardship, and continued, "This response was not beyond their capabilities in the past."55 Taking up the matter of the female presence, she added:

Presumably, the local command has been able to maintain sufficient disciplinary control over the masculine element to avoid undue unpleasantness for Navy Nurses, dependents of the other services, and civilian school teachers aboard the base.

The most telling argument against the assignment of women to Iwakuni is not their ability to adjust to unusual or difficult circumstances but the negative attitude expressed at all levels of command in WestPac toward their presence at Iwakuni. This attitude is hardly conducive to their welcome reception and normal uneventful adjustment.56*

Colonel Bishop and the Sergeant Major of Women Marines, First Sergeant Evelyn E. Albert, made a trip to WestPac to confer with the commands and to inspect the available barracks. At Iwakuni all the briefings were designed to discourage the plan. In response to a question on the controversy, the former director wrote in a letter to the History and Museums Division in 1977:

Controversial is an understatement of the assignment of women to the Far East—particularly to Japan. Okinawa was no great problem — nor Vietnam, but the CO of the Air Station in Japan was unbelievable in his efforts to prevent this "catastrophe." (He made my trip interesting tho by having me dragged through an assortment of bars and what not as an indoctrination to the horrors of the Far East. I still have a fan presented to me by an aging proprietress of one of those establishments to show she bore no ill will to the women.)57

1stLt Anne Tallman (center), officer-in-charge of the first woman Marine contingent to arrive on Okinawa, stops to confer with members of her group upon arrival at Kadena Air Base in November 1966.

Captain Marilyn E. Wallace became the first woman Marine to serve in the Far East, reporting to the Marine Corps Air Station, Iwakuni on 15 October 1966. Assigned as station disbursing officer, she was billeted in a BOQ housing Navy nurses.58 Five months later, on 23 Match 1967, the arrival of the first enlisted women Marines raised the air station distaff strength to seven. The WMs, Gunnery Sergeant Frances J. Fisher, Staff Sergeants Carmen Adams and Mary L. McLain, and Sergeants Elva M. Pounders, Patricia Malnat, and

Donna K. Duncan were accompanied on the last leg of their journey from Okinawa to Japan by Major Jane L. Wallis, senior WM in the Fat East.59

At Iwakuni, Colonel William M. Lundin, station commanding officer; Lieutenant Colonel Robert W. Taylor, station executive officer; Sergeant Major J. F. Moote, station sergeant major; and First Sergeant K. L. Ford of Headquarters and Headquarters Squadron were on hand to greet the women Marines and to take them to lunch. They were taken on a tour of the station ending with a welcome aboard gathering where they met the officers for whom they would work. Staff Sergeant Adams wrote to the Director of Woman Marines, "These Marines over here just can't seem to do enough for us."60 The WMs received thorough briefings on customs, laws, and Japanese religions. Interviews were arranged with the Japanese press explaining the work of the women Marines to dispel any notions that they were taking jobs away from Japanese women.61

The welcome accorded the WMs at Iwakuni in 1967, in the wake of the bitter opposition voiced at the prospect of their assignment, was not unlike the reception given the first Regulars in 1948. Once the decision was final and the presence of women Marines was a fait accompli, Marines, with few exceptions, accepted the situation with good grace.

Marine Corps Air Station, Futema, Okinawa

Within days of Captain Wallace's arrival at Iwakuni in October 1966, First Lieutenant Anne S. Tallman and nine enlisted WMs reported to Travis Air Force Base, California, for transportation to Okinawa.62 Arriving at Kadena Air Force Base not far from Futema on Saturday, 22 October, they were greeted by Major John D. Way, administrative officer; Captain George A. Kinset, personnel officer; and Sergeant Major John W. Arnby, the facility sergeant major. Included in the first group were Sergeant Carol A. Kindig; Corporals Joan A. Carey, San Crosby, Patricia Hurlbutt, Elizabeth Turner, and Ronelle Wuerch; and Lance Corporals Maryann Burger, Suzanne Davis, and Diana Savage. First Lieutenant Tallman took up the duties of informational officer and the enlisted women were assigned to operations, disbursing, supply, weather service, and communications.63

The women Marines were attached to Headquarters and Headquarters Squadron. The senior WM officer functioned as the WM liaison to the commanding officer of the Marine Corps Air Facility. When more officers arrived, the senior woman officer became, as an additional duty, the officer in charge of the WMs. She reported to the commanding officer of the squadron and helped him with duty assignments, inspections, and matters related to the distaff Marines. The officers and staff noncommissioned officers (due to a lack of adequate space) lived in BOQ 217. The enlisted women lived in a small barracks, ideally situated behind the post exchange, and next to the swimming pool, theater, and gymnasium.64

Marine Corps Base, Camp Butler, Okinawa

The renovation of a barracks at Camp Smedley D. Butler delayed the arrival of WMs for a few months. The first aboard were Major Jane L. Wallis and Second Lieutenant Doris M. Keeler, reporting in on 10 December 1966. Major Wallis, assistant base adjutant, was in addition officer in charge of the women Marines. Second Lieutenant Keeler, formerly enlisted, was assigned as communications officer.65

BGen Ronald R. Van Stockum, assisted by Maj Jane L. Wallis, WM Company commander, Camp Butler, Okinawa cuts the birthday cake in November 1967.

Between 1967 and 1973, 36 women Marines served in South Vietnam. Capt Elaine E. Filkins (left) and Sgt Doris Denton (right) tour Saigon in a cyclo on a rare afternoon off.

On Monday, 16 January 1967, a contingent of 18 enlisted WMs arrived on Okinawa for assignment to Camp Butler and Futema. On hand to meet the arrivals were Brigadier General Ronald R. Van Stockum, Commanding General, FMFPac (Forward); Colonel Robert B. Laing, Sr., Futema Marine Corps Air Facility commander; Colonel James A. Gallo, Jr., Camp Butler executive officer; and Major Wallis, the senior woman Marine on the island. The 9th Marine Amphibious Brigade Band from Camp Hansen serenaded the women during the welcoming ceremony. The first enlisted women to be assigned at Camp Butler were Staff Sergeant Helen A. Dowd; Corporals Kathleen Wright,* Sharon Lynn Bowe, Suzanne T. Guyman, Susan W. Blair, and Mary J. Andlott; and Lance Corporals Linda C. (nee Jaquet) Beck, Virginia Emaline Baker, and Brenda Ray Brown.66

* Sergeant Wright became the first Camp Butler woman Marine to receive a Certificate of Commendation for outstanding performance of duty. The certificate was presented by Major General John G. Bouker in February 1968.

At work in the adjutant's office, Major Wallis saw much of the correspondence dealing with the opposition of the command toward the assignment of WMs to Okinawa. Yet, the welcome the women received was characteristically cordial. Major Wallis believes the Marines were sincere as they performed small acts of courtesy and consideration beyond the routine. As an example, at the time it was unofficially accepted that the men of each unit had their own table at the Staff Noncommissioned Officers Club, leaving the women SNCOs with literally no place to sit except the bar. When Master Sergeant Sarah N. Thornton arrived, men from several of the units invited her to join their group whenever she came to the club. The WMs further found that once on the job, they soon became indispensable. Their work sections did not easily release women on Saturdays or Mondays, making weekend liberty trips difficult.67 It was a bittersweet compliment.

Women Marines on Okinawa had a uniform problem since they wore the two-piece summer cord dress all year and it was often quite cold. The raincoat did not provide a satisfactory answer as it was too hot and sticky in the humid weather. Major Wallis and Second Lieutenant Keeler designed a green, V-necked cardigan sweater that fit under the lapels of the uniform. The small standard green buttons normally worn on the epaulets of the summer uniform were used on the non-regulation sweater. It cost about $15 to have one custom made, and Colonel Bishop gave permission to wear it on Okinawa only.68

WMs stationed at Camp Butler and Futema joined together to celebrate Christmas in Japan in 1967. Major Wallis and one enlisted woman flew to Camp Fuji to check the facilities. The question was, "Could 17 women live in one hootch (quonset hut) with only one shower?" They decided they certainly could manage for 72 hours. Marines moved out, doubled up, and turned over their hootch to the WMs. The medical dispensary was made into quarters for the women officers and staff noncommissioned officers. In all, 25 WMs spent the holidays at the Camp Fuji Range Company. Time was spent climbing the slopes of Mt. Fuji, skiing, and ice skating, but the highlight of the trip was a Christmas Eve party at the Seibi Yamanaka Orphanage. The Marines, men and women, arrived laden with pots of spaghetti and meatballs, orange soda, chocolate cake, and gaily wrapped presents for the 51 orphan boys. After the party the group returned to Camp Fuji to carol and to decorate the trees in the mess hall and the clubs. Late in the afternoon of Christmas Day, the Marines enjoyed a family-style traditional Christmas dinner.68

February 1968 marked the 25th anniversary of the women Marines and Major Wallis' tour was extended to complete plans for a special celebration. It was planned to have WMs from all WestPac commands attend, and a search was made to find as many former WMs as possible from among the dependents. At the last moment, the WMs from Vietnam could not leave the country due to the Tet offensive of 1968.

Women Marines from Camp Butler, Futema, and Iwakuni gathered at Kadena's Airmen's Open Mess along with their guests. The traditional cake was cut by Major General John G. Bouker, who presented the first piece to Master Sergeant Thornton, oldest WM at the party, and the second to Lance Corporal Maureen McGauren, the youngest.70

Women Marines in Vietnam

Companion to greater opportunity is greater responsibility and for women in the Marine Corps in the 1960s that meant service in the war-torn Republic of , Vietnam. The announcement was made and plans were set in 1967 for one officer and nine enlisted women to fill desk billets with the Military Assistance Command, Vietnam (MACV), based in Saigon. Generally, they were to work with the Marine Corps Personnel Section on the staff of the Commander, Naval Forces, Vietnam. The section provided administrative support to Marines assigned as far north as the Demilitarized Zone (DMZ). Later, another officer billet was added and Lieutenant Colonels Ruth J. O'Holleran and Ruth F. Reinholz eventually served as historians with the Military History Branch, Secretary Joint Staff, MACV.

Care was taken to select mature, stable WMs who could be expected to adapt to strange surroundings and cope in an emergency. Interested women Marines were asked to volunteer by notifying their commanding officer or by indicating their desire to serve in Vietnam on their fitness reports. There was no shortage of volunteers, but not all met the criteria. Then there was a number of women who would willingly accept, but not volunteer for orders to a combat zone. Theoretically, all WMs who served in Vietnam were volunteers in that nearly all had expressed their willingness to go and none objected.71 When Master Sergeant Bridget V. Connolly was asked what made her volunteer for duty in Saigon, she laughed and said, "Who volunteered? I received my orders in the guard mail." She became a legitimate volunteer when her initial tour ended and she extended for an additional six months.72

The first woman Marine to report to Vietnam for duty was Master Sergeant Barbara J. Dulinsky, who arrived on 18 March 1967. After an 18-hour flight, she landed at dusk at Bien Hoa, about 30 miles north of Saigon. Travel was restricted after dark on the unsecure roads, so she was billeted overnight at the airfield. The next morning she was taken by bus and armed escort to Koeppler Compound in Saigon and there her tour began with a security lecture. The briefing was not concerned with security of classified material as one might expect, but with security in day-to-day living in Vietnam, such as recognizing booby traps, and checking cabs upon entering to ensure there was a handle inside. Arrival procedures were similar for most WMs.73

At first, the enlisted women were quartered in the Ambassador Hotel, and later they moved to the Plaza, a hotel-dormitory, two to a room. Women of other services and several hundred men called the Plaza home.

By spring 1968, the enlisted women were moved to the Billings Bachelor Enlisted Quarters (BEQ), located near MACV Headquarters and Tan Son Nhut Airbase.

Generally, the women officers were billeted in Le Qui Don, a hotel-like Bachelor Officers Quarters (BOQ). Company grade officers were usually assigned two to a room; WMs and WAVES billeted together.

Like the Plaza and Billings BEQ, Le Qui Don Hotel was air conditioned, but electricity was a sometime thing.

There were no eating facilities in either the Billings BEQ or the Le Qui Don BOQ. Most of the women cooked in their room on hot plates or with electric skillets. When the power was out, they managed with charcoal-grilled meals served by candlelight.74

There were no laundry facilities, but for about $15 a month, each woman hired a maid who cleaned her room, and washed and pressed her uniforms. Before leaving the United States the women Marines were cautioned to bring an ample supply of nylons, sturdy cotton lingerie, and summer uniforms. Not only were these items scarce in the post exchange that catered to male troops, but the maids were unduly hard on them. Lieutenant Colonel Elaine E. Filkins (later Davies) spoke of looking out her window to see the maid laundering her nylon stockings and lingerie in a creek by pounding them with rocks. The garments that survived were a mass of torn, short elastic threads. Girdles and bras were short-lived "in the combat zone."75 Nylon hosiery was a luxury. Women of some services were even excused from wearing them when in uniform, a privilege not extended to women Marines. Vietnamese women were fascinated by the sheer stockings and Lieutenant Colonel Vera M. Jones told of walking down the streets of Saigon and being startled by the touch of a Vietnamese woman feeling her stockings.76

SSgt Ermelinda Salazar, nominated by the Veterans of Foreign Wars Auxiliary for the 1970 Unsung Heroine Award, recognizing her assistance to children of the St. Vincent De Paul Orphanage, Saigon, is the subject of this painting by artist Cliff Young.

The women were advised to arrive with four to six pairs of dress pumps for uniform wear because the streets were hard on shoes and repair service was unsatisfactory. In the "Information on Saigon" booklet provided each woman before leaving the United States was written, ". . . bring a dozen sets of heel lifts. . . . Heels can easily be extracted with a pair of pliers and new ones inserted with little difficulty."77

For the most part the WMs worked in Saigon, but on occasion duty took them outside the city. In January 1969, Captain Filkins, in a letter to the Director of Women Marines, wrote:

In early December, Corporal Spaatz and I traveled to Da Nang with nearly 100 SRB/OQRs [service record books/officer qualification records] to conduct an audit of the service records of the men stationed in the north. The Army I Corps had been most kind in aiding us in our efforts to provide administrative assistance to our widely scattered men. Corporal Spaatz is a fine representative for the WMs with her professional handling of the audit. It was obvious that the men enjoyed the unfamiliar click of the female high heeled shoes. The weather was on our side so we were able to wear the dress with pumps the entire visit.78

When the weather was unusually wet or when the city was under attack, the women wore utilities and oxfords. In addition the Army issued field uniforms and combat boots to any woman required to wear them for duty.

The Tet offensive of January-February 1968, a large-scale enemy attack that disrupted the city, brought some changes to the lives of WMs in Saigon. At the time enlisted women were still quartered at the Plaza which received automatic weapons fire. Bus service to many of the BOQs and BEQs was cut off, confining the women to their quarters.

Captain Jones was unable to leave the Le Qui Don for a day and a half before bus service, with armed escorts, resumed. Excerpts of a letter from Captain Jones to Colonel Bishop told something of the situation:

3 February 1968. It's hard to believe that a war is going on around me. I sit here calmly typing this letter and yet can get up, walk to a window, and watch the helicopters making machine gun and rocket strikes in the area of the golf course which is about three blocks away. At night, I lie in bed and listen to the mortar rounds going off. The streets, which are normally crowded with traffic, are virtually bare MSgt Dulinsky, Cpl Hensley, and Cpl Wilson finally got into work this afternoon. Cpls Hensley and Wilson plan to spend the night. 79

Excerpts from a letter from Master Sergeant Dulinsky elaborated:

9 February 1968. We are still on a 24-hour curfew, with all hands in utilities MACV personnel (women included) were bussed down to Koeppler compound and issued 3 pair of jungle fatigues and a pair of jungle boots.

Right now, most of us don't look the picture of "The New Image." Whew! Hardly! I can't determine at night, if I'm pooped from the work day or from carrying around these anvils tied to my feet called combat boots.

Our Young-uns (and me too inside) were scared; but you'd have been proud of them. They turned to in the mess, cashiering, washing dishes, serving and clearing tables.80

Although the Tet offensive kept the women from attending the celebration of the silver anniversary of the women Marines in Okinawa, they were not without a celebration. Thanks to a WAVE and male Marines, they had a cake in the office and the traditional cake-cutting ceremony.

The command expected each person to work 60 productive hours a week. Time off was precious, and recreational facilities were limited. Bowling was a popular sport, and old American television shows were broadcast a few hours each evening. The city was often under curfew with the Americans back in their quarters by 2000 or 2200. Movies were available several nights a week in some of the BEQs and BOQs. A number of the women kept busy during their off-duty hours by working at the Armed Forces Television Station, helping at various orphanages, and visiting Vietnamese families. Captain Jones, the only woman Marine who attended Vietnamese language school, taught English to a class of Vietnamese policemen.

Captain Filkins, interested in an orphanage for blind girls, solicited soap, clothing, linens, toys, and supplies from the women Marine companies at home. In her letter she wrote, "They are rather confined in their small, dark world of the orphanage so they seem quite thrilled when visitors come to see them Many of these children are lucky if they are picked up and held for a few minutes each week.81

Assigned to administrative duties in Saigon, GySgt Donna Hollowell Murray, shown here in Tanh Anh, Vietnam, in 1970, gave time to work with children in outlying areas.

One woman Marine in particular, Staff Sergeant Ermelinda Salazar (later Esquibel), who touched the lives of Vietnamese orphans, was nominated for the 1970 Unsung Heroine Award sponsored by the Veterans of Foreign Wars Auxiliary, and was immortalized in a painting by Marine artist Cliff Young. During her 15 months in Saigon, Staff Sergeant Salazar essentially took over a MACV civic action project involving the St. Vincent de Paul orphanage.

In a letter dated 10 September 1969, to Gunnery Sergeant Helen A. Dowd, she told of her work with the children:

I don't remember if I mentioned to you that I had been working with the orphanage supported by MACV. It is not a big one —only 75 children ages from a few weeks old to about 11 or 12 years of age. They are precious and quite lively. . . . This whole orphanage is taken care of by two Catholic sisters. . . . One of them is rather advanced in age (about in her 60's) and the other is quite young and active. Still and all, Gunny, these two souls work themselves to death. . . . The two sisters are Vietnamese who speak no English at all. . . . And me? I know a limited number of broken phrases and words in Vietnamese. . .

Since I've been working at the orphanage, I've had to overcome much repugnance. There's a lot of sickness and disease here in Vietnam. . So when I say the orphanage it doesn't have the same connotation that it does back in the states where the children are well fed . . . and healthy for at least they have medical facilities and medicines available. These children have nothing! If the WM company is wondering about any projects for Christmas here is something you can think about. Anything and everything is needed.82

Determined that these children would have a party, Staff Sergeant Salazar personally contacted Marine units for contributions, arranged a site and bus transportation, enlisted interested people to help, and wrapped individual gifts for each child. Her interest continued after the holidays and in spite of 11-hour workdays, six days a week, she was able to influence other Marines to follow her lead in working at the orphanage. Nominating her for the Unsung Heroine Award, her commanding officer wrote: "Her unusual and untiring efforts to assist these otherwise forgotten children reflect great credit upon herself, the United States Marine Corps, this command, and the United States."83

Staff Sergeant Salazar was awarded the Joint Service Commendation Medal for meritorious achievement in the performance of her duties during the period 10 October 1969 to 10 January 1970 while serving with the Military History Branch, Secretary Joint Staff, U.S. Military Assistance Command, Vietnam. In addition, the Republic of Vietnam awarded her the Vietnamese Service Medal for her work with the orphans.

Women Marines in Vietnam normally numbered eight or 10 enlisted women and one or two officers at any one time for a total of about 28 enlisted women and eight officers between 1967 and 1973. Their letters and interviews reveal their apprehension before arriving in Saigon, their satisfaction with their tour, and their increased sense of being a Marine.

Women Marines in Marine Security Guard Battalion

Traditionally, women Marines had not been assigned to the Marine Security Guard Battalion, commonly referred to as embassy duty. The primary mission of an embassy Marine is to safeguard classified material vital to the United States' interests and to protect American lives and property abroad. In 1967 the first two women officers joined the Marine Security Guard Battalion, not as guards, but as personnel officers. First Lieutenant Charlene M. Summers (later Itchkawich) served with Company C, Manila, Philippines, and Warrant Officer Mary E. Pease was assigned to Company D, Panama Canal Zone. The following year, Captain Gail M. Reals reported to Company B, Beirut, Lebanon.84

Women Marines Overseas — Summary

Opportunities for women Marines to serve outside the continental United States had been extremely limited from World War II to 1966. Billets available in Europe never accommodated more than nine or 10 women, officers and enlisted. Until October 1966, Hawaii was the only location in the Pacific at which WMs could serve. On 30 June 1966, 3.7 percent, or 63 women Marines, 56 in Hawaii and seven at foreign locations, were serving outside the continental limits.85 On 30 June 1971, 9-3 percent, or 209 women were serving in the following locations:86

Sgt Doris Denton receives the Joint Service Commendation Medal from MajGen Richard F. Shaffer, USA, assistant chief of staff, J-5, in Saigon, South Vietnam, on 5 March 1969.

Location / Officer / Enlisted

MCAF, Futema, Okinawa / 3 / 20

MCB, Camp Butler, Okinawa / 6 / 37

MCAS, Iwakuni, Japan / 5 / 34

FMFPac, Camp Smith, Hawaii / 14 / 59

MCAS, Kaneohe, Hawaii / 5 / 9

AFSE, Naples, Italy / 1 / 1

EUCOM, Stuttgart, Germany / 1 / 3

MarDet, London, England / 0 / 1

MAS NATO Brussels, Belgium / 1 / 0

MACV, Saigon, Vietnam / 2 / 6

MarSecGdBn, Hong Kong / 1 / 0

TOTAL / 39 / 170

The location of the billets and the numerical requirements change from time to time but the policy of expanded overseas assignments for women in the Marine Corps made during the years 1966-1972, following the recommendations of the Pepper Board, has persisted.

These years saw remarkable changes made in the utilization, training, and assignment of women Marines and marked success in recruiting, officer procurement, and retention efforts. The Pepper Board reported its findings and recommendations to improve the effectiveness of women Marines in 1965 at a time when the war in Vietnam demanded maximum effort and performance of each Marine. Many questioned the price tag that would accompany implementation of the study group's recommendations; others recognized the costliness of inadequately trained and disillusioned Marines. Largely due to the leadership and untiring efforts of the Commandant of the Marine Corps, General Greene; the chairman of the Woman Marine Program Study Group, Lieutenant General Pepper; and the Director of Women Marines, Colonel Bishop, notable progress was made and the status of women placed on a firmer footing than any time previously in the history of the Corps.

CHAPTER 7

Utilization and Numbers: Snell Committee, 1973-1977

Strength, 1973-1977 — New Occupational Fields — Military Police — Presiding Judges — Breaking the Tradition Bandsmen — Women Marines in the Fleet Marine Force — Women in Command — 1973-1977 Summary

There was, in the early 1970s, an increased awareness of the phenomenon called equal opportunity for women.1 It permeated the family, the schoolroom, business, religion, and the military. In all fairness, laws, customs, and prejudices notwithstanding, a case can be made for the advantageous position of servicewomen compared to women in education, business, and industry. There were, however, recognized shortcomings which had to be dealt with. The advent of the all-volunteer force and the national women's liberation movement were leading to increased use of women in the military. On 1 September 1972, the Chief of Naval Operations, Admiral Elmo R. Zumwalt, Jr., recommended a plan tailored to meet a goal stated as "allowing women an equal opportunity to contribute their talents and to achieve full professional status in the Navy."2 The Marine Corps had no such plan.

One week later, the Secretary of Defense, Melvin R. Laird, directed the services to develop by 30 November 1972 detailed equal opportunity/affirmative action plans for minorities and servicewomen. As a result, the Deputy Chief of Staff (Manpower) of the Marine Corps, Lieutenant General Ormond R. Simpson, proposed an ad hoc committee to be chaired by Colonel Albert W. Snell. The committee was tasked with developing a plan of action, objectives, and milestones for a program to increase equal opportunity for women Marines.

The membership of Colonel Snell's committee varied from time to time but included representatives of the Assistant Chief of Staff, G-l; Deputy Director of Personnel; Director Division of Reserve; and Director Women Marines. Included were Lieutenant Colonel Jenny Wrenn and Major Barbara E. Dolyak. At the initial, formal meetings, the committee established the goal to "increase the effectiveness and utilization for all women Marines to fully utilize their abilities in support of Marine Corps objectives." Five specific objectives identified to accomplish the goal were:

a. To identify and eliminate all discrimination based solely on sex.

b. To ensure to women Marines equal opportunity for assignment to and within noncombat occupational fields.

c. To provide the opportunity for women Marines to obtain technical and professional schooling at all levels.

d. To provide equal opportunity to women Marines for progression and advancement through duty assignments.

e. To ensure equal economic opportunity for women Marines.3

It happened that the Office of the Assistant Secretary of Defense (Manpower and Reserve Affairs) Central All-Volunteer Task Force on the Utilization of Military Women, headed by Colonel Helen A. Wilson, USMCR, published a separate but related study in December 1972. This report specifically recommended that the Marine Corps:

(1) Intensify its recruiting efforts for enlisted women.

(2) Open additional job specialties to women.

(3) Take action to reduce attrition rates to a level more comparable to that being experienced by the other services.

(4) Advise . . . after six months the results achieved in (1), (2), and (3) above and how these results affect its FY 1974 plans for female military strength in Marine Corps.4

A further consideration by the Snell Committee was the report of a task group chaired by the Judge Advocate General of the Navy to review the portion of Titles 10 and 37 of the United States Code which differentiated between the treatment of men and women.

Taking all into consideration, the Snell Committee identified 17 separate tasks needed to attain its objectives. A background position paper containing the 17 tasks was then staffed to appropriate Headquarters agencies for comment. Colonel Margaret A. Brewer was given the job of reviewing the comments, summarizing the recommendations, and making appropriate modifications.

The recommendations that evolved included several concerning promotion boards that would require legislative action. Most, however, challenged the Marine Corps' policies and regulations that barred women from occupational fields or schools based solely on sex. The fields of logistics, military police and corrections, and aircraft maintenance, all closed to women, were singled out as possibilities for immediate action while all other noncombat fields would be studied to determine their appropriateness for women Marines. Two of the most unorthodox ideas presented were the plan that a pilot program be established to assign women to stateside Fleet Marine Forces and the recommendation that:

. . . the prohibition in the Marine Corps Manual which limits women officers to succeeding to command only at those activities which have the administration of Women Marines as their primary function be eliminated.5

According to Lieutenant Colonel Barbara Dolyak, a member of the Snell Committee, it came as a surprise when the Commandant approved all recommendations on 14 November 1973- On the final page of the report, General Robert E. Cushman, Jr., penned, "O.K. —let's move out!"6

Strength, 1973-1977

In April 1973 a goal was set of 3,100 women Marines by 30 June 1977.7 This represented a 30 percent increase of women's strength and completely disregarded the traditional figure of one percent of total Marine Corps enlisted strength. Subsequently, the target date was moved up to 1 January 1976. During the summer of 1976, the Commandant, General Louis H. Wilson, Jr., responding to requests from commanders for additional women, to the improved effectiveness of women in the Corps, and to the realities of the all-volunteer force, approved an additional increase in the size of the woman Marine force.8 The change was planned to be implemented over a six-year period beginning 1 October 1976, with a recruiting goal for the year of 1,700 women or 164 over the current annual input. Beginning with fiscal year 1978, in October 1977 the Corps aimed to recruit 2,500 women annually. Then in March 1977, appearing before a House Armed Services subcommittee, General Wilson made the surprise announcement that the Marine Corps expected to have 10,000 women in its ranks by 1985-e Incremental increases were planned based on logistical limitations related to uniform supplies and billeting space rather than on need or availability of qualified applicants. In 1975 18 percent of all women who enlisted in the Marine Corps had attended college and some had baccalaureate degrees.10 In 1977, both recruiting and officer procurement quotas were easily met with many fine young women being turned away. On 30June 1977, the strength of the active duty women Marines was 407 officers and 3,423 enlisted women for a total of 3,830.

The reenlistment and retention rate for women improved to the point where in 1974, the rate of retention for first-term WMs bettered that of male Marines, 9-9 percent to 7.9 percent. In 1975, it was 10.4 percent for women compared to 7.9 percent for the total Marine Corps.11 No one factor is responsible for the improved recruiting and retention of women. The indications point to a generation of women awakened to new horizons, improvements in the woman Marine program brought on by the Pepper Board and the Snell Committee, and the positive action taken by the Commandants to publicize to all Marines the role of women in the Marine Corps.

New Occupational Fields

The Snell Committee had recommended that the Marine Corps regulations and policies not governed by law be reviewed to revise or eliminate those which discriminated solely on the basis of sex without rational and valid reason, and that all noncombat MOSs be examined to determine which could be made available to women. Since a task analysis of all noncombat occupational fields was already underway at Headquarters and would not be completed for several years, it was further recommended that certain fields be opened immediately as a sign of good faith. For officers, logistics, military police and corrections, and aircraft maintenance were suggested, and for enlisted women, the same three fields plus utilities and electronics. Because of some disagreement and in view of the ongoing study of all noncombat MOSs, only logistics and military police and corrections were approved for officers and utilities and military police and corrections for enlisted women.

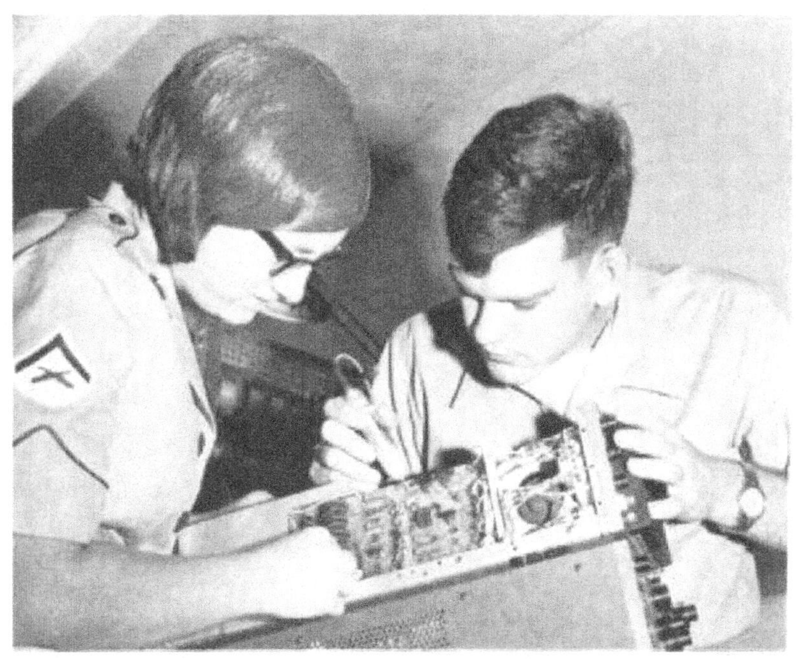

LCpl Brenda Hockenhull, in 1972 the first woman Marine to graduate from the Test Instrument Course, Albany, Georgia, examines a piece of electronic equipment with fellow student, LCpl William Day.

Sgt Karen Cottingham, a trained telephone switchboard repairman, checks the level of battery acid in the standby power source, at the Marine Corps Base, Twentynine Palms, California, on 4 February 1977.

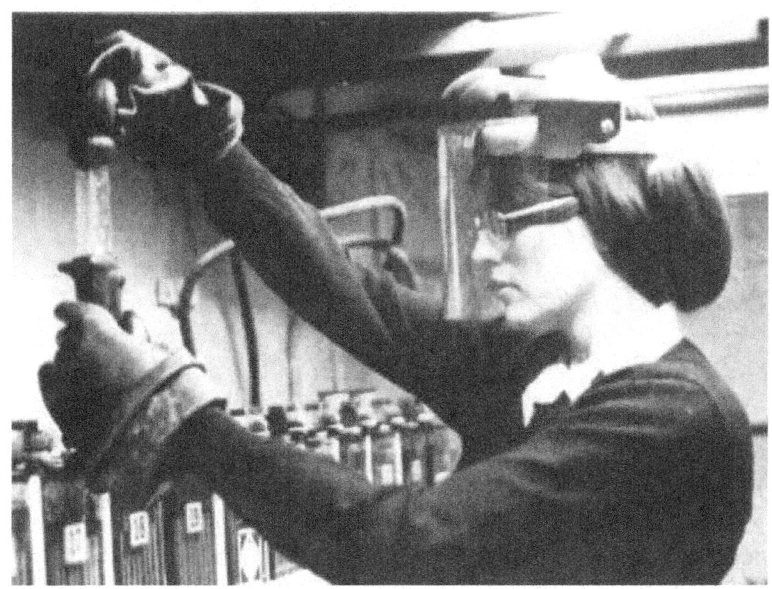

PFC Regina T. Musser, first woman Marine tank mechanic, works on the optic unit of a tank turret while assigned to the Tracked Vehicle Maintenance Unit at Camp Pendleton, California, in 1974.

The final breakthrough, dropping all barriers except those grounded in law, was made on 15 July 1975 when the Commandant, General Wilson, approved the assignment of women to all occupational fields except the four considered combat-related, infantry (03), artillery (08), armor (18), and flight crews (75). Management limitations, preservation of a rotation base for male Marines, equal opportunity regardless of sex for job assignments and promotions, need for adequate facilities and housing for WMs, and availability of nondeployable billets, of necessity, affected the number of women assigned to some fields, but this was truly a decisive change.12

Military Police

Records indicate that there were five women with a military police MOS in 1952 but a search of the records failed to reveal who they were or what duties they performed. It is likely that they were former WRs since the policy after 1948 had been not to assign women to this field.

The Corps' first known post-World War II military policewoman, in January 1974, was Lance Corporal Harriett F. Voisine, a WM who had a bachelor of science degree in criminology with a major in police science and administration. She had worked with the Police Department in Westminster, California, before enlisting in July 1971 and, after recruit training, served for two and one-half years in the Provost Marshal Office at Parris Island. Taking courses on her own in juvenile delinquency; vice and narcotics; criminal law; and arrest, search, and seizure procedures, she was a natural candidate for the military police field when it was finally opened to women Marines13 Lance Corporal Voisine, given on-the-job training by the recruit depot's MPs, was used on the desk, on traffic control details, and on motorized patrols.

Two women Marines, Privates M. B. Ogborn and J. E. Welchel, were the first to attend the seven-week Military Police School at Fort Gordon, Georgia, graduating in April 1975.14 Private Mary F. Bungcayo, who graduated from the same course the following month was assigned to the Marine Corps Air Station, Cherry Point, for duty. In a 1977 interview, Corporal Bungcayo stated that she met some male opposition at first, but no restrictions. She worked on the desk and on patrol; she responded to fires and flight emergencies; and she stood guard on the gate. Corporal Bungcayo, who joined the Marine Corps with the guarantee of military police work, believed that on the job she was given the same responsibilities as the male MPs.15

Second Lieutenant Debra J. Baughman, the first woman officer in the military police field, was assigned to the Provost Marshal Office at Camp Lejeune after graduation from the 35th Woman Officer Basic Course in March 1975. She entered the field with a degree in corrections but no experience. At Camp Lejeune she was assigned as platoon leader for a platoon of MPs and in the opinion of Colonel Valeria F. Hilgart, the base G-l, "She did a topnotch job."16

The next two officers to enter the 5800 field, military police, were Second Lieutenants Mary A. Krusa and Judith A. Cataldo. Neither had any police experience but both had majored in criminology and the police science field in college. In January 1976 all three attended the Military Police Officer Orientation Course at Fort McClellan, Alabama, to obtain formally the 5803 MOS. After graduation in February 1976, Second Lieutenant Krusa reported to El Toro as the assistant operations officer for the Provost Marshal Office and Second Lieutenant Cataldo reported to Cherry Point for assignment as the officer in charge of the Traffic Investigation, Traffic Control, and Pass and Identification Section. Second Lieutenant Baughman returned to Camp Lejeune. Each of the three officers had received more extensive training in their MOS to include attendance at Northwestern University's Traffic Institute at Evanston, Illinois.17

On the subject of police work for women, Second Lieutenant Cataldo, in March 1977, wrote:

Speaking for myself, I love the field. It is a constantly changing challenge. Twenty-five male MPs work for me and I am given a great deal of responsibility. I feel that after the initial testing and proving period I have been fully accepted. I would recommend the field to other women trained in it as it is still growing and developing professionally. . It frequently demands 24 hour duty (PMO duty officer) five days per month and proficiency with various weapons. . . . For women interested in the police field it offers a great deal.18

Presiding Judges

There were seldom more than one or two women Marine lawyers on active duty at one time, and it was news when in 1970, First Lieutenant Patricia Murphy was named a certified military judge. But in 1974, it was Captain Eileen M. Albertson, second woman to be certified a military judge, who became the first to preside in a courtroom. A graduate of Bloomsburg State College and the Marshall Wythe School of Law at the College of William and Mary, she served in the Marine Corps Reserve for a six-year tour before going on active duty. She served nine months in Judge Advocate General School for military lawyers at Charlottesville, Virginia; 14 months on Okinawa as prosecutor and foreign claims commissioner; and some months as defense counsel at Quantico.19

1stLt Debra J. Baughman, first woman officer in the military police field, inspects her platoon at Marine Corps Base, Camp Lejeune, North Carolina, in the summer of 1975.

Capt Eileen M. Albertson, first woman Marine military judge to preside in a courtroom, administered the foreign claims section and acted as trial counsel at the Camp Smedley D. Butler Law Center in 1972.

As a judge, Captain Albertson was praised by her colleague, Captain David A. Schneider, who said, "I would give her the highest compliment —I'd call her a professional. She shows that she is more interested in justice and fairness than formality or speed . . . ."20 Her former commanding officer, Colonel Joseph R. Motelewski, commented bluntly, "She is one of the finest lawyers I've ever worked with."21

In an effort to attract persons of needed skills, the Marine Corps inaugurated a program of direct Reserve commissions for those who met the criteria. Reserve Marine Major Sara J. Harper, a judge of the Municipal Court of Cleveland, Ohio, entered the Corps as a lawyer and served a number of tours on active duty over a four-year period. Then in 1977, she was appointed a military judge by General Louis H. Wilson, in ceremonies in his office.22

Breaking the Tradition

Improved educational level of women recruits, a changed attitude of society toward the role of working women, especially in technical and professional fields, and an openmindedness in the Corps brought on by the Pepper Board and fostered by the Snell Committee, and finally the Commandant's key decision in July 1975, combined to increase the assignments of women to a greater variety of occupational fields. For example:

In November 1973, Second Lieutenant Patricia M. Zaudtke was assigned as one of the first two WM motor transport officers.23

In June 1974, Captain Shirley L. Bowen was the only woman and the first woman Marine to graduate from the 34-week Advanced Communication Officer Course.24

Private Mary P. McKeown made history at the Army's Ordnance Center and School, Aberdeen, Maryland, when she became the first WM to attend the Metal Body Repair Course. Her classroom instruction included practical work in gas welding, exterior finishing of metal bodies, glass cutting, and instruction in inert gas metal welding techniques.25 First Lieutenant Dian S. George, in 1975, was the first woman Marine to be assigned to the inspector-instructor staff of an all-male Reserve unit, Headquarters and Service Company, Supply Battalion, 4th Force Service Support Group, at Newport News, Virginia. Previously she had served as the assistant SASSY officer at Cherry Point, North Carolina. SASSY is the acronym for Supported Activity Supply System, which was, at the time, a new computerized way of keeping track of all Marine Corps equipment. Thus it was not merely coincidental that First Lieutenant George found herself at the Newport News unit, the first Reserve company to have the SASSY system, one which tied into the computer at Camp Lejeune. During drill weekend she worked on the organization and supervision of the training program which included computer programming and key punch operations skills. In addition she served as personnel, public relations, and recruiting officer on the staff headed by Lieutenant Colonel Robert J. Esposito. For the lieutenant, being in an all-male outfit was not entirely new since she had participated in the 1974 pilot program permitting women to serve in the Fleet Marine Forces.26 Private First Class Cathy E. Smith was the first woman Marine to attend the Water Supply and Plumbing Course at Camp Lejeune. The training which began on 14 July 1975 was concerned mainly with water purification, i.e., supplying fresh water to Marines in the field.27

On 28 January 1977, Sergeant Deborah A. Rubel, a mechanic in the fuel and electrical shop, Motor Transport and Maintenance Company, 2d Maintenance Battalion, Force Troops, 2d Force Service Support Group, was named Force Troops 2d FSSG Marine of the Quarter, high praise for a woman serving in the FMF in a nontraditional job.28

Second Lieutenant Jo Anne Kelly became, in January 1977, the first of four women in her occupational field to qualify for the 7210 MOS, Air Defense Control Officer. She finished initial training at Twenty-nine Palms in August 1976 and then reported to the Marine Corps Air Station, Beaufort, where she completed the required number of live intercepts in tactical flight missions.29

On 9 January 1977, three WMs, Sergeants Connie Dehart and Cynthia Martin, and Corporal Geneva Jones, were reported to be the first women to earn their wings while serving as flight attendants on the C-9B Skytrain. After a two-week familiarization course at the McDonnell Douglas School, the women's duties included loading baggage and cargo, and serving meals. In an interview in March 1977, Sergeant Jones indicated that there was no resentment shown by male Marines with whom she worked, but at least one lieutenant colonel was uncomfortable about her work as he ordered her out of the cargo compartment and loaded his own baggage.30

Private First Class Pamela Loper, the first woman Marine to hold a tractor-trailer license at Camp Lejeune since World War II, was described in April 1977 by Lieutenant Colonel John F. Drummond, base motor transport officer, as " . a much better driver than some of our experienced men." Private First Class Loper drove a large tractor-trailer rig, known as a "semi" or "18 wheeler." She obtained her license after passing tests on handling the vehicle and hooking up and unhooking the trailer.31

Private First Class Katie Jones Dixon, Headquarters and Maintenance Squadron-32's first WM jet mechanic, worked on jet engines and components which MAG-32's squadrons sent to its power plant for repair. Extensive schooling prepared her to do the type of intermediate maintenance that the squadrons were not authorized to perform.32

Private First Class Gail Faith Morise, first enlisted woman to attend the 12-week Automotive Mechanics School at Camp Lejeune, was also the first WM to be assigned to Cherry Point's Motor Transport Division.33

Bandsmen

Well before the final verdict was in on opening new occupational fields to women, an old one became available once more. Until 1973, the musical MOS 5500 was designated for wartime duty only. Women Marine bandsmen were a rare sight after the demobilization of Camp Lejeune's renowned MCWR band of World War II. In 1967, Colonel Bishop reported that Corporals Donna L. Correll and Marjorie W. Groht had joined the Marine Corps Supply Center band at Albany and played in ceremonies on 10 November.34 These two Marines, members of the first group of WMs to report to Albany, played the clarinet and trumpet and were believed to be the only women performing with a Marine band at the time. In 1969, Lance Corporal Judy A. Tiffany volunteered on a part-time basis as a cymbal player with the newly formed Drum and Bugle Team at the Marine Barracks, Treasure Island, California. And then, in 1971, five WMs, Corporals Sue Redding and Nancy Wright, Lance Corporals Sue Deleskiewicz and Joan Mahaffey, and Private First Class Martha Eveland became the first WM musical unit since World War II when they formed the WM Drum Section of Treasure Island's Drum and Bugle Team.35

Private Jay C. Clark was assigned the 5500 MOS in February 1973 while in recruit training at Parris Island.

Sgt J. S. Burke, a tractor-trailer driver with Base Material Battalion, Camp Pendleton, California, adjusts the chains of her rig on 11 February 1977.

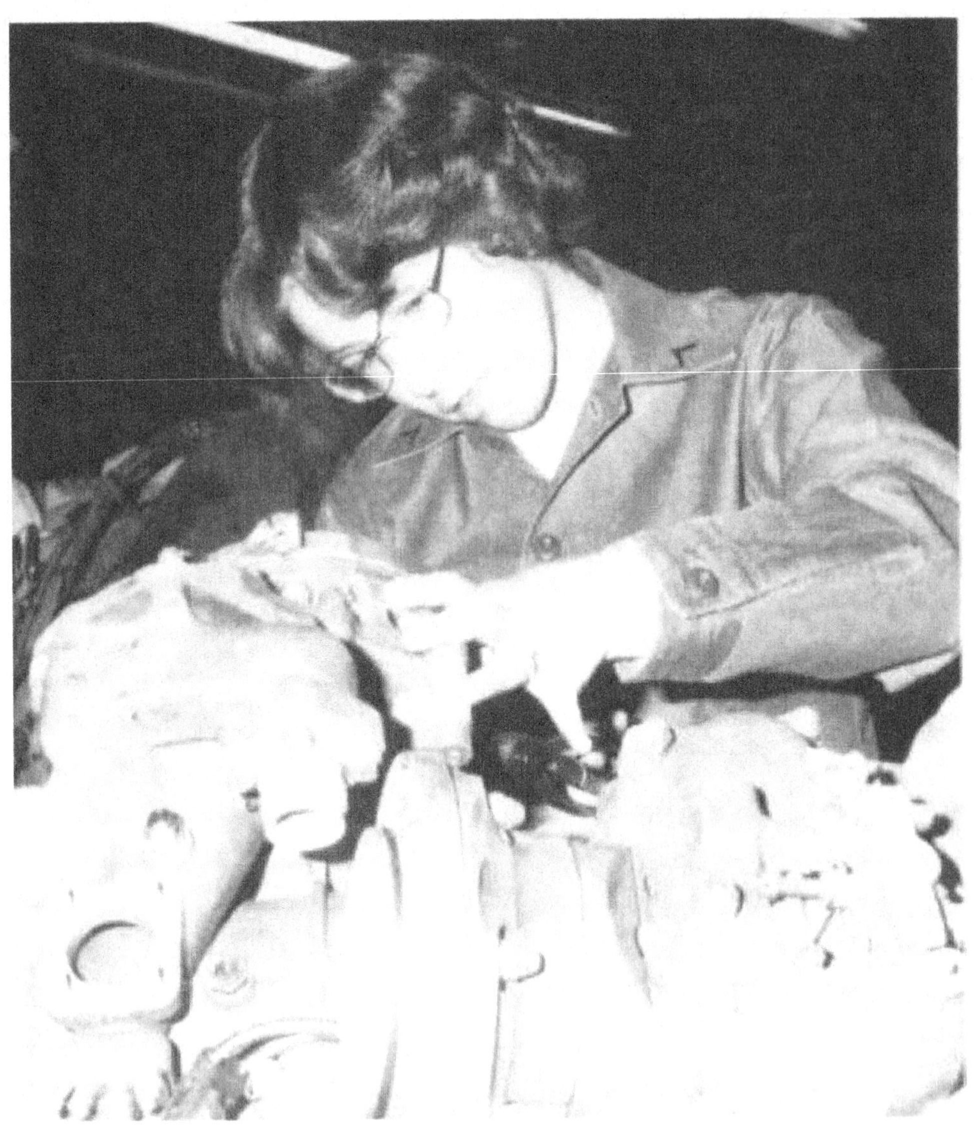

PFC Katie J. Dixon, H&MS-32 mechanic, safety wires the fuel control of an A-4 Skyhawk power plant in the squadron's powerplant section, Marine Corps Air Station, Cherry Point, North Carolina, in 1977.

She was assigned to the post band and later sent to Basic Music School in Little Creek, Virginia. Upon completion of the six-month course, she served in the bands in Hawaii and at the Recruit Depot at San Diego, California.

The famed U.S. Marine Band of Washington, D.C, however, remained an all-male bastion until 1973, when, due to a critical shortage of certain instrumentalists, the band sought and received permission to enlist women.36 Elizabeth A. Eitel, an oboist and University of Montana student, became, in April 1973, the first woman to audition and to be accepted. Before she graduated and subsequently enlisted on 30 July, another young woman, Ruth S. Johnson, a University of Michigan graduate, joined the band on 16 May, becoming its first woman member. Like all members of the band, the women were appointed to the rank of staff sergeant and were not required to attend recruit training. Gunnery Sergeant Johnson, in 1977, was the Marine Band's principal French hornist.37

At first there were several conditions imposed by the band. The women, for example, were to wear the male bandsmen uniforms. Colonel Margaret A. Brewer, Director of Women Marines, satisfied that this new opportunity was available to women, prudently offered no opposition. It was soon obvious that the men's trousers were ill-fitting and difficult to tailor for the women, so new uniforms, following the traditional pattern but proportioned for the female figure, were designed. Eventually long skirts were added to the wardrobe. The WM hat posed some problems, especially in wet weather as it required careful blocking to keep in shape. The band had a white vinyl model designed and asked Colonel Brewer for her opinion. With its gold emblem, red cap cord, and semi-shiny fabric, she found it unattractive at first, but agreed to a test period. The vinyl hat not only looked fine when worn during performances, but it solved the maintenance problem. Recognizing the practicality of a hat that can withstand rain and snow, the white vinyl was later copied for use by women MPs.38

By July 1977, the Marine Band counted in its ranks the following 10 women musicians:39

Gunnery Sergeant Gail A. Bowlin .flute

Gunnery Sergeant Elizabeth A. Eitel .oboe

Staff Sergeant Elnora Teopaco Figueroa violin

Staff Sergeant Michelle Foley .oboe

Gunnery Sergeant Carol Hayes viola

Gunnery Sergeant Ruth S. Johnson French horn

Staff Sergeant Denna S. Purdie .cello

Staff Sergeant Linda D. Stolarchyk .cello

Staff Sergeant Vickie J. Yanics .violin

Staff Sergeant Dyane Wright .bassoon

Women Marines in the Fleet Marine Force

The Snell Committee recommended that a pilot program be established to assign women to stateside division, wing, or force service regiment headquarters in noncombat rear echelon billets such as disbursing, data systems, administration, etc. General Cushman, Commandant of the Marine Corps, approved the concept on 14 November 1973.40 In February 1974, a message was sent to FMF commanders notifying them of a yet-to-be published change in policy which would permit the assignment of women to FMF billets involving service support, aviation support, or communication occupational specialties that would not require them to deploy with the assault echelon of the command if a contingency arose. The legal restrictions that women not be assigned duty in aircraft that are engaged in combat missions nor on vessels of the Navy other than hospital ships and transports were included.

The 2d Marine Aircraft Wing and the 1st Marine Division were designated as the commands to participate in a six-month pilot program, and they were provided information on the grade and MOSs of the women selected for FMF assignments. The message stated, "These Marines will be joined on the rolls of, and administered by, the headquarters indicated. Their duties will be consistent with the requirement of the billet to which assigned."41 This simple statement, referring to Marines without the usual modifier, women, bespoke an important change in attitude. As an adjunct to the pilot program, all FMF commanders were asked to identify billets within their headquarters considered suitable for women Marines.

Originally, 13 women were selected to take part in the experiment: seven to the 2d Marine Aircraft Wing and six to the 1st Marine Division. Actually, nine WMs, four officers and five enlisted women, were assigned to the wing. They were:

First Lieutenant Maralee J. Johnson

First Lieutenant Dian S. George

Second Lieutenant Vicki B. Taylor

Second Lieutenant Margaret A. Humphrey

Gunnery Sergeant Sharyl E. Sheftz

Sergeant Charlene K. Wiese

Corporal Pamela S. Scott

Corporal Eva J. Lugo

Lance Corporal Marsha A. Douglas

In an interview published in the Windsock, the Cherry Point newspaper, in July 1974, Corporal Scott said, "At first I heard there might be some problems because men didn't want women in the Wing, but everyone here has been helpful, and I haven't had any problem at all."42 Sergeant Wiese, accounting analyst with the comptroller section, 2d Marine Aircraft Wing said, "There was a lot of apprehension between myself and the Marine I was working with, but it's gone now and things are great."43 Others commented on the changes brought by being administratively attached to the wing rather than Woman Marine Detachment 2, a small unit where everyone knew everyone else.

The six women assigned to the 1st Marine Division at Camp Pendleton were Captain Karyl L. Moesel, First Lieutenant Maria T. Hernandez, Second Lieutenant Mary S. Burns, Gunnery Sergeant Esther F. Peters, Sergeant Judith A. Alexander, and Sergeant Lynn J. Powell.

First woman Marine music unit since 1945 was the drum section of the Marine Barracks, Treasure Island Drum and Bugle Team, 1970-1971: (left to right) Cpls Sue Conley and Nancy Wright, LCpl Sue Deleskiewicz, PFC Martha Eveland, and LCpl Joan Mahaffey.

At the end of the six-month experimental period, in November 1974, the Commanding General of the 1st Marine Division, Brigadier General William L. McCulloch, reported that, ". . . the WMs have managed to assimilate necessary knowledge of FMF-peculiar systems to allow them to be assets to their respective sections"44 and, he continued:

It is this command's interpretation . . . that WMs assigned to FMF commands are deployable to advanced areas as long as they are not deployed with assault echelon . . . and are, therefore, not necessarily bound to rear echelon . . . billets This command enthusiastically supports assignments of WMs to CONUS FMF commands and foresees no insurmountable problems associated with program. Assignment of WMs would provide source of talent and critical skills and would ease skill shortages within the First MARDIV.45

The Commanding General, 2d Marine Aircraft Wing, Major General Ralph H. Spanjer, in his assessment of the pilot program, noted that the nine WMs were rapidly assimilated into the wing staff, and no problems were observed in military courtesy, appearance, or bearing. The physical fitness testing had been conducted by the senior woman officer without difficulty and with notable success. He continued that the small number involved precluded any effect on deployment and during field exercises, the women Marines had a positive effect on the headquarters by remaining in garrison and continuing the daily administrative routine. Finally, he submitted:

The pilot program of assigning Women Marines to 2d Marine Aircraft Wing has thus far been successful in terms of orientation, capability, and performance. Realizing the practicality of assigning Woman Marines to CONUS Fleet Marine Force Commands, it is felt that the program should be continued.49

The commanding general of FMFPac, on the subject of women in ConUS FMF commands, wrote: "This headquarters regards utilization of women Marines in FMF commands both feasible and desirable providing such assignment does not adversely affect combat readiness. . . ." And he offered the recommendation that:

. . . Marine Corps education and training programs be modified to:

1. Increase emphasis on FMF-related instruction and training for women Marines, to include extension school courses and, if possible additional quotas to intermediate and high level schools.

2. Incorporate into Human Relations and Leadership training consideration of the role of women Marines in the FME47

As part of the pilot program, the commanders of the division, aircraft wings, force troops, and force service regiments identified rear echelon billets totaling 75 officer and 450 enlisted that could be filled by women without requiring them to deploy with the assault echelon. The billets included supply, disbursing, communications, intelligence, administration, data systems, and legal specialties. When new MOSs were opened to women by the 1975 decision, even more FMF billets were considered suitable for women Marines.

Women in the 1st Marine Division were featured in an article published in the Los Angeles Times in September 1976. Among those mentioned were Second Lieutenant Michele D. Venne, combat engineer officer, who was the first woman officer to attend Combat Engineer School and finished first in her class; Lance Corporal Victoria Carrillo, a plumber and water supplyman who, at the time, was the only woman water purification expert in the Marine Corps; Second Lieutenant Carol Sue Lamb, the only female motor transport officer in the FMF, who was serving as assistant division motor transport officer and later served as a division supply group platoon commander; Corporal Cynthia Robinson, an electrician, who performed duties such as pole line construction and the stringing of power lines; Second Lieutenant Laura A. Hull, headquarters battalion adjutant; and Lance Corporal Kimberly Greene, only woman coxswain in the Marine Corps. Lance Corporal Greene, who grew up on Narragansett Bay in Rhode Island, practiced her seamanship in the Corps by handling a 58-foot landing craft which could carry up to 40 combat-loaded Marines for an assault on an enemy beach.

GySgts Ruth Johnson (left) and Beth Eitel (right), first women members of the U.S. Marine Band, frequently performed with the Band's Woodwind Quintet.

There were at the time, 42 women in the 1st Marine Division, and their commanding officer, Lieutenant Colonel Robert D. White, confessed that while the obvious problems such as restroom facilities and billeting were nettlesome, they were not difficult. The women Marines lived in motel-like BEQs with their male colleagues, since it was thought that segregated barracks would run counter to unit integrity.

The men found that women tend to keep their quarters better policed, but Colonel White soon learned that:

. . . there is a greater sense of urgency from the women when equipment, such as washing machines, fails. The women seem to be more conscious of how they look in uniform . . . and when it comes to wearing sidearms which might make a hippy woman look hippier, an option of uniform is allowed. They can wear either skirts or utility outfits.48

Anticipated problems resulting from men and women living in the same barracks did not materialize as the division men seemed to take a protective attitude toward the WMs. Barracks and office language was noticeably improved, but the feminine presence apparently caused little resentment on that score, since Lieutenant Colonel White was quoted as saying, "The division is more fun with the girls."49

The women unanimously endorsed FMF assignments for WMs. Lance Corporal Debora Pederson, a correspondence clerk in the headquarters battalion adjutant's office, said, ". . . at Pendleton, we are treated as Marines, not specified as women Marines."50 First Lieutenant Venne found senior officers dubious when she was assigned as a division engineer, responsible for equipment used in bridge building, grading roads, and other construction projects associated with combat. But the skepticism was because she was a lieutenant and not because she was a woman.

In July 1977, there were 610 women Marines serving in the FMF, 96 officers and 514 enlisted women.51 The policy to assign them only to stateside organizations was still in effect, but individual exceptions had been made where FMF commanders overseas had specifically asked for women Marines.

Women in Command

The Marine Corps Manual, from 1948 until 1973, laid down the rule that women could command only those units that were predominantly female. At least one exception was made when Captain Jeanne Fleming was assigned as the commanding officer of Company B, Headquarters Battalion, Marine Corps Schools, Quantico, from July 1956 until September 1958. The company consisted of all officer students at Quantico, less those attending The Basic School. Her duties were primarily administrative, but it was quite unusual, nevertheless, for men to report in and find a woman commanding officer. One of them was Major Albert W. Snell, later to head the Ad Hoc Committee in 1973.

After approving the Snell Committee recommendation that women be permitted to command units other than woman Marine companies, General Cush-man announced the new policy at a press conference in southern California in December 1973. He added, as a side comment, that, indeed, Camp Pendleton was soon to make such an assignment. According to the woman destined to become the Marine Corps' first woman commander of a nearly all male battalion, Colonel Mary E. Bane, the general's pronouncement was news to the command at Camp Pendleton. The press picked up on the Commandant's statement immediately and all other topics of his news conference were forgotten.

Colonel Bane, who had been filling a colonel's billet as an assistant chief of staff for personnel services, was informed by the Assistant Chief of Staff (Manpower), "You have been selected to sacrifice, Evie."52 The day following the Commandant's announcement, the commanding general, Brigadier General Robert L. Nichols, named Colonel Bane to be Commanding Officer, Headquarters and Service Battalion, Marine Corps Base, Camp Pendleton, California. The furor was astonishing. In less than 24 hours, she had to change her telephone to an unlisted number. She had spent a sleepless night answering calls from the media, women's liberation organizations, cranks, and friends. In a short time she received over 300 letters, both congratulatory and abusive. There were requests for autographed photographs and an 80-year-old reared Navy chief petty officer wrote to General Earl E. Anderson, Assistant Commandant, and asked for a set of Colonel Bane's first lieutenant bars. Mail came from Germany, Vietnam, Korea, and the Philippines, and from such diverse sources as the American Nazi Party and the National Organization of Women. In fact, the letters continued to arrive two years after she left the command.

Headquarters and Service Battalion was a unit of 1,700 Marines, including a woman Marine company. Colonel Bane's immediate staff, the executive officer, Lieutenant Colonel Robert W. Topping, and the battalion sergeant major, were all very supportive. She, herself, felt unprepared for the billet and resented being assigned because of sex rather than qualifications. In due time the commotion subsided, and business at the battalion went on as usual. Eleven months later, Brigadier General Paul Graham assumed command of Marine Corps Base, Camp Pendleton, and reassigned Colonel Bane for, in her words, ". . . precisely the same reason for which I was assigned — because I was a woman."53 He just did not want a woman as the commanding officer of a headquarters battalion. In fact, he did not want a woman in a colonel's billet and Colonel Bane, who had held the responsible position of an assistant chief of staff and had been a battalion commander for 11 months, was reassigned as the base human affairs officer, a major's billet.54

When Captain Kathleen V. Abbott Abies took command of Supply Company, Headquarters and Service Battalion, Marine Corps Base, Twentynine Palms, California, on 7 March 1975, there was none of the hoopla that accompanied Colonel Bane's appointment. It was, just the same, an historic event, a woman in command of a predominantly male company. Looking back, Major Abies was not certain what prompted the battalion commander to assign a woman to the job. The billet was open, and she was the next senior captain in the battalion. She wrote, "The prevailing attitude was that it was my job as a cap-rain, and that I could and would handle it professionally."55

The company first sergeant, Gayle R. Heitman, made it known to the NCOs and SNCOs that he had worked with Captain Abies before and their expressed fears were unfounded. Only the company clerk, a sergeant, had real difficulty accepting a woman commanding officer, and he went to the battalion commander several rimes, in vain, to ask for a transfer.

In the beginning, as might be expected, inspections were the cause of some concern. Personnel inspections had been held without weapons at Supply Company so that when Captain Abies arrived on the scene she merely had to learn the details of male uniform regulations and personal appearance standards. As for quarters inspections, it was not difficult to respect the privacy of Marine shift workers who were apt to be sleeping or relaxing in the barracks during the day since the battalion was billeted in motel-style rooms rather than in open squadbays. First Sergeant Heitman would knock and if there was no answer, he would unlock the door and go in. If the room was empty, Captain Abies followed him in to inspect. The procedure was reversed in the women's BEQ. Male Marines learned something about a woman's idea of a clean barracks. In a 1977 letter, Major Abies wrote:

Capt Kathleen V. Ables takes command of a predominantly male unit, Supply Company, Headquarters and Service Battalion, Marine Corps Base, Twentynine Palms, in 1975.

BEQ inspections caused some heartburn in the company for about a month after I became commanding officer. With two of us inspecting, a large number of previously undetected discrepancies were found. One morning, we arrived at one room to find one of the occupants leaning over a table with a cloth in his hand. I made some comment about making the final touchup, and he replied, "Yes, m'am. We hear you're a real stickler on dust."56

Nonjudicial punishment is always unpleasant but with a woman commanding officer could be awkward as well, depending upon the nature of the offense. One case involved language that neither the accused nor the witnesses wanted to use in front of a lady. A relatively simple solution was found: the offending statement was written out and all parties read and signed it.

Five months after taking over Supply Company, Captain Abies was assigned as commanding officer of her second and larger nearly all-male company, Headquarters Company, Headquarters and Service Battalion, which consisted of about 330 men and 40 women. Again, the first sergeant, Gene A. Lafond, was a key to a successful tour. Integrated battalions and companies such as this one gave rise to some interesting adjustments, notably in the area of physical training. In this instance, the battalion organized a competitive seven-mile conditioning hike. The course included a climb over hills behind the main camp, but because the WMs did not have adequate boots for the cross-country portion, a seven-mile road march was planned for them to be led by Captain Abies. The battalion commander had arranged to take her company himself. The women's platoons from each company were combined to form a single WM unit and scheduled to hike on the day before Captain Abies' Headquarters Company.

Having finished her portion of training, Captain Abies was challenged by her husband, Major Charles K. Abies, to lead her own company the next day. She admitted that it was a struggle to run-walk to keep from straggling. It happened that she was not only not the last to complete the course, but she helped to push a Marine over the finish line, and Headquarters Company won the competition. Afterwards, it was decided that future company hikes would be conducted with men and women participating together, maintaining unit integrity.

An interesting aspect of Captain Abies' experience as a commanding officer is the fact that her husband was a member of her command, no doubt a unique situation in Marine Corps history.

In addition to the command tours of Colonel Bane and Captain Abies, other assignments evidenced some change in philosophy and policy. In 1974, Lieutenant Colonel Annie M. Trowsdale was assigned as executive officer of Headquarters and Headquarters Squadron, Marine Corps Air Station, El Toro, and Sergeant Major Eleanor L. Judge was named sergeant major of Headquarters and Headquarters Squadron, Marine Corps Air Station, Cherry Point. Gunnery Sergeant Frances Gonzales, in 1975, became the first sergeant of Casual Company, Headquarters and Service Battalion, Marine Corps Recruit Depot, San Diego.57

1973-1977 Summary

The Snell Committee report, approved in November 1973, challenged the Marine Corps to take a new look at its use of womanpower, and the zero draft situation for military services demanded it. Combined with the women's movement, changing attitudes in American society, and successful recruiting in terms of quality as well as numbers, these factors added up to a role of increased importance to be played by women in the Marine Corps.

CHAPTER 8

Reserves After Korea

Deactivation of the WR Platoons - Woman Special Enlistment Program - Strength Women Reserve Officers - Formal Training for Women Reservists

Following the Korean War, the Woman Marine Organized Reserve program was reestablished and expanded. The extraordinary success of the original 13 platoons activated in 1949-1950 and mobilized by August 1950 demonstrated the wisdom and practicality of the plan to maintain a trained cadre of women. Accordingly, when the Reservists completed their tour of duty and the Korean emergency neared settlement, Headquarters set an objective of 18 women's platoons having a strength of two officers and 50 enlisted women each.

Their mission explicitly was ". . . to provide trained women reservists to meet initial mobilization needs of the Marine Corps."1 To this end, each of these post-Korean platoons was assigned a specialty determined by mobilization needs. The original plans called for units trained in administration, supply, classification, and disbursing. In 1953, First Lieutenant Margaret A. Brewer, a future Director of Women Marines, organized a communication platoon of 10 officers and 47 enlisted women in Brooklyn, bringing the total up to 19 WR units. Later, a 20th platoon was activated in Miami, Florida. Unlike the pre-Korea Reserve program, these women not only participated in formal specialty training at their home armory, but they attended summer training at Marine Corps posts and stations.

The WR platoons were attached to the parent Reserve unit and came under the command of the male commanding officer. Women officers were designated as platoon leaders and assistant platoon leaders, but were commonly referred to as the commanding officer and executive officer by the women members. Active duty women Marines, one officer and one or two enlisted women were assigned to the inspector-instructor staff to assist the Reserve platoon leader.

The women's platoon was responsible for its own internal administration, recruitment, adherence to rank and military occupational specialty distribution of the members, training, and mobilization state of readiness. Additionally, to make up for the increased work of the parent unit caused by the WR platoon, the women were directed to assume part of the administrative work of the male organization.

Forty-eight two-hour training sessions per year were required. Training of the WRs took several forms: basic general military information for women with no prior service; refresher courses for former servicewomen; and formal classes in the unit's specialty. Summer camp was the highlight of the training program, not only because of the benefit of the classes, but because it provided military experiences (e.g., squadbay accommodations, restrictive liberty hours, liberty cards, standing duty watches, field night, barracks inspections, male drill instructors, mess halls, and reveille), unknown and impossible to acquire at the home armory. For some of the inexperienced Reservists, unaccustomed to military routine, the overnight change from civilian to Marine was jolting. They learned quickly that a merely clean sink was not good enough and that returning from liberty a few minutes late was tantamount to a calamity. As a rule, liberty at summer camp expired at 2200 for women below the rank of corporal and some of these lower ranking Marines carried an alarm clock in their purse to avoid being late.2

The annual two-week training period included combat demonstrations, gas mask drill, classes, participation in a parade or review, as well as softball games and picnics with the regular WMs. At each post where women Reservists trained, a Woman Reserve liaison officer was assigned to coordinate the unit activities. She conducted the annual pretraining conference in the spring, attended by inspector-instructors and the platoon officers, and she assisted the unit during the actual training session.

At home, the Reservists enlarged the intended scope of the program with numerous recreational and public relations activities. Rifle, bowling, and softball teams were the rule. The WR platoons participated in parades on Armed Forces Day, Memorial Day, and in celebration of local holidays. They were asked to attend movie premieres in the days when John Wayne and Marine Corps movies were common; and they helped the Marine Reserve Toys for Tots campaign by laundering and mending doll clothes, wrapping gifts, and posing for publicity photographs. It was not unusual for enthusiastic women Reservists to spend several evenings a week at the armory rather than the required two hours.3

The first post-Korea WR platoon to be established was the Woman Marine Classification Platoon, 2d Infantry Battalion, in Boston, which was activated on 13 January 1952.4 "Boston's Own" was so successful that on 16 November 1955 it was redesignated a company with an authorized strength of three officers and 103 enlisted women. At the ceremony in honor of the first Woman Marine Reserve company, the unit was awarded two recently won trophies, the Katherine Towle Trophy given each year to the Woman Reserve platoon attaining the highest percentage of attendance at annual field training and the Commanding Officer's trophy annually awarded to the best Woman Marine platoon attending summer training at Parris Island based on scholastic standing, percentage of attendance, and military bearing. The platoon had already made history as the first to win the Ruth Cheney Streeter trophy for attaining the highest percentage of combined officer and enlisted woman attendance at drill periods during 1952, a feat repeated in 1953. To the already impressive collection, the Boston Reservists added the National Women Reserve Rifle Team Trophy.5

A list of the 20 post-Korea, WM platoons in the Organized Reserve showing their dates of activation, and the names of the platoon leaders upon activation appears as a table on page 103. 6

Future brigadier general, 1stLt Margaret A. Brewer (seated second from left), was inspector-instructor, WM Communication Platoon, 2d Communications Company, Brooklyn, New York. Capt Mary E. Roach (seated third from left) was the platoon commander in 1954.

Unit	Date	Leader
WM Classification Platoon, 2d Infantry Battalion Boston, Massachusetts	13Jan52	Captain Olive P. McCarty, I&I, served as interim platoon leader.
WM Administrative Platoon, 3d Infantry Battalion St. Louis, Missouri	13Feb52	Captain Leontone A. Meyer
WM Administrative Platoon, 5th Infantry Battalion Detroit, Michigan	6Mar52	Major Evelyn J. Greathouse
WM Classification Platoon, 2d 105mm Howitzer Battalion Los Angeles, California	25Mar52	Captain Christine S. Strain
WM Classification Platoon 1st Air and Naval Gunfire Liaison Company Fort Schuyler, New York	17Apr52	Major Mildred D. Gannon
WM Classification Platoon, 9th Infantry Battalion Chicago, Illinois	24Apr52	Captain Mary R. Jason
WM Supply Platoon, 2d Depot Supply Battalion Philadelphia, Pennsylvania	24Apr52	First Lieutenant Florence E. Lovelace
WM Classification Platoon, 10th Infantry Battalion Seattle, Washington	1May52	Captain Virginia B. Strong
WM Disbursing Platoon, 2d Depot Supply Battalion Philadelphia, Pennsylvania (deactivated 1Dec55)	22May52	Unknown
WM Disbursing Platoon, 1st Amphibian Tractor Battalion Tampa, Florida	27May52	Captain Margaret E. Meyers
WM Classification Platoon, 1st Engineer Battalion Baltimore, Maryland	12Aug52	Major Betty F. Coy
WM Administrative Platoon, 1st 4.5-inch Rocket Battalion Dallas, Texas	30Aug52	Captain Hazel C. Tyler
WM Administrative Platoon, 4th Infantry Battalion Minneapolis, Minnesota	5Sep52	Captain Florence I. Haasarud
WM Supply Platoon, 11th Infantry Battalion Cleveland, Ohio	2Dec52	Captain Bernice V. Carpenter
WM Supply Platoon, 7th Infantry Battalion San Bruno, California (later moved to 1st Antiaircraft Artillery, Automatic Weapons Battalion, San Francisco, California)	28Feb53	Captain Marjorie J. Woolman
WM Disbursing Platoon, 13th Infantry Battalion Washington, D.C.	28Apr53	Captain A. Taylor
WM Disbursing Platoon, 1st 155mm Gun Battalion Denver, Colorado	28Apr53	Second Lieutenant Marilyn J. Standage
WM Communications Platoon, 2d Communications Battalion Brooklyn, New York	19Nov53	Captain Janet M. Lowrie
WM Disbursing Platoon, 1st Communications Company Worcester, Massachusetts (formerly at Philadelphia)	1Dec53	First Lieutenant Marjorie B. MacKinnon
WM Supply Platoon, 10th Automatic Weapons Battery Kansas City, Missouri	7Mar54	First Lieutenant Virginia A. Hajek, I&I, served as interim platoon leader; Major Helen A. Wilson, platoon leader
WM Administrative Platoon, 2d 105mm Gun Battalion Miami, Florida	31Jul55	First Lieutenant Mabel A. Pauley

Deactivation of the WR Platoons

As a result of fiscal limitations and a desire to increase male enlisted strength to meet mobilization requirements, the Reserve Structure Board, meeting in May 1958, recommended the deactivation of the WR platoons. Two units, Kansas City and Tampa, had already been deactivated, leaving only 18 in 1957. At the time of the proposed dissolution of the platoons the total strength was 29 officers and 618 enlisted women as opposed to an authorized strength of 34 and 687. The strength of the WR platoons had peaked in 1955 with 35 officers and 664 enlisted women Marines.7

The undersigned does not concur with the recommendation of the Reserve Structure Board that the Woman Marine Reserve units be disbanded and the membership in the Organized Marine Corps Reserve units be restricted to male personnel, or to the arguments given to support such a recommendation.

The board report emphasized the decreasing strength of the platoons since 1955 and the cost involved in training women. The point was made that the same amount of money would support 200 additional six-month trainees (male). Lieutenant Colonel Elsie E. Hill, Head of the Women's Branch, Division of Reserve, took exception to the report and on 14 May 1958 submitted her views which were:

She continued:

Inasmuch as the statement is made that a strength of 45,000 is sufficient to provide all of the initial requirements for desired augmentation of the Fleet Marine Force upon mobilization it is assumed that numbers of trained personnel become of paramount importance. From just the standpoint of numbers alone, it becomes obvious that 600 women is a larger number of trained personnel than the 200 six-month trainees. . . .8

She argued that the 600 women could be used for administrative support during the early stages of mobilization, thus releasing a like number of Regulars who, she wrote. ". . . are not only highly trained, but at the optimum of training." Referring to the issue of the $200,000 spent each year on the women's program, she pointed out that in 1957, two women had to be enlisted for a net gain of one, while five men had to be enlisted to produce the same result.

Lieutenant Colonel Hill concluded that to continue the organized program for women was the only economical course to follow. As might be expected, the Director of Women Marines, Colonel Julia E. Hamblet, the one person most directly responsible for the activation of WR platoons, did not agree with the board's recommendations and added the comments:

The basic problem appears to the undersigned to boil down to the following: which will be more important in the early stages of mobilization —approximately 600 trained or partially trained administrative personnel or a somewhat lesser number of potential combat Marines in various stages of training. It is believed that it would be impossible to mobilize a Selected Reserve of the size indicated . in the time contemplated without prior or simultaneous augmentation of administrative personnel at Mobilization Stations, Joint Examining and Induction Stations, District Headquarters and Processing Centers. It is my belief that the male administrative personnel in the Organized Reserve will be needed in the numbers available in the FMF and other operating force units with an early deployment schedule, and that the women will be needed as part of the required immediate administrative back-up. . . .9

The women's protests notwithstanding, it was decided to disband the units and to allow 227 women Reservists (one half of one percent of the authorized strength of the Organized Reserve) to remain in a drill pay status, affiliated with male Reserve units.10 There was a great deal of bitterness on the part of women Reservists who had faithfully served in the Reserve for as many as 11 years. Retired Lieutenant Colonel Mary E. Roddy recalls hearing the news of deactivation while she was at summer training with her platoon at San Diego. The Dallas women were finishing up an enjoyable and profitable two weeks and she was reluctant to tell them of the impending disbandment of the program. On the night before leaving for home, she broke the news so that she would be the first to tell them. A final inspection at deactivation ceremonies for the unit was held at the Dallas Naval and Marine Corps Reserve Training Center on Saturday, 27 September 1958. Joining Major Roddy for the inspection was Lieutenant Colonel Joe B. Griffith, Jr., commanding officer of the 1st 4.5-inch Rocket Battalion.1 1

At first there was spirited competition for the coveted 227 billets but by 1967 the number of women participating in a paid status with the Organized Reserve dwindled to two officers and 74 enlisted women.12 Between 1958 and 1967 there was no Reserve program for WMs.

Woman Special Enlistment Program

An outgrowth of the Woman Marine Program Study Group of 1964 (General Pepper Board) was the creation of an Ad Hoc Committee in 1966 to study Reserve training for women Marines. This committee recommended the creation of three women's platoons, and the enlistment of women without prior service who would be sent to Parris Island for a 10-week period of training (an adaptation of the six-month training program in effect at the time for male Marines).13

The platoon idea was quickly discarded as being too expensive and too restrictive geographically. The Director of Women Marines, Colonel Barbara J. Bishop, did not approve of the plan to train Reservists at Parris Island due to the lack of space at the Woman Recruit Training Battalion. So, it was not until 10 June 1971, nearly four years after the submission of the committee report, that the Woman Marine Special Enlistment Program was established in the Marine Corps Reserve. Marine Corps Order 1001R.47 provided for an initial quota of 88 women to be recruited and enlisted by Organized Reserve units (ground and aviation). These women, integrated with platoons of regular WMs, received ten weeks of active duty. Training of varying periods was offered after completion of basic training.

Reservists then returned home and attended regular drills and training periods with their units for the remainder of a three-year enlistment.14

From that time on, the assignment and utilization of women Reservists paralleled that of the Regulars. In 1973 when the Commandant approved a pilot program to assign women Marines to division, wing, and force service regiment headquarters based in the United States, women Reservists moved into those units in the Organized Reserve. By May 1976, one and one-half percent (i.e., 30 officer and 400 enlisted billets) of the members of the 4th Marine Division/Wing were women.15

In the year in which the prohibition which limited women officers to succeeding to command only of units made up primarily of women was lifted, 1973, the way was opened for women to command Organized Reserve units. One of the first to do so was Major Jeanne B. Botwright Humphrey, Commanding Officer, Truck Company, 4th Service Battalion, Erie, Pennsylvania.

Strength

As early as 1948, a strength goal for women Marines was set at one percent of the authorized enlisted strength of the Marine Corps even though the law allowed for a maximum of two percent. The same figures dictated the number of women allowed to participate in the Reserve. In 1967, Public Law 90-130 removed the percentage restrictions and has allowed for a steady increase in the number of women Marines, Regular and Reserve. In 1975, the Director of the Division of Reserve, Major General Michael P. Ryan, acting on a request from the Commanding General, 4th Marine Division, stated that it would be possible and advantageous to increase the number of women to five percent of the authorized strength of the Organized Reserve. But due to the desirability of an incremental rate of growth, he asked that the ceiling for fiscal year 1976 be increased to three percent. This translated into 1,937 women.16 By 1977, ahead of the schedule, a maximum of five percent was authorized. Actual figures on 30 June 1977 were 40 officers and 668 enlisted women in the 4th Marine Division and 4th Marine Aircraft Wing.

Women Reserve Officers

There remained the perplexing problems of providing adequate training for women Reserve officers. While organized units were willing and often anxious to join enlisted women, most of whom had administrative skills, few units could find a place for the officers, especially if they were above the rank of captain. Major General Ryan encouraged the male units to join women officers.*

LtCol Joe B. Griffith, Jr., and Maj Mary E. Roddy conduct inspection at the deactivation ceremony in 1958 of the WR Platoon, 1st 4.5-inch Rocket Battalion, Dallas, Texas.

* The positive attitude of Major General Ryan was based upon his personal knowledge of the utilization of WRs in World War II. He estimated that at least 18,000 women would be needed again in an emergency, and he believed in the importance of their training. This tends to support a contention of Colonel Hamblet, that the men who served in World War II recognized the contribution of the WRs and that as these men retired, women Marines received less and less consideration.

Believing that the most profitable training comes from experience in an organized unit, he took positive steps to make this opportunity available to the women. In 1976 a message was sent from Headquarters Marine Corps to the Commanding Generals, 4th Marine Division and 4th Marine Aircraft Wing authorizing them to exceed authorized officer strength by joining WM officers in numbers not to exceed five percent of total authorized officer strength. Since these are combat-ready units, the women could not be included in their mobilization plans, but upon mobilization would be reassigned individually to base units to replace male Marines who would in turn augment the Reserve units. Women Reservists who had been openly critical of the lack of meaningful training opportunities found reason for optimism in the message and especially the final paragraph which put teeth into the plan and read:

As the majority of available WM officer assets are in the administrative and supply fields, this is an opportunity for individual commanders to improve administrative and supply efforts.

Request this headquarters be advised of results of this program. Request you reply no later than 31 December 1976.17

Formal Training for Women Reservists

Beyond unit training, increased numbers of women Reservists received orders to formal technical and professional schools. In 1971, four years after the first Regular woman officer entered the midlevel Amphibious Warfare School at Quantico, Major Patricia A. Hook and Captain Elizabeth D. Doize were assigned to Phase I of the shortened Reserve version of that course. Major Hook returned to Quantico the following summer to complete Phase II and became the first woman Reserve officer to graduate from the Reserve Officers' Amphibious Warfare Course. In 1973, Lieutenant Colonel Patricia A. Meid and Major Hook attended the special Reserve course offered by the Command and Staff College, becoming the first women Reservists to do so.18

The most dramatic manifestation of a change in attitude and policy resulting in broader and unusual opportunities for women Reservists was the assignment of the military occupational specialty of air delivery to Private Beth Ann Fraser. Having joined the Reserve under the Special Enlistment Program, her three-year contract provided for initial recruit training at Parris Island followed by specialist training. In Private Fraser's case, that meant three weeks at the Army Airborne School ("jump school") at Fort Benning, Georgia.

She graduated with Platoon 9A, Woman Recruit Training Command, on 15 November 1976. Even before her basic training began she had been preparing herself for the physical rigors of jump school by running two miles several days a week. At Parris Island she performed extra physical training and unlike the other women, she wore combat boots and utilities during the required run.

Private Fraser entered the Airborne School on 16 November where the training included physical conditioning, practicing parachute landing falls, tower jumps, and finally actual jumps from an airplane. The chief instructor at the airborne battalion, Master Sergeant D. W. Fischer, described Fraser as ". . . physically strong, a bit above average, with lots of esprit de corps."19 Her platoon sergeant, Sergeant First Class Thomas Rowe, said of her, "We don't often get women through here who are in such good physical shape or have her 'can do' attitude. She is definitely representative of what I think a Marine stands for."20 Private Fraser attributed her success to the Marines of her home unit of whom she said, "Those guys really helped. They had me running, pulling-up, sitting-up, the works."21

To demonstrate the Corps' pride in her accomplishment, Brigadier General Jack M. Frisbie, commanding general of the 4th Force Service Support Group, not only attended Private Fraser's graduation but also promoted her to private first class. Additionally her former drill instructor from Parris Island, Sergeant Kathy A. Potter, made a special trip to congratulate the first woman Marine to graduate from Army Airborne School.

Private First Class Fraser returned to her Reserve unit, the Beach and Port Operations Company, Headquarters and Service Battalion, 4th Force Service Support Group in San Jose, California, to serve the remainder of her contract. Her MOS is an example of the type of rear echelon duty that can be performed by women, delivering supplies by air. Since she graduated, several women Regulars have attended the same school.

The cited examples, Major Humphrey, commanding officer of a truck company; Private First Class Fraser, assigned to air delivery; and the number of WMs serving in organized units along with male Marines, testify to a more total integration of women into the Marine Corps Reserve and the recognition of their potential value as a source of trained Marines in the event of war or national emergency.

Pvt Diane Curtis smiles as she receives her Marine Corps emblem during graduation exercises at Marine Corps Recruit Depot, Parris Island, South Carolina in March 1967. The emblem-pinning ceremony signifies the woman has successfully completed recruit training.

CHAPTER 9

Recruit Training

Mission — The Training Program — Arrival at Parris Island — The Daily Routine — Recruit Regulations - The Drill Instructor-Recruit Evaluation and Awards — WM Complex — Command Reorganized

Enlisted women Marines begin their service at the Marine Corps Recruit Depot, Parris Island. The women's battalion had been known, at different times, as the 3d Recruit Training Battalion, the Woman Recruit Training Battalion, and the Woman Recruit Training Command. Boot camp has varied in length from six to 10 weeks, but certain things remain unchanged. The schedule is rigorous; the drill instructors seem bigger than life; and for the recruit, no matter what motivated her to enlist, on graduation day, being called a Marine is enough.

Mission

Woman recruit training has been designed ". . . to produce a basic woman Marine who is able to function effectively in garrison and instinctively practice those traits that distinguish her as a Marine."1 The specific objectives of recruit training were listed in 1976 as:

a. Self-discipline. A state of discipline which assures respect for authority; instant willing obedience to orders and the self-reliance to maintain or improve those traits that distinguish a Marine.

b. Military Skills. To teach individual proficiency in selected basic military skills.

c. Physical Fitness. The ability to maintain physical fitness, endurance, and weight-distribution.

d. Military Bearing. The ability to properly wear and maintain uniforms and practice personal hygiene.

e. Esprit de Corps. To instill the spirit of comradeship among all Marines for each other and the Marine Corps.2

Fundamentally, they differ very little from the aims set by Captain Henderson and her staff in 1949-

The Training Program

Originally, recruits completed a six-week course consisting of basic military and administrative subjects. By 1949, when the 3d Recruit Training Battalion was activated, Marines had become accustomed to the mature WR of World War II who entered the Corps with certain basic skills, and it was hoped —especially by the men —that this short course would produce a woman Marine ready to take her place in nearly any Marine Corps office. At first the recruits were at least 20 years old and as a rule they had some business experience. After the age limit was lowered to 18 years and the requirement of a high school diploma was dropped in 1950, a longer period of training was deemed necessary.

Major Beckley, Commanding Officer, 3d Recruit Training Battalion in 1951, asked that boot camp be lengthened to eight weeks and that instruction in group living, character guidance, career guidance, and typing be added to the program.3 Her recommendation reflected the frustration felt by the women Marines who had entered the service during World War II. Confronted with a younger recruit —probably away from home for the first time, motivated more by a sense of adventure than a sense of patriotism, and unaccustomed to the discipline of even a civilian job —they worried about the qualifications of the "new breed."

In a letter to Colonel Towle, Major Beckley described the problem of finding suitable assignments for women with low mental scores or who had had little career training. Conceding that the women consistently scored higher on intelligence tests than male recruits, nevertheless, she observed:

Male recruits who have low GCT scores can be fitted into many types of work and prove most valuable. Women Marines are automatically restricted in performance of heavy manual duties. They fill billets involving "white collar" work where at least average ability, a neat appearance, and military bearing are requisites.4

The discovery in one platoon of three women who listed their civilian occupations as sheepherder, gill net fisherman, and motorcyclist strengthened her case for more careful screening and a change in recruit training.5

Colonel Towle endorsed the basic proposal, but because of her great interest in advanced training added:

It is assumed that inclusion in the proposed revised training program of basic typing for all recruits, as outlined . . . will not be taken as indicative that every woman Marine is a potential typist or preclude assignment to the Clerk Typist School in cases where such further training is considered desirable and necessary.6

Recruits at Parris Island undergo tear gas exercises during recruit training in 1950.

The new program lengthening recruit training from six to eight weeks became effective on 1 October 1952. 7

Since that time the length of the training cycle has varied from seven to 10 weeks with three major program changes. The first was the introduction of a General Office Procedures Course in 1958.8 Essentially, at that time recruit training was separated into two elements: six weeks of basic military indoctrination and four weeks of administration. During the initial military indoctrination phase, the recruit underwent traditional training. She then moved her personal belongings to another barracks and, under less supervision, completed the General Office Procedures Course. The commanding officer, Lieutenant Colonel Barbara J. Bishop, recommended the new program in order to make the women more valuable to a command from the minute they reported for duty and also to give them a chance to move gradually from the strict supervision of recruit training into the relative freedom enjoyed by permanent personnel.9

This latter aim emphasized one of the major problems encountered by graduate woman recruits. Whereas the male Marine traditionally moved from recruit training to advanced infantry training with an attendant let-up in supervision, the woman normally went directly from recruit to permanent personnel status. Oftentimes, after arrival at her new command, the period of adjustment was as difficult for the woman's first sergeant as for the woman herself.

After the General Office Procedures Course was inaugurated, graduation from boot camp was not quite the same sad, emotion-packed event that it had been. A simple ceremony was held on the parade ground behind the battalion administration building, and it was followed by the move out of recruit barracks. The most noticeable changes for the new graduates were granting of base liberty from 1700 to 2400 on weekdays and 1145 to 2400 on weekends, reveille at the more civilized hour of 0600, and a work day that ended at 1630. 10

Chief Warrant Officer Ruth L. Wood, who had been a teacher before joining the Marine Corps in 1943, was head of the new administrative course which included 44 hours of typing, and classes in the Marine Corps Directive System, business English, spelling, correspondence, publications, security of military information, office etiquette, and the duties of a receptionist. On the small, hand-picked staff were Technical Sergeants Lillian J. West and Eileen P. Phelan, both former school teachers, and Technical Sergeant Grace A. Carle — later Sergeant Major of Women Marines—who had had civilian experience as an instructor.11

The dual training program —first boot camp and then the General Office Procedures Course—was not entirely satisfactory in that it took a considerable amount of administrative work to transfer the women from recruit to student status, and more importantly, it shortened the screening and observation time. Since only recruits could be separated by an aptitude board, the disposition of marginal and problem students became particularly difficult. Thus in 1961, Lieutenant Colonel Hill, then Commanding Officer, Woman Recruit Training Battalion, asked that the 10-week dual program be combined into a nine-week course of two phases, with the important proviso that the women remain in a recruit status and under the supervision of the recruit company staff during the entire period.12

The second major program change in Marine Corps woman recruit training was the introduction in 1967 of the Image Development Course, part of a larger plan to teach grooming to recruits, officer candidates, and permanent personnel. The decision to adopt this program was based on three premises: first, the improvement of the woman Marine image would enhance the prestige of the WM program in the eyes of the public and within the Marine Corps; second, that emphasis on the feminine aspects of a servicewoman's life would counteract the unappealing impression of military service and therefore improve recruitment; and finally, that heightened self-confidence and poise would reflect advantageously on the duty performance of the woman Marine.

Lectures of this sort had always been a part of woman Marine training, but the new approach to teaching techniques of proper makeup, hair and nail care, wardrobe selection, posture, wig selection and care, social etiquette, wearing the uniform, and grooming practices involved a personal program to meet the individual's needs. It was designed to enhance each woman's poise and social grace. To start the effort on a sound footing, 20 women Marines, officer and enlisted, were trained at the Pan American World Airways International Stewardess College. They would serve as instructors. Beautifully decorated, professionally outfitted grooming facilities were installed at Quantico in 1967 and at Parris Island in 1970.13

The "peanut suit," a one-piece seersucker exercise uniform with drawstring bloomers held over from World War II and in the system until 1960, is worn by women recruits.

1stLt Patricia Watson, recruit platoon commander, takes daily inspection in 1956.

The Image Development Course, which fluctuated from 12 to 31 hours in length was conducted in a more relaxed manner than other phases of recruit training and proved to be a popular addition to the schedule, particularly from the recruits' point of view. One of the most important parts of the course covered the proper application and reapplication of cosmetics throughout the day. The recruits were inspected as before, but in addition to the shine on the shoes, press of the uniform, and police of the barracks, they had to be concerned with their makeup. The natural look—appropriate makeup for a career women—was emphasized as the proper standard.

The finale of the course was an evaluation period held several days before graduation. Selected Marines, dependents, and civilians from the depot were invited to participate at a social hour and recruits were judged on their poise, courtesy, and appearance. The guest list changed but traditionally included, among others, a senior officer and his wife, several staff noncommissioned officers —students and staff—from Recruiter's School and the Personnel Administration School, a chaplain, and a medical officer. Individual grades were not given, but obvious problems and weak areas were noted and when necessary the recruit was given additional help.14

The course, as may be expected, was not wholeheartedly received at all levels. Generally speaking, the women drill instructors were less enthusiastic than the recruits and the command. Primarily they objected to the requirement for DIs to wear makeup while on duty. According to Sergeant Major Judge, who was first sergeant of Recruit Company, and Master Sergeant Bridget V. Connolly, who as a staff sergeant was a DI during the initial stages of the program, there was some muttering in the ranks. First Sergeant Judge, who had never before worn eye makeup, told the commanding officer, Lieutenant Colonel Ruth J. O'Holleran, that if her family could see her they would call her a "hussy."15 In Staff Sergeant Connolly's view, it was an added burden on the drill instructor who had to be up, dressed, and in the recruit barracks before 0500 to be expected to appear in full makeup. It also meant, of course, that she could not freshen up quickly during the day.16 Despite these difficulties, there was general agreement that the Image Development Course improved the appearance and poise of women Marines and achieved its intended goals.

The third major change in women's recruit training involved the forming period and occurred in 1968. In order to give drill instructors time off to rest themselves physically and to prepare themselves mentally to make the transition from working with a graduate platoon to another platoon of new recruits, the initial processing was put in the hands of other members of the permanent personnel unit. This team welcomed the new arrivals and supervised the multitude of details incidental to preparing recruits for training. Only on the first scheduled training day did the DI meet her recruits.17

As they have for years, the majority of recruits arrived during the night. Under the new procedures, they were offered a snack, and shown to their already made-up bunk. Overhead lights were kept off to avoid disturbing other sleeping recruits. The latercomers were allowed to sleep to the very last minute in the morning, getting up only in time to eat before the mess hall secured. While it had been proven that recruits react more quickly and assimilate instructions better when they are less tired and less frightened, old ways die hard, and veteran DIs believed that something was lost in the way of initial discipline. The forming period, while still a difficult adjustment for civilians, was planned to instill a positive attitude toward Marine Corps training at the onset.18

Arrival at Parris Island

These forming period procedures of 1968 bear little resemblance to those remembered by women Marines who attended boot camp from 1949 to I968. In 1949, recruits arriving by train were met by the DIs at Port Royal, South Carolina. In later years, the terminal point of a rail trip was Yemessee, about 26 miles from Parris Island. Unfortunately, the most lasting impression for many of these women arriving from northern states was the segregation of "white" from "colored" on the train south of Baltimore and at the station at Yernessee. Major Joan M. Collins remembered that in 1953, on the way to boot camp, a Puerto Rican recruit, Sunny Ramos, was separated from her group and asked to sit in a compartment by herself. The women protested, but the conductor told them not to make any trouble.19

Women arriving by train were usually taken by bus along with male recruits to the recruit depot. If a male DI was on hand at the station he normally succeeded in scaring the life out of the women, even if he totally ignored them and directed all his attention at the men. Lieutenant Colonel Gail M. Reals remembered that she and one other woman were the only females on board a bus driven by a civilian who amused himself all the way from Yernessee to Parris Island asking the young women why they had done such a foolish thing and personally guaranteeing that they would regret it.20

As a rule, the bus delivered the male recruits first and at each stop the women witnessed the traditional brusque ceremony of the DI greeting his recruits for the first time so that by the time they arrived at the women's battalion, they feared the worst.

The "worst" for the women recruits meant rush and pressure. Most recruits, tired and apprehensive, arrived after midnight, made up their bunks, dropped into bed, and then awoke at 0500 with the lights blazing and the duty NCO shouting, "Hit the deck." For several days they were kept busy with administrative tasks such as endorsing orders, filling out forms, and writing their autobiography. They received shots, a PX issue, and an initial clothing issue — normally utilities and exercise suits. Time was spent sewing name tags in their clothes, hemming the utility slacks, and learning how to give a Marine Corps shine to their oxfords. Until black shoes were adopted in 1964, groups of recruits were taken outdoors to dye the issue brown a darker cordovan shade. For many women Marines, the first "chewing out" was brought on by spilling shoe dye on one of the new uniforms.

Women Marines who were impressed by the "sharp" appearance of the recruiter in her attractive dress blue uniforms were invariably let down when, during forming, they received their clothing issue. A hold-over from World War II that remained in the system until I960 was the exercise suit of tan seersucker —a one-piece bloomer outfit with a matching buttoned front skirt appropriately nicknamed "the peanut suit." The World War

II bib overalls, white T-shirt, and long-sleeve jacket made up the utility uniform until the mid-50s, but the most unpopular items, by far, were the heavy cotton lisle hose worn by WMs in training until 1968, and the very practical oxfords*

* See Chapter 14 for a discussion of woman Marine uniforms, 1946-1977.

These shoes, with their two-inch Cuban heels were, for obvious reasons, known as "grandmas." In the 1950s a more modern, lower heeled oxford was adopted for drill and certain types of work, and until the old supply stocks ran out, each recruit was issued one pair of "grandmas" and was then taken by bus to Mickey's Bootery in the nearby city of Beaufort to purchase the newer shoe—which WMs naturally called "Mickeys."

The basics of military courtesy were instilled during the forming period. In order to give practice in saluting, recruits were required to be covered at all times when outdoors. For a number of years, recruits who had not yet been issued a uniform cap were instructed to wear a civilian hat or scarf, even if only going to the clothes line behind the barracks, and so it was not uncommon to see a WM dressed in a peanut suit, hair neatly covered by a flowered scarf, rendering the hand salute.

Women recruits spent long hours in the classroom mastering administrative subjects. GySgt Frances A. Curwen teaches a typing course in the early 1960s.

Recruits display issued clothing for a "junk on the bunk" inspection in the early 1960s.

The Daily Routine

Traditionally, women recruits bounded from their bunks at 0500, ate breakfast, policed the barracks, and prepared for morning inspection. The daily inspections by the drill instructors varied —that is, personnel, barracks, locker box, or clothing rack—but always included general grooming. Classes were scheduled until the noon meal and again from 1300 to 1700. Evenings were devoted to studying, laundry, shoe shining, and letter writing. Recruits also could be found practicing salutes in front of a mirror or perfecting movements in close order drill alone or in small groups. They were assigned to the duty roster and took turns at standing the watch from the end of the class day until reveille. Classes were held until noon on Saturday.

Liberty, for many years, was granted sparingly, and then only to recruits visited by close family members. In the 1970s, as a result of a study of the woman Marine program, a look at the basic training of the other services, and in order to ease the transition from recruit status to the environment of the first duty station, limited liberty hours were extended to all. Women recruits were authorized depot liberty Sundays and holidays from 1000-1500; Saturdays and Sundays prior to graduation 1330-1930; and Thursday and Friday of final week 1800-2000.21

On one night the routine differed from all the rest —field night. The evening before important inspections (which graduated weekly from the junior drill instructor through all levels of the command up to the battalion commander) was spent in furious activity scrubbing and shining every inch of the barracks and neatly arranging locker boxes and clothing racks to conform to regulations. A clean white towel folded lengthwise in even thirds and a clean white wash cloth folded evenly in half and centered over the towel were displayed at the end of each bunk. In the squadbay, bunks and locker boxes were lined up exactly, and in the laundry, irons were arranged as precisely as Marines in formation. In preparing for inspections, the recruit learned a lesson of lasting value; she learned the importance of team work, because the platoon passed or failed as a unit. Inspecting drill instructors and officers had their individual methods of showing displeasure, but few were more effective than the technique of tearing up poorly made bunks and gathering all the gear left "adrift" and displaying it in the center of the squadbay.

The outdoor equivalent of "field night" is the "garden party." New recruits who found garden party on the schedule were often genuinely disappointed to find rakes, clippers, and lawn mowers where they expected barbecue grills and hot dogs. It was one of the mischievous pleasures of the DI to shout, "Put on your peanut suits, ladies; we're going to have a garden party." Over the years, only the uniform changed; the garden party still translated into mowing, clipping, and trimming.

For all of the nonstop activity of a recruit's day, it ended on a serene and peaceful note. A custom traced to the early 1950s was the singing of "The Lord's Prayer" at taps. Colonel Hamblet, when she was Director of Women Marines, visited Parris Island and later wrote:

. . . having heard of a custom that had developed in the Woman Recruit Company, I returned to hear taps. The bugle notes sounded:

Day is done

Gone the sun

From the lakes

From the hills

From the sky

All is well

Safely rest

God is nigh

One by one lights in the barracks went out. At other Marine bases a hush would then fall. But here, as the last note of the bugle faded in the distance, came not silence but the sound of voices in song.

They started softly in the Senior Platoon area on the second deck (floor) of the barracks, were picked up by another platoon topside, then by the recruits on the first deck. The song swelled in volume as each group joined in, filling the darkened barracks and spilling over into the street outside.

From their bunks the women recruits were singing "The Lord's Prayer". They sang spontaneously, their young voices, untrained and unrehearsed, blended in reverence. They were not required to sing. They did so because they chose to. It had become their tradition, a new group learning by listening to the others.22

Recruit Regulations

The recruit regulations published in 1949 scarcely changed over the years. There was a proper, established procedure for nearly every activity; deviations from the norm, no matter how minor, were not acceptable. A recruit immediately learned that she did not rise before reveille nor sit on, rest on, or get into her bunk before taps. Bulletin boards were to be read several times daily and she initialed every roster on which her name appeared. She moved quickly, but did not run in the passageways; came to attention whenever someone other than a recruit entered the squadbay; and called "gangway" while backing up to the bulkhead when someone other than a recruit approached.23

Only clean clothing, with all buttons buttoned, zippers zipped, and buckles buckled could be displayed. The one exception was a pair of untied oxfords and the unbuttoned raincoat to facilitate a hasty exit in case of fire. Unauthorized personal items were stowed in the luggage room. Keys, clothing, cosmetics, shoe polish, or notebooks left lying about were deposited in the "lucky box" and could be claimed only after the hapless recruit admitted her carelessness to her DI.

The vertical dryers, rectangular ironing tables, and stationary ironing boards found in a typical woman Marine barracks laundry room were well used during recruit training.

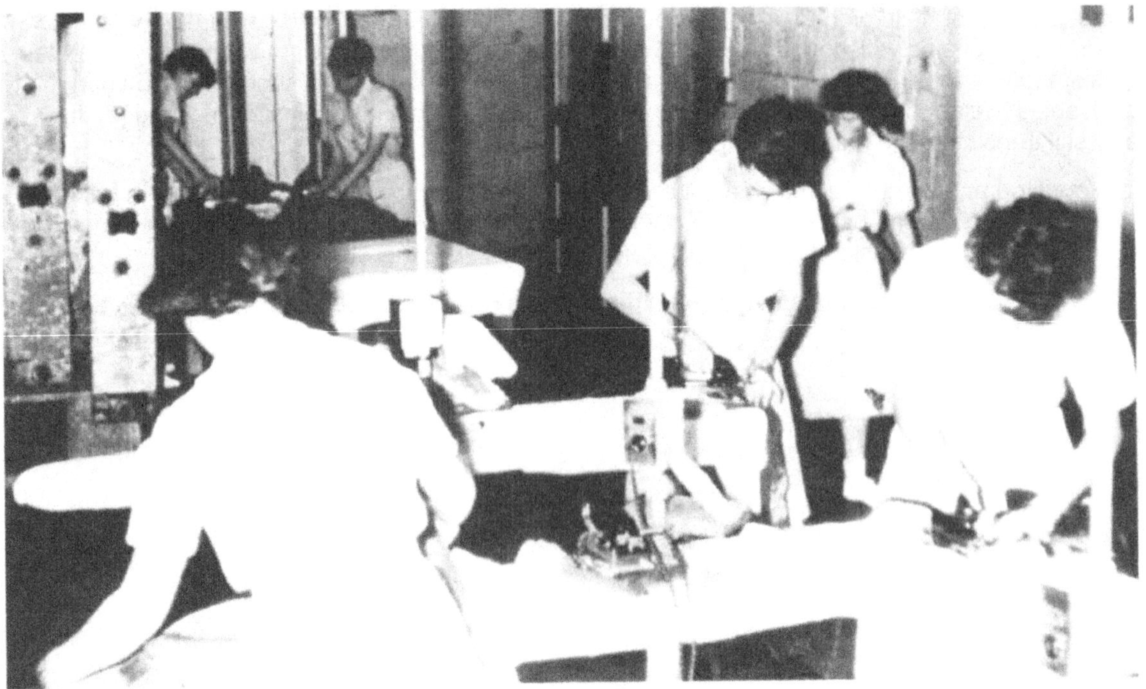

Mail call was the highlight of a recruit's day unless she received contraband items from well-meaning family and friends. Packages were opened in front of witnesses and any food, candy, or gum was returned to the sender, thrown away, or donated to the Red Cross.

Smoking was limited to designated areas at specified times; drinking beer or hard liquor was taboo; borrowing, lending, or giving clothing away was forbidden; and hair was rolled only at prescribed times. Neat, clean, and orderly was the rule. Laundry bags were washed, bleached, starched, and ironed frequently. Singing in the laundry was encouraged, but talking was prohibited. That these seemingly irksome regulations remained virtually unchanged for so long a time testified to their effectiveness in teaching discipline, respect for authority, and the value of teamwork.

The Drill Instructor

These recruits are entrusted to my care. I will train them to the best of my ability. I will develop them into smartly disciplined, physically fit, basically trained Marines, thoroughly indoctrinated in love of Corps and Country. I will demand of them, and demonstrate by my own example, the highest standards of personal conduct, morality and professional skill.

The Drill Instructor's Pledge 24

The drill instructor was the key to recruit training and was directly responsible for the training, physical fitness, discipline, welfare, and morale of her recruits and her junior drill instructors. The assignment was considered by many enlisted WMs to be the most exhausting, frustrating, yet satisfying job in the Marine Corps. Her role and responsibility resembled that of the male DI, but her training and the evolution of her title moved along a different path.

Until 1976, with one short-lived exception, women did not attend Drill Instructor School and those involved in recruit training were officially called platoon sergeants or platoon leaders. WMs, themselves, unofficially consistently used the more familiar term of DI.

Competent, mature, willing noncommissioned officers in excellent physical condition and with impeccable military records were essential to the conduct of recruit training. Due primarily to the small number of women Marines and proportionally fewer NCOs, and a reluctance to release women from their primary occupational specialty for periods of two years —normal tour length for a DI —there persisted a shortage of women DIs. Colonel Barbara J. Bishop, when she was Director of Women Marines, 1964-1969, tried in vain to come to a mutually acceptable arrangement with the assignment branch at Headquarters whereby they would notify her of the impending transfer of senior enlisted WMs. Then, if DIs were needed at Parris Island, Colonel Bishop proposed to fill those vacancies on a priority basis. Her plan met with opposition and for many years much of the burden of training was carried by a group of NCOs who served two and in some cases three tours of duty at the Woman Recruit Training Battalion.25

Recruit learns to shine shoes from drill instructor.

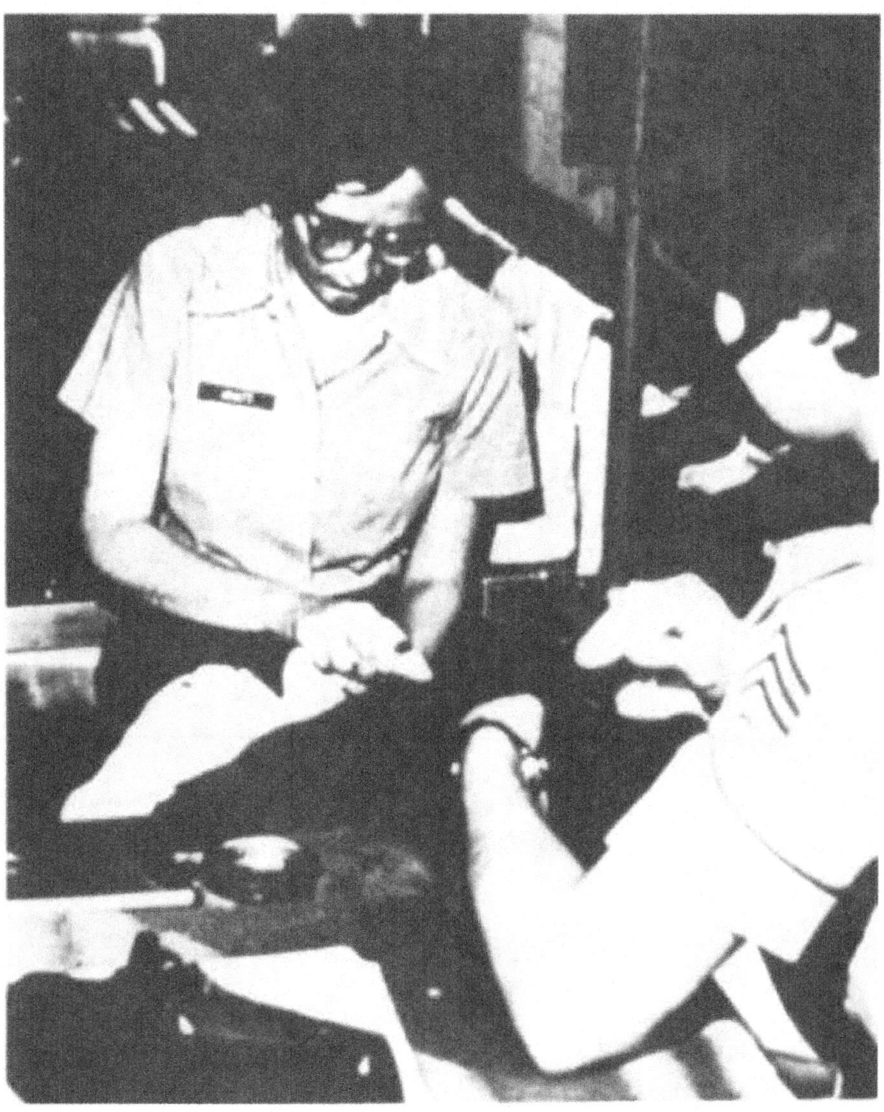

The policy had normally been to assign a staff noncommissioned officer as the senior DI with sergeants or corporals as junior DIs, but, it was not uncommon in the early 1950s to have lower rated women in these jobs. The process of selection from 1949 until 1976 was to order NCOs to the women's recruit battalion for screening by a medical doctor, psychiatrist, the battalion commander, the recruit company commander, and perhaps a battalion screening board. Having satisfactorily moved through this chain, a prospective DI began on-the-job training and was in a probationary status for the period of one training cycle. Only then did she receive the coveted MOS 8511. 26

"Welcome to the Pig Pen." A drill instructor tore up the squadbay and left this message taped to a chair for her recruits after an unsatisfactory inspection in the early 1960s.

Each platoon had a male DI to teach close order drill and military customs and courtesies. Recruits in 1961, wearing the one-piece dacron dress, render a hand salute.

With assignment of women to Drill Instructor School beginning in January 1976, certain procedures changed. The formal course was in itself a screening process, eliminating the need for battalion involvement; the successful graduates were immediately assigned the drill instructor's MOS; and they were not considered to be in a probationary status. Furthermore, Headquarters regularly sent two or three women to each scheduled class, taking the Director of Women Marines out of the assignment business, and assuring a steady and more satisfactory flow of DIs into recruit training.27

Whether or not women should attend the formal school was heatedly debated for a number of years. Lieutenant Colonel Elsie Hill, twice commanding officer of the recruit battalion, believed that the school would give uniformity to the training and arranged for five WMs to enroll at DI school in October 1955.28 The women, Sergeant Ida J. Reinemond and Corporals Marion M. Moran, Edith M. Reeves, Dorothy Rzepny, and Lillian Hagener underwent the prescribed course with only one concession; they did not carry a rifle during the drill sessions.29 According to Lieutenant Colonel Hill, the women did well at school and as battalion commander, she was satisfied with their subsequent performance as DIs, but Headquarters was evidently uneasy about a loss of femininity and the WM image and put an end to the idea.30

The issue lay dormant for 21 years, but in January 1976, once again, five WMs entered DI school: Sergeants Mary E. Gibbs and Jeanette M. Plourde and Corporals Victoria Goodrich, Veda R. James, and Erlene A. Thomas. WMs continued to attend the course and were involved in all academic studies, training, and drill except individual combat training and the complete marksmanship program. They were not required to qualify with the M-16 service rifle or the .45 caliber pistol, but they fired them for familiarization. At graduation, the women graduates, in place of the traditional DI hat, were presented with scarlet epaulets, worn by WM DIs since 1970.31

The DI was in direct control of the recruits in her platoon and shouldered the greatest responsibility in their training. For many years, the senior drill instructor was required to be with her platoon at all times during the first three weeks of training. In the late 1960s, this requisite was eased somewhat and her presence was necessary at key times like clothing issue and inspections and at all periods of instruction where the recruits' health or physical wellbeing was involved, such as physical fitness and swimming classes. More routine events could be supervised by the junior drill instructors.32

In reality, the recruit was seldom out of view of her DIs. One of the team was in the squadbay before reveille and again after lights out. While her charges slept, the DI examined the next day's schedule, made notes about the number of required uniform changes, checked transportation arrangements, filled out evaluation forms, and wrestled with administration matters and personal problems of her recruits. Like the recruit, she had to launder and iron several uniforms and shine her shoes. For the DI the day began at 0430 and ended well after midnight. With rare exceptions, she was a Marine totally committed to her task and accepted the fact that for two years, she would have very little life of her own. A DI of the early 1950s, Corporal Constance A. Shafer, wrote of her tour, "A gruelling pace, but it had its own reward. At least one of the 4 platoons 1 had made Honor Platoon, and the satisfaction of seeing my hard work come to fruition made up for the loss of sleep."33 Master Sergeant Bridget Connolly and Lieutenant Colonel Gail Reals, two of Corporal Shafer's recruits, were still on active duty in 1977.

A three-mile run concludes the fitness test taken by recruits at Parris Island in 1974.

A drill instructor wearing scarlet epaulets in place of the traditional male DI hat calls cadence for recruits dressed in the blue utility uniform in the 1970s.

Lt Vera M. Jones, Recruit Company commander, ties three streamers, symbols of training excellence, to the Platoon 1A guidon. SSgt M. M. Gruetzemacher looks on in 1965.

Recruit Evaluation and Awards

The evaluation and awards program was meant to screen recruits for graduation as basic women Marines and to recognize outstanding performance. The criteria used to judge the women was much the same as it was in 1949, but a more sophisticated system of awards evolved. Individually, recruits were graded in three main areas: academic, performance, and attitude. The first was the easiest to document as it was a numerical value based on the results of objective examinations. Performance and attitude marks are by nature subjective and so were derived from a composite of the entire staffs contact with the recruit, with emphasis on inspection results, drill aptitude, physical fitness, weight control, image development, and leadership ability.34

In one way or another, the guidon, a flag with the platoon's designation carried by the platoon guide, had long been associated with the platoon's performance. New platoons normally had been identified by a bare guidon staff. After successful completion of specified inspection or milestone, pennants were added with appropriate ceremony. The gold guidon marked the junior platoon or series, and for some time had to be earned by passing the junior DI's inspection. The scarlet guidon had nearly always been awarded by the senior DI after a satisfactory formal inspection, which in 1977 was scheduled for the third week in training. Traditionally, poor platoon performance was noted by the command to furl the guidon, the ultimate sign of the DI's displeasure.

Colorful streamers, symbols of excellence, were added to the WM guidon staff for the first time in March 1968, when First Lieutenant Vera M. Jones, then Recruit Company commanding officer, presented three streamers to Platoon 1-A for achievement in swimming, drill, and physical fitness.35 Streamers in 1977 were presented in recognition of exceptional platoon performance in the areas shown in the chart elsewhere on this page.

The Marine Corps emblem, most visible outward symbol of a Marine, had normally been given as an award rather than an unearned right to be taken for granted. Sometime in the 1950s the practice of issuing emblems along with the uniforms was stopped and the recruit had to pass the Recruit Company commander's inspection before she received the highly prized "globe and anchor." The emblem ceremony, beginning in 1966, had become a part of the graduation day events. At a company formation early in the morning, each graduate held her emblems in her gloved hand and the company commander and DIs personally affixed them to her uniform.35

The American Spirit Honor Medal, highest available individual distinction, was given to the recruit who displayed, to a high degree, outstanding leadership qualities best expressing "The American Spirit" of honor, initiative, and loyalty and who set an example in conduct and performance of duty. The award, consisting of a medal and certificate, was made available by the Citizens Committee of the Army, Navy, and Air Force through the Department of Defense. A recruit who won the American Spirit Honor Medal was automatically designated the Honor Graduate or Outstanding Recruit* and additionally received the Leatherneck Award and the Dress Blue Uniform Award.

* The terms Honor Graduate and Outstanding Recruit have been used interchangeably.

Private Mary E. Gillespie, in October 1950, was the first woman Marine to be awarded the American Spirit Honor Medal.37 The uncommon excellence associated with this medal was underscored by the fact that several years could pass without a recommended recipient.

The Honor Graduate, known in the past as the Outstanding Recruit of the platoon, was the woman who had demonstrated the desirable attributes of a Marine to a degree not displayed by any other member of the platoon. The certificate accompanying this award noted not only her academic accomplishment, but leadership ability, integrity, honor, and loyalty.

For many years Leatherneck magazine awarded a complete dress blue uniform with all accessories to the outstanding male recruit of each platoon. In 1962, the WM DIs, feeling that their recruits were slighted, looked into the matter, and since that time, women have been included in this tradition. Private First Class Sonia Nelson, Platoon 15-A, meritoriously promoted at graduation in December 1962, was the first Honor Graduate to receive the Leatherneck Dress Blue Uniform award.38 Leatherneck magazine, in 1972, changed the Honor Graduate award to a wristwatch and the Dress Blue Uniform Award was thereafter presented by the Marine Corps Recruit Depot.

Area / Color / Criteria

Physical Fitness Test / gold / 95 percent platoon performance

Academic / red / 85 percent platoon performance

Drill / green / 250 points

Chief DI Inspection / purple / 75 percent platoon performance

Series Officer Inspection / light blue / 80 percent platoon performance

CO, WRTC Inspection / blue 85 percent platoon performance

The chart is based on the 1976 WRTC SOP. Streamer colors and criteria have varied slightly over the years.

Lt Vera M. Jones awards the Marine Corps emblem, visible symbol of a Marine, to recruits who have passed the company commander's inspection in 1965.

PFC Sonia Nelson, in 1962, was the first woman Honor Graduate to receive the Leatherneck *Dress Blue Uniform Award. LtCol Doris V. Kleberger makes the presentation while Recruit Company Commander, Capt Mary L. Vertalino (later Stremlow), looks on.*

A 1975 air view of newly constructed woman Marine recruit complex at Parris Island.

Families and friends were encouraged to attend the graduation exercises —an event marked by pride, happiness, and tears. Recruits laughed and cried as they reminisced about their boot camp days, and said farewell to platoon mates; they sang joyously; and they stepped off smartly as they marched together for the last time. Graduation, for the most part, included some sort of outdoor review or drill exhibition. For a brief time, 1960-1963, the ceremony was held in a classroom. On 25 September 1963, however, Platoon 11-A began a new tradition by holding its final review on the parade field behind building 914 in the old WM area.39

WM Complex

By 1977, where the yellow-stuccoed barracks, home of the 3d Recruit Training Battalion and the Women Recruit Training Battalion, once stood, only open fields were found. Two buildings remained. No. 900, formerly the mess hall, later a craft shop, and No. 903, which housed the senior series of WM recruits. The junior series was billeted in the WM complex, built within view of the old area.

Suggestions had been made to rehabilitate and air-condition the World War II barracks, but the public works officer found that the cost would exceed 50 percent of the replacement value of the buildings. Consequently, at a meeting on 27 July 1967 the Depot Development Board directed that an entire new complex for WMs be programmed at Parris Island.40

Groundbreaking ceremonies were held on 26 January 1973 and construction was begun. For two years the women Marines watched patiently across the field. Finally on 8 February 1975, they made the big move.41 The new complex, completely self-contained, was designed to house Parris Island's permanent women personnel as well as the women recruits. In actuality, increases in strength of WMs resulted in the retention of the old barracks for recruits. By the time the complex was opened, plans were already underway for an addition.42

Among the facilities included in the WM complex were a fully equipped gymnasium, headquarters areas for the battalion and recruit company, a dining facility, storage areas, a conference room, four classrooms, a laundromat, clothing issue area, sickbay, tennis courts, volleyball court, and television and telephones on each level of the three-story barracks. The structure was built in a square, leaving a central courtyard area open with the flagpole in front of the battalion headquarters. Permanent personnel enjoyed a patio with a fountain, rooms of one to three occupants, and new, motel-like furnishings. Beds replaced metal bunks, closets replaced lockers, and the women were allowed to decorate their rooms with colorful bed spreads, rugs, flowers, photographs, and other personal touches. Recruits in 1977 still lived in austere, albeit more modern and comfortable, squadbays.

Command Reorganized

The Woman Recruit Training Battalion became the Woman Recruit Training Command on 28 May 1976 when Headquarters Company was disestablished. Consistent with Marine Corps-wide policy at the time, personnel assigned to Headquarters Company were administratively transferred to the command under which their work section fell, but remained billeted in the WM complex. Thus reorganization efforts completed a full cycle. In February 1949 the 3d Recruit Training Battalion, under Captain Henderson, consisted of one company of 50 recruits and the 15 WMs to train them. In May 1976 Woman Recruit Training Command, once again embodied only a recruit company, but of 300 recruits and 32 WMs to train them.

CHAPTER 10

Officer Training

Location — Training Program — Traditions — Awards — 1975-1977 — Towards Total Integration - Second Platoon, Company C, BC 3-77

Marine officer training, conducted at Quantico, Virginia, is the sum of the precommissioning officer candidate course and the postcommissioning basic course. From 1949 to 1973 the women trained separately from the men, under the auspices of a women's unit, called at various times: Woman Officer Training Detachment (1949-1955), Women Marines Training Detachment (1955-1958), Women Marines Detachment (1958-1965), and Woman Officer School (1965-1974). Customarily, a woman lieutenant colonel, heading a female staff, was responsible for the administration and training of the students. From 1949 to 1954 the Woman Officer Training Detachment was under the control of The Basic School for matters pertaining to training, and under Headquarters Battalion, Marine Corps Schools for all else* The name was changed to Women Marines Training Detachment in 1955 and the G-3, Marine Corps Schools, took over the responsibilities formerly held by The Basic School.

* The command at Quantico was reorganized in 1968, and the title was changed from Marine Corps Schools to Marine Corps Development and Education Command.

For nearly two years, until 17 December 1958, the woman Marine company, Company D, made up of the post troops was a component of Headquarters Battalion. Then the Women Marines Detachment was activated, a two-part women's unit composed of Headquarters Company and the Woman Officer Training Class. The name changed once more in 1965 to the Woman Officer School and the training functions came under the cognizance of the Marine Corps Education Center, but the woman Marine company remained a part of the unit.

Organizationally, the most significant change came on 12 June 1973 when the Woman Officer School was designated a school under the Education Center, and not a command. The former commanding officer, Lieutenant Colonel Carolyn J. Walsh, became the director and the functions of the woman Marine company were transferred to Headquarters Battalion where they first began in the days before Korea. On 20 December 1974, the Woman Officer School was disestablished; the training of candidates became the responsibility of the formerly all-male Officer Candidates School; and the newly commissioned women lieutenants moved to The Basic School at Camp Barrett, an outpost of the main command at Quantico.

Location

Women Marine officers lived and trained from 1948 to 1973 in the southeast corner of the base in an area bordered on one side by the Potomac River and on another by the town of Quantico. The commanding officer and her staff moved from Building 3091 across from the mess hall to 3094 down the street and back again. For almost the entire period, candidates were quartered in Barracks 3076. Suitable billeting space for the women once commissioned always posed a problem as the choices were limited. Some classes of student officers remained in the same barracks, living in open squadbays as they had as candidates; others moved to Building 3091 where semiprivate rooms were available, if there were not too many staff noncommissioned officers on board. A few classes were quartered at the Cinder City BOQ which in later years became the base Hostess House.

This perplexing problem was brought on by the small number of classes involved. Never did more than two classes of officer candidates train in one year, and more often there was only one. Since the billeting space was vacant for as much as six months of the year, it was not economical to set aside quarters for the women lieutenants comparable to the BOQs enjoyed by the men.

The WM area at Quantico was nearly self-contained: barracks, mess hall, small dispensary (when officer candidates were on board), drill field, and classroom. Early classes, at least until the mid-1950s, received their uniform issue in the sweltering hut behind the barracks while later groups were bused mainside to the clothing warehouse.

Whenever available, the air-conditioned classrooms of Breckenridge or Geiger Halls were used rather than the uncomfortable barracks classroom. Lieutenant Colonel Emma H. Clowers, twice commanding officer of the training detachment, wrote:

I remember how we begged and pleaded, and yes, fought to get just one air-conditioned classroom —in the barracks or anywhere — large enough to accommodate the WOTC students during those hot summer days of training. And how we envied Educational Center and even Basic School, with their fine air-conditioned, well designed classrooms, with all necessary training aids and facilities.1

Again the small numbers involved mitigated against any large expenditures of money. The male programs not only trained many times the number of candidates, but they operated on a year-round schedule, making efficient use of all facilities.

Training Program

Judging from the numerous organizational adjustments, one would expect to find parallel changes in the training of officer candidates, but that did not generally happen. With only one exception, the training of women lieutenants was done on a schedule of 12 weeks' candidates training and six weeks' basic course from 1949 until 1962. In 1951, because of the Korean War and the critical shortage of Marines, the basic course was shortened to four weeks. The 12 weeks precommissioning portion did not vary for the 13-year period. It was divided into a junior and senior course with college sophomores eligible to attend the first six weeks, and college seniors and graduates completing the entire course in one summer. The sophomore who successfully made it through the junior phase was then able to return another summer to finish the senior phase. College graduates and former enlisted women were commissioned and continued on to the basic course located in the same area, and conducted by the same staff as the candidate training.

College students and graduates arrive at Marine Corps Schools, Quantico, Virginia, in June 1953 to begin their summer training program with the Women Officers Training Class. The students being checked in by staff member WO Ruth L. Wood are (left to right) future Cols Ellen B. Moroney and Mary L. Vertalino, and June E. Palmer, Joan G. Bantzhaff, Mary E. Lane, Helen L. Fiocca, Jean M. Byrnes, and Antoinette S. Willard.

Several changes were made from 1962 to 1973 which resulted in a shortened candidate course varying from seven to 10 weeks and a lengthened basic course of up to nine weeks.

During the initial stages of training, the daily routine, candidate regulations, and course material was not significantly different from what was found in recruit training. The most obvious dissimilarities were the assignment of officer platoon leaders at Quantico versus the women platoon sergeants at Parris Island and the liberty granted to candidates.

At Quantico, the goal was twofold: first, to produce a basic Marine and develop her leadership potential. Secondly, the candidate course was considered a screening process, a place to observe each potential new woman officer. To this end, officer candidates were allowed a measure of freedom in the form of liberty one or two nights a week and on weekends. Those with good sense used it wisely. Additionally, candidates were given a number of leadership assignments, duties which set each woman apart from the group and which demanded, in their execution, the use of good judgement, initiative, and force.

After commissioning, during the phase of training originally known as the Woman Officer Indoctrination Course (WOIC) and in 1962 changed to the Woman Officer Basic Course (WOBC), the lieutenants were given extra doses of freedom and responsibility. They arose, not at reveille, but in time to accomplish their chores and be ready for inspection at the appointed minute. At night, they turned in not at lights out, but in time to get sufficient rest to prepare them for a day of training. Classroom lectures and demonstrations emphasized their role as a leader and much time was spent in problem-solving seminars, often chaired by the commanding officer. The second lieutenants accompanied the regularly assigned duty officer on her tours, took personnel and barracks inspections, and delivered prepared lectures to their classmates.

Traditions

Traditions of the type seen at recruit training never developed around either the officer candidate course or the basic course. Again, numbers may be a factor. With only one class in session at a time, there was no opportunity for a junior platoon to emulate a senior platoon. The staff members closest to the candidates, the platoon leaders, and instructors, seldom worked with more than one platoon. At Parris Island, on the other hand, the drill instructors, both senior and junior, graduated one platoon and immediately picked up another. There was a thread of continuity unknown at Quantico.

"Hitting the beach" are members of the Women Officers Training Class at the Marine Corps Schools, Quantico, Virginia, during an amphibious landing exercise in 1959.

Officer candidates play volleyball behind the barracks at Quantico in the early 1950s.

DIs were the only male members on the staff of the Woman Officer Candidate School. In this 1955 photograph the drill instructor shows a candidate the proper distance she must maintain while marching.

There were, however, two occasions generally remembered by officers commissioned in the 1950s and 1960s. The first was the WOTC picnic held just before graduation, and highlighted by the students' impersonations of staff members. The second was the official call made by the lieutenants at the home of the commanding officer.

A long-standing military custom held that each officer, upon arriving at a new base should call, formally, on his commanding officer. Protocol dictated that the visit be made in civilian clothes with a hat (although some authorities called for the dress uniform); the visit should last precisely 20 minutes; and the proper number of engraved calling cards had to be deposited in a waiting tray. Until the 1970s the tradition was rigidly adhered to at the Quantico women's detachment. It gave the second lieutenants an opportunity to practice the procedure and gave the commanding officer a chance to see the young officer in a somewhat formal social situation.

Officer candidates were advised to bring a hat to training, but not many complied. The few hats per platoon made many calls on the commanding officer. The students were scheduled to call in small groups and as one contingent left, their hats were passed on to those waiting outside. The commanding officer, meanwhile, greeted each guest, with a straight face and an inner smile. White gloves, often in short supply, were sometimes doled out one glove per student, each one trying to hold the single glove as inconspicuously as possible.

At the call, drinks were offered and although a second was suggested, the lieutenants were expected to refuse and to bring the call gracefully to a close. Sometimes the commanding officer would tactfully help, but often the young women were on their own to excuse themselves, say goodbye, and drop their cards as if they did that sort of thing every day. As awkward as the new officers felt, it probably never occurred to them that at times the commanding officer was equally uneasy. Colonel Hamblet recalled her tour at the Woman Officer Training Detachment in 1951 when she presided at the formal calls in her suite at the senior officers' BOQ, Harry Lee Hall. Major Dorothy M. Knox, the executive officer, was there to help and the two, somewhat apprehensively, awaited the arrival of the second lieutenants. The meeting got off to a poor start when one of the guests was asked if she would like to remove her coat, and she answered she was not wearing one —she had on a coat-styled dress.2 By the 1970s, the calls became far more casual, even replaced by group cookouts at the home of the commanding officer. When the training of women officers was integrated with the male officers, large groups made calls in dress uniforms at one of the officers' clubs on the base.

Awards

Awards for honor graduates of the officer candidate and basic courses have varied with none standing out in the manner of a tradition. The Marine Corps Association has from time to time given wrist watches or dress emblems to the candidate finishing first in her class. The Women Marines Association, for some years, presented the honor woman with a statuette of Molly Marine.

1973-1977

The Woman Officer Candidate Course and Woman Officer Basic Course underwent numerous stylistic but no philosophical changes for 25 years. It must be said that women officers were being prepared for the limited duties they were allowed to perform. The expanded role played by women in the Corps in the years after the Pepper Board, increased interest in careers even by married women officers, improved retention, and unprecedented procurement success, all led to some new thinking about the training of women. It also happened that in 1972 the Commandant of the Marine Corps, General Cushman, directed the Marine Corps Development and Education Command at Quantico to convene a panel to study the programs and goals for the education of Marines to determine if they, in fact, supported Marine Corps needs.3 The results, submitted on 31 May 1972 by the chairman, Colonel William F. Saunders, Jr., included the recommendation that when facilities permitted the WOBC and The Basic School should be merged into a single command and male and female officer candidates be trained in a single course. The action would mean the disestablishment of WOS and the activation of a woman Marine company in Headquarters Battalion, MCDEC.4

Officer candidates shared a messhall with the permanent personnel of the WM Company. The future lieutenants could be identified by the "OC" pins worn on their lapels.

The major part of the candidate's day was spent in the classroom. The women pictured here wearing the two-piece seersucker uniform and cotton lisle hose are members of the first post-World War II Woman Officer Training Class held at Quantico, in 1949.

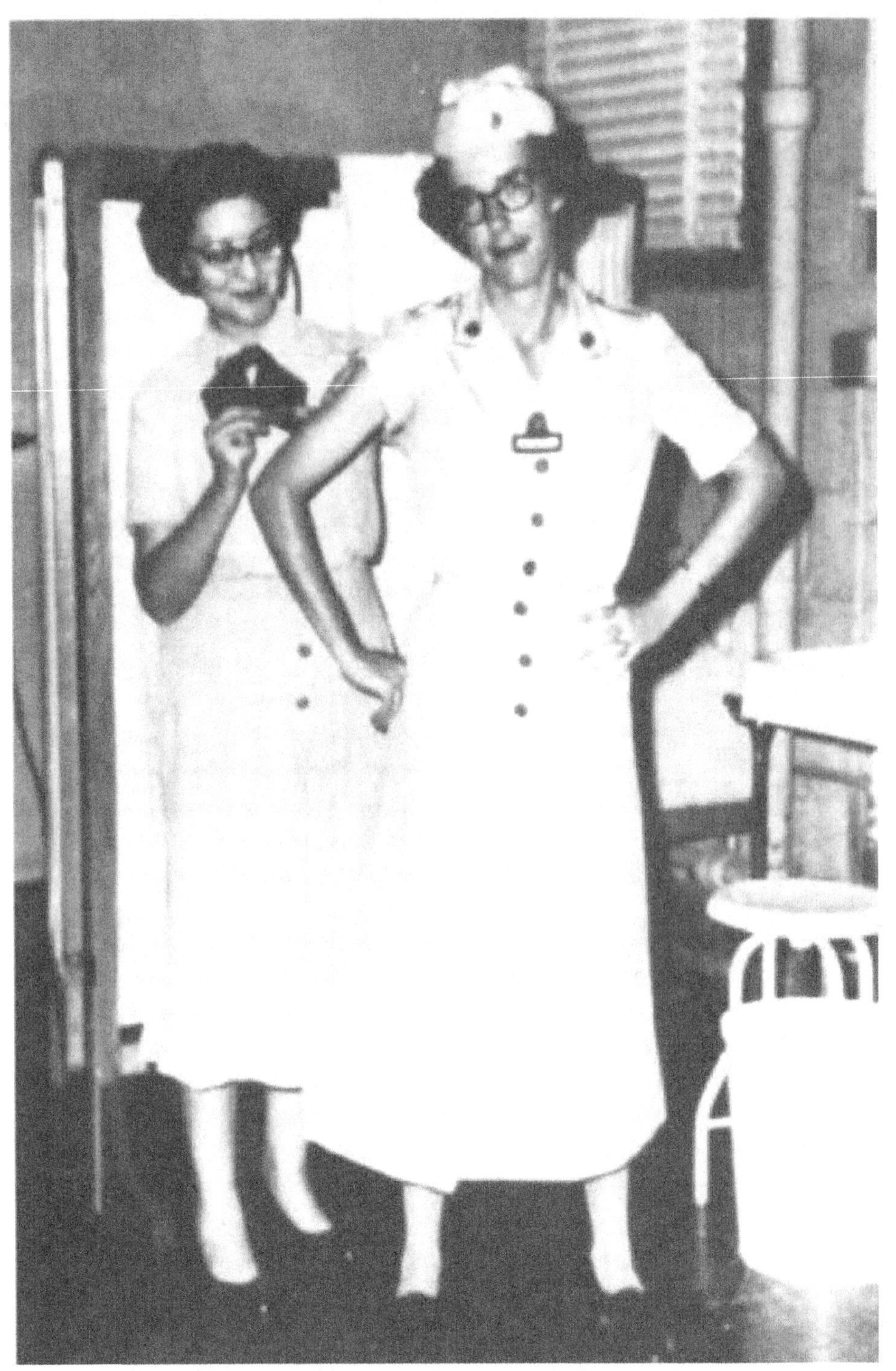

Navy nurse "Miss Mattie" innoculates officer candidate Nancy A. Carroll in the woman Marine dispensary at Marine Corps Schools, Quantico, in October 1957.

Regarding the section of the study pertaining to the women's schools, the Commandant, on 20 February 1973, approved the idea to relocate WOBC to Camp Barrett when facilities would allow and the integration of portions of the instruction given by the two schools. He specifically stated, "The disestablishment of the Woman Officer School is not anticipated."5 His final words, "The study . . . will have far-reaching impact on shaping Marine Corps professional and academic education in the future,"6 proved prophetic for women Marines.

Lieutenant General Robert P. Keller, Commanding General, MCDEC, finding the operation of WOS as a separate entity to be inefficient, transferred the company of women Marines from the cognizance of WOS to Headquarters Battalion as Company B on 11 June 1973.7 The next day WOS was disestablished as a command and redesignated as a school within the education center, and its commanding officer became the director.

Concurrently, the administration but not the training of women officer candidates was placed under the control of the Director of the Officer Candidates School. The 32d Woman Officer Candidate Class (WOCC) was entered into the records as Company W, with both WOS and the Officer Candidates School performing the administration. On 13 August 1973, the academic section of WOS moved to The Basic School and two days later the newly commissioned officers of the 32d WOBC moved into quarters at Graves Hall, Camp Barrett.8 From that time until January 1977 the women officer students were trained in separate, independent companies, receiving selected academic and leadership instruction from The Basic School staff. Course curriculum varied in length from 10 to 12 weeks.

Closer ties were made with the Officer Candidates School when the reporting date for the 35th WOCC was scheduled so that its graduation date would coincide with that of the 90th OCC on 20 December 1974. The two separate classes shared related training, participated in a combined parade on 19 December 1974 at Brown Field, and graduated together the following day. Once again, to save personnel and to avoid duplication of training effort, the Commanding General, MCDEC, had recommended that WOS be dissolved, suggesting 20 December, graduation day of the 35th WOCC, as a target date.9 Accordingly, WOS was disestablished and the WOCC and the WOBC were maintained as separate courses under the direction of the Officer Candidates School and The Basic School respectively.

Candidates board a "cattle car" for weekly swimming class at Quantico in late 1950s.

Future BGen Margaret A. Brewer, then a captain, inspects officer candidates at MCS, Quantico in 1959.

Towards Total Integration

At The Basic School, Company L (Lima Company), became the company of student women officers. In 1976 Major Barbara E. Dolyak, in the course of being briefed for her duties as company commander, questioned the differences in training given male and female officers. At the time, WOBC was 12 weeks compared to 26 weeks for the men's basic course. Just as she was wondering, "Why can't the women do it?,"10 the Commandant of the Marine Corps, General Wilson, published White Letter No. 5-76 on the subject of Women Marines, and addressed it to all general officers, commanding officers, and officers in charge.11 In it he stressed the fact that increased opportunities for women demanded positive leadership and management action on the part of commanders relative to their assignment, training, utilization, and welfare. He suggested that the requirement for separate women's units be reviewed, and continued, "In the same view, commanders who are responsible for the conduct of professional schools should review curricula to ensure that the training offered prepares Marines to lead, irrespective of sex."12

The promulgation of the White Letter prompted Colonel Clyde D. Dean, Commanding Officer at The Basic School, to discuss its possible ramifications with Major Dolyak. And so, at this time, the summer of 1976, the thought of combined training for men and women officers was in the serious talking stage. It gained momentum with the arrival in August of the lieutenants of the 38th WOBC, several of whom had completed totally integrated Naval Reserve Officers' Training Corps (NROTC) in college. In Major Dolyak's words, "These women were ready to go."13 They were enthusiastic and like a good many women of their generation, they expected a more integrated training program.

During a talk to the students of TBS, the Commanding General of MCDEC, Lieutenant General Joseph C. Fegan, Jr., was questioned by the women on their abbreviated course. They were not satisfied with the answer. Later, participating in a combined field exercise which required carrying but not firing a weapon, the women were incensed when they were issued rubber rifles.

Coincidentally, Lieutenant Colonel Edward M. Mockler, at The Basic School, was conducting a review of the program of instruction for male lieutenants. Traditionally, the mission of the school had been to:

. . . educate newly commissioned officers in the high standards of professional knowledge, esprit de corps and leadership traditional in the Marine Corps to prepare them for duties of a company grade officer in the Fleet Marine Force, with particular emphasis on duties of a rifle platoon commander.14

In order to pass the swimming qualification test all 1960s women officer candidates were required to jump from the high platform into the pool at Quantico.

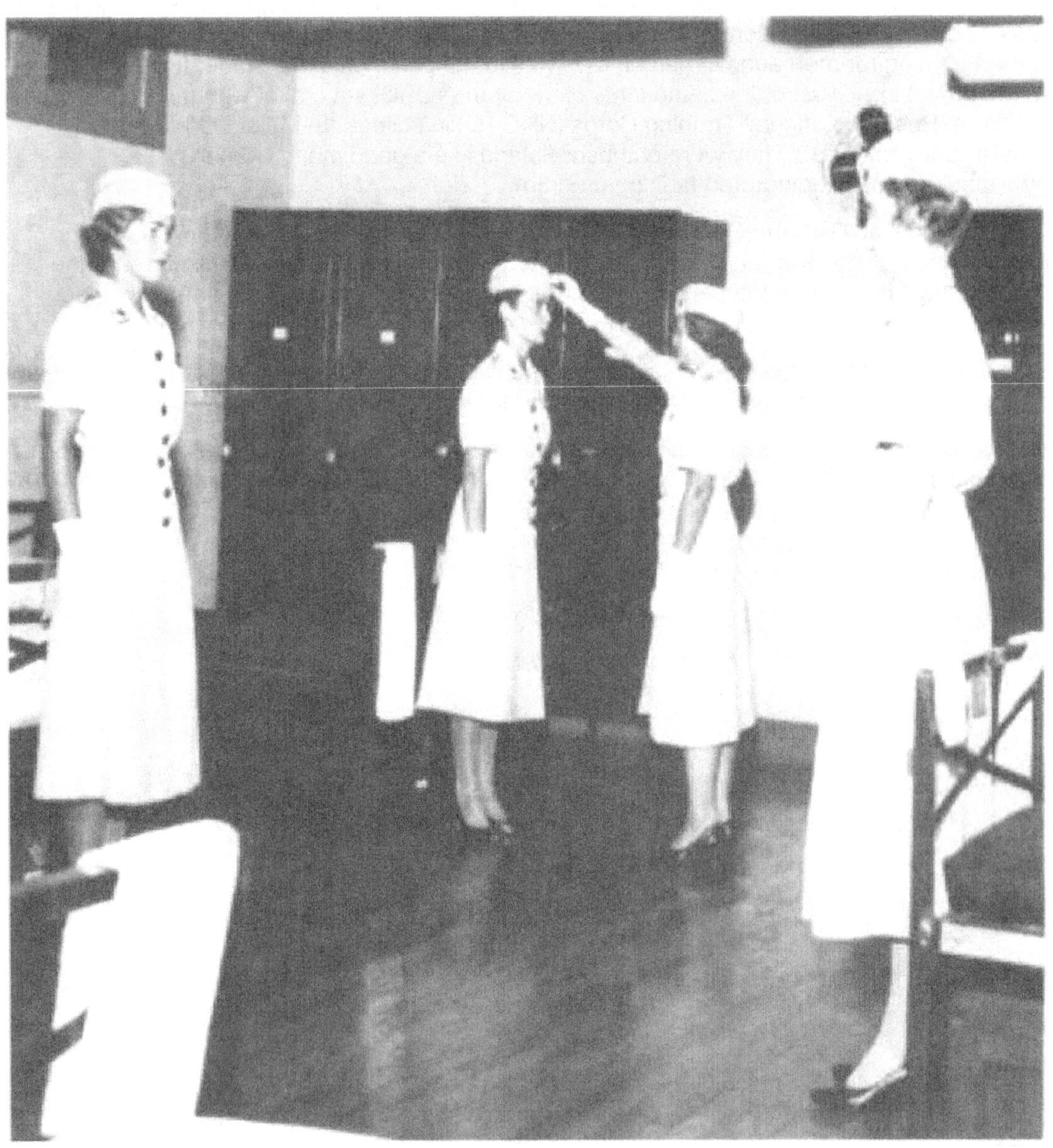

Daily personnel inspection was held in officer candidate barracks at Quantico, Virginia, in 1960s.

However, in 1976, only 18 percent of the newly commissioned male officers were classified as infantry officers, and in 1977 the projection was to be only 12 percent. The remaining 82 percent were assigned to aviation, combat support, and combat service elements, all of whom exist solely to support the infantry unit. Plans were being made to shorten the male officer basic course from 26 weeks to 21 weeks and to create an advanced infantry officer course as follow-on training for those assigned an infantry MOS. In this way, all male officers, sharing a common education and mindful of the interdependence between combat and support units, would be better prepared to lead the Marines under their command.

In the course of staff briefings on the reduced syllabus, Major Dolyak posed the incisive question, "If it is essential that male Marine lawyers and supply officers share this commonality of experience with the infantryman, why isn't it important for the women?"15 Lieutenant Colonel Mockler responded, "You've got me, I don't have a logical answer."18

In Lieutenant Colonel Dolyak's view, that was the turning point in the training of women officers. Her question was mulled over and discussed but not immediately acted upon.

The Basic School carried through with the proposal for a 21-week course, briefing first Brigadier General Paul X. Kelley, Director of the Education Center and then Lieutenant General Fegan on 20 October 1976. The plan was sent to the Commandant in early November 1976, and on the 24th it was approved in concept. The possibility of a combined male/female class was not yet broached in either briefings or correspondence.

Future Col Vea J. Smith (left), then an officer candidate, takes a sailing lesson from Lt Patsy A. Twilley, shown hoisting the sail at the Quantico docks in the summer of 1957.

Grooming instructor, Lt Ruth Walsh (later Woidyla) conducts class in personal makeup for newly commissioned women officers at Quantico, in April 1969.

Officer candidates prepare for inspection with a coin and a ruler. Blankets pulled tightly enough to allow the coin to bounce and an eight-inch top sheet fold are two marks of a properly made military bunk.

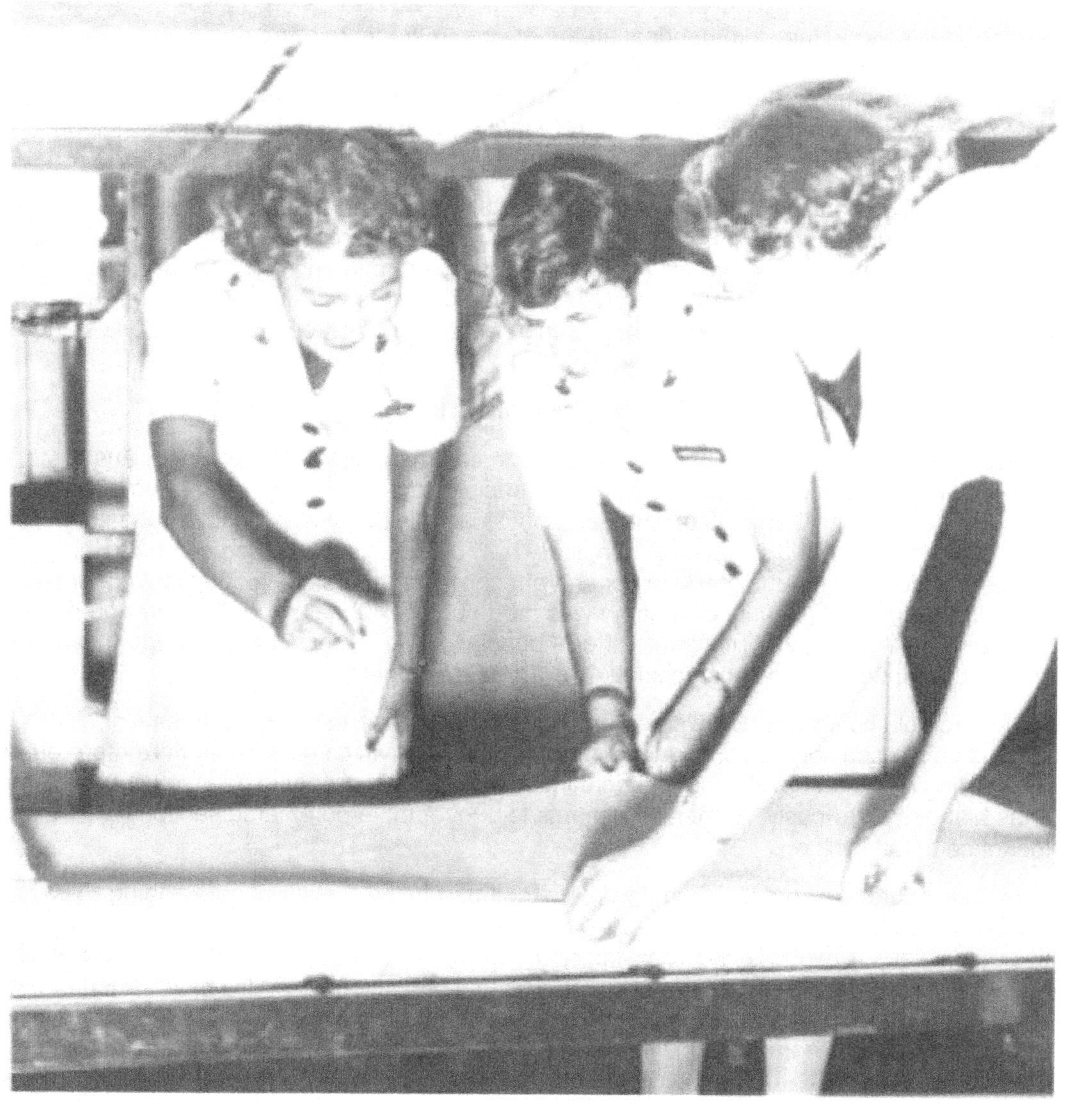

During November and December, The Basic School staff reviewed the new 21-week syllabus with an eye toward a combined class. With this in mind, Major Dolyak visited the United States Naval Academy and the Army's combined Officer Candidates School at Fort Benning, Georgia, to discuss lessons they had learned in the process of integrating training. Then, on 20 December, Lieutenant General Fegan wrote the Commandant of his intention to conduct a pilot consolidated male/female Basic Course beginning with Basic Class 3-77 (BC 3-77) on 4 January 1977.17 The Commandant's White Letter 5-76 was referenced as the basis for an evaluation of the training at TBS. The conclusion drawn was that the 60-day course for women was not comparable to the 105-day course offered male officers. General Fegan reasoned:

In order for the woman officer to provide the Marines under her command with knowledgeable, professional leadership, it is considered that she, too, must develop an awareness and understanding of such fundamental subjects as the Fleet Marine Force, Marine air-ground task forces, and the field environment.18

Timing was crucial. WOBC-39 was scheduled to begin in two weeks on 4 January and there would not be another class of women until August. Quantico intended to move quickly and needed waivers of Marine Corps policies that prohibited women from firing the rifle and pistol for qualification and from participating in field exercises. There was never any intent to train women for combat, but, rather, ". . . to provide each woman officer with . . . commonality of origin, experience, and education in order to broaden her perspective and make her a more effective leader of those Marines placed in her charge."19

In reply to General Fegan's letter, the Commandant stated his commitment to preparing women for their increasing duties and responsibilities associated with their support role. But, he added, ". . . in conducting the pilot program, due consideration must be given to the noncombatant role of women and to the physiological differences between men and women."20 Regarding weapons and tactics skills, guidance dictated an emphasis on orientation, familiarization, and defensive training.

The fact that the women lieutenants had not received comparable physical conditioning during the candidate course was of some concern to all parties. For the pilot program, the women participated in all exercises but were graded on the physical fitness program for WMs in which they ran one and one-half miles rather than the three-mile course prescribed for men. And, the obstacle course grades were weighted differently. Because of these limitations, as well as the experimental nature of the combined class, the class standings were delineated by sex.

Second Platoon, Company C, BC 3-77 (January 1977-26 May 1977)

The second platoon, Company C, BC 3-77, under staff platoon commander Captain Robin L. Austin, plunged into a training course made up of such subjects as basic tactics, patrolling, vertical envelopment operations, tank-infantry operations, amphibious warfare, physical training, aviation and ground support, infantry weapons, supporting arms, land navigation, military law, communications, and combat intelligence. The 22 women were divided into groups of five or six and attached to the remaining five male platoons for field exercises. In all, Company C (Charlie Company) was made up of 243 male and 22 female lieutenants commanded by Major Guy A. Pete, Jr. Nicknamed after a popular 1977 TV show based on the experiences of three women detectives, 2d platoon became known as "Charlie's Angels."

Aside from exposure to field conditions, the women gained first-hand experience in leadership positions. They took their turns as platoon sergeants, squad leaders, and guides, which gave them heretofore out-of-reach practice in leading men and developing the techniques and tact necessary in dealing with problems men encounter as Marines. Previously, women lieutenants took over male-dominated sections without having this experience to fall back on.

Like thousands of male lieutenants before them, the WMs took part in the Basic School Landing Exercise (BaScoLEx) in which a company of student officers storms ashore on Onslow Beach at Camp Lejeune during a practice amphibious assault. To their consternation the women were bused from Quantico to Camp Lejeune while the men made the trip by sea. The law forbade their service on board ship, so when at 0900, 20 April 1977, about 200 male lieutenants swept across Onslow Beach, they were confronted by the 2d Platoon (women) and the 5th Platoon (men) playing the role of inland aggressors.

Women lieutenants of the 2d Platoon, Company C, the first integrated Basic School unit, debark an amtrack during exercises at Quantico, Virginia, on 20 April 1977.

The new twist to the BaScoLEx prompted a number of remarks of a sexist nature from the men. A few said the women should not be in the field at all. Others thought it unfair that the law prevented them from taking part in the entire exercise. Most of the men, at any rate, seemed to support the women's efforts and liked to see them do well in the field.

The platoon commander, Captain Austin, acknowledged some prejudice in the company, but she also cited a contradictory incident which had occurred three days before the BaScoLEx. "We all completed a 12-mile forced march and 4-mile run," she explained. "Following the run, a male lieutenant regarded as the company's worst chauvinist, gave us a smile and the okay sign. We felt accepted."21

There were some problems at the outset, most of which were expected. The women tended to straggle and bring up the rear on the long marches, but eventually made it. Some suffered stress fractures of the lower leg just as the women at the military academies had. A woman lieutenant on crutches was not an unfamiliar sight. As the pilot program progressed, emphasis on conditioning was stressed during scheduled periods of physical training and by the midpoint of the program the female officer students were able to keep up with their male counterparts during field problems, conditioning hikes, and company runs.22

One factor that had not been anticipated and that affected training to a degree was the intense and continuous interest of the news media. Initial stories were expected, but not 21 weeks of interminable coverage. It became tiring for the women, distracting for the men, and a source of resentment dividing the sexes. Charlie Company found itself on the front page of The Washington Post and in newspapers around the world. Brigadier General Kelley was questioned repeatedly on the purpose of the combined training. He summed up the prevailing philosophy, saying:

Our decision is based on a firm conviction that our young women officers must be informed on all facets of our Corps, to include rigors of field environment, if we expect them to fulfill the broad variety of tasks we have and will assign to them in our Fleet Marine Force.23

The members of the history-making 2d Platoon, Company C, BC 3-77 were: 24

Second Lieutenant Linds L. Belanger

Second Lieutenant Christine A. Benson

Second Lieutenant Patricia P. Blaha

Second Lieutenant Diana C. Day

Second Lieutenant Mary A. Devlin

Second Lieutenant June M. Dignan

Second Lieutenant Colleen M. Flynn

Second Lieutenant Robin C. Garrett

Second Lieutenant Megan A. Gillespie

Second Lieutenant Gayle W. Hanley

Second Lieutenant Georgia J. Jobusch

Second Lieutenant Bonnie J. Joseph

Second Lieutenant Rosa K. Knight

Second Lieutenant Janie D. Loftis

Second Lieutenant Bonnie L. MacPherson

Second Lieutenant Jennifer J. Martell

Second Lieutenant Ann M. Milinovich

Second Lieutenant Angelica V. Ritscher

Second Lieutenant Judith C. Shaw

Second Lieutenant Gloria M. Stottlemyre

Second Lieutenant Jo Ann Taylor

CHAPTER 11

Administration of Women

Supervision and Guidance of Women Marines — Barracks — Daily Routine — Discipline

The Woman Marine Company was long a standard unit on posts and stations wherever WMs served. It was Colonel Towle's expressed policy that no woman Marine would serve alone and that a woman officer would be assigned wherever enlisted women were located.1 Since it was bothersome to arrange billeting for a small number of women, it naturally evolved that women were only assigned to bases that could utilize and support a sizable number and where women could be organized into a single WM unit. Women Marines have long been considered an integral part of the Marine Corps, and the WM company was fitted into the existing command structure. For administrative purposes all WMs were carried on the rolls of the Woman Marine Company, which normally was part of Headquarters or Headquarters and Service Battalion. The table of organization of a typical WM company indicated only the personnel required to command and administer it: the commanding officer, the executive officer, the first sergeant, clerks, and a police and property NCO. The strength of the company bore no relation to the table of organization as the women making up the company were filling other authorized billets throughout the base.

There has been a certain amount of confusion over the name of WM units. Colonel Hamblet, when she was Director of Women Marines, settled the issue in 1958, drawing attention to the variety of titles in existence. She cited such examples as Women Marine Company, Headquarters and Service Battalion, Camp Pendleton; Women Marines Detachment Two, Marine Corps Air Station, Cherry Point; and Woman Marine Company, Headquarters and Service Battalion, Marine Corps Recruit Depot, San Diego. In the interest of uniformity, it was decided to use the words "Woman" with an "a" and "Marine" without an "s" in the title designations.2 Once in a while the WM companies were given letter names —most often Company D, which lent itself to the nickname, "Dolly Company." In one instance, at Pearl Harbor in 1952-1956, the women Marines were Company A— no recorded nickname. At Marine Corps air stations, the women were organized into a detachment, which was a squadron-level unit. In these cases, the table of organization called for a sergeant major rather than a first sergeant.

Administratively, this plan of grouping all WMs into one company while they worked throughout the command, differed from the organization of male Marines who were attached to a company within the same battalion for which they worked. For the male Marine, his work supervisor and his company commander were in the same chain of command; for the WM, her work supervisor could belong to one battalion while her commanding officer belonged to another. A cooperative spirit among commands was absolutely essential since often the interests of the work supervisor and those of the commanding officer clashed. Leave and liberty, for example, were granted by the commanding officer, based upon a written release by the work supervisor. Company duty assignments, inspections, and barracks field nights infringed on women's work responsibilities and vice versa. On matters of discipline, if a work supervisor put a woman on report, it was handled not within his chain of command, but through her company and, when necessary, battalion.

In spite of these areas of potential conflict, the system worked relatively smoothly from 1948 until 1974 when an emphasis on a "total Marine Corps" brought into question the need for separate women's commands. An ad hoc committee met in 1973 and made a number of proposals which opened new career opportunities for women in the Marine Corps and also recommended changes in policies that tend to set the women apart as if a separate entity. As women moved into more and more previously all-male fields, commanders challenged the tradition of woman Marine companies. From posts and stations came the suggestion to disband the units and to treat the women as all other Marines. The Commandant's White Letter No. 5-76 also addressed this matter:

With the achievement of more complete integration of women, the requirement for separate women's units should be reviewed. Positive benefits can be derived from assigning women Marines administratively to their duty units. During transition periods, you may find it desirable to establish additional duty billets for a woman officer or staff noncommissioned officer to work as "Special Assistants" in providing guidance relative to woman Marine matters.3

In June 1977 only three WM companies remained—at Henderson Hall, at Norfolk, and at Camp Lejeune. The others had been deactivated upon the request and justification of the commanding generals of the bases at which the WM units had been located.

Where no woman Marine company existed, women were administratively attached to the unit for which they worked, but the billeting was handled in one of several ways. They could be billeted in a barracks which came under the jurisdiction of the command to which they were assigned. A prime example was Base Materiel Battalion at Camp Lejeune, where in 1976 the commanding officer, Lieutenant Colonel George J. Ballard, asked to have the WMs working in his battalion transferred to, and billeted with his unit. Although a company for all other WMs was still maintained, the women of Base Materiel Battalion were transferred. The battalion occupied a new motel-like barracks in which all rooms had outside entrances. Lounges, laundries, and other common areas were shared by men and women. The WMs, as was their habit, decorated their rooms and displayed colored towels, and according to Major Gerald W. Sims, the executive officer, the male Marines had not objected. The company commander, Captain Vernon C. Graham, and First Sergeant Charlie L. Boyd of Headquarters and Service Company were enthusiastic about the value of having complete control of and responsibility for all Marines in the command. In the spring of 1977, members of the staff admitted that this was a new idea for the Marine Corps and in some way an experiment. Some procedures were being changed. Weekly training, for example, found the women drilling and inspected as a separate platoon, and thought was being given to integrating the women into the male platoons.4

Following a long-standing tradition, the visiting Director of Women Marines, Col Katherine A. Towle, is entertained at a tea held in the barracks at Parris Island in 1951. The colonel is flanked by MSgt Lotus T. Mort (left) and Maj Nita Bob Warner (right).

At Quantico, things were handled differently. After the deactivation of the WM company in 1976 women Marines from 11 Marine Corps Development and Education Center units lived in three barracks. That fall it was decided to put the women under one roof again and a new Bachelor Enlisted Quarters was renovated for them.5 This system paralleled the one in existence in 1977 at Cherry Point where the WM detachment was deactivated on 31 December 1974. The women were administratively transferred to the various squadrons and the 2d Marine Aircraft Wing, but they remained in the same barracks they had previously occupied. Under this arrangement, a woman NCO was responsible for the barracks, its cleanliness, maintenance, and security. She checked women in and out, held linen call, and prepared duty rosters. On a three-month assignment, she was away from her regular job for that length of time.6

These barracks NCOs, like Corporal Kay Frazier at Twentynine Palms in 1975, Staff Sergeant Sandra Hoolailo at Quantico, and Sergeant Carol Fox at Cherry Point in 1977 found that they were involved in many areas formerly handled by women commanding officers or first sergeants. Disputes between roommates, personal problems, and work dissatisfaction were some of the matters brought to the NCO. Infractions of barracks regulations and the preparation of duty rosters still required coordination between the battalion or squadron maintaining the barracks and the duty units of the women.

Sergeant Fox, who was stationed at Cherry Point when WMD-2 was active, and who carried the colors at the deactivation ceremonies, compared both systems. In her view, the women had more esprit and were a closer unit when under one command. The commanding officer and first sergeant knew the women personally and were interested in them as individuals. Since the deactivation of the detachment, Sergeant Fox felt that unit pride had virtually disappeared; the barracks was no longer a scrupulously clean showplace; WM activities, like picnics or ball games, were nonexistent; and the women never paraded or marched as a unit. She particularly recalled the spirit and pride they had felt in the past after events such as IG inspections.7 Private First Class Katie Jones Dixon and Lance Corporal Judith Coy, interviewed at Cherry Point were, on the other hand, quite satisfied with the arrangement and voiced no complaints.8

One found, in 1977, senior WMs, officer and enlisted, who were unsure of the merits of the newer way for two reasons: first, deactivation of WM companies eliminated the primary source of command experience for company grade officers; and second, the WM company was a source of group spirit and pride for the women Marines. A not uncommon sentiment was that women would never truly be accepted as Marines by male Marines, and therefore they needed some visible unit to identify with. Others —most often junior WMs —saw the deactivation of WM companies as a sign that women Marines were truly Marines and not a separate corps.

An offshoot of the deactivation of WM companies was the new experience for women having male commanding officers and the novel experience for the men —commanding women. Staffs of mixed gender were no longer unusual, and male Marines were not apt to suffer fits of apoplexy when reporting in and finding the company clerk or executive officer wearing a skirt.

Colonel Margaret A. Brewer, the Director of Women Marines during this period of change, when asked if she thought that the venture of integrating women into male units was successful, answered that much depended upon the quality of the leadership. Where the commanding officers took positive steps to integrate the women and to make them feel welcome, the system worked.9 Women Marines told her that they felt more like Marines —like they belonged. More importantly, the men took the trouble to learn about WMs, their regulations, concerns, and problems. It happened less frequently that male Marines called on WM officers and SNCOs to handle the routine matters involving women: uniform discrepancies, poor work habits, and lapses in military courtesy. Some "old salts" discovered that the presence of a few WMs had a beneficial effect on behavior, language, and discipline of the entire unit.

Supervision and Guidance of Women Marines

A long-standing tradition, wherever WM companies were found, was that all women Marine officers and staff noncommissioned officers regardless of their assignment, accepted some responsibility for the company. The commanding officer naturally had the primary responsibility of administration, discipline, training, morale, and billeting of the enlisted WMs, but all company grade officers, SNCOs, and NCOs stood WM company duty; took their turn giving lectures on the training schedule; were apt to be assigned as platoon leaders; and attended all company-sponsored athletic and social happenings. Every WM second lieutenant left Quantico well indoctrinated with the idea that the health, happiness, performance, and appearance of all WMs junior to her were matters of her concern, and the same theme was reiterated in all phases of NCO training.

Colonel Towle set the example in the very beginning when, in 1949, she invited all newly integrated WM officers to her apartment for tea. Lieutenant Colonel Munn remembers the care with which they dressed — hat and gloves —and in 1977 reflected on how wise it was of the colonel to bring them all together, even though they worked throughout the Headquarters.

Colonel Hamblet, who succeeded Colonel Towle as Director of Women Marines, believed that senior women Marines, officer and enlisted, in their relationship with juniors, should be concerned with the "total" person and her development. The receptions that women Marines customarily gave for the Director when she made her annual visit were a part of this philosophy. The purpose was not only to give the women and the Director an opportunity to meet informally and look each other over, but it was an enjoyable way to learn something about entertaining, extending invitations, making introductions, and carrying on social conversations. In most cases, the work supervisors and their wives were invited and in Colonel Hamblet's view, it was beneficial for them to see the WMs in their own environment —often leading to a better understanding between the sexes.

To be sure, not all the women wanted to get involved in these affairs, but gentle persuasion and a little well-directed leadership on the part of the commanding officer and the firsr sergeant worked wonders. Very often, younger women were uncomfortable with the prospect of entertaining senior Marines and this accounted for their apparent disinterest. When the party was over, obviously a success, and when the women received the compliments of the invited Marines and their ladies, they were in Colonel Hamblet's words, ". . . pleased as punch."

All women staff noncommissioned officers rook an active role in the supervision and guidance of younger WMs. They were considered a vital link between the commanding officer and her women, spotting potential problems and alert to changes in mood and morale. During the 13-year period between the time postwar enlistment was opened to nonveterans in January 1949 until World War II WMs began to retire in 1962, there existed a group of staff noncommissioned officers, older and more experienced, who felt a real obligation to the younger Marines. Due to the fact that there was no recruiting of women from 1945 to 1949, and because the WMs were at least 20 years old when they enlisted during the war, the age difference was quite pronounced. First Sergeant Schultz remembers that when the enlistment age was lowered to 18, the officers and NCOs felt a real obligation to ". . . these youngsters."10

Women Marines who served in the 1950s and early 1960s tell many anecdotes that attest to the concern of these SNCOs for the WMs junior to them. One name often mentioned was that of Master Sergeant Lucretia E. Williams, retired in 1976, a supply NCO who was known to buy items for the barracks and mess hall out of her own money. When the WMs scheduled ball games or hikes, she often arranged for cool drinks and then carried the large thermos jugs to the field herself.11 Colonel Hilgart remembers a time as the commanding officer of WMD-1 when a snafu held up a check meant to pay for a WM ball team trip and Master Sergeant Williams appeared at the company office with a personal check for over $200.12

Another woman remembered by many is Master Sergeant Catherine G. Murray who on 30 November 1962 became the first enlisted woman Marine to transfer to the Fleet Marine Corps Reserve at the completion of nearly 20 years of service. Master Sergeant Murray could be found in the barracks every Sunday morning rousing up all the Roman Catholics and driving them to Mass. Returning with one group from the early service, she gathered up more for the next one. All women with obvious Irish or Italian names were presumed Catholics and taken to church. Major Joan Collins, as an enlisted WM at Quantico, was a member of Master Sergeant Murray's "Volunteer" group that helped the nuns prepare the altar at nearby St. Francis parish in Triangle, Virginia. A Lutheran with an Irish name, she nonetheless spent three consecutive Saturdays cleaning and arranging altar cloths.13

Warrant Officer Eileen R. Scanlon relates another story that typifies the relationship of these women to the WM company. On a bitter cold day in January 1961, the women Marines of Henderson Hall marched in President Kennedy's inaugural parade. The women having been instructed to dress warmly, layered flannel pajamas, woolen Bermuda shorts, and whatever else they could fit under their uniforms. Not able to wear boots in a parade, they wore woolen socks cut off at the top so as not to show above the oxfords. But simple advice was not enough. Before leaving the barracks, all the SNCOs went through the squadbays inspecting each woman to ensure she had carried out the instructions.14

Several factors have combined to change the role played by women officers and staff noncommissioned officers in the supervision and guidance of women Marines and the very personal concern evidenced in the incidents related above is now relatively rare. In the late 1960s, as a result of recommendations made by the Woman Marine Program Study Group, women SNCOs were allowed to move out of the barracks, and more officers were given permission to move off base, making them far less accessible.15 Attrition was much higher in the 1950s and 1960s before the change in regulations which allowed women with children to remain on active duty, thereby causing a shortage of older, mature SNCOs. Finally, the World War II WMs began to retire in 1962 and the women Marines lost this nucleus of officers and noncommissioned officers which for many years felt a special motherly responsibility to new WMs and to the success of the WM program.

Barracks

Marines have never disputed the philosophy that men are different from women. But even acknowledging this or expecting it in no way lessened the initial jolt to a male "old salt" the first time he set foot in a WM barracks. Women are vitally concerned with their living areas, they spend more time in their quarters, and they have needs unique to the distaff community.

Colonel Streeter and her officers in World War II recognized these things early on and even in the midst of a war felt it was important to insist upon certain amenities for the women. A guest lounge became standard. One room, usually furnished with comfortable chairs, sofa, TV (later), and record player was set aside to greet and entertain male guests. The regulations regarding proper attire and behavior were quite strict: Marines, men and women, had to dress in full uniforms or comparable civilian clothing. For the women, sportswear, shorts, or slacks were definitely not considered appropriate for the guest lounge.

Very often the barracks boasted a sewing room, hair dryers, refrigerators, and some cooking equipment. Adequate laundry appliances were the subject of no small number of memoranda from the Director's office. It had to be explained that women, as opposed to men, do not send personal clothing to commercial laundries and therefore needed more washing machines, dryers, and ironing boards than government specifications allowed. There was some feeling among WMs of that era that, in the end, the men's barracks had been improved and better equipped as an outgrowth of the women's insistence on nicer living conditions.

Early in the 1950s women were issued a dresser and permitted to display one stuffed animal per bunk as shown in this photograph taken at Camp Lejeune, North Carolina.

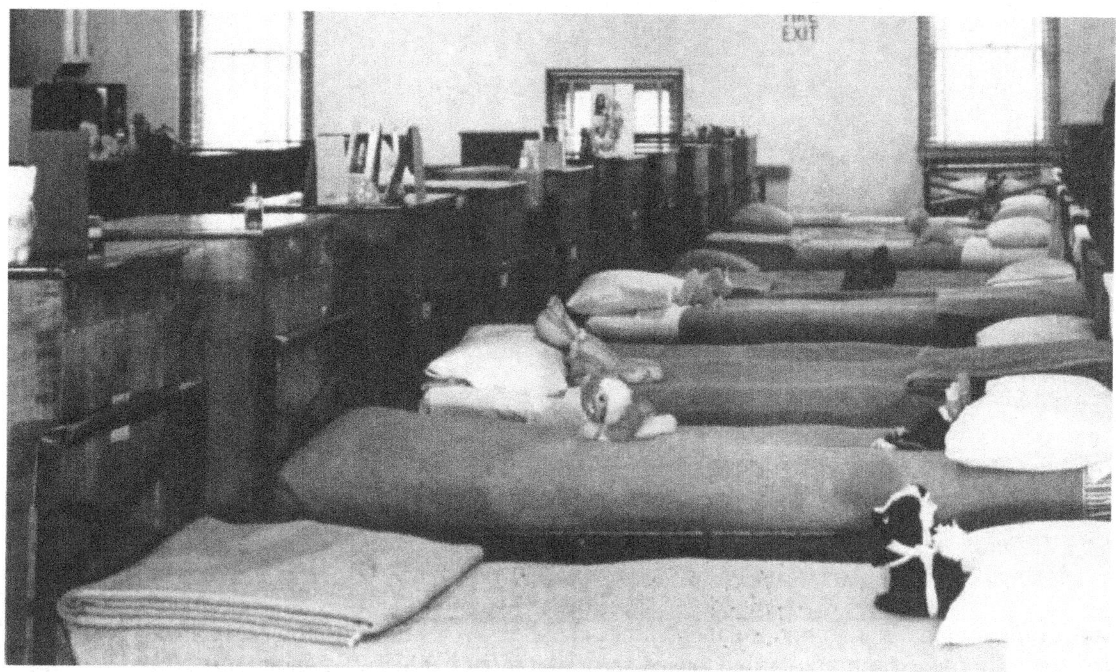

Barracks life in the days of the open squadbays offered little privacy, so whenever possible, the commanding officer would set aside a "quiet room." It was a place to read, to study, to write letters, or to cry: it helped fulfill a woman's need to just be alone. For privacy's sake another distinguishing mark of the distaff barracks took hold — the fence. Discreetly, a fence hid from public view the dainty unmentionables drying on the clothes line while at the same time providing a spot for sunbathing.

Where the WMs excelled at making a squadbay a home was in the decoration of their individual areas. Before the Department of Defense regulations requiring more space and privacy were published in 1973, most Marines were quartered in open squad rooms outfitted with double metal bunks, lockers, and locker boxes.[16] Wooden dressers were a concession to the women, and normally had to be shared. Much ingenuity went into the arrangement of the furniture to form cubicles, thereby assuring a measure of privacy to the several occupants.

A persuasive commanding officer could often talk the battalion commander and S-4 into pastel colored paint—a very radical innovation in the 1950s. Colored rugs, bedspreads, and towels; perfume bottles, prayer books, and photos on the dressers; and finally stuffed animals on the bunks were all privileges eventually won, but often not easily. To keep some semblance of order, the company regulations specified how many items per dresser, and how many stuffed dolls by size per bunk.

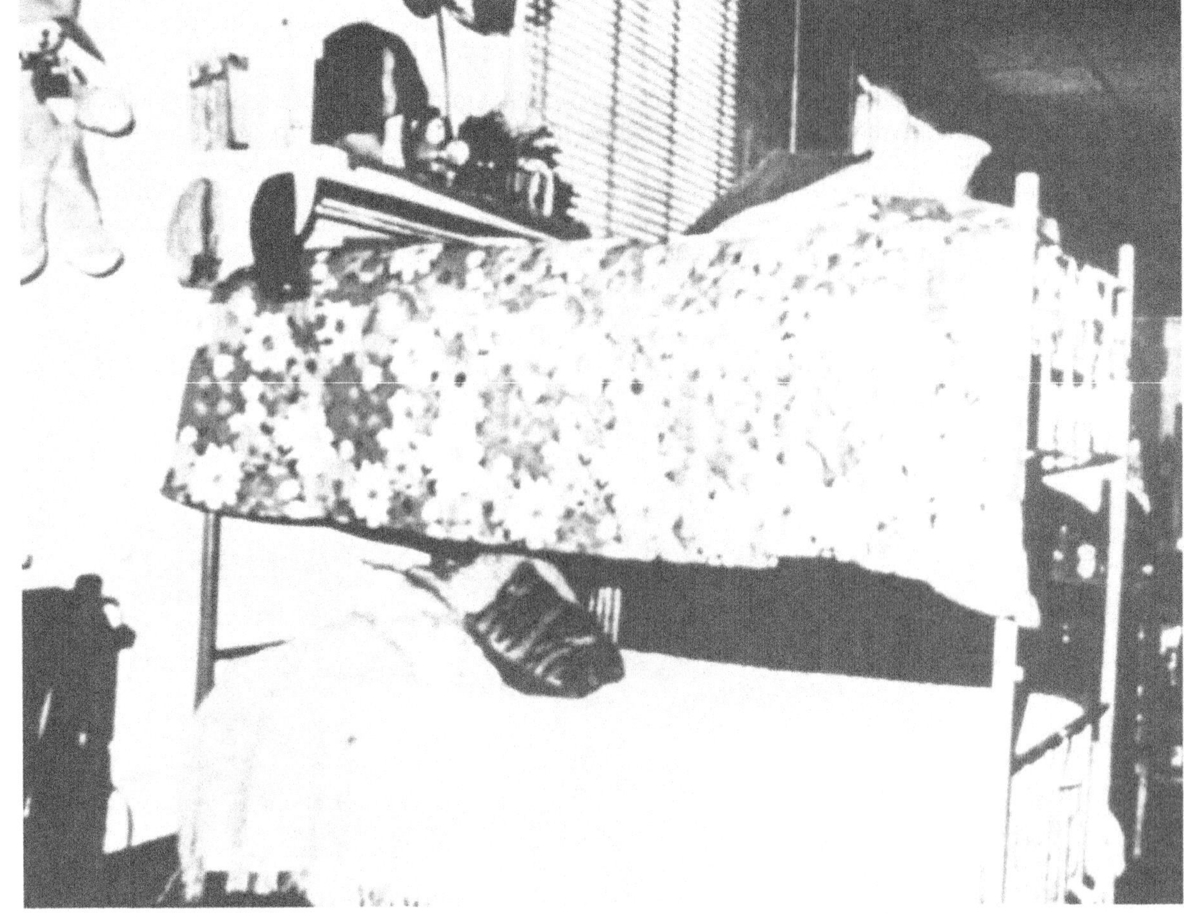

In the 1970s, a move from less military to more feminine and personalized decorating was allowed in the WM barracks. Colorful bed spreads as pictured here were popular.

Understandably, many male Marines had a difficult time adjusting to this desecration of a barracks. Before long, however, the idea gained remarkable acceptance, and at most posts and stations the WM barracks was a mainstay on the itinerary of visiting dignitaries.

Daily Routine

Life on board a Marine base in 1977 would have been only vaguely familiar to the WM of 1949 or even 1959. The most obvious difference would have focused on the barracks building itself, apt to be motel-like with outside entrances for each room or hotel-like with rooms opening on a long passageway. Closets and dressers would have replaced lockers and locker boxes and the metal double bunks would have become unknown items of the past. Reveille would still come too soon, but would be more likely to be announced over a public address system than by means of a bugle.

WMs, until the mid-1950s, held an outdoor formation at roll call each morning, summer and winter, in utilities. Since then roll calls have become less and less regimented and are generally taken by an NCO with the Marines standing by in their areas.17

Mess halls, once furnished with long tables and benches, have become known as dining facilities and feature restaurant-style tables and chairs. Mandatory chow formations for the morning and evening meals are all but a memory since I960. The requirement to wear a uniform to the mess hall was eased to allow civilian clothing first on weekends, then for the evening meal, and finally for all meals. In 1977, at Henderson Hall, appropriate attire for the dining facility permitted neat, but not frayed jeans and excluded only shorts, halters, tank tops, and physical training outfits.18

Liberty cards and liberty logs also had joined "Old Corps" lore by 1970. Before that time all Marines signed out with the barracks duty NCO, and each was closely inspected to see that he or she was properly dressed. WM company regulations generally went a step further. At most commands women Marines could not sign out on liberty after a certain time, perhaps 2130 or 2200, and liberty often expired within an hour after the service clubs closed. Cinderella liberty, as it was called, and the motherly concern of commanding officers, served to challenge the inventiveness of the women who found some ingenious ways to circumvent the rules.

The WM of 1977 walked out of the barracks at will. Dressed in slacks, she did not find it necessary to prove that she was going to participate in an active sport. Shorts did not have to be covered by a modest skirt, and wearing jeans was not strictly limited to car washing in the immediate vicinity of the barracks. She was expected to be back on time by reveille, but beyond that she was largely her own boss.

By 1975 at a few bases women were assigned motel-like rooms as the one pictured here.

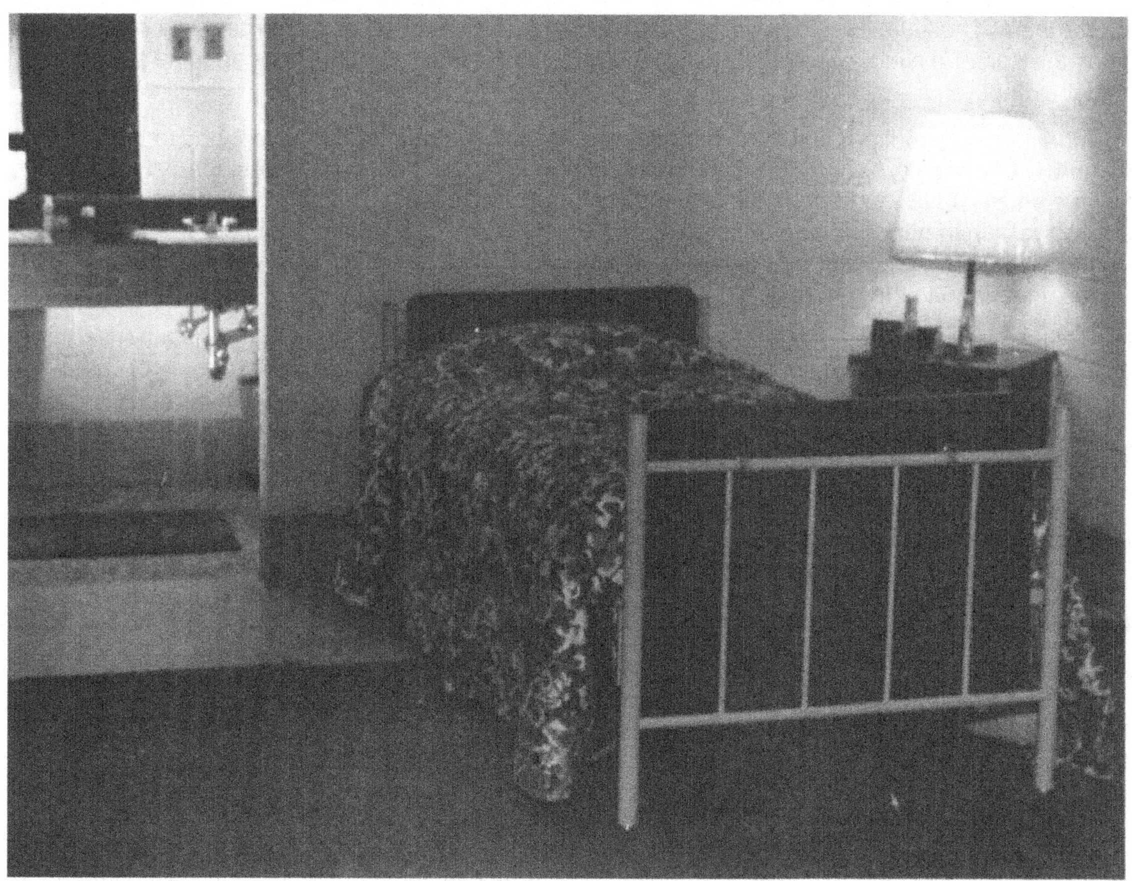

Discipline

Regulations regarding apprehension, arrest, restrictions, and confinement, from a technical standpoint have been equally applicable to all Marines, however, philosophical and practical consideration have dictated unequal enforcement. The differences primarily involve investigative procedures and confinement policies. Since women did not have a military obligation, there was a tacit agreement that the best interests of the Marine Corps were served by removal of habitual offenders. WMs who just could not adjust to military life, who caused more work than they produced, and who had a negative effect on command morale and discipline were, when possible, administratively discharged. The Marine Corps expeditious discharge program, which was initiated in 1975 to improve the quality of personnel serving in the Corps, was based on much the same idea.

The interrogation of women poses problems for both civilian and military police. In order to protect women from abuse and at the same time to protect the police from false accusations, authorities usually demand the attendance of a woman witness during the questioning. It had been Marine Corps policy to require on these occasions the presence of a woman officer or mature staff noncommissioned officer—senior to the woman being interrogated—who could counsel and advise the suspect. The accused could waive this privilege as long as it was done in writing and before a woman officer or her own commanding officer.

For a time it was planned to train enough women investigators so that each post and station would have available a capable officer or NCO to assist the provost marshal when necessary. There was no intention to assign these women to any sort of police duty. Second Lieutenant Marjorie E. O'Hanlon and Ruth F. Reinholz were the first two women Marine officers to attend Provost Marshal General's School—Investigative Officers Course at Camp Gordon, Georgia, from 6 July to 2 September 1953. The two-month class covered surveillance techniques, photography, fingerprinting, and interrogation. The women were well trained but the idea backfired. No one, not even their best friends, trusted the new investigators, and after sending women Marines to several more classes, the project was abandoned.19

There always existed a reluctance to confine women, and policy prohibited the use of brigs and guardhouses for them. Those guilty of civil crimes could be sent to civilian prisons. Women who rated confinement as a result of a court martial were more apt to be restricted to the barracks and fined —a punishment that did not require posting a guard.

When WM companies were routine, and if the offense was serious, women could be confined in the barracks. A number of barracks had a room set aside specifically for that purpose. It was sparsely furnished, had a door with a small window, and could be locked from the passageway. The confinement of a woman Marine in the barracks invariably affected the morale of the entire unit. Guards were posted around the clock causing many extra duty assignments for the NCOs; meals had to be brought in; and merely passing the locked door was unnerving to the others.20

With the disbandment of WM companies and the resultant loss of appropriate barracks, confinement posed additional problems. Punishment had not necessarily been diminished; on the contrary, policy changes have allowed a more liberal use of civilian jails. In 1977, a woman Marine convicted by a court martial could face restriction plus a fine or detention in an approved civilian prison —depending upon the judgment of the commanding officer.

Based on the number of courts martial per total strength, the woman Marine disciplinary rate was less than one percent.21 Although there have been few cases, each one is disproportionately magnified due to the very rarity of occurrence and the lingering hesitancy to confine women.

CHAPTER 12

Promotions

Public Law 90-130 - Enlisted Promotions

By law women officers had always been selected for promotion under a different process and by separate board action from their male colleagues. The provisions of the Armed Forces Integration Act of 1948 held until 1967 when certain restrictions were lifted.1

For 20 years women in the Marine Corps as well as the other Services could aspire to no higher permanent rank than lieutenant colonel. Additionally, the number of women allowed to serve in the grades of major and lieutenant colonel was rigidly limited by the number of regular women officers on active duty. As the women officers who integrated in the 1948-1950 period moved into the field grade ranks, two things occurred: it became irksome to them to stagnate for years in one rank as the male officers passed them by; and the upper ranks were virtually closed until the mid-1960s when these women became eligible to retire. During these years, women were selected for promotion by a separate board convened to consider all women officer ranks. The limited duty officer program, a major opportunity open to male enlisted Marines to achieve commissioned rank, was legally closed to women Marines.

Warrant officer status has been available to women and the early history of the first women Marine warrant officers is told in a letter from CWO-4 Ruth L. Wood:

Of course the biggest event for me was being selected for warrant officer. On 14 April 1952 we took the 3-hour examination. I believe there were about 57 women applicants, and Lillian Hartley (Disbursing) and I

(Administration) were the two lucky ones selected. We took the same exam the men did, at the same time, which included making decisions on questions whether to dig a one-man or a two-man fox hole, when to retreat from an air strip and by whose authority, etc.! A couple of years later when the Marine Corps decided to select another woman warrant, the Testing and Education Unit at Quantico called me, as I was stationed at Quantico, to say they couldn't find a copy of the "women's exam" and were quite astonished when I told them we took the men's exam. They proceeded to make a separate exam for the women.

Lillian Hartley was stationed at HQMC so she received her warrant soon after selection. Mine didn't come so Colonel Hamblet called HQMC to ask about it as she wanted to assign me as adjutant and instructor at the Women Officer Training Detachment there before the next class began. At the time, Lieutenant Colonel Hamblet was the commanding officer of the detachment and not Director of Women Marines. When they told her the delay in my warrant was due to the breakdown of the "fancy typewriter," she suggested they write it in longhand if necessary to get it down here! It soon came typed, but not in the "fancy type."

Lillian Hartley's and my date of rank was 13 June 1952, but in the "Blue Book" {Combined Lineal List of Officers on Active Duty) I was listed first for some reason, with a man next, and then Lillian Hartley, so I am the senior woman warrant officer. Three years later we made CWO-2. That same year we had the opportunity to apply for permanent warrant officer, and on 16 Dec 1955 the list came out showing we had been selected over again with a permanent date of rank of 1 July 1954, and Lotus Mort was selected with a permanent date of 14 Dec 1955. Margaret Robertson was selected in 1956, Alice Mclntyre in 1957, Elaine Freeman in 1958, and Mary Thompson in 1959, none in I960, then one a year for some time thereafter.

When on 1 Jan 1961 I was the first woman promoted to CWO-4, they made a big event of it (altho' I had been the first CWO-2 and CWO-3 also so it was quite logical!), and I made permanent CWO-4 on 13 June 1967.2

A change was made in the warrant officer program in 1975 when for the first time women warrant officers attended the Warrant Officer Basic School with their male counterparts.

Public Law 90-130

The first significant change in law directly affecting servicewomen occurred when Congress enacted Public Law 90-130. In a colorful ceremony in the East Room of the White House, President Lyndon B. Johnson on 8 November 1967 signed into law the bill giving women officers in the armed forces equal opportunity for promotion with their male colleagues. Present at the signing were servicewomen and former servicewomen, including directors and former directors of the WAC, WAVES, WAF, Women Marines, the three Nurse Corps, and three Women's Medical Service Corps. High-ranking male officers were there as well, including members of the Joint Chiefs of Staff.

The Marine Band, which normally plays at Presidential ceremonies, relinquished the stage for the occasion to the 14th U.S. Army Band, the only all-women official band in the Armed Forces. The United States flag and the flags of the various services were carried by a color guard of enlisted women, and the President entered the East Room through a cordon of 50 women from all branches of the Services, including 12 women Marines.

Heading the list of Marines present at the ceremony was General Wallace M. Greene, Jr., then Commandant. Four of the five women who had held appointment as Director of Women Marines were in attendance: Colonels Ruth Cheney Streeter, Julia E. Hamblet, Margaret M. Henderson, and Barbara J. Bishop. Sergeant Majors Ouida Craddock and Rosa Harrington topped the roster of enlisted women Marines at the historic ceremony.3

Significant among the President's remarks was the statement that:

Our Armed Forces literally could not operate effectively or efficiently without our women . So, both as President and as the Commander in Chief, I am very pleased and very proud to have this measure sent to me by the Congress.4

This long-awaited law repealed the legal limitations on the number of women in the Armed Services and also removed some, but not all, of the assignment and promotion restrictions. There were still certain legal limitations such as the prohibition against the appointment of women as limited duty officers, the legal limitations on the promotion of women officers to flag and general officer rank in the Navy and Marine Corps, and the differences in the criteria for the involuntary separation of male and female officers who were not selected for promotion. In the Marine Corps, a male first lieutenant or captain was involuntarily separated if he was considered as having twice failed selection for promotion to the next higher grade. Historically, due to the upper rank promotion restrictions for women, a female first lieutenant or captain was not involuntarily separated until she had completed seven or 13 years of commissioned service, respectively, and was not on a promotion list.

The law also precluded female commissioned officers in the Marine Corps from competing for promotion with male officers. This restriction combined with the smaller numbers of women officers made it difficult to maintain an equitable rank structure. As a result, women officers by the 1970s were sometimes promoted earlier than their male contemporaries. In order to achieve comparability, a goal was set to slow down the women's promotions and to "age them in grade." A selection board was not convened in 1976 to consider women for the rank of colonel nor in 1977 to consider selections to lieutenant colonel. In some cases, as a result, a few women served more time in grade than average.

WO Lillian Hartley, one of the first two women Marines to be promoted to warrant officer, receives congratulations from Col Katherine A. Towle, WM Director, on 7 August 1952.

Although the law required selection boards for male and female Marine officers, women since August 1974 had been selected for promotion by the same board membership as the men with the addition of a woman officer. If that woman officer was a colonel, she also served as a member of the male officer selection board.

The law further precluded the selection of a woman officer to flag and general officer rank in the Navy and Marine Corps although there was a provision for temporary appointment as a rear admiral or brigadier general while serving in specific billets.5

On the positive side, PL 90-130 allowed for permanent promotions to colonel for women. In April 1968, some six months after it was enacted, selection boards were convened at Headquarters Marine Corps to select Regular and Reserve women lieutenant colonels for promotion. Colonels Towle and Hamblet were called from retirement to sit on these boards. The Director of Women Marines, Colonel Barbara Bishop, and Lieutenant Colonel Jeanette Sustad, former Deputy Director of Women Marines, were the first Regular women officers selected for permanent promotion to the grade of colonel. Of the six Reserve officers selected, two, Lieutenant Colonel Hazel E. Benn, deputy head of the Special Services Branch at Headquarters, and Lieutenant Colonel Ruth H. Broe, special projects officer for the Division of Information, were serving on active duty. The four remaining Reserve colonels were Lieutenant Colonels Mary L. Condon, Helen A. Wilson, Dorothy R. Dietz, and Rilda M. Stuart.6

Lotus T. Mort, third woman Marine to be appointed a permanent warrant officer, receives her new insignia from Col Julia E. Hamblet (left), Director of Women Marines, and LtCol Pauline B. Beckley, in a ceremony at Headquarters Marine Corps, in January 1956.

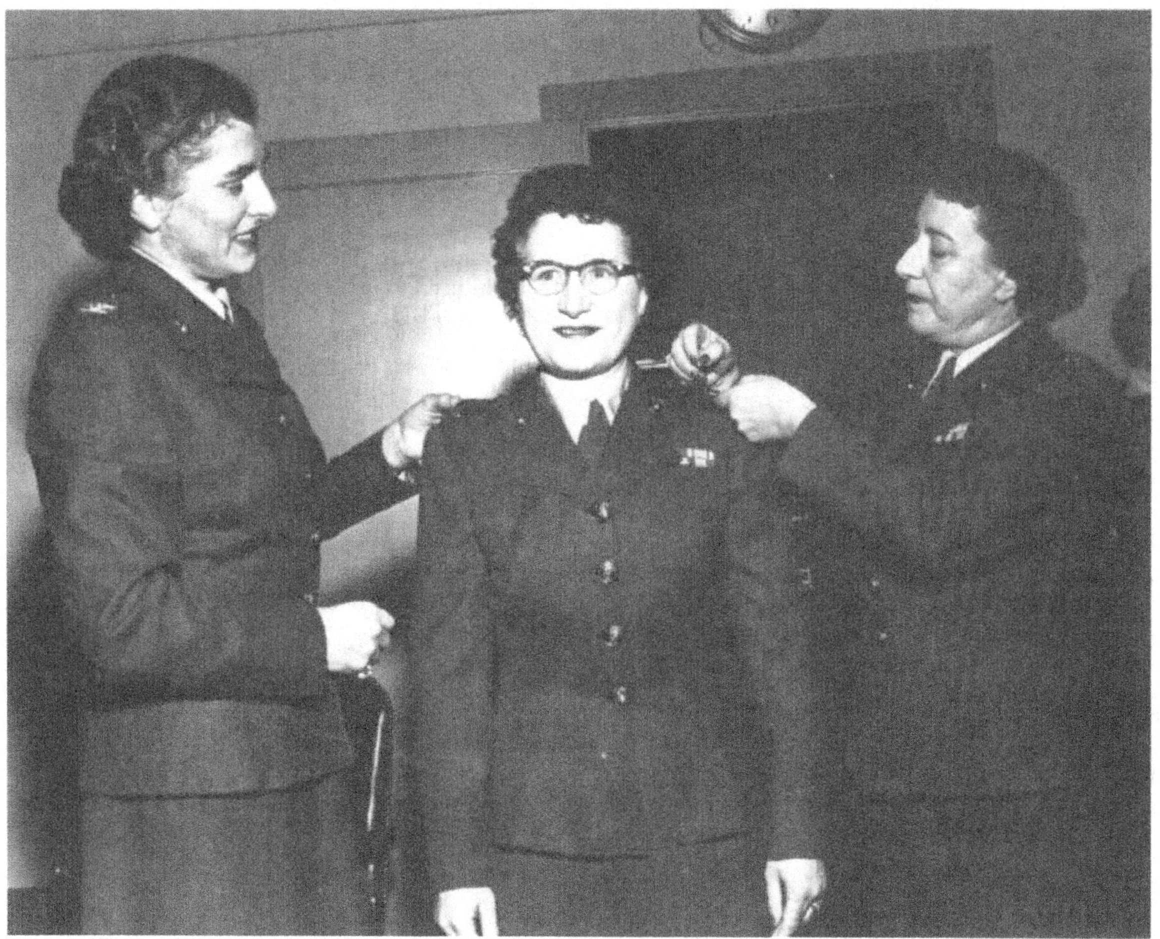

Enlisted Promotions

For the most part, promotions for enlisted women in the Marine Corps were made under the same policies and by the same boards as for the men. Except in scattered individual cases, there has never existed the dissatisfaction or charges of sex discrimination—voiced either by WMs who felt held back or by male Marines who thought the women to be favored —that was evident in the case of officer promotions.

The notable exception was the first sergeant and sergeant major program opened by the Marine Corps in 1955. At first only male Marines were eligible and the Director, Colonel Hamblet, fought the exclusion for three years. In a report dated 21 September 1956, after noting the defined duties of the first sergeants and sergeants major, she reasoned that all of them apply equally to men and women Marines. She continued:

Paragraph 4 g, however, denies the program to women on the basis that the "senior NCO present must have the capability of leading the unit in a combat, or other type situation.

It is felt that it is unrealistic to deny the first sergeant/sergeant major program to women on the basis that they cannot supervise a unit in the field nor lead a unit in combat. The mission of male Marines, officer and enlisted, is preparedness for combat; however, we do not refuse to commission women officers because they cannot lead combat platoons nor do we fail to promote enlisted women from private to master sergeant because they cannot serve "in the field."

Attention is invited to the fact that women Marines did attend First Sergeants School, were designated first sergeants/sergeant major, and did wear the distinctive insignia of those ranks during World War II; consequently, a precedent for the appointment of women Marines to first sergeants/sergeant major definitely exists.7

Recognizing the futility of her cause at the time, Colonel Hamblet made two practical recommendations that were in the realm of possibility. She asked that the:

. . . first sergeant/sergeant major program be opened to women Marines in event of national emergency when not only would the increased strength and billets in the women's program justify their selection, but undoubtedly women would, as they did during World War II, replace male first sergeants/sergeants major who were ordered to combat duty.8

and that:

. . . the policy be continued that women's units will have billets designated for first sergeants/sergeants major and the women assigned to these billets will hold the billet title while so serving even though they are not authorized the distinctive insignia.9

Two years later, on 20 November 1958, she personally brought her case to the Commandant, General Pate, and on the following day she submitted a report of the conversation to the chief of staff. She wrote:

The pros and cons of selecting women Marines for the permanent rank of sergeant major and first sergeant to fill sergeant major and first sergeant billets existing within the women's program were discussed. The Commandant and the undersigned were in accord that because of the limited number of these billets (probably 3 sergeants major and 10 first sergeants) it would not be in the best interests of the Marine Corps to select women to these ranks and restrict their assignment to the few billets in the women's program. Instead, it would appear more advantageous to have the women filling these billets have the rank, pay, title, and insignia while so assigned. It was agreed that the selection of women for these billets would rest with the Director of Women Marines.10

The brevet system discussed by the Commandant and Colonel Hamblet materialized when Marine Corps Order 1421.6, dated 3 May I960, was published allowing for temporary appointments to first sergeant and sergeant major for women. They were not considered to be promotions as the women eligible for them had to be master gunnery sergeant in order to move into the sergeant major slot or master sergeants to become first sergeants —actually comparable pay grades.

These top-rated enlisted women held the appointment, wore the appropriate chevrons, and received full pay and the privileges of the rank as long as they were in the designated billets and reverted to their permanent rank on transfer out of the jobs. At the time, there were three sergeants major billets: the senior enlisted women at the Woman Recruit Training Battalion at Parris Island; the Women Marines Detachment at Quantico; and in the office of the Director of Women Marines. There were 10 first sergeant spots, one at each of the existing women Marine companies which were then located at: Headquarters Marine Corps; Quantico; Norfolk; Cherry Point; Camp Lejeune; Parris Island; San Diego; Camp Pendleton; El Toro; and FMFPac, Hawaii.11

By modern standards, the policy appears restrictive, but, in fact, the brevet system was adopted to protect the women. The policies governing assignments of women at the time prohibited them from serving in these billets in male organizations. Had the appointment been permanent, the 13 women would have been limited to these billets, thereby restricting their potential utilization and at the same time, precluding others from serving as sergeants major and first sergeants.

As it turned out, for a number of years, there were so few women master gunnery sergeants that it was not until December 1964 that a woman Marine eligible for a sergeant major appointment reported to Parris

Island. Sergeant Major Doris Derrick was the first WM to be authorized the chevrons, pay, and privileges inherent in the title of Sergeant Major, Woman Recruit Training Battalion.12

Women who served in the temporary positions could, upon retirement, ask for a permanent appointment to first sergeant or sergeant major as appropriate, providing they had performed satisfactorily in the rank for at least a year.

The brevet system was in effect for 12 years. Surprisingly, the suggestion that women be promoted permanently to the top enlisted ranks came from a man, the Sergeant Major of the Marine Corps, Joseph W. Daily. In a memorandum to the Commandant dated 1 November 1971, the sergeant major stated:

It is realized that billets for Women Marine First Sergeants/Sergeants Major are few. However, I feel the Women Marines are treated unfairly, not being able to compete on the same promotion system as Male Marines. This subject was brought up as an agenda item at the SNCO Symposium. The vote was 95 percent in favor for Women Marines to be promoted to First Sergeant/Sergeant Major the same as Male Marines. It was surprising to learn the number of Male Marines who were unaware of the fact that Women Marines were not promoted the same as males in those two ranks.13

Furthermore, the Sergeant Major endorsed the idea of women filling these positions in male units as he continued:

If Women Marines were ever promoted in First Sergeant/Sergeant Major, they could fill other billets as they are now interchangeable in many jobs with Male Marines. This would also help the Woman Marine become more professional in the First Sergeant/Sergeant Major billet.

It is strongly recommended that Women Marines be given the same opportunity as Male Marines in our promotion system and that it should commence with the Fiscal Year 1972 Board. . . ."14

CWO4 Ruth L. Wood, the first woman Marine to achieve that grade, has her insignia of rank pinned on by Col Clifford P. Quilici and Col Charles E. Dobson, in 1966.

A debate on the issue ensued finding the Director of Women Marines, Colonel Sustad, opposed due to the short time given WMs to consider career alternatives. Directives at the time allowed male gunnery sergeants to indicate on their fitness reports their preference for promotion to either master sergeant or first sergeant

—the selection having a bearing on their future assignments. Colonel Sustad recommended that action be deferred until a study could be conducted to determine whether a permanent system or the brevet system was actually best fitted for women Marines.15

In due time, the colonel was on the side of permanent promotions, and her stand received timely support by way of a memorandum signed by Roger T. Kelley, Assistant Secretary of Defense, Manpower and Reserve Affairs, directing the Services to eliminate inequities. On 31 July 1972, the Commandant of the Marine Corps approved the selection of an unlimited number of women Marines as designated sergeants major and first sergeants. The new policy was implemented by the E-8/E-9 promotion board already in session, having convened on 18 July.18

Apart from the particular designations as sergeant major and first sergeant, the ninth pay grade was opened to women in the spring of l960 when Geraldine M. Moran became the first and only WM at the time to hold the rank of master gunnery sergeant. She was promoted to that rank in April l960 by Captain Valeria F. Hilgart, commanding officer of Woman Marine Detachment 1, El Toro.17 Master Gunnery Sergeant Mary G. Vaughn, believed to be the first black woman Marine E-9, received her promotion warrant from Lieutenant General John N. McLaughlin, Commanding General, Fleet Marine Force, Pacific, in Hawaii in April 1977.

CHAPTER 13

Marriage, Motherhood, and Dependent Husbands

Marriage — Motherhood — Dependency Regulations — The Military Couple — Marine Wife, Civilian Husband

Right from the start, Colonel Towle had to field questions from newspeople insinuating that the Marine Corps was against matrimony for women Marines. Tactfully, she, and then later, her successors, Colonels Hamblet and Henderson, assured the reporters that Marines certainly were not anti-marriage. The laws, Department of Defense regulations, and Marine Corps regulations of the time supported their statements: marriage was indeed acceptable; husbands and children, however, posed some problems. Generally, it can be said that from 1948 until 1964 a woman Marine could marry, and almost immediately ask for a discharge; the acquisition of natural, adopted, foster, or stepchildren under 18 years of age, in fact required discharge. Husbands were not considered dependents unless they were actually dependent upon the wife for more than 50 percent of their support.

Marriage

Under the policy in effect from 1949 until the Vietnam War, enlisted WMs who married could ask for an administrative discharge based solely on marriage. Providing they had completed one year of their enlistment beyond basic training, they were discharged for the convenience of the government. Regular officers were eligible for release two years after their appointment. During the Korean War, regulations were more stringent, but were relaxed immediately after the emergency.1 This liberal view toward discharges and release from contractual obligations reflected society's negative attitude toward working wives. Needless to say, it contributed to instability in the WM program.

With changing values, a manpower crisis in the 1960s, and a need to improve the attrition rate of women Marines, Colonel Barbara J. Bishop, by then the Director, led the fight to tighten the rules. Colonel Bishop reasoned that women must honor their enlistment contract. To make it easier, husbands and wives, whenever possible, would be stationed at the same or nearby bases. A joint household policy was put into effect on 14 July 1964 which stated:

A married enlisted Woman Marine may be discharged at her written request, provided she is not stationed at or sufficiently close to the duty station or residence of her husband to permit the maintenance of a joint residence, and provided she meets all of the following conditions.

a. A transfer request to the same or nearby duty station or place of residence of her husband has been submitted to the Commandant of the Marine Corps and has been denied.

b. The separation of husband and wife has exceeded 18 months.

c. The enlisted woman is not serving on an extension of enlistment or reenlistment entered into subsequent to marriage.

d. The enlisted woman has completed 24 months of service subsequent to completion of a service school if the length of school was more than 24 weeks.

A married woman Marine officer does not become eligible for separation or release from active duty, simply because of her marital status, until she has completed her period of obligated service (3 years).2

In August of the following year, 1965, due to the demands of the Vietnam War, discharges based upon marriage were suspended regardless of place of residence. Then, once again, on 31 October 1966, the joint household policy was reinstated.

The desired effect of these new regulations —to lengthen the service of many WMs—was realized almost immediately. The rate of discharges for reasons of marriage was dramatically reduced from 18.6 percent in fiscal year 1964 to 6.3 percent in fiscal year 1965 and, finally, to 2.3 percent in fiscal year 1966.3

Motherhood

A study group in 1948 meeting to discuss proposed regulations governing the discharge of women stated:

It is believed that pregnancy and motherhood ipso facto interfere with military duties. . . . Granting of maternity leave would result in having ineffectives; replacement could not be procured while the woman remained on the active list; and the mother of a small child would not be readily available for reassignment. Necessary rotation of duty assignments would require the family unit to be broken up for considerable periods of time, or at least until the husband made the necessary provisions to establish the home at the mother's new duty station It is believed that a woman who is pregnant or a mother should not be a member of the armed forces and should devote herself to the responsibilities which she had assumed, remaining with her husband and child as a family unit.4

This sort of reasoning, typical of the times, formed the basis for Marine Corps regulations on the subject until 1970. The rules were very strictly enforced, and any responsibility for children forced the separation of a woman Marine from the service.

The first step toward a more liberal view was taken in the fall of 1970 when Headquarters announced that a WM who is the stepparent of, or who has personal custody of, or adopts, a child could ask to stay on active duty. Each case had to be reviewed, taking into consideration such factors as length of service, performance record, ages and number of children involved, and the commanding officer's evaluation of the situation. Waivers were granted if it could be determined that parenthood would not interfere with the Marine's job.5

On 12 August 1970, Colonel Jeanette I. Sustad, Director of Women Marines, startled the women attending the Women Marines Association Convention in Philadelphia by predicting the possibility of allowing natural mothers to continue on active duty. It was, in fact, due to her personal efforts that many of the long-standing regulations were set aside. Times had changed, women had changed, mores had changed. It was 1970 and women no longer accepted the old order as dogma.

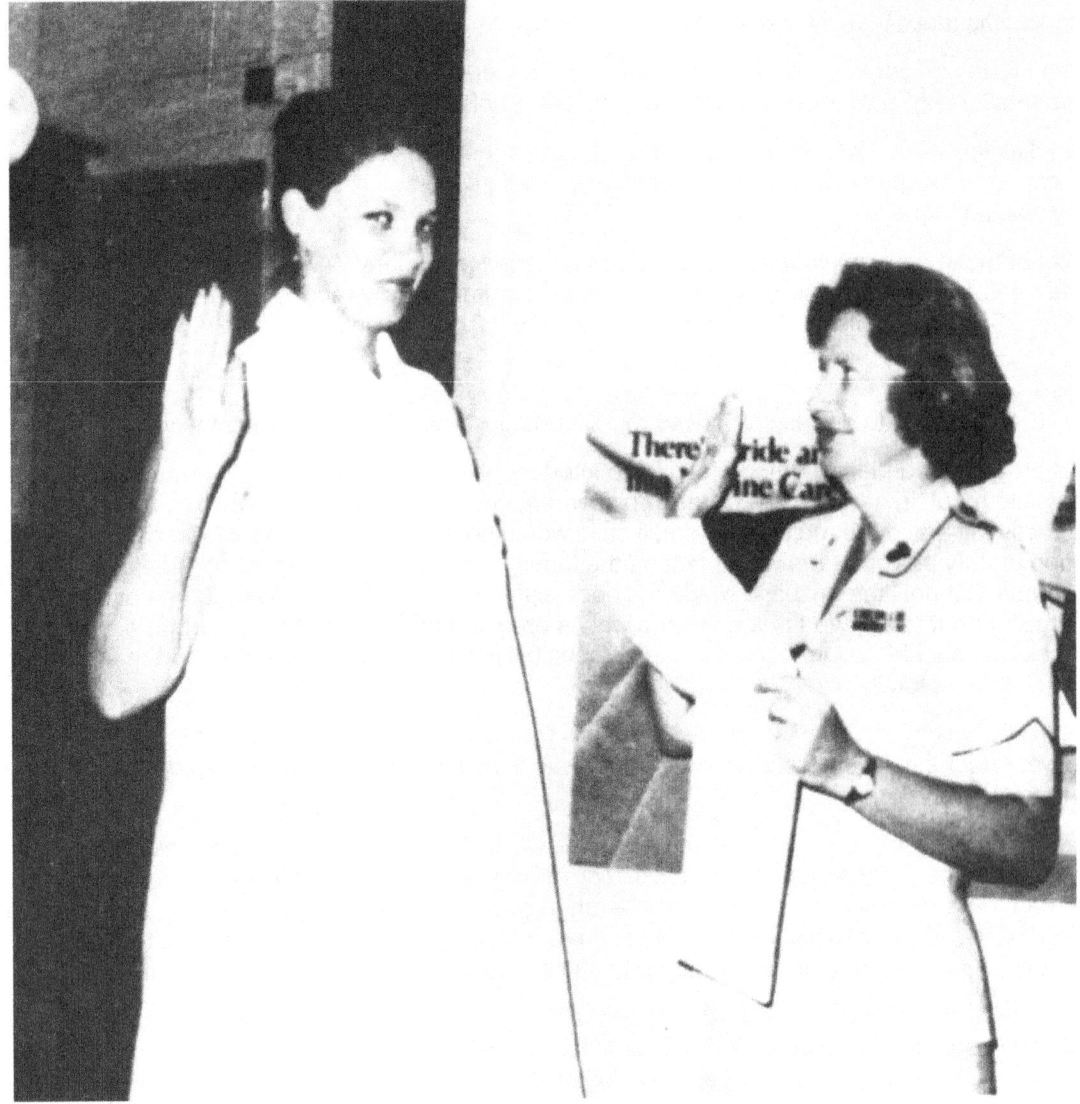

In 1971 a change in regulations allowed natural mothers to continue on active duty service. Capt Joan Collins, company commander, reenlists pregnant GySgt Donna Murray.

Colonel Sustad invested a great deal of her time locating and attempting to gain acceptance of this view at Headquarters. Colonel John L. Ostby of the Legal Division was her trusted advisor and mentor, supplying her with facts, legal interpretations, and whatever ammunition she needed to get by each stumbling block. Certain that success was within reach, Colonel Sustad kept at least one Reserve officer's separation papers in staffing—lost in the administrative maze — until the regulations were changed allowing for a more favorable disposition of her case.6

And, change did come in 1971 when a waiver policy for natural mothers was tested. Again, each case was carefully considered by Headquarters and women with good records who were able to show that they could adequately care for the child were allowed to remain on duty.7 Gunnery Sergeant Frances L. Gonzales, the first WM to take advantage of the program, never missed a day of work other than annual leave and the travel time involved with her transfer at the time.8 Lieutenant Colonel Carolyn Auldridge Walsh, the first officer to remain on active duty after having a child, lost little time as well. Colonel Sustad credits the positive example of these first cases with helping to calm the fears of some, but not all, of the opponents to the idea.9

Women who had been discharged from the Marine Corps for pregnancy took new hope, and some asked to be allowed to return. Major Mary Sue Stevens League, separated in March 1970 because of pregnancy, was one of these former WMs who sought to regain her commission. On 24 January 1972, she was given the commissioning oath in the Marine Corps Reserve by her husband, Lieutenant Commander William C. League, a Navy chaplain, in ceremonies at the Marine Barracks in the Naval Shipyard at Portsmouth, Virginia. She reportedly was the first woman Marine to regain her commission after becoming pregnant and being separated.10

The Department of Defense in 1975 published instructions which precluded the involuntary separation of servicewomen on the sole basis of pregnancy. Marine Corps Order 5000.12, dated 16 July 1975, specified that WMs who are pregnant may, upon request, be discharged or retained on active duty if otherwise qualified. Women who chose to remain in the Service were cautioned that parenthood did not entitle them to special treatment or consideration in duty assignments, and commanding officers had the obligation to initiate action for discharge in cases where women failed to carry out their duties after the birth of the child.11

Pregnant WMs could wear civilian clothes when the uniform no longer looked appropriate. The seemingly unlikely prospect of a regulation maternity outfit was under study by the military services and later approved.

Under normal circumstances, and based upon the advice of a medical officer, a pregnant servicewoman was expected to lose no more than 10 weeks of duty-four before delivery and six after. If the mother wanted more time off, for reasons other than medical, she could ask for annual leave. A 1977 study showed that even with time off for maternity leave and other strictly female matters, servicewomen lost much less time than men because of their lower incidence of absence without leave, desertion, and drug- and alcohol-related problems.12

Finally, in respect to the demands of both motherhood and her job, if a Marine asked to remain on duty, but later found it impossible to do justice to her responsibilities, she could ask for an administrative discharge.

In early 1949, when the policies were being formulated that would eventually cause the discharge of all pregnant servicewomen, Rear Admiral Clifford A. Swanson, Chief of the Bureau of Medicine and Surgery, Department of the Navy, stood alone in an attempt to protect the careers of women in the military. Taking a somewhat radical position, one not even espoused by the leading military women of the day, he wrote:

Inasmuch as pregnancy is a normal biological phenomenon in women in the military age group it must be assumed that the possibility that women entering the regular military service become pregnant was recognized by Congress when reference (a) [Women's Armed Services Integration Act of 1948] was enacted. It would appear to this Bureau that the apparent purpose . . . was to afford women an opportunity to enter into and remain in the military service as a career and that the subject proposed regulation is inconsistent with this apparent purpose of the Women's Armed Services Integration Act of 1948.

In connection with the foregoing, it cannot be presumed to be the policy of the military service to regard either the institution of marriage or the raising of a family with disfavor. However, it is recognized that if such personal interests seriously interfere with military duties, or if female military personnel desire to give up their military career voluntarily in order to raise a family . it would be desirable to have means available whereby such personnel can be expeditiously separated from the service. Aside from these considerations there would appear to this Bureau to be no reason for terminating the service of personnel who are pregnant but physically able to perform their duties. . . .'3

Admiral Swanson made specific recommendations regarding time off, maternity leave, and discharges, and while the regulations published 27 years later are not precisely his, the philosophy is unmistakable.

Dependency Regulations

In a report to the House Armed Services Committee on 6 March 1972, Colonel Sustad wrote:

Title 37 contains different criteria for defining dependents of men and women military members. This results in an inequality of treatment between the married military man and the married military woman. It also causes a difference in treatment between the military man married to a civilian and the military man married to a military woman.

To this simple statement of fact, she added her personal view, "The present law is clearly unfair to the military woman. In recent years this inequity has become the primary complaint among women in the Marine Corps."14

The question of dependency had long been an irritant causing ever increasing dissatisfaction to those who found themselves adversely affected by the law and policies. When women first entered military service, the traditional American family concept was that of a unit financially supported by the male member. For many years, women accepted the inequities with only a minimal amount of grumbling; but few, if any, considered challenging the law until the era of women's rights — approximately 1970.

Chaplain (LCdr) William C. League, USN, pins leaves on his wife, Maj Mary Sue League, the first woman to regain her commission after being separated for pregnancy. Joining in the ceremony are Maj Nannette I. Beavers, USMCR (second from right), and her mother, Mrs. Leola A. Beavers (far right), a World War I Marine, on 24 January 1972.

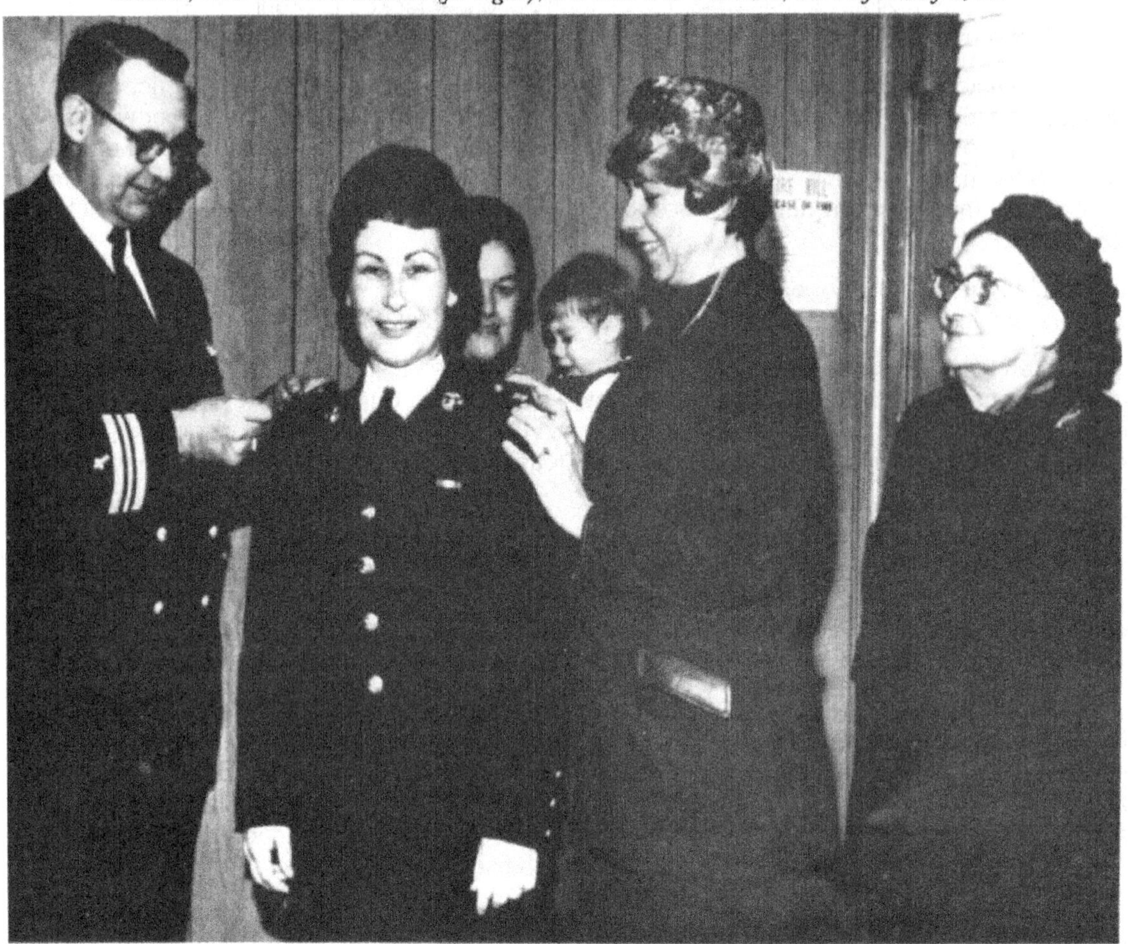

The Military Couple

For WMs married to servicemen the problems focused on quarters and the basic allowance for quarters (BAQ) normally provided to members of the Armed Forces with dependents. Since the Marine wife in a military family received military pay, she was not considered a dependent. It then followed that the husband was entitled only to the lower BAQ provided to members without dependents. Furthermore, if the husband was assigned to sea duty, field duty, FMF duty, or combat, where presumably adequate quarters were furnished him, even the without-dependents allowance was denied to him as it was denied to all of the bachelors. The wife was not entitled to any allowance for quarters unless she was a major or above, and unless there was no available space for her in the Bachelor Officers' Quarters (BOQ).

Put into effect, this policy financially penalized not only WMs, but their service husbands. The experience of two lieutenants stationed at Camp Lejeune in the mid-1960s is typical of the inconvenience caused many. Since there was at Camp Lejeune a BOQ for women with plenty of available space, the WM lieutenant, although married, was assigned a room. She, therefore, was not entitled to a monetary allowance. Her Marine husband, because he was married, was not required to live in the BOQ, but since his wife was a Marine, he was paid BAQ at the rate of a single man. They rented a house together and she merely ignored the assigned quarters. When the husband left for a six-month Mediterranean cruise, his entitlement to an allowance stopped and they were left with two alternatives: maintain the house anyway or put their furnishings in storage at their own expense for six months, and have the wife move into the BOQ. They kept their house.

As to public quarters for families on board a base, when they were available, only the husband was eligible, and the assignment was based upon his grade regardless of who was senior.

Marine Wife — Civilian Husband

During the legislative hearings that preceded the passage of the Women's Armed Services Integration Act of 1948, much attention was paid to the question of military women with civilian husbands. There was, in the minds of many, a real fear of an army of indigent men —camp followers, in effect—who would take unscrupulous advantage of the largesse of the United States Government and military wives. The ensuing laws, Title 10 and 37 of the United States Code, laid down specific tests of dependency which were interpreted for 25 years to mean that a civilian husband was not the dependent of his military wife unless he was dependent upon her for more than 50 percent of his support due to total and permanent mental or physical disability. The ramifications were considerable, and especially difficult for young Marines who upon discharge enrolled in college while their Marine wives continued on active duty.

The civilian husband had no type of identification card and hence had to obtain a visitor's pass each time he came on the base, and could not, of course, go to the service club, post exchange, or commissary, or use any recreational facilities such as the swimming pool, golf course, or theater unless accompanied by his wife as her guest. Additionally, he was not entitled to medical care. The couple was not eligible for family housing, travel and transportation allowances for the husband, dislocation allowance, overseas station allowances, or a family separation allowance.15

Because of a quirk in commissary regulations which used the term "authorized agent" rather than "dependent," occasionally local authorities ruled that civilian husbands could, with a special pass, shop for groceries. Other times, under stricter interpretations, the man was given a pass that only allowed him to accompany his wife into the store and help her carry out the purchase, but not to shop on his own. Most often, the civilian husband was not allowed to enter the commissary at all. The Armed Services Exchange Regulations, on the other hand, specifically limited the use of post exchanges to dependents, thereby summarily barring all civilian husbands of servicewomen.16

Lieutenant Colonel Clowers, perhaps the only woman Marine officer of her time to be married to a civilian husband for the majority of her career, was never permitted to live on board a Marine base with her husband. In fact, although she was always permitted to draw the single quarters allowance, she lived under the constant threat of being assigned quarters in a BOQ and losing that entitlement. In 1956, the colonel was ordered to Parris Island to take command of the Woman Recruit Training Battalion and she was advised of the commanding general's desire that all battalion commanders live on board the base. The Quartermaster General at Headquarters, however, ruled that her husband absolutely could not live with her on base except for visits of a maximum of 30 days since he was not dependent on her due to mental and physical incompetence. In the end, the dilemma was solved by cancelling Lieutenant Colonel Clower's orders to Parris Island, and sending her instead to Quantico to command the Women Officers Training Detachment.

The first major change in interpretation of the law came on 3 July 1972 when it was ruled that a husband could be considered a dependent when there is sufficient evidence to establish his dependence on his service wife for over half of his support without regard to his mental or physical capacity to support himself. Thus, a student husband, for example, if his veteran's benefits did not make up more than 50 percent of his support, became eligible for an identification card and the attendant privileges.

Women Marines, as all married servicewomen, still resented the narrow interpretation of the term "dependent" since wives of servicemen were automatically granted all privileges regardless of their financial, physical, or mental status. Morale was significantly raised in the female ranks therefore, when on 14 May 1973, in the Frontiero vs. Richardson case, the Supreme Court ruled that servicewomen were eligible for all benefits, privileges, and rights granted servicemen under the same circumstances. Furthermore, former or retired servicewomen could file claims for retroactive payment of with-dependents quarters allowances for periods of active duty during which they were married but not receiving the increased allowances.19 The single, major complaint of WMs at the time of the ruling was thus resolved.

CHAPTER 14

Uniforms

The Beginnings of Change, 1950 - The Mainbocher Wardrobe, 1950-1952 — After Mainbocher - Grooming and Personal Appearance — Utilities

A composite of the 1943 Marine Corps Women's Reserve uniform regulations with several changes made during World War II was published on 30 April 1945 as Uniform Regulations, U.S. Marine Women's Reserve, 1945 > These regulations remained in force until 1952 when newly designed uniforms were introduced. When women joined the Regular Marine Corps in November 1948, the subject of uniforms was on their minds since fashions had changed, most noticeably skirt lengths. From short knee-length styles, hems dropped to midcalf with the coming of the "New Look." Male Marines responsible for supplies and money were unshakeable. There would be no new uniforms until the wartime stocks were depleted.

Generally, women Marines, officer and enlisted, wore identically styled uniforms of the same fabric. This was not true of male Marines. Women officers wore green, detachable epaulets on the shoulder straps of summer uniforms and had additional dress uniforms. For dress, officers wore gilt and silver-colored emblems traditionally worn by Marine officers while the enlisted women wore the gilt emblems of enlisted Marines. Both wore the bronze eagle, globe, and anchor on their service uniforms. While the vertical axis of the hemisphere paralleled the crease line of the jacket collar for officers, it was worn perpendicular to the floor for enlisted women. Coats, caps, shoes, gloves, handbags, and mufflers were the same for all ranks. Enlisted women wore the same large chevrons as the men.

Winter Service: The winter service uniform consisted of a man-tailored jacket and straight-lined skirt made of forest green serge. A long-sleeved khaki shirt with four-in-hand necktie, green cap, brown shoes and gloves, and bronze metal buttons completed the outfit. A heavy green overcoat or khaki trenchcoat with detachable lining, and a red wool muffler were worn when needed. All women Marines were required to maintain a pair of plain black galoshes, boots, or rubbers to fit the oxfords.

Officer Winter Dress: Women Marines did not have a dress blue uniform until 1952. During World War II and the seven years following, officers turned the winter service uniform into a dress uniform by exchanging the khaki shirt for one of white and the khaki necktie for one of forest green. Enlisted women had no comparable dress outfit.

Summer Service: The summer service uniform was a two-piece green and white seersucker or plisse dress. It was V-necked and was fastened with green plastic buttons. The jacket came in both short and long sleeves. The traditional dress cap in matching green, with white cap cord and bronze buttons, or a garrison style cap in the same shade was worn with the summer service uniform. Shoes, oxfords or pumps, were brown. When the trenchcoat was worn, a white rayon muffler was required.

Officers' uniforms were distinguished by green shoulder boards worn over the regular epaulets and held in place by the shoulder strap button and rank insignia.

Summer Dress: Perhaps the favorite uniform of World War II WRs was the short-sleeved, V-necked white twill uniform worn with gilt buttons on the jacket and cap, dress emblems, and white pumps. The stiffly starched uniform never failed to evoke compliments. Enlisted women Marines were disappointed when a white uniform was not included in the new 1952 wardrobe. It was discontinued because male enlisted Marines had no equivalent uniform.

Officer Summer Dress: Officers had three summer dress uniforms: the one worn by the enlisted women with the green shoulder straps, summer dress "B," and summer undress "C." The latter two were made of white twill, worsted, or palm beach fabric. Both were worn with a short-sleeved white blouse, and without a necktie or shoulder strap. The "C" uniform was long-sleeved and collarless. On these two uniforms the dress uniform emblems were worn, not on the collar as usual, but on the epaulet, three-fourths of an inch from the armhole seam. The insignia of rank was then centered between the ornament and epaulet button. Lieutenant Colonel Nita Bob Warner remembered that even a lieutenant looked like a four-star general with so much metal on her shoulders.2

Handbags, Shoes, and Hose: There was only one handbag, a brown, rough textured leather purse with a spring closure and shoulder strap. It was always worn over the left shoulder, leaving the right arm free to salute, and until 1952 the strap could be worn either over or under the epaulets of coats. A green cover and strap were added for wear with the summer service and summer dress uniforms.

The woman Marine winter service "A" uniform is modeled by "PFC" Sgt Mary Ann Kennedy, in 1952.

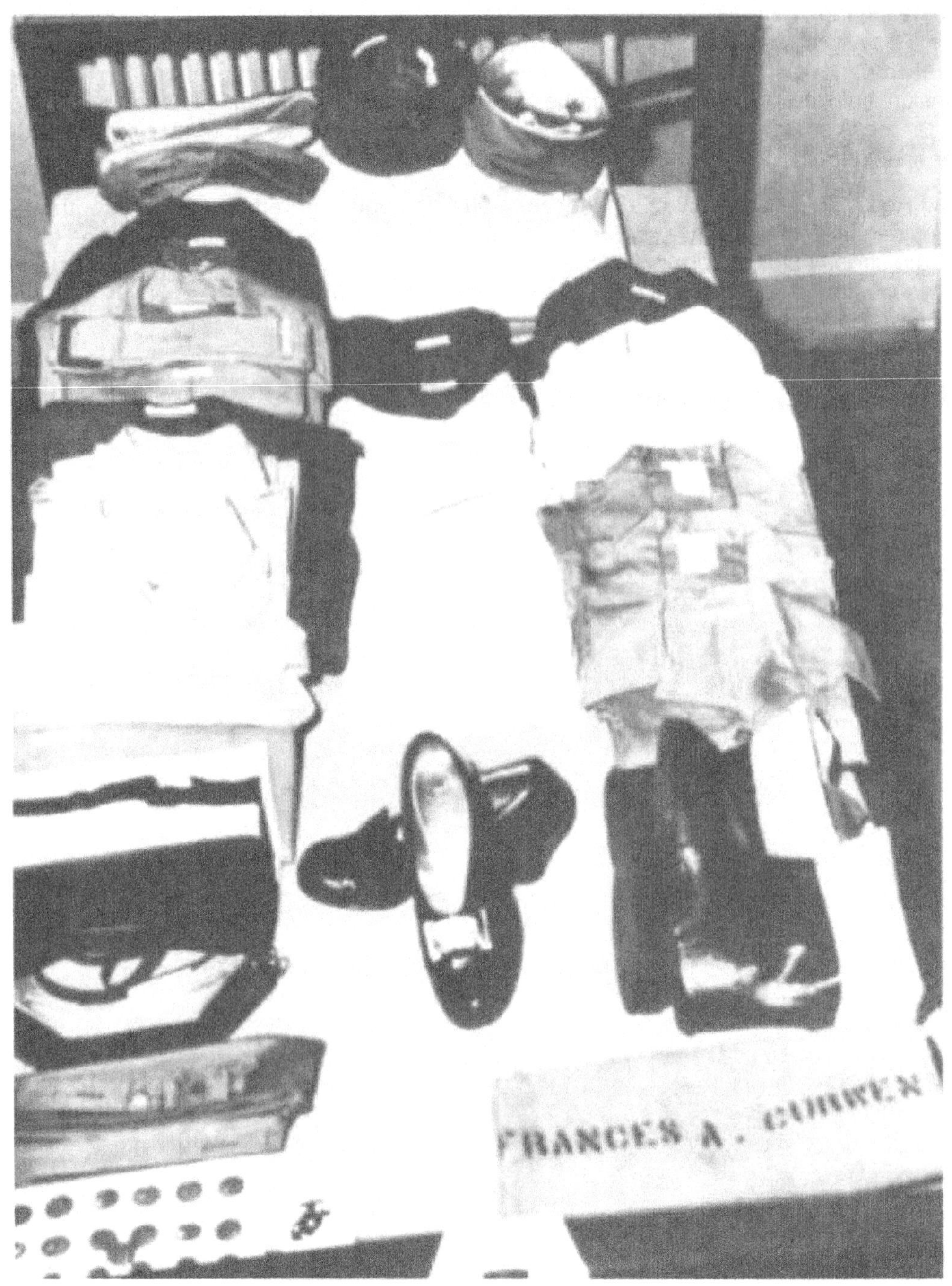

Issued uniform items and gear, cleaned, ironed, and labeled are displayed according to regulations for a "junk on the bunk" inspection in the early 1950s.

Women Marines wore smooth leather oxfords or pumps in dark brown, dark russet, or cordovan color with the service uniform. The pumps, with heels between one and one-half and two and one-half inches were trimmed with a flat bow. Similar white pumps were prescribed for wear with the summer dress uniforms.

Full length, beige stockings were worn with all uniforms. Mesh and seamless hose were prohibited, and cotton hose were worn in ranks. When, during World War II and immediately after, nylon, rayon, and silk stockings were rationed, some women in the other Services used leg makeup, but the Directors of the Women Marines remained firm. Women in the Marine Corps would wear stockings, but never with more than three runs.3

Utilities and Exercise Suits: During World War II, WRs had covert slacks which could be worn for certain duties. The most common work uniform, however, was the olive-drab, cotton utility uniform. The trousers were topped by a bib front and long crossed straps in back. A short-sleeved, matching shirt was worn underneath, and a long-sleeved jacket over all. Enlisted women stenciled their rank on the shirt and jacket sleeves.

The exercise suit was a light beige, seersucker, one-piece bloomer outfit covered by a front-buttoned skirt. Known as the peanut suit, because of the color and the crinkled appearance, it was issued until the late 1950s.

Grooming, Handkerchiefs, and Unmentionables: During this period, the regulations specified that, if worn, lipstick and nail polish would harmonize with the color of the red cap cord on the winter service cap. The same rule applied in the summer, even though the red cap cord was stored out of sight for the season. Rouge, mascara, and hair tints, if used, had to be inconspicuous. It was nearly impossible for a woman to color or bleach her hair since it had to be the color indicated on her identification card. Hair could touch, but not cover, the collar.

Officer summer dress "A" adorned 2dLt Marcella J. Greene in 1950. Emblems are worn on the epaulets.

Col Katherine A. Towle poses in the evening dress suggested for women officers. The uniform designed by Mainbocher was patterned after the evening dress uniform of the men. It was officially adopted one day prior to the Marine Corps' 175th birthday celebration.

Slips and girdles were required in uniform. At the time, the regulations did not specify color or style. Handkerchiefs could be khaki when the khaki shirt was worn, otherwise, they had to be white.

The Beginnings of Change — 1950 Formal Evening/Mess Dress Uniforms

Officers: A new uniform was added in November 1950 when the famed designer, Mainbocher, designed a formal evening dress uniform for Colonel Towle. She wore it, the first time, to the Marine Corps Birthday Ball on 10 November, held at the Sail Loft of the Naval Gun Factory in Washington, D.C.

Tall and stately, Colonel Towle wore the uniform beautifully, and Major Harry D. Elms, a member of the Uniform Board at the time, remembers that Mainbocher was much taken with Colonel Towle's appearance and demeanor.4 When she suggested to the couturier that the uniform fit too closely, Mainbocher told her "Just remember, Colonel, when you drink a martini, do not eat the olive."5

Patterned after the full dress uniform of the men, Colonel Towle's uniform consisted of a midnight blue mess jacket with a straight, formal skirt slightly flared at the hem, over a tailored blouse of white silk, trimmed at the waist with a scarlet silk cummerbund. The jacket, which bore an even dozen gilt buttons, six on each side, was worn open. Its scarlet collar and the cuffs of the sleeves were adorned with gold and silver bullion embroidery in the form of oak leaves and acorns.

A broad, square-tipped tie was worn at the neck, held with a silver ring bearing the Marine Corps officer's dress ornament.

Colonel Towle's insignia of rank, the eagle, was embroidered in silver bullion on the shoulder tabs. Also in silver and gold bullion were small replicas of the Marine insignia on the collar points. The headpiece was a scarlet wool tiara, also embroidered. Colonel Towle carried a small, envelope-style handbag of her own on which she pinned her insignia of rank. A cloak was not designed so she borrowed a male officer's boat cloak for the occasion. Newspaper accounts spoke of the stunning ensemble and dazzled guests.6

The evening dress uniform was initially intended to be worn by women officers at state and diplomatic functions, but its manufacture presented some problems. The original had been made, in the manner of high fashion, expressly for Colonel Towle. There was no pattern to be adopted for general use. All the embroidery had been done by hand by an Italian woman in New "fork City and mass production was out of the question.7

When Colonel Hamblet became Director of Women Marines in 1953, she had a similar uniform made up by Rienzi in Philadelphia. She selected a softer, more feminine shirt with a pleated front to conceal the buttons.8 She felt, however, that the new uniform fit her poorly, so Mainbocher was commissioned to make another and she subsequently gave the Rienzi uniform to Colonel Henderson, her successor. When Colonel Hamblet left for Naples in 1959, it was discovered that there was no sample woman's cloak at the Marine Corps Uniform Board, so she left her own behind. The third Director of Women Marines, Colonel Henderson, borrowed the cloak on the occasions when she wore the evening dress uniform. Between 1950 and 1964, only two evening dress uniforms for women were made: one for Colonel Towle and the other for Colonel Hamblet.9

Colonel Henderson was not completely satisfied with the tiara. To begin with, the scarlet color was not becoming to the redheaded Director. During her tenure a black tiara was made optional, a uniform modification that caused no concern since only the Director was required to have the formal dress outfit. When asked by the President of the Uniform Board for comments on the evening dress uniform, she submitted:

Tiara—It is suggested that an attempt be made to slightly redesign this tiara. As it is presently designed, the wearer has difficulty in keeping it on her head. In addition, the extreme points on the tiara makes the wearer feel as if she had wings or horns on her head—depending upon her mood.10

The tiara was not redesigned. When in 1964 evening dress uniforms finally became available to all officers, a plain unembroidered one in keeping with tradition was made for company grade officers. Field grade officers still wore the tiara decorated with gold bullion embroidery. Finally, in 1973, to the pleasure of some, and the dismay of others, it was deleted as a uniform item.

In 1964, Major Jenny Wrenn, on her own initiative, designed an evening dress uniform that resembled a long, formal, evening suit. It was much less complicated than the Mainbocher model. Master Sergeant Barbara Jean Dulinsky made the sketches which were sent to the Marine Corps Supply Depot at Philadelphia for evaluation. The Marine Corps tailors made a uniform, of Major Wrenn's design, for the Director of Women Marines, Colonel Barbara J. Bishop.11

The Wrenn uniform included a white mess dress jacket, as well as the midnight blue evening dress jacket, both trimmed with a scarlet collar. The collar of the field grade model was lightly embroidered. Rank insignia and Marine emblems were the standard detachable type rather than of embroidered gold bullion. A short skirt was added for less formal occasions and a plain black envelope style handbag was carried. Shoes were black suede or fabric.

In November of 1964, when Lyndon B. Johnson was elected President, the Presidential Inaugural Committee asked for Marine field grade officers to act as military aides during the Inaugural events. For the first time, two women were nominated, Lieutenant Colonels Wrenn and Mary E. Bane. Since neither owned the requisite evening dress uniform, the Marine Corps tailors in Philadelphia again made up the Wrenn-designed uniform. There was little time between the election and the Inauguration, so the women had to make several quick round trips to Philadelphia and at the very last moment the uniforms were delivered to them in Washington by staff car. Unfortunately, the beautifully tailored uniforms were not worn for the intended occasion as the women officers were assigned to less formal functions, a reception for the governors and a distinguished ladies reception at the National Gallery of Art to which they wore their dress blues.12

By 1966, the pattern and a kit of fabric and findings was available to women officers. Due to the small number involved no manufacturer was interested in making the uniform, so each had to find a willing tailor. It was not an easy task because the pattern and specifications resembled a technical manual. The kit cost between $70 and $100, depending upon rank. The tailoring could run an additional $500.

Staff Noncommissioned Officers: On 11 May 1972, the Commandant of the Marine Corps, General Cushman, approved a recommendation of the Uniform Board that an experimental staff noncommissioned officer evening/mess dress uniform be made for, and tested by the Sergeant Major of the Women Marines. It was styled after the officer uniform with a few modifications. There were no shoulder straps, nor collar or cuff ornamentation. The sleeves were finished with the traditional peaked cuffs. Since male staff noncommissioned officers had no corresponding formal uniform, it was decided to forego the long skirt. The dress insignia of grade, gold on scarlet, was sewn on the sleeves. Gilt Marine Corps emblems were worn.

Sergeant Major June V. Andler was the first to wear the test uniform. She introduced it at the Marine Corps League Banquet on 11 August 1972 in Anaheim, California, and at the Woman Marine Association convention a week later in Hawaii. She took it on inspection trips and modeled it for the WMs at Parris Island, El Toro, Camp Pendleton, San Diego, Hawaii, and, of course at Headquarters Marine Corps. The response was enthusiastic and the uniform was approved on 30 May 1973. Subsequently, long skirts became very stylish and acceptable at even casual affairs, a fashion change that prompted the Marine Corps to add a long skirt to the staff noncommissioned officers' evening dress uniform on 13 September 1976.

The Mainbocher Wardrobe, 1950-1952

The Commandant, General Clifton B. Cates, wanted dress blue uniforms for the women Marines. In the fall of 1950 well-known American designers were contacted, and First Lieutenant Ben Alice Day (later Munn), a World War II supply officer, and Captain Harry Elms of the Uniform Board personally interviewed couturiers including Hattie Carnegie and Mainbocher.13 Mainbocher was the unanimous choice of the Uniform Board, Quartermaster General of the Marine Corps, and the Director of Women Marines. The Chicago-born designer, most expensive of the world's dressmakers, was not very interested, but his enormous respect for Colonel Towle prevailed and he accepted. Lieutenant Colonel Munn believes his lack of enthusiasm stemmed from the fact that when he designed the World War II WAVE uniform he was not paid the one dollar stipulated in the contract and would have liked it as a remembrance. When the new WM uniforms were finished, Lieutenant Day and Captain Elms made a point of presenting him a framed dollar bill, the price agreed upon.

Col Barbara J. Bishop, the Director of Women Marines, wears the officer mess dress uniform with a short black skirt, a red cummerbund, white gloves, and white jacket trimmed with scarlet collar, in June 1964.

SgtMaj June V. Andler, Sergeant Major of Women Marines, is photographed in 1972 wearing the staff noncommissioned officer evening dress uniform with short skirt, red cummerbund, and miniature medals.

Mainbocher, once involved, asked to do an entire new wardrobe, redesigning the current uniforms to be more feminine and more becoming. Further, he wanted to work with the accessories, to include chevrons and service stripes, which he found too large and out of proportion for women. One item he did not change was the cap which Mainbocher said was the most attractive hat worn by women of any service.

He not only designed the uniform but coordinated manufacturing and fabric selection. He personally supervised every run at the manufacturers, since at the time quality control was not yet a standard business practice.

Lieutenant Day and Captain Elms visited his elegant salon in New York bringing with them photographs of the male Marines' complete wardrobe as well as historical prints of old Marine Corps uniforms. Working with these and aware of Marine Corps traditions and standards of appearance, he produced a blue uniform, winter and summer service uniform, raincoat and overcoat for all WMs along with new chevrons for the enlisted women and a white uniform for the officers.

When interviewed by the press, Mainbocher expressed his theories on feminine uniforms thus:

Whether a woman is wearing a custom designed suit or a uniform, she should look feminine. That was the thought I kept in mind while working on the Marine uniforms, and it was quite a job, considering all the traditions that had to be incorporated in the design.14

The final designs, approved on 27 December 1951, went into production, with the exception of the officer's white uniform. Mainbocher supervised all fittings and was a meticulous taskmaster not only of his tailors, but of the women Marine models. With a glance, by the drape of the uniform, he could tell whether or not a model was wearing a girdle and slip. He never allowed his fashions to be worn without either item no matter how thin and svelte the wearer. When all was ready, a formal presentation was held on 28 August 1952 in the auditorium of the Marine Barracks, 8th & I Streets, Washington, DC. The Commandant sent invitations to a selected guest list including all the Marine Corps general officers in the area. At the showing, each model was escorted by a male Marine in comparable uniform. Colonel Towle modeled her formal evening dress ensemble.

Sergeant Mary Ann Kennedy modeled the summer uniform, a one-piece shirtwaist dress of green and white striped nylon-dacron, with a matching long-sleeved jacket. The jacket worn over the short sleeved dress had a nipped-in waist and its collar, epaulets, and cuffs were outlined in green piping. The accompanying overseas cap was of the same fabric. Washing ease and wrinkle resistance were the chief features of the new summer fabric.

Sergeant Lois King modeled the forest green serge winter uniform. The fitted jacket featured sleeves finished with the traditional peaked cuff. A six-gore skirt, an entirely new pale green cotton broadcloth skirtwaist, and an ascot-shaped forest green necktie completed the outfit.

Technical Sergeant Margaret Babcock introduced the new dress blue uniform of a design similar to the green serge. Inspiration for the trim was provided by a print of an 1859 Marine officer's overcoat. Scarlet piping emphasized the collar and shoulder detail of the blue jacket, traditional Marine bracket-shaped cuffs had three gold buttons. Chevrons for the enlisted women were gold on scarlet. A short-sleeved, action-backed dacron shirtwaist was worn with a blue, ascot-shaped tie.

Sergeant Patricia Norman modeled the lightweight, green raincoat of nylon and rayon. It featured a squared-off collar rather than points, bone buttons, and a full belt.

Sergeant Jo Anne Monette wore the forest green double breasted overcoat of kersey. Of a modified princess design, a box pleat held in by a belt gave fullness in the back.

Designed by Mainbocher in 1952, new uniforms are modeled on the lawn of the National Capitol by PFC Margaret Keefe and Sgts Margaret Dill and Jo Anne Monette.

The fashion show over, the guests attended a sunset parade followed by a reception at Quarters 1 hosted by the Assistant Commandant of the Marine Corps, Lieutenant General Gerald C. Thomas and Mrs.

Thomas.15 This was the same General Thomas who, as the Director, Plans and Policy Division in 1946, opposed so steadfastly the integration of women into the Regular Marine Corps.

The new uniforms were well received and a model in dress blues was featured on the cover of Parade, the Sunday picture magazine, on 31 August 1952.

Mainbocher was willing to design a utility uniform but since there were plans for a standardized utility uniform among the services, his offer was declined. Rather, Headquarters Marine Corps had the bib overalls redesigned. The bib was removed and the olive green slacks were made of the male Marines' utility fabric. The aim was to keep it simple. The overseas cap was redesigned slightly to follow the new dacron one which fit the women better. To get a manufacturer to accept such a small order, it was appended to a much more lucrative order for men's uniforms, a ploy often used in procuring WM uniform items.

Male Marines at Headquarters became uncommonly interested in the new uniforms, not because of style but due to the new fabrics. Dupont Corporation sent a team of scientists to demonstrate the properties of dacron, a new material at the time. It was a pure, fireproof fabric and the men were greatly impressed. They could picture its usefulness for men's uniforms to save laundry expense and for combat purposes. When first introduced this particular dacron was used to make firehoses.

Eventually the World War II uniforms were declared obsolete; old summer uniforms could not be worn after December 1956, winter uniforms after June 1957.

Officers' Dress White Uniform: Mainbocher designed a white uniform at the time he did the new wardrobe in 1952. Distribution was delayed until 1958 due to difficulty in obtaining a suitable wash-and-wear fabric that would remain white. The uniform was styled after the winter service uniform, and worn with the same white short-sleeved dacron shirt prescribed for the dress blues. A bright blue-green cap, ascot shaped tie, and white pumps completed the outfit. At first, a green cover was worn over the brown handbag, just as was done in World War II. When the brown handbag was later replaced by a new style, a small envelope-styled purse was adopted for certain dress uniforms. When carried with the whites, it was, of course, slipped into a blue-green cover.

The white uniform is worn only by officers, in keeping with Marine Corps tradition. During World War II, enlisted WRs had a dress white uniform while the men did not. Conversely, the men had a dress blue uniform while the women did not.

After Mainbocher

The Mainbocher wardrobe was the only large-scale uniform change for women Marines. His theories on dressing military women have proved sound since at least two of his designs, the dress blue and winter service uniforms, have remained virtually unchanged for the 25 years from 1952 until this writing. Ensuing changes came piecemeal and usually were directed by economy rather than style.

The Department of Defense plan to standardize certain items and fabrics made their impact on WM uniforms in the early 1960s.

Summer Uniforms 1961-1977: There was no middle ground for the acceptance of the one-piece dress. Either a woman liked it or did not. For those who were long- or short-waisted, the summer uniform with its band at the waist was nearly impossible to alter properly. But the fabric was all it was touted to be. After wearing and caring for the easily wrinkled seersucker uniform which by custom was starched so that a skirt could stand at attention, unsupported on the laundry room floor, the women Marines found the dacron dress to be truly carefree. One could wear it all day, get caught in the rain, and still look fresh. Unfortunately, the fabric became scarce and expensive and the Marine Corps had no choice but to consider a material shared by the other services since the increased quantity ordered reduced the price. Colonel Margaret M. Henderson remembers that one of her most disappointing days as Director of Women Marines was one when she had to acquiesce on the fabric for the summer uniforms.18

In 1962, a dacron-cotton cloth used by the Women's Army Corps was approved for use by women Marines. Logistically, it became very complicated since uniforms of mixed fabric could not be worn. The dress, jacket, and cap had to match, and supplies available for each issue to recruits varied from one item to another and from one size to another. When the fabric was again changed to polyester-cotton, more confusion resulted.

In 1966, an entirely new two-piece dress made of the same polyester-cotton, corded, green-and-white striped material was approved. Recruits began to receive it in July 1967. The old-style uniform became obsolete and could no longer be worn after 1 July 1972. Women officers did not wear rank insignia on their new summer caps. Because male Marines continued to wear rank ornaments on their garrison caps, this difference for the women caused a certain amount of confusion. Marines who failed to salute were justified in their claim that it was difficult to recognize women officers. On 20 October 1971, the rank insignia officially was reinstated on the women officers' caps.

Another change involving summer uniforms was seen in 1966 when women officers were authorized to wear the summer dress cap, a bright green version of the winter service and dress blue cap, as an optional item when on leave or liberty. When worn with summer uniform, bronze buttons and insignia were worn rather than gilt buttons and dress insignia. Field grade officers, if they elected to wear the dress cap with the service uniform, were required to wear one with a plain visor, without gold embroidery. In 1969, the regulations were broadened and officers could wear the dress cap on an everyday basis except when in formation. This privilege was extended to staff noncommissioned officers in 1971.

Coats: In time the nipped-in waist and full-pleated back of the Mainbocher coat went out of style. Furthermore, the complicated styling, and excess fabric made it expensive to manufacture. It clearly did not flatter short, stocky figures. In 1966 Mario Mariani, the Marine Corps' designer, introduced a straight-lined, serge overcoat styled after the civilian coats in vogue at the time.17 By the winter of 1967, as old stocks were depleted the new overcoat was issued to recruits.

Shoes: In 1954 the bows on the brown dress shoes became optional except that they could not be removed from the issue pumps. By 1962, long after they became socially acceptable, women Marines were allowed to wear seamless hose as an optional item, but never in formation. The regulation was reversed in 1965 when hose with seams became optional and could not be worn in formation. Finally in 1966, snag-proof, run-resistant stockings of inconspicuous mesh were authorized. In January 1971, the color of hose to be worn with dress blues changed from everyday beige to a gray, smoke shade.

The cotton hose worn by WRs in World War II and for years by WM recruits and officer candidates were universally unpopular. Because of the extreme heat and strenuous schedule followed at both training commands, the absorbent property of cotton stockings was long considered to be a health and comfort feature. Civilian women, upon arriving at Parris Island or Quantico and seeing staff members wearing the unbecoming lisle hose were disbelieving that anyone younger than a grandmother would allow themselves to be seen in public in such an item. It was not an unwelcome announcement that Colonel Bishop made in the Woman Marine Newsletter, Winter 1968, when she wrote:

A traditional article of clothing—not altogether appreciated by the recruits wearing them—will be obsolete when the current stock of cotton hose is exhausted. The old lisle or cotton hose were a necessity for WRs when nylons "went to war". . . . Discarded years before by other women's services, the Marine Corps —always long on tradition—became the "sole user" of cotton hose. At some future date this year, Women Marine recruits may have "lighter" pocketbooks and tender feet, but higher morale and trimmer limbs.18

Umbrellas: All Marines know that umbrellas are not a military item. There is a theory that several armies of old who carried umbrellas went down in defeat because they were more concerned with keeping dry than winning the battle. Women Marines had a plastic cover called a havelock that fit over their cap and a hood that matched their raincoat, but there was always some question about wearing them without the outer coat. The havelocks were difficult to procure and tore easily; the rainhoods were not authorized with the overcoat. Clearly, many WMs wanted an umbrella. In 1972, the Commandant authorized WMs to carry an all-black, plain, standard or folding umbrella as an optional item. The announcement included the caution to carry the umbrella in the left hand so that salutes could be properly rendered. They were not permitted in formation. A story circulated that Colonel Sustad, Director of Women Marines, in her effort to have the umbrella adopted as a uniform item, slipped the proposal through the Commandant by asking him to approve a red umbrella to harmonize with the red cord. He was said to have replied, 'Absolutely not! They'll carry a black umbrella," thereby sanctioning its use. When asked about the story, Colonel Sustad disclaimed it saying, "I would never have been so fresh with the Commandant."19

A green dacron raincoat worn with the winter red wool scarf is modeled by Cpl Carla J. Sacco in 1959.

The green utility uniform with rank stenciled on the sleeves is worn by Sgt Mary A. Kennedy in 1952.

The woman officer white dress "A" uniform with a green tie, purse, and field grade gold embroidered hat, is modeled by Maj Adele Graham in 1971.

Handbags: When black accessories became mandatory, and women of all services adopted a single handbag, WMs lost the rough-textured leather bag for a black vinyl model. In 1970 regulations changed to permit the individual option to carrying the handbag over the left shoulder as usual or with a shortened strap, over the arm. A woman sergeant major asked, "How can you stand at attention for morning colors with a handbag over your arm?" The question remains unanswered.

Grooming and Personal Appearance

The grooming and personal appearance of women Marines changed slowly. World War II regulations prevailed for nearly 30 years. Bright red lipstick, "Montezuma Red," created by Elizabeth Arden for the WRs, and later Revlon's "Certainly Red" were the only shades sold at post exchanges that catered to WMs. The policy was clear: lipstick had to harmonize with the red cap cord of the blue and green caps and the scarlet trim on the formal evening dress uniform, even when the wearer was in the green and white summer uniform or dress whites. In 1971, the regulations were relaxed to allow others shades of lipstick in the summer. Extremes of lavender, purple, white, or flesh color remained prohibited. Nail polish, if worn, had to harmonize with the lipstick or be colorless.

Hairstyles and Wigs: The first major change to hair styles and color regulations came in 1970 when specific hairstyles were not prohibited as long as they were feminine and allowed for the proper wearing of the cap. One reason for the change was the popularity of the Afro hairdo worn by young black women. It also accommodated chignons and twists. Hair tints and bleaches were no longer taboo but were required to harmonize with the person's complexion and color tone. Natural looking wigs were permitted as long as they conformed to regulations.

Lingerie: Girdles and light-colored, full-length slips were the modest underpinning of WMs for 30 years. Paula W. Sentipal remembers that when she reported to boot camp in 1950 she was so thin that with a girdle on her uniform could not be taken in enough to fit her, so she was ordered to buy a larger girdle that would not hold her in.20 Bras were one unmentionable that did not have to be mentioned. Until the women's liberation movement made going braless fashionable in the 1970s, it was never an issue. The uniform regulations of 1976, in the spirit of the times, stated:

Adequate undergarments to include support garments shall be worn to ensure the proper fit, appearance, and opaqueness of the uniform. The conservative appearance of the uniform shall be maintained and undergarments shall not be conspicuously visible.21

Hem lengths: The style of the uniform was able to withstand fashion changes from 1952 to 1977, but hem lengths were as controversial for servicewomen as civilians. When the Mainbocher wardrobe was issued, the regulations specified that skirts would be of a conventional sweep and length, approximately mid-calf.

By the early 1960s, fashion dictated shorter skirts, but regulations persisted. At one point, Lieutenant Colonel Elsie E. Hill, Commanding Officer, Woman Recruit Training Battalion, wrote to the Director of Woman Marines, Colonel Henderson, and asked for guidelines since she agreed with the women that ". . . we look like a bunch of hicks from the sticks."22 Women's fashions being fickle, Headquarters did not want to give specific rules that would necessitate printed changes as skirts went up and down, so in 1963, following the phrase "midcalf' a parenthetical guideline was added that read, "(adjusted to current styles but not extreme)."23 At the same time, the Director's office passed the word informally that two inches below the knee was officially considered acceptable. In more than one women Marine company, skirt shortening parties were held under the watchful eyes of staff noncommissioned officers and officers, who, on their knees and using the width of two fingers as a measuring device, passed judgement on the length of uniform skirts, dresses, and coats.

The green and white striped two-piece summer service dacron uniform with black handbag and pumps was worn by officers and enlisted women in the 1970s.

Skirts continued to rise to the mini-length, and all services except the Marine Corps relented. In a Woman Marine Newsletter of 1970, Colonel Bishop wrote:

. . . conventional sweep and length is currently interpreted as mid-knee, i.e., between the top of the knee and the bottom of the knee. Since the skirt can be worn anywhere between the top of the knee and the bottom of the knee, this allows for some flexibility so that the individual can wear her skirt the length that is most becoming to her.

No doubt the young WMs hoped for more flexibility since civilian skirts were being worn 4 to 6 inches above the knee, but the message from the top woman Marine clearly marked the limits.

The 1976 regulations called for knee-length skirts, not more than one inch above the top of the knee cap nor one inch below the bottom of the knee cap. Alas, as the order was being printed, civilian skirts were back down to mid-calf, completing the full cycle.

Utilities

The hastily designed green utilities available in the early 1950s were not beautiful, but they served their intended purpose as a work uniform. Unfortunately, they were part of the woman Marine wardrobe when most WMs were working in offices. Wearing utilities was vigorously discouraged except when considered absolutely essential because the effect was too masculine. Great pains were taken to keep them out of view and it was an unwritten law that photographs of WMs in utilities were not to be published. The standardization of uniforms by the four services resulted in a common blue utility outfit, dark blue slacks, cap, and sweater, and a light blue shirt. Recruits received the new blue utilities in July 1967 and the green ones were not permitted after July 1971. The new uniform, while more feminine in appearance, was never truly accepted by WMs because it made them look like WAVEs and was not durable. Even male Marines who were chauvinistic about keeping the Marine Corps for men found the blue uniform offensive and decided that they preferred their women Marines to look like Marines. At first, the black insignia of service was worn on the blue cap but the dark color lacked contrast and the gold emblem was adopted on the utility cap in 1970.

The blue utilities were threadbare by the time a woman graduated from boot camp and commanders made their dissatisfaction known to Headquarters. With women Marines subject to assignment as heavy equipment operators, welders, and to similar occupations, a more functional work uniform was needed. On 22 September 1975 the Commandant authorized as an interim measure, a supplementary allowance of male utilities to women to be worn under restricted conditions depending upon their job.24 Wear-testing of several styles began in an effort to find a suitable uniform to replace the blue, which by 1975 had been abandoned by all the other services. In June 1977, General Wilson approved the wearing by women of the male camouflaged field uniform. Combat boots replaced the black oxfords and cushion-sole socks took the place of anklets for WMs at work in certain jobs and in training.25

Consistent with an age when male/female roles were less clearly defined, there appeared to be less urgency to prove that service women were feminine. Photographs of the jet mechanics, welders, and officer candidates wearing utilities were taken and published and only the older officers and staff noncommissioned officers were scandalized.

CHAPTER 15

Laurels and Traditions

Legion of Merit — Navy and Marine Corps Medal — Bronze Star Medal — Joint Service Commendation Medal - Dominican Republic — WM Anniversary — Women Marines and Mess Night - Molly Marine — Women Marines Association

Women Marines recognized for meritorious performance and bravery have been awarded many of the same medals, ribbons, and letters of appreciation and commendation presented to male Marines under similar circumstances. The highest decoration, at this writing, worn by women in the Corps is the Legion of Merit. A few are privileged to wear the Navy and Marine Corps Medal, Bronze Star, and the Navy Commendation Medal, and a number have been awarded the Joint Service Commendation Medal and the Navy Achievement Medal.

Legion of Merit

Following a tradition set in World War II, the Legion of Merit, the Navy's fifth ranking decoration, falling immediately below the Silver Star and conferred on individuals ". . . who have distinguished themselves by exceptionally meritorious conduct in the performance of outstanding services. . . ." has been awarded to all Directors of Women Marines. Their citations underscore the particular challenges faced by each one, and read consecutively, they trace the history of women in the Marine Corps through the stages of organization, expansion, and total integration.1

Only one woman Marine, other than the Directors, was the recipient of the Legion of Merit. Upon retirement in May 1975, Colonel Hazel E. Benn, Head, Educational Services Branch, was cited for her work in formulating educational programs for both officers and enlisted Marines.2

Colonel Benn's career was unique in that as a Reserve officer on active duty, she worked for 24 years at the same job. She was the Marine Corps' expert on education and as new programs developed, her responsibilities increased. A member of the second officer candidate class at Mount Holyoke College in 1943, she served as a personnel/administrative officer in World War II. Following the war, after receiving a graduate degree in education, she worked for the Navy as an education specialist, and in 1951, was asked to return to the Marine Corps. A principal architect of the Serviceman's Opportunity College, she helped to develop the concept that removed the traditional academic barrier in the areas of residency, transfer of credit by examination, and acceptance of service schools and service experience for academic credit, thereby easing the road to college degrees for countless Marines.3 Colonel Benn was among the first women Marines to be promoted to colonel in 1968, only months after that rank was opened to women.

Navy and Marine Corps Medal

The Navy and Marine Corps Medal, ranking eighth in precedence —between the Distinguished Flying Cross and the Bronze Star —and the Naval Service's highest recognition for heroism not involving combat has been awarded to four women Marines. Staff Sergeant Barbara O. Barnwell, first woman ever to win the medal, was decorated on 7 August 1953 by General Lemuel C. Shepherd, Jr., Commandant of the Marine Corps, for saving a Marine's life in the Atlantic Ocean off Camp Lejeune. A Marine since May 1949, she was attached to the staff of the Inspector-Instructor, 1st Air and Naval Gunfire Liaison Company at Fort Schuyler, New York, at the time of the incident.4 Her citation reads:

Hearing a cry for help from a man struggling in the heavy surf some 50 feet outward from her position while she was swimming in deep water approximately 120 yards from the shore, Sergeant Barnwell immediately swam to the rescue and, although severely scratched on the arm and repeatedly dragged beneath the surface by the drowning Marine, secured a hold on him and commenced to swim to the beach. Despite the treacherous undertow which constantly carried her outward from the shore, she bravely maintained her hold until she had reached shallow water and, assisted by a lifeguard, succeeded in bringing the unconscious man to the safety of the beach. By her exceptional courage, daring initiative and selfless efforts on behalf of another in face of grave peril. Sergeant Barnwell was directly instrumental in saving the Marine's life and upheld the highest traditions of the United States Naval Service.5

Staff Sergeant Barnwell struggled for 20 exhausting minutes to rescue Private First Class Frederick Hernandez Roman. Once she saw that artificial respiration was successful and that the man was going to live, she walked away without even giving her name. Roman's was, after all, the third life she had saved. When she herself was only a child of 11 she saved a seven-year-old from drowning. Later, at 16 she brought a young woman safely to shore.

In addition to the medal presentation in the Commandant's office, Staff Sergeant Barnwell was honored, along with six male officers, at a retreat ceremony at the Marine Barracks, Washington, D.C. It was the first time that a woman was so honored.8

Gunnery Sergeant Dorothy L. Kearns became the second woman Marine in history to receive the Navy and Marine Corps Medal when it was presented to her by Colonel Margaret M. Henderson, Director of Women Marines, on 25 June 1963 at a parade at the Iwo Jima Memorial in Arlington.7 The award read:

For heroic conduct on the morning of 5 February 1961 while serving with the United States Marine Corps Recruiting Station, San Francisco, California. Hearing cries from help emanating from an upstairs apartment in the same building in which she resided, Gunnery Sergeant Kearns immediately rushed to the assistance of a woman who was being attacked with a knife by a mentally deranged man. After pulling the assailant from the victim, disarming him, and forcing him away, she rendered first aid to the victim and attempted to calm the attacker. She then telephoned the hospital which, in turn, notified the police. While Gunnery Sergeant Kearns was admitting the police at the apartment building entrance, the deranged man again armed himself and succeeded in inflicting fatal wounds upon the victim as the police were entering the room. By her courageous and selfless efforts in the face of grave personal risk, Gunnery Sergeant Kearns upheld the highest traditions of the United States Naval Service.8

A World War II Marine, Gunnery Sergeant Kearns had been one of the women retained at Headquarters Marine Corps after the war, serving continuously until her retirement in May 1966.

In 1955, Maj Hazel E. Benn, USMCR, was head of Education and Information Section, Special Services, Personnel Department, HQMC. She received the Legion of Merit upon retirement in 1975 for formulating innovative educational programs for Marines.

SSgt Barbara O. Barnwell (third from left) was awarded the Navy and Marine Corps Medal on 7 August 1953 by Gen Lemuel C. Shepherd, Jr., for saving a Marine's life in the Atlantic Ocean off Camp Lejeune. Director Col Julia E. Hamblet (right) attended.

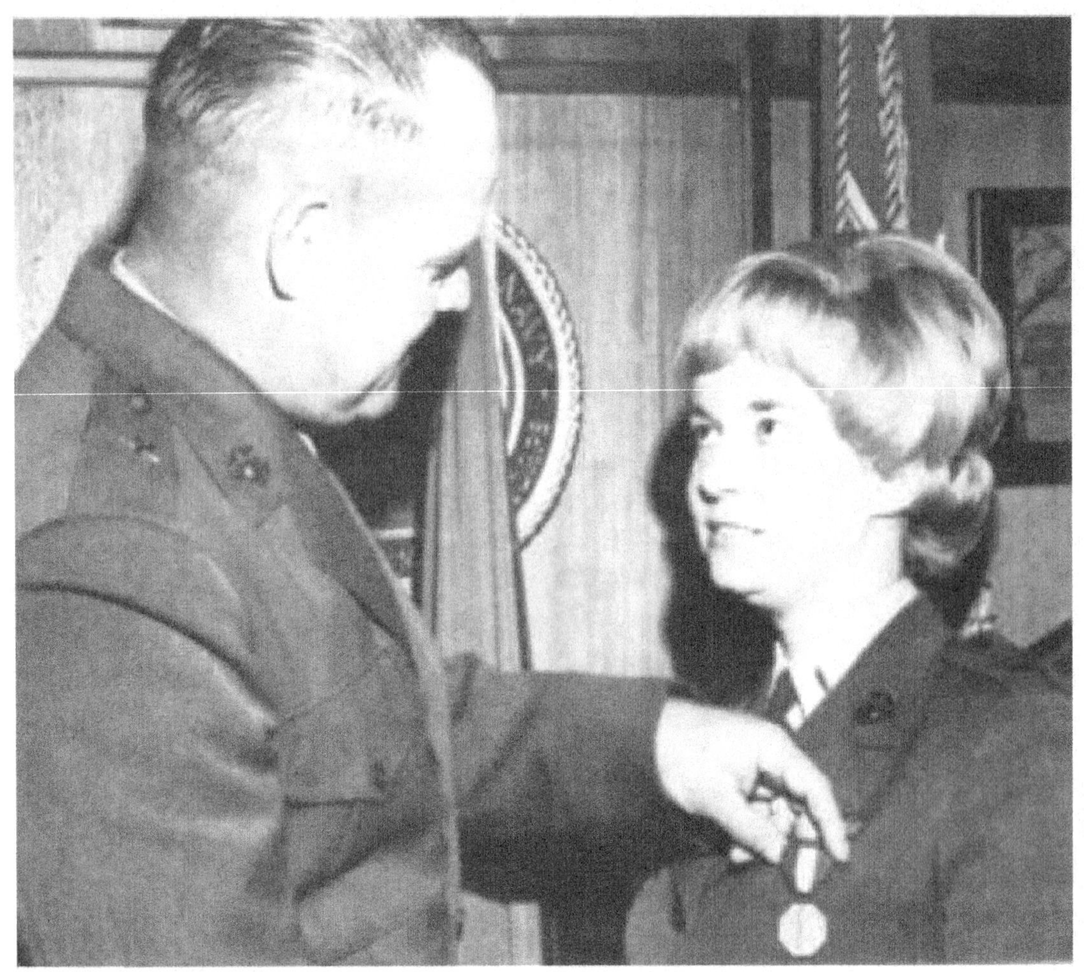

1stLt Vanda K. Brame was presented the Navy and Marine Corps Medal by BGen Harry C. Olson, Commanding General, Marine Corps Supply Center, Barstow, California, on 24 November 1970, for heroism in thwarting the holdup of a blind man's shop in Iowa.

GySgt Dorothy L. Kearns is presented the Navy and Marine Corps Medal by Col Margaret M. Henderson, Director of Women Marines, in 25 June 1963 ceremonies, for rushing to the assistance of a woman being attacked with a knife by a mentally deranged man.

First Lieutenant Vanda K. Brame (later Bresnan), serving at the Marine Corps Officer Selection Office in Des Moines, Iowa, was awarded the Navy and Marine Corps Medal for thwarting the holdup of a blind man's shop on 10 April 1970. Having lunch in the Federal Building Lunch Shop, the petite lieutenant saw a man taking money from an unattended cash drawer while an accomplice stood guard. The citation describing her heroic reaction read:

Immediately realizing that the owner was unaware of the attempted robbery and helpless to defend his property, First Lieutenant Brame unhesitantly, and without regard for her own safety, pursued, seized, and threw the thief to the floor. The accomplice became unnerved by her aggressive action and fled. The thief succeeded in breaking away, but he dropped the stolen money as he attempted to escape on foot. She continued to pursue him and attracted the attention of several onlookers who joined the chase and apprehended the man after he had run several blocks. It was through her courageous and heroic determination in the face of danger that the handicapped owner was saved from bodily harm and personal loss, and the thief was captured, placed in the hands of the police, and finally identified as a potentially dangerous user of narcotics. First Lieutenant Brame's heroic action reflected great credit upon herself and upheld the highest traditions of the Marine Corps and the United States Naval Service.9

Brigadier General Harry C. Olson, Commanding General, Marine Corps Supply Center, Barstow, presented the medal to Lieutenant Brame, then commanding officer of the Woman Marine Company there, at an awards and retirement parade on 25 November 1970.10

Lance Corporal Sheryl L. Young received the highest noncombat decoration for heroism in June 1977 for her part in freeing a mother and two small children from a wrecked car moments before it exploded. On 15 October 1976, while students at the Legal Services School at Camp Pendleton, then Private Young and a companion, Private First Class Thomas J. Maue, were walking in town when they heard a crash. Running to the intersection, they heard cries from an auto engulfed in flames. Private First Class Maue removed the occupants one by one, handed them to Private Young, and both Marines administered first aid and comforted the victims until the police and fire departments arrived."

LCpl Sheryl L. Young was presented the Navy and Marine Corps Medal by BGen Robert J. Chadwick, Director, Judge Advocate Division, in June 1977, for her part in freeing a mother and two small children from a wrecked car moments before it exploded.

Brigadier General Robert J. Chadwick, Director of the Judge Advocate Division, presented the Navy and Marine Corps Medal to Lance Corporal Young on behalf of the President of the United States for the daring rescue. Her citation read:

Upon arriving at the scene of a traffic accident in Ocean-side, which left three victims pinned in a burning automobile, Lance Corporal Young, with complete disregard for her own safety and fully aware of the personal dangers involved, unhesitatingly assisted her Marine companion in removing the victims from the vehicle before the gas tank exploded. Her courageous and prompt actions in the face of great personal risk undoubtedly saved three lives; thereby reflecting great credit upon herself and upholding the highest traditions of the Marine Corps and the United States Naval Service.12

Bronze Star Medal

The Bronze Star, with combat "V," awarded to per-, sons who have distinguished themselves by heroic or meritorious achievement or service in connection with military operations against an armed enemy, has been awarded to three women Marine officers, all of whom served in Vietnam. The first recipient, Captain Shirley E. Leaverton, served as the Marine Corps Officer in Charge, Marine Corps Personnel Section, on the staff of the Commander, Naval Forces, Vietnam, from April 1970 until 1971. Serving as Historians, Military History Branch, Secretary, Joint Staff, United States Military Assistance Command, Vietnam, Lieutenant Colonel Ruth J. O'Holleran and later Lieutenant Colonel Ruth F. Reinholz were also awarded the Bronze Star Medal.13

Joint Service Commendation Medal

Women Marines recognized for superior performance on joint staffs, especially for duty in Europe and in Vietnam, have often been awarded the Joint Service Commendation Medal. The first recipient, Captain Elaine I. Primeau, who was fatally injured in an automobile accident while on duty on the staff of the Commander in Chief, U. S. Forces, Europe, was decorated posthumously in the spring of 1964.14

Dominican Republic

The first woman Marine to be assigned attache duty coincidentally became the first to serve under hostile fire. Staff Sergeant Josephine S. Gebers (later Davis), intelligence specialist and administrative assistant to the Air Force attache, reported to Santo Domingo in July 1963. During the turmoil that followed the overthrow of the government in April 1965, Staff Sergeant Gebers was offered the opportunity to leave with the American women and children but chose to remain at her post. She assisted in the evacuation and then, in addition to her duties, took charge of the commissary to ensure equitable distribution of available supplies; prepared food armed with only an electric fry pan, a toaster, and a hot plate; brought meals to the ambassador twice daily; and took turns at the embassy switchboard.15

At the outbreak of the revolt, rebels surrounded the embassy complex and the staff was confined for nearly 10 days until the 6th Marine Expeditionary Unit landed. In a letter to Staff Sergeant Joan S. Ambrose, dated 7 May 1965, Staff Sergeant Gebers wrote:

I have been living in the Attache office, sleeping on the floor, chair or anything I can grab, fixing chow for the attaches and male clerks etc., running across the street with messages as the telephones were out under gunfire, wandering around in the dark . no electricity or water, everything was out. Almost all the Americans here have invested in freezers and we all lost hundreds of dollars of frozen foods. I managed to get back to my apartment in time to give all my frozen food to my Dominican neighbors, so I don't feel it was a total loss. My apartment is located in a neutral zone and has not been the center of activity. My landlord and neighbors are watching my apartment so no one can loot it.

Joannie, I still can't believe all that has happened. The first day, the Marines landed of course, was quite a thrill and all so exciting. They drove in in trucks, jeeps, tanks, LVTs, etc. and scattered into their positions all around the embassy. Of course that night and for a few days following, it wasn't so thrilling as we were being fired on by nearby snipers.16

On 1 September 1966, in a ceremony in his office, General Wallace M. Greene, Jr., presented the Joint Service Commendation Medal to Gunnery Sergeant Gebers, then administrative chief to the Commandant. Additionally, she was authorized to wear the Armed Forces Expeditionary Medal and later, the Combat

Action Ribbon —reportedly the first WM to do so. First Sergeant Josephine Gebers Davis remained on active duty until August 1971.17

SSgt Josephine S. Gebers, who later was authorized to wear the Armed Forces Expeditionary Medal and Combat Action Ribbon as a result of hostile action in the overthrow of the Dominican Republic government in April 1965, reads the Commandant's Marine Corps birthday message on 10 November 1965, at the U.S. Embassy, Santo Domingo.

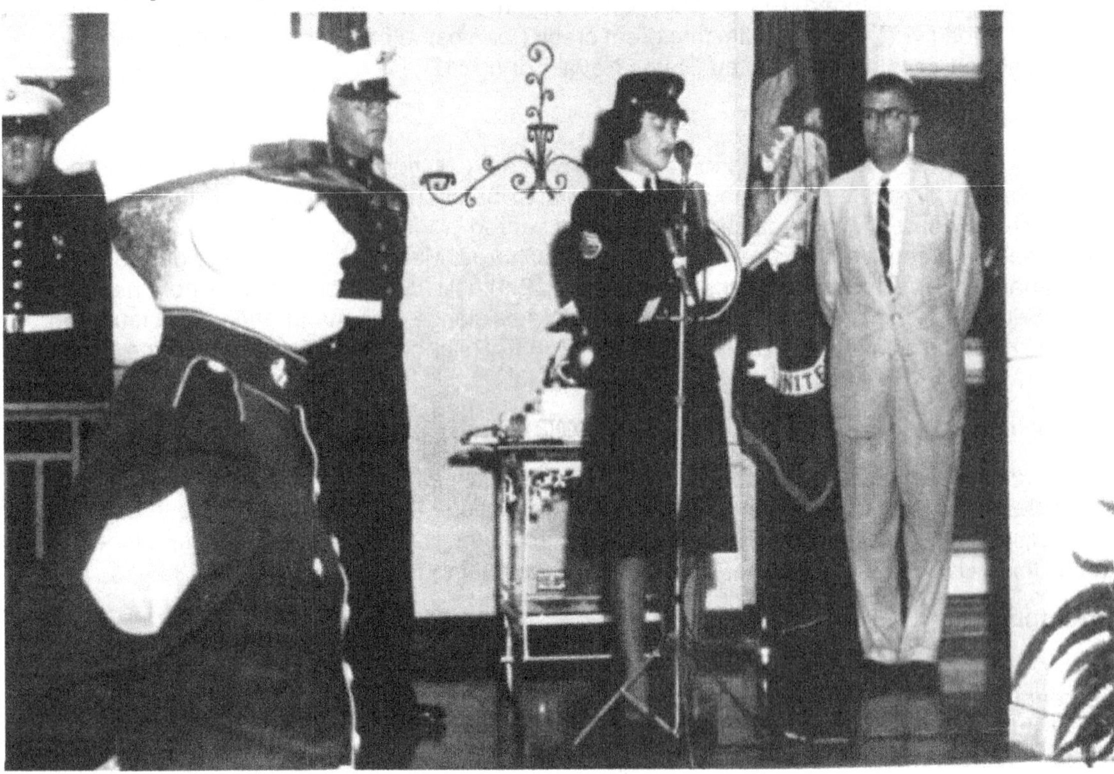

WM Anniversary

The tradition began on 13 February 1944 when much was made of the first anniversary of the entry of women into the Marine Corps. Mrs. Franklin D. Roosevelt, wife of the President; Acting Secretary of the Navy Ralph A. Baird; the Commandant of the Marine Corps, General Vandegrift; and Colonel Streeter headed the list of dignitaries at a ceremony conducted at Fort Myer, Virginia.18 Since then, the anniversary of the women Marines has been the subject of some controversy—at times celebrated with much encouragement and at other times purposely neglected by the upper levels at Headquarters in an effort to encourage all Marines to acknowledge one birthday, the 10th of November. To further complicate the issue, the women who served in World War I questioned the use of 1943 as a point of reference. Colonel Towle wrote a memorandum on the subject in 1951 stating:

The formation of the Marine Corps Women's Reserve of World War II was officially announced by the CMC, General Thomas Holcomb, on 13 February 1943, under the provisions of the Naval Reserve Act of 1938, as amended. It is that anniversary which is recognized each year by women who served in World War II; hence the Eighth Anniversary, 13 February 1951.19

During World War II and immediately after, the celebration of the occasion was an effective way to raise morale, keep up the interest of former WMs, and in general to enhance the prestige of women in the service. Celebrations have varied according to local customs, but normally included a cake-cutting ceremony attended by the commanding general, the battalion commander, and all WMs, officers and enlisted, at the noon meal at the mess hall; formal messages from the Commandant and the Director of Women Marines; a women Marine color guard to raise the flag; and an evening party, often a formal dance. A sizable number of male Marines took up the habit of joining the women in celebrating the anniversary. Long after he retired, former Commandant General Greene continued to call the Director of Women Marines on 13 February to wish her a "Happy Anniversary."20

Mrs. John B. Cook, wife of Brigadier General Cook, said that she never can forget the date of the WM anniversary since it coincides with her wedding anniversary. Twice the battalion commander of women Marines, the general made it a point to celebrate their mutual anniversaries together. Mrs. Cook remembers that one 13 February in Philadelphia, when he was not commanding women Marines, the general took her to a restaurant for dinner, but as soon as the meal was finished, he said, "Well, let's go the club and have a drink with the WMs."21

Colonel Randolph McC. Pate, Director of Division of Reserve during the post-World War II period, inaugurated the tradition of giving red roses to the Director of Women Marines on 13 February—one for each year being commemorated. Major Hamblet, as Director of the Women's Reserve, received the first bouquet. Later, when the Director became a member of the Commandant's staff, each succeeding Commandant continued the custom 22 Sometime in the 1970s, as emphasis on a separate anniversary for women waned, Colonel Sustad received the last bouquet of red roses from General Cushman.

In addition to the roses, for many years, the Commandant sent a formal message to all women Marines to mark the special day. On the occasion of the eighth anniversary of the founding of the Women's Reserve, General Cates, then Commandant, wrote gallantly to Colonel Towle:

It was a proud day in the annals of the Corps when the women joined us in 194}. Your record of achievement since then well merited the permanent recognition of Women Marines. The filling of your ranks by Regulars and Reserves since the outbreak in Korea has greatly aided our Corps to attain new glories. All ranks in the Corps join me today in a fond salute to our "lady Marines."23

In 1933, Headquarters encouraged all commands to promote, celebrate, and publicize the observance, but in 1954, the Chief of Staff directed that nothing should ". . . emanate from this Headquarters in connection with the 11th anniversary of the women Marines, 13 February 1954."24 Two years later, the Commandant, General Pate sent a similar message to the Director which stated:

I have directed no specific Marine Corps-wide observance of the 13th Anniversary of the service of women in our Corps. This was for the sound and satisfying reason that Women Marines are now a completely integrated part of our Corps. I felt certain that as a permanent and integral part of our Corps and sharing alike in all our traditions, our Women Marines would consider a separate celebration to be inappropriate.

However, I cannot let this occasion pass without extending a greeting to you as the representative of all Women Marines. I should also like to congratulate you on the splendid manner in which you are discharging this responsibility.

My very best wishes to you and all Women Marines for the future.25

The local celebrations continued, nevertheless, and General Pate relented by resuming the habit of sending greetings to all women Marines in the ensuing years.

Apparently, when General David M. Shoup became Commandant the propriety of the observance was again questioned. Colonel Henderson, the director, prepared a year-by-year study of the celebrations and concluded with the thoughts:

Woman Marine anniversary cake prepared by the Mess Hall, Camp Pendleton, California, in February 1966.

The women Marines of Camp Pendleton are aided in celebrating their 28th anniversary at the traditional cake-cutting ceremony by Col Emil J. Radics, base chief of staff. From left are PFCs Julia Krauss and Brenda Baker, Col Radics, and Maj Georgia Swickheimer.

It is my personal belief that the Women Marines think of 13 February 1943 not as a birthday, but as the date which commemorates the opportunity given them to become a part of the Marine Corps and to share in all its traditions. Because of this belief and their esprit de corps, I recommend that they continue to celebrate their anniversary.

I know that it will please every woman in the Corps to have a personal message of recognition from the Commandant and make her prouder than ever of being a woman Marine.26

And so it went until the question was settled once and for all in 1974. The Commandant made known that in the future only 10 November would be acknowledged by a CMC message. Colonel Brewer, Director of Women Marines, agreed with the theory that, with ". . . increased effectiveness in the utilization of women Marines as an integral part of the Corps, it is appropriate and timely to discontinue the practice of publishing 'WM Anniversary' messages by the Commandant and the Director of Women Marines."27 Referring, however, to the wide reaching changes in policy approved by the Commandant in 1973, she reasoned that a final message would be an excellent way to reemphasize the increased opportunities for women Marines and to announce the discontinuance of the tradition.28 General Cushman, therefore, in the final anniversary message, said:

With each passing year, we Marines working together will meet the challenges of the future, willing and able to fulfill our responsibilities as the "Nation's Force In Readiness."

In recognition of the role of the women members of our Corps in fulfilling this mission, and since all Marines share one Birthday, it seems appropriate to recognize your achievements for this, the last time, as a separate, special occasion. Accordingly, we pause today to reflect on the day 31 years ago when women became members of our Marine Corps team ready to meet all challenges.29

Women Marines and Mess Night

For a number of years, it was generally understood that formal mess nights were for men only.30 Women officers did not expect to be included and indeed they were not. As women were assigned to more and more billets outside the WM program, the situation became increasingly awkward, and on rare occasions, they were invited to take part in the ancient social custom. The first woman to attend a mess night was probably Colonel Helen A. Wilson.*

* "In August, 1957, while on active duty for training at the Marine Corps Base, Camp Pendleton, to attend the U.S. Marine Corps Reserve Administrative Course, I took part in a formal mess night. The announcement was made that I was the first woman in history to participate in this ancient and solemn ceremony. For me, it was almost a terrifying experience, having been direly warned and incriminated by my fellow Marines as to the solemnity of the occasion. They coached me and warned me of the deep significance of a formal mess night, and the importance of my role on this auspicious occasion. My memorized speech dissolved into a few halting (but sincere) phrases memorializing the important event itself, and the Marine Corps. After the meat was declared "fit for human consumption," the feast began, the wine flowed freely—and glasses were raised in countless toasts, each more fervent than the last. Then, as I quivered, my turn came—"Gentlemen —a toast to the Director of Women Marines!"—which was by then most enthusiastically received. In my "memento box" I still have the cigar they gave me that night, carefully wrapped and labeled —and unsmoked!" Col Helen A. Wilson comments on draft manuscript, dtd 1 Jan 80.

The date of the first formal mess night sponsored by a WM unit is known —12 February 1970. To celebrate the 27th anniversary of the women Marines, officers of the Women Marine Recruit Training Battalion, Parris Island, and the women officers of the neighboring Marine Corps Air Station at Beaufort, gathered at the officers' club and followed the time-honored procedures under the direction of Major Roberta N. Roberts (later Patrick), Madam President. Madam Vice, the junior officer present, was Chief Warrant Officer Bertha Peters Billeb, who had been one of the original staff members when the battalion was activated in 1943, and later in 1961 became the first Sergeant Major of Women Marines.

The battalion commander, Lieutenant Colonel Jenny Wrenn, invited the guests of honor, Major General Oscar F. Peatross, Commanding General, Marine Corps Recruit Depot, and Colonel Richard J. Schriver, Commanding Officer, Marine Corps Air Station. In his remarks, General Peatross praised the women for their patriotism. He said:

You have no obligation to serve in the military. You are not subject to the draft or to any other impetus to serve except your own patriotism and desire to serve your country and fellow man. You must be counted as the most patriotic among the citizens of our nation.31

Subsequently, the most frequent WM-sponsored mess nights occurred at The Basic School, Quantico, when the training schedule precluded a joint affair. With the complete integration of women into the Basic School program in 1977, scheduling problems disappeared and separate mess nights along with them. At all commands where women now serve, they take their place at formal mess nights along with their male colleagues.

Molly Marine

"Molly" is the nickname of a statue which has stood at the intersection of Elk Place and Canal Street in downtown New Orleans, Louisiana, since it was originally dedicated on the Marine Corps Birthday in 194 3.32 Originally cast in marble chips and granite because of wartime restrictions, Molly had become weather beaten. In 1961, a local committee decided to erect a monument to women who had served in all branches of the service in all wars, but, they proposed to erect their monument on Molly's beachhead, and remove the statue of the woman Marine.

Molly's many friends blocked this action. Heading the long list of her benefactors was Mr. Frank Zito, Jr., former State Commandant, Marine Corps League, Louisiana, who pledged that Molly would be bronzed and placed on a new pedestal. Thus, Mr. Zito established the Molly Restoration Fund for her refurbishing.

The tradition of giving red roses, one for each year, to the Director of Women Marines on 13 February was begun by Col Randolph McC. Pate, post-World War II Director of Reserve. Col Jeanette I. Sustad receives the bouquet of roses from the Commandant, Gen Leonard F. Chapman, Jr., in the early 1970s.

LtCol Jenny Wrenn, Commanding Officer, Woman Recruit Training Battalion, Parris Island, presides at the first Mess Night sponsored by a woman Marine unit, in 1970.

During the ensuing controversy, it was pointed out that New Orleans was the site of the first statue of a woman in the United States, that of Margaret Haughery, erected in 1884; that the first statue of a woman in uniform anywhere in the world was Joan of Arc, in her armor, in Orleans, France; that New Orleans was the namesake of Orleans, France; and that therefore, it was appropriate that Molly Marine, the first statue of a woman in uniform in the United States, should remain in New Orleans.

At the 1964 national convention for the Women Marines Association and the Marine Corps League, both organizations unanimously passed resolutions pledging support to the restoration project. The Marine Corps Reserve Officers Association added its aid with a Support the Restoration of Molly Marine resolution passed by the national delegates in 1966 at Houston, Texas. Through the efforts of the New Orleans Cajun Chapter of the Women Marines Association, and local friends of the Corps, a full-scale drive was launched for the final completion of Molly.

After many years of working and waiting, Molly received her new dress. She was taken from her post to be returned dressed in her new bronze finery where she awaited her unveiling which took place during the Women Marine Association National Convention, 29 June-1 July 1966.

On hand for the occasion, as personal representative of the Commandant, was Brigadier General Edward H. Hurst, Director, Marine Corps Landing Force Development Center, Quantico, who as a major in 1943 had been the commanding officer of the Marine Training Detachment, Naval Reserve Midshipmen School (WR), Northampton, Massachusetts, and later the commanding officer of the Officer Training School, MCWR, Camp Lejeune; Colonel Barbara J. Bishop, Director of Women Marines; and Gunnery Sergeant Helen Hannah Campbell, USMCR, President, Women Marines Association. Many of Molly's benefactors were at the ceremonies to see the culmination of their efforts in the restoration.

The original inscription, which read:

Molly Marine, monument in New Orleans, dedicated to women who served as Marines.

Dedicated by the People of New Orleans

TO THE WOMEN OF AMERICA

In the U.S. Marine Corps Women's Reserve

for recognition of the patriotic service rendered their country

10 November 1943

was changed to:

Molly Marine

November 10, 1943

FREE A MARINE TO FIGHT

REDEDICATED JULY 1, 1966 IN HONOR OF

WOMEN MARINES WHO SERVE THEIR COUNTRY IN KEEPING WITH THE HIGHEST TRADITIONS

OF THE UNITED STATES MARINE CORPS

Women Marines Association

The Women Marines Association (WMA) traces its origin to a 1923 dream of a couple of World War I veterans, Florence Miller and Louise Budge, who tried without success to organize the "Girl Marine Veterans."33 The idea lay dormant for years until a handful of members at large met at the first WMA convention in Denver in l960. The founders who laid the groundwork for the unofficial organization of women Marines were headed by Reserve Major Jean Durfee and included former WRs Marion A. Hooper Swope, Maryjeane Olson Nelson, June F. Hansen, Lois Lighthall, Ila Doolittle Clark, and Barbara Kees Meeks. Colonel Margaret M. Henderson, the Director of Women Marines, attended the convention and gave her support and encouragement.

A constitution was adopted, setting forth WMA objectives and providing for biennial conventions, national officers and directors were elected; and the attendees returned home to mount a vigorous membership campaign which netted approximately 350 charter members by February 1961. Shortly thereafter, the first issue of a quarterly newsletter, WMA Nouncements appeared. Subsequent conventions were held in Cleveland, Saint Louis, New Orleans, San Francisco, Philadelphia, Honolulu, Galveston, and in 1976, the nation's bicentennial birthday, in Boston. For the first time in WMA history, the women were addressed by a Commandant of the Marine Corps, General Robert E. Cushman, Jr., at the 1974 Texas meeting. The WMA is the only national organization open exclusively to women who serve or have served as United States Marines.

CHAPTER 16

The Sergeants Major of Women Marines

Bertha L. Peters — Evelyn E. Albert — Ouida W. Craddock — Mabel A.R. Otten — June V. Andler — Grace A. Carle

With the publication of MCO 1421.6 in April l960, three WM sergeant major billets were designated, one of which was marked for the senior enlisted woman in the office of the Director of Women Marines. The system at that time provided for the temporary appointment to sergeant major of women already in the ninth pay grade, master gunnery sergeant. The first woman to be promoted to master gunnery sergeant, Geraldine M. Moran, was stationed at El Toro where no billet for a WM sergeant major existed. The second woman to be selected for the top enlisted pay grade was Bertha Peters (later Billeb), who at the time was in the Director's office. Promoted on 18 January 1961 to master gunnery sergeant, Peters coincidentally became eligible and was appointed as the first Sergeant Major of Women Marines.

Officially, no special provisions were made for the billet, but much ceremony and publicity attended the appointment. Colonel Henderson strongly believed that an experienced staff noncommissioned officer, through close liaison with enlisted WMs in the field, could provide the Director with valuable insights which would help in the development of meaningful policies concerning women Marines. She enhanced the prestige and position of the sergeant major most notably by taking her on trips to inspect women Marine units. The top enlisted WM visited the women on the job and in their barracks. She spoke to work supervisors and the WM company staff. Back at Headquarters, she made public appearances and she was the expert in residence on enlisted women Marine matters.

Selection of the succeeding sergeants major was done by a special board convened at Headquarters. The senior member was a woman officer and the Director of Women Marines was an advisor. The guidance given board members describing the desirable qualifications specified:

1. In personal appearance, an outstanding representative woman Marine for her age and grade. Feminine in mannerism and person; impeccable in uniform and knowledgeable in presenting an appearance in civilian clothing appropriate to any social occasion.

2. Poised and mature in military presence; socially aware and approachable; tactful and capable of achieving a nicely balanced relationship with officers, senior staff NCOs, and personnel of lower pay grades, men and women.

3. Possessed of an excellent ability to communicate orally and in writing; particularly well qualified to speak before a sizable audience.

4. A Marine Corps career of widest possible experience, particularly in regard to billets in the women's program and in contrast to assignments limited solely to duty in her MOS. Consideration should be given to her performance in her OF and to the past selection for such other assignments as instructor, recruiter, DI, or as 1stSgt/SgtMaj.1

Six women were eventually designated through 1976 as Sergeant Major of Women Marines. They are:

Sergeant Major Bertha L. Peters (Billeb) -18 Jan 1961-13 Nov 1963

Sergeant Major Evelyn E. Albert - 13 Nov 1963-1 Dec 1966

Sergeant Major Ouida W. Craddock - 1 Dec 1966-1 Aug 1969

Sergeant Major Mabel A. R. Otten - 1 Aug 1969-30 Apr 1972

Sergeant Major June V. Andler - 30 Apr 1972-30 Apr 1974

Sergeant Major Grace A. Carle - 30 Apr 1974-30 Oct 1975

Sergeant Major Bertha L. Peters

Sergeant Major Bertha L. Peters (Billeb) of Wasco, California, having been recruited by Lieutenant Colonel Lily H. Gridley (who was still in a WAVES uniform) in San Francisco, was enlisted in the Marine Corps Reserve on 5 March 1943 and entered training on 19 April 1943 in the second recruit class of WRs at Hunter College in New "fork. She served on continuous active duty at Headquarters Marine Corps in the Division of Aviation throughout World War II. On 10 November 1948 she was one of the first eight enlisted WRs to be sworn into the regular Marine Corps by General Clifton B. Cates.

In February 1949, she was transferred to Parris Island where she became the Battalion Chief Clerk for the newly organized 3d Recruit Training Battalion. Upon the discharge of MSgt Elsie Miller, the Battalion Sergeant Major, GySgt Peters assumed the duties of Sergeant Major. Subsequently she was assigned as Sergeant Major of the Woman Marines Officer Training Command, Quantico; First Sergeant, Company A, Pearl Harbor, and in 1955 once again, as Sergeant Major, Women Recruit Training Battalion. In 1959 she was selected and assigned to the senior enlisted woman Marine billet, Office of the Director of Woman Marines. She was selected for promotion to master gunnery sergeant in 1961 and redesignated as sergeant major. She became the first Sergeant Major of Women Marines. After her marriage in 1962 to Gunnery Sergeant William N. Billeb she joined her husband at Quantico and was assigned for the second time as Sergeant Major, Women Officers Training. In 1966 after her husband had been promoted to warrant officer (temporary) she accepted promotion to warrant officer (temporary) and was transferred to her third tour of duty with the Woman Recruit Training Battalion, Parris Island, where she was assigned to the billet of Battalion adjutant. In 1970 the Billebs, both commissioned officers, reverted to their permanent ranks.

Master Gunnery Sergeant Bertha Billeb was transferred to MCB, Camp Pendleton. She was redesignated to permanent sergeant major in 1972 when all women Marines who held that rank were given permanent warrants. At this time the Billebs were the only husband-wife sergeant major team in the Marine Corps. In 1973, Sergeant Major Bertha Billeb, being the first woman to complete 30 years' continuous active duty, was retired with honors at MCB, Camp Pendleton. She requested and was placed on the retired list as a commissioned warrant officer.

Bertha L. Peters, Sergeant Major of Women Marines 18 January 1961-13 November 1963.

Evelyn E. Albert, Sergeant Major of Women Marines 13 November 1963-1 December 1966.

Sergeant Major Evelyn E. Albert

Sergeant Major Evelyn E. Albert assumed the assignment as Sergeant Major of Women Marines, Headquarters Marine Corps, on 13 November 1963. She was the second woman to hold that billet since its creation in April 1960.

A 1943 graduate of Wagner College, Staten Island, New York, with a BA degree in English, Sergeant Major Albert enlisted from her native New Jersey in April 1943, following the call to active duty of the Marine Corps

Women's Reserve in February. She was in the third class of WRs to train at the Naval Training School at Hunter College prior to the transfer of the WR training to Camp Lejeune. One of the first WRs assigned to Camp Lejeune, she served there until July 1943, when she was transferred to the Marine Corps Air Station, Cherry Point.

While at Cherry Point, she was temporarily detached to the Aerological School Training Unit at the Naval Air Station, Lakehurst, New Jersey. Upon completion of school, she was promoted to corporal and returned to Cherry Point as an aerographer. She remained there until the general demobilization of the Marine Corps Women's Reserve in December 1945. On her return to civilian life, she completed the Executive Secretary Course at Berkley School in New York City.

In July 1948, Staff Sergeant Albert enlisted in the Inactive Reserve and, following the 1948 Women's Armed Forces Integration Act, enlisted in the U.S. Marine Corps and returned to active duty. She was the first woman Marine to serve as a receptionist to the Secretary of Defense. She served in this capacity until December 1951 under Secretaries Louis A. Johnson, George C. Marshall, and Robert A. Lovett.

After serving as a recruiter for a few years she attended Personnel Administration School at Parris Island and upon graduation she was assigned to Marine Corps Schools, Quantico, as first sergeant of the Woman Marine Company.

From December 1958 until December I960, Albert served on the staff of Commander in Chief, Allied Forces, Southern Europe, Naples, Italy, where she was promoted to master sergeant. She then served as Sergeant Major, Woman Recruit Training Battalion, Parris Island, and during this tour was promoted to first sergeant in February 1961. In October 1963, she was detached from her duties and reported to Headquarters as Sergeant Major of Women Marines. At the end of her tour she was transferred to the Marine Corps Air Station Facility, Santa Ana, where she was promoted to master gunnery sergeant. From January 1968 until her retirement in December 1969, she served with the Awards Unit, Force Adjutant Section, FMFPac.

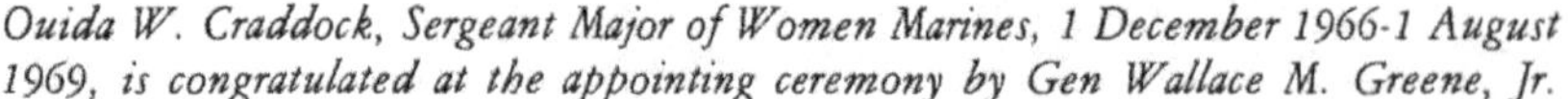

Ouida W. Craddock, Sergeant Major of Women Marines, 1 December 1966-1 August 1969, is congratulated at the appointing ceremony by Gen Wallace M. Greene, Jr.

Sergeant Major Ouida W. Craddock

Ouida Wells Craddock was born in Haskell, Oklahoma, and grew up in Oakland, California. During World War II she enlisted in the U.S. Marine Corps Reserve at San Francisco and served on active duty as a private first class in San Francisco and El Toro until discharged in April 1946.

She reenlisted in July 1949 and was integrated into the Regular Marine Corps in August 1951. Assigned to active duty, she served as electric accounting machine operator, and later, noncommissioned officer in charge, Civilian Payroll and Fiscal Accounts, Machine Records Section, San Francisco, California. She was promoted to staff sergeant in June 1952 and to technical sergeant in May 1953.

From August 1953 until July 1954, Sergeant Craddock served at Headquarters as assistant projects planner, and later, as supply accountant. She attended the Recruiters School, then was transferred to the 12th Marine Corps Reserve and Recruitment District, San Francisco, where she served as WM recruiter from September 1954 until October 1958.

She returned to Parris Island and joined the Woman Recruit Training Battalion, serving as recruit platoon sergeant. She attended Noncommissioned Officer Leadership School at Quantico and then was assigned duty as chief drill instructor back at the Woman Recruit Company, serving in that capacity from August 1959 until September I960.

For the next three years she saw duty with the Woman Marine Company at Camp Smith, Hawaii. She served first as project planner and later became the first woman to be designated as a data processing installation chief. While serving in Hawaii, she was promoted to master sergeant in January 1962.

In January 1964, Sergeant Craddock returned to Headquarters and was assigned as operation analyst, Operation Management Branch, Data Processing Division. Transferred in February 1965, she was assigned duty once again as recruiter in San Francisco. While there, she was selected as the top ranking noncommissioned woman Marine in the Corps, with the rank of sergeant major. At the time of her selection she was the senior enlisted woman in the data processing field, and was the first woman to be promoted to the senior pay grade from outside of the administrative field.

Sergeant Major Craddock served as Sergeant Major of Women Marines until she retired on 2 August 1969.

Sergeant Major Mabel A. R. Otten

Sergeant Major Mabel Annie Rosa Otten became the fourth Sergeant Major of Women Marines in ceremonies held at Headquarters on 1 August 1969. Born in Centerville, Illinois, she graduated from Dupo Community High School. She enlisted in the Marine Corps Reserve during the national emergency on 16 May 1944, in St. Louis, Missouri, and received recruit training at the Marine Corps Base, Camp Lejeune.

During World War II, she served at the Depot of Supplies in San Francisco, in Hawaii, at Mare Island, and again at the Depot of Supplies, San Francisco. While stationed in San Francisco, she was discharged as a sergeant following demobilization of the Marine Corps Women's Reserve in August 1946.

In April 1947, she reenlisted in the Marine Corps Reserve and in November 1948 integrated into the Regular Marine Corps. Following her return to active duty, Staff Sergeant Otten served in the disbursing field at Headquarters from April 1948 to October 1951 and at Cherry Point from October 1951 to June 1954, where she was promoted to master sergeant on 1 June 1952. Master Sergeant Otten completed Recruiters School in August 1954, then served on recruiting duty at South Charleston, West Virginia.

In October 1957, she became disbursing chief at Quantico and in March I960 was assigned duty as S-3 operations chief at the Woman Recruit Training Battalion at Parris Island serving there until June 1962.

For the next seven years, she served as disbursing chief consecutively at Camp Lejeune, Treasure Island, and at Futema in Okinawa. She was promoted to master gunnery sergeant on 1 August 1967 and returned to the United States in June 1969.

Sergeant Major Otten served as Sergeant Major of Women Marines until she retired on 30 April 1972.

Mabel A. R. Otten, Sergeant Major of Women Marines
1 August 1969-30 April 1972

June V. Andler, Sergeant Major of Women Marines
30 April 1972-30 April 1974

Sergeant Major June V. Andler

Sergeant Major June (Judy) V. Andler became the fifth Sergeant Major of Women Marines on 30 April 1972. Born in St. Paul, Minnesota, she graduated from St. Paul High School in 1940. She enlisted in the Marine Corps Reserve on 9 March 1944 and received recruit training at Camp Lejeune. During the war, she served at Quantico and at Headquarters Marine Corps.

In 1948, she integrated into the Regular Marine Corps and in February 1949 was transferred to Parris Island as one of the original members of the staff of the 3d Recruit Training Battalion. She served there until September 1952, first as battalion chief clerk, then as a drill instructor. While at Parris Island, she completed the Personnel and Administrative Course in 1950.

Transferred to the Marine Corps Base, Camp Pendleton, California, she saw duty as Chief Clerk, Officer Personnel Section and, later, served as an investigator in the Base Provost Marshal's Office. During this assignment, in 1953, she attended the Noncommissioned Officers Leadership School at Camp Lejeune and the Criminal Investigation Course at Camp Gordon, Georgia. For the next 28 months, she saw duty as administrative chief of the Woman Marine Company at Camp H. M. Smith in Hawaii.

Promoted to gunnery sergeant in December 1959, during the same month she was assigned to El Toro and subsequently served as administrative chief of Woman Marine Detachment One. From April 1962 until November 1963, Gunnery Sergeant Andler served, successively, as First Sergeant, Woman Officers Candidate Class, and Administrative Chief of Woman Marines Detachment at Quantico.

Following this assignment, she returned to Camp Pendleton for duty as noncommissioned officer in charge, Officer Personnel Section, Marine Corps Base, and later as administrative chief of Headquarters Regiment. She was promoted to master sergeant in June 1966, and that September, became S-3, operations/special subjects instructor for the Woman Recruit Training Battalion at Parris Island.

Transferred to the Marine Corps Recruit Depot at San Diego, she served from April 1969 until February 1970 as First Sergeant, Woman Marine Company. She was promoted to first sergeant on 1 May 1969- Upon promotion to master gunnery sergeant on 1 February 1970, she became the Headquarters and Service Battalion administrative chief.

In January 1971, Master Gunnery Sergeant Andler assumed duty as Personnel Chief, Marine Corps Communications Electronics School at Twentynine Palms. While serving in this capacity, she was named the fifth Sergeant Major of Women Marines.

Completing 30 years of continuous active duty, Sergeant Major Andler retired on 30 April 1974.

Sergeant Major Grace A. Carle

Sergeant Major Grace A. Carle became the sixth and last Sergeant Major of Women Marines in ceremonies held at Marine Barracks, Washington, D.C., on 30 April 1974. Born in Yankton, South Dakota, she graduated from Pender High School, Pender, Nebraska, in 1940. She enlisted in the Marine Corps in April 1943 and was a member of the last regiment trained at Hunter College, New York. During World War II, she saw service at Headquarters Marine Corps and in Hawaii. She was released from active duty in November 1945.

The all-woman Volunteer Training Unit which she joined in 1948 became the nucleus of the WR Platoon, 13th Infantry Battalion and was mobilized in 1950 at the beginning of the Korean War. Before leaving for San Francisco, she, along with others in the platoon, was ordered to the home armory for two weeks active duty during which the women helped the men to pack and to get their paperwork in order. Initially, she served in San Francisco as a Reservist and then integrated into the Regular Marine Corps in 1951. 2

Other duty assignments took her to El Toro, Parris Island, Camp Pendleton, and to New Orleans, as assistant to the woman officer selection officer. She served as first sergeant of the Woman Marine Companies at Camp Lejeune and on Okinawa. At the time of her selection as Sergeant Major of Women Marines, she was Sergeant Major, Woman Officer School, Quantico.

At the end of her tour as Sergeant Major of Women Marines, a woman Marine mess night was held at the Sheraton Hotel on 29 October 1976, an occasion attended by women Marine officers and enlisted, from all

East Coast posts. The next day, upon retirement, she was awarded the Navy Achievement Medal and honored at parade at the Marine Barracks, 8th and I Streets, Washington, DC.

Grace A. Carle, Sergeant Major of Women Marines
30 April 1974-30 October 1976

An era ends as the last Sergeant Major of Women Marines, Grace A. Carle retires at ceremonies held at Marine Barracks, 8th and I, Washington, on 30 October 1976.

CHAPTER 17

The Directors of Women Marines

Katherine A. Towle — Julia E. Hamblet — Margaret M. Henderson — Barbara J. Bishop — Jeanette I. Sustad - Margaret A. Brewer — The Position

Colonel Katherine A. Towle

Originally of Vermont stock, Colonel Katherine Amelia Towle was born in Towle, California, a lumber mill hamlet in the Sierras founded by her grandfather. She earned her bachelor's degree in 1920 at the University of California at Berkeley with honors in political science and received her master's degree there in 1935. Prior to 13 February 1943, she had served successively as an assistant in the admissions office at the University of California; resident dean and headmistress of Miss Ronsom and Miss Bridges School for Girls at Piedmont, California; a teaching fellow in political science at the University of California; and senior editor of the University of California Press.1

On 15 March 1943, she accepted an appointment as captain in the Marine Corps Reserve with rank as of 24 February. Having never attended basic training of any sort, Colonel Towle in later years laughingly remarked that she was not even a 90-day wonder. After six days of indoctrination with the Division of Reserve at Headquarters Marine Corps, Captain Towle was assigned as a staff officer (WR) with the Training Brigade, Marine Training Detachment, U.S. Naval Training School, Bronx, New York.

When the WR battalion was established at Camp Lejeune in June 1943, she was transferred there and became the senior Marine Corps Women's Reserve School officer and assistant executive officer. In that position, she was promoted to major on 2 February 1944, and in September of that year she became Colonel Streeter's assistant at Headquarters Marine Corps.

She remained at Headquarters, was appointed a lieutenant colonel on 15 March 1945, and succeeded Colonel Streeter as Director nine months later on 8 December. A colonel by virtue of her billet, she spent her remaining months in the Marine Corps directing the demobilization of the women Reservists and laying plans and policies for a postwar Marine Corps Women's Reserve.

On 14 June 1946, certain that all World War II WRs would be released within a few months, Colonel Towle returned to the Berkeley campus as assistant dean of women. For her meritorious wartime service, she carried with her the Letter of Commendation with ribbon by the Secretary of Navy and a letter of appreciation from General Alexander A. Vandegrift, the Commandant of the Marine Corps.

When Congress provided for Regular components of women in the Armed Forces, General Clifton B. Cates, then Commandant, asked Colonel Towle to direct the new Regular women Marines. She returned to Washington as one of the first 20 women Regular officers and became the first Director of Women Marines.

Recruit and officer training programs were organized and a gradual buildup of women in the Regular Marine Corps began. At the same time, 13 women's platoons were established in the Marine Corps Organized Reserve. Colonel Towle was particularly proud of the response of these women and the low percentage of deferments among women Reservists upon mobilization in 1950. Following the Korean War the Reserve units were reorganized, this time with a total of 19 platoons.

Col Katherine A. Towle, Director of Women Marines
18 October 1948-1 May 1953

Col Katherine A. Towle, Director of Women Marines, reviews a parade in honor of her retirement on 1 May 1953. Commandant of the Marine Corps Gen Lemuel C. Shepherd, Jr., stands in the rank behind her with (from left to right) LtCol Julia E. Hamblet, Col Towle's successor; LtCol Foster La Hue, aide-de-camp to the Commandant; and Col Jack C. Juhan, commanding officer of Marine Barracks, Eighth and I, Washington, D.C.

As an educator, Colonel Towle recognized the value of formal training and continually worked for increased school opportunities for WMs. Her national stature in the academic community enhanced the prestige of the women Marines and contributed to her success in gaining access to colleges and universities to recruit women officers. Among her honors is the Doctor of Laws conferred on her by Mills College in June 1952.

The Oakland Tribune said of her, "Behind the formidably admirable public record is one of the most charming women in the world,"2 Colonel Towle, a lady of style and grace who loved feminine hats, was a paradox in the overtly masculine Marine Corps. Yet, in the opinion of Colonel Hamblet, "She was the perfect one for the job at the time/13 She had made her reputation as an able administrator and commander in World War II. She was firm but never aggressive and won the respect of Marines — irrespective of their personal views of women in military service.

To a newsman's question regarding the acceptance of women in the Marine Corps by senior officers, Colonel Towle frankly answered that there were varying degrees of enthusiasm but with one or two exceptions the feminine presence had been taken with good grace. The day after the interview was published nearly every general officer at Headquarters stopped by her office, poked in his head, and asked, "You didn't mean me, did you, Colonel?" The Colonel replied, "Oh no, sir, of course not," but by the end of the day neither she nor her administrative assistant, Lieutenant Colonel Kleberger, could keep a straight face as the parade by her office continued.4

On 1 May 1952, Colonel Towle was retired under the statutory age provision of the Women's Armed Services Integration Act of 1948 which required retirement for colonels at age 55. A special sunset parade had been held in her honor the evening before at the Marine Barracks in Washington, D.C., and for the first time in the history of the famous barracks, a platoon of women Marines joined the contingent of Marines who passed in review. Upon retirement, the colonel was awarded a Letter of Commendation from the Commandant of the Marine Corps and a Legion of Merit from the President of the United States.*

* Colonel Towle returned to the University of California at Berkeley as the dean of women and associate dean of students. Later she filled the very demanding post of dean of students during the famous free speech movement and anti-war demonstrations on the Berkeley campus.

Colonel Julia E. Hamblet

The third Director of the Marine Corps Women's Reserve and the second Director of Women Marines was Colonel Julia Estelle Hamblet, called Judy by her friends. Born in Winchester, Massachusetts, Colonel Hamblet attended the Hartridge School in Plainfield, New Jersey, and graduated from Vassar College in 1937 with a bachelor of arts degree.5 The first woman Marine to be afforded the opportunity to attend graduate school while on active duty, she earned a master of science degree in public administration at Ohio State University in 1951. Appropriately, her thesis was entitled, "The Utilization of Women in the Marine Corps."

Colonel Hamblet worked for the U.S. Information Service in Washington, D.C., from 1937 until 1943 when she became the first woman from the nation's capital to join the Marine Corps. Her motive for entering military service, like thousands of Americans during those critical days, was a patriotic desire to do her part. Her reason for choosing the Marine Corps was less noble; with one brother in the Army and another in the Navy, she wanted to remain impartial.

Graduating from the first woman officer training class on 4 May 1943, she, along with several of her classmates, was commissioned a first lieutenant. Captain Towle, then senior woman officer on the staff at the Marine Corps Training Detachment in the Bronx, personally selected Lieutenant Hamblet to fill the billet of adjutant of that unit. She served in that post at Hunter College and later at Camp Lejeune when the Women's Reserve schools were transferred there in July 1943. Her subsequent tours during World War II included six months with the Marine Corps Women's Reserve Battalion at Camp Lejeune, first as adjutant and then as executive officer; adjutant and executive officer, Women's Reserve Battalion, Camp Pendleton; commanding officer, Women's Reserve Battalion, Quantico; assistant for the Women's Reserve on the staff of the commanding general at Quantico; and finally commanding officer, Aviation Women's Reserve Group 1, Cherry Point. For her services during World War II, she was awarded a letter of commendation.

In a distinguished career marked by numerous achievements, one stands out as having the most direct impact on the entire Marine Corps. As a major and the Director of the postwar Women's Reserve, 1946-1948, she was responsible for maintaining the interest of the WRs during those critical years and for organizing the WR platoons, all of which were ready when the Korean War erupted.

The year of graduate work was followed by a tour of duty in Honolulu as the assistant G-1, FMFPac. Lieutenant Colonel Hamblet was the first WM to return to Hawaii since the departure of the WRs in 1946. In less than a year, she was assigned as officer in charge of the Women Officer Training Detachment at Quantico.

On 1 May 1953, she assumed the position of the second Director of Women Marines, again succeeding Colonel Towle, who was retiring. Only 37 years old, she was the youngest director of women in the armed services. Colonel Towle, in praising her successor said, "She has had practically every type of duty a woman Marine officer can have. I have followed her military career since her assignment as my adjutant. She has brains, ability, personality, and looks."8 Colonel Hamblet held the post of Director until March 1959, longer than any other woman.

Col Julia E. Hamblet, Director of Women Marines
1 May 1953-2 March 1959

Legal provisions at the time prohibited women, other than the Director, to serve in the rank of colonel, so Colonel Hamblet reverted to her permanent rank of lieutenant colonel and was then transferred to Naples, Italy, where she served as military secretary to the Commander in Chief, Allied Forces, Southern Europe. Before leaving, her friends feted her with a "demotion" party which featured a large cake decorated with an eagle flying away.

Lieutenant Colonel Hamblet, uncommonly attractive and poised, became a favorite among the servicewomen at Naples. When the enlisted women gave a New Year's party in 1961 to which many officers, American and foreign, were invited, she was the only woman officer to accept. "In fact," said Sergeant Major Judge, a WM in Naples at the time, "she was the only woman officer to give us the time of day. She was so gracious; she didn't just come to say hello, she stayed and had a good time. No one forgot that. It was mentioned for a long time by the WAVEs and the WACs."7

In April 1962, Lieutenant Colonel Hamblet was transferred to Parris Island, where she was commanding officer, Woman Recruit Training Battalion, until her retirement on 1 May 1965. Colonel Hamblet was awarded the Legion of Merit and according to regulations, upon retirement she was reappointed to the rank of colonel, the highest rank in which she served.

Colonel Margaret M. Henderson

Colonel Margaret Henderson became the fourth Director of Women Marines on 2 March 1959, succeeding Colonel Hamblet. Born in Cameron, Texas, Colonel Henderson earned a bachelor of business administration degree from the University of Texas in 1932 and taught in the secondary schools of Lubbock, Texas, before her enlistment in the Marine Corps in 1943.8

After completing the Marine Corps Women's Reserve Officer Training School at Mount Holyoke, Massachusetts, she was commissioned a second lieutenant in the Reserve on 29 June 1943. Lieutenant Henderson began her career as a general subjects instructor at the Marine Corps Women's Reserve Schools at Camp Lejeune and was later assigned as officer in charge of the Business School, Marine Corps Institute, Washington, DC In later years, Colonel Streeter wrote:

As this was a teaching job, it was natural enough for her to be assigned to it; but it soon became evident that her capacity was far greater than this job would give her opportunity to develop. Unfortunately, she was doing it so well that her Commanding Officer would not let her be transferred! Willie and I put our heads together and she finally wheedled him into letting Margaret go to a better job, where she promptly showed her fine qualities.*

* Willie, referred to by Colonel Streeter, was Major Cornelia D. T. Williams, World War II detail officer.

The "better job" was that of executive officer, Marine Corps Women's Reserve Battalion, Camp Lejeune. On 14 June 1946, Captain Henderson was released from active duty.

She went home to Lubbock where she taught at Texas Technological College for two years. Selected to be one of the first 20 Regular woman Marine officers, Captain Henderson returned to the Marine Corps in December 1948.

Her academic and professional background made her the obvious choice to head the embryonic 3d Recruit Training Battalion. Interviews with officers and enlisted members of the original staff confirm the wisdom of the assignment. From Parris Island, Major Henderson was transferred in 1950 to the Division of Plans and Policy at Headquarters Marine Corps where, in addition to her regular duties, she was concerned with developing personnel and assignment policies for the newly integrated WMs. She played an important role in the return of women Marines to posts and stations during the Korean War.

During subsequent tours she served consecutively as commanding officer, Woman Officer Training Detachment; assistant G-l, Marine Corps Base, Camp Pendleton; and as head, Women's Affairs Section, Division of Plans and Policy at Headquarters Marine Corps.

As Director of Women Marines, Colonel Henderson worked to establish the billet for Sergeant Major of Women Marines, since she believed that enlisted women would speak more freely to the Sergeant Major than to the Director. Sergeant Major Bertha L. Peters (later Billeb), already assigned to the Director's office since June 1959, was elevated to the new position of Sergeant Major of Women Marines in January 1961.

Col Margaret M. Henderson
Director of Women Marines
2 March 1959-3 January 1964

Completing her tour as Director in January 1964, and, once again a lieutenant colonel, she was assigned as assistant G-I, Marine Corps Recruit Depot, San Diego. Colonel Henderson, reappointed to the rank of colonel, received the Legion of Merit, by the commanding general, Major General Bruno A. Hochmuth, at a parade marking her retirement on 31 January 1966. 9

Colonel Barbara J. Bishop

Colonel Barbara J. Bishop, the fifth Director of Women Marines, was born in Boston, schooled in Everett, Massachusetts, and graduated from Yale University in January 1943 with a bachelor of fine arts degree.10

She enlisted in the Marine Corps on 18 February 1943, just five days after the public announcement of the new Women's Reserve program. Colonel Bishop received her Marine officer training as a member of the second officer candidate class at Mount Holyoke and was commissioned a Reserve second lieutenant on 1 June 1943.

Throughout World War II Lieutenant Bishop held a variety of command and administrative assignments: commanding officer, Marine Training Detachment at the University of Indiana; executive officer, Marine Aviation Detachment at the Naval Air Station in Atlanta, Georgia; commanding officer, Aviation Women's Squadron 21 at Quantico; and officer-in-charge, S&C Files, Division of Aviation, Headquarters, U.S. Marine Corps. She was released to inactive duty on 10 November 1946 with the rank of captain.

Col Barbara J. Bishop, Director of Women Marines
3 January 1964-31 January 1969

During the next two years, Captain Bishop earned a master of arts degree at the University of Chicago and was working toward a doctorate when, following the passage of the Women's Armed Services Integration Act, she returned to active duty, selected as one of the original 20 Regular women officers. She served at Headquarters as officer-in-charge, S&C Files, until January 1952 when she went to Headquarters, Fleet Marine Force, Pacific, in Hawaii.

In September 1953 she assumed command of the Woman Marine Company at Camp Lejeune, and was reassigned to Headquarters in 1955 as head, Women's Branch, Division of Reserve, with the additional duty as Deputy Director of Women Marines. A lieutenant colonel, she returned to the field in October 1956 for consecutive tours as commanding officer, Woman Recruit Training Battalion, Parris Island; and assistant G-I, Marine Corps Schools, Quantico. In March 1962 she went to Europe, reporting for duty in Naples, Italy, as military secretary to the Commander in Chief, Allied Forces, Southern Europe.

From Italy, she was once again assigned to Headquarters, this time to succeed Colonel Henderson as the leading woman Marine on 3 January 1964. Colonel Bishop served as Director during a time of sweeping changes in programs and policies affecting women Marines. When she was named Director there were about 1,500 WMs serving at 10 Marine Corps posts and stations throughout the United States and in a few overseas billets. Four years later, there were 2,600 active duty WMs serving 25 posts and stations as well as in Europe, the Philippines, Okinawa, Japan, and the Republic of Vietnam.

Colonel Bishop worked toward improving the living accommodations of women Marines, increasing their assignment opportunities, and raising the rate of their retention. During her tour, women officers for the first time were assigned to career military schools.

When Public Law 90-130 was signed by President Johnson on 8 November 1967, removing certain restrictions to the promotion to field grade of women officers, Colonel Bishop was among the first group of WMs to be selected for promotion to the permanent rank of colonel. Therefore, she, unlike Colonels Hamblet and Henderson, retained her rank when she eventually left the position of Director of Women Marines on 31 January 1969.

Colonel Bishop, whose last assignment was congressional liaison officer to the Senate, retired in November 1969 and was awarded the Legion of Merit during ceremonies held in the office of the Commandant of the Marine Corps, General Leonard F. Chapman, Jr. Colonel Sustad, her successor, presented Colonel Bishop a citation lauding her for her service to the women in the Marine Corps. The unofficial award was signed by all active duty WM officers and was given in recognition of personal efforts on their behalf.

Colonel Jeanette I. Sustad

Colonel Jeanette I. Sustad, sixth Director of Women Marines, was born in Minneapolis, Minnesota, and raised in Tacoma, Washington. She earned a bachelor of arts degree in sociology at the University of Washington in Seattle in 1943.11 On 8 May of that year she enlisted in the Marine Corps Women's Reserve, received officer training at Camp Lejeune, and was commissioned a Reserve second lieutenant on 27 December.

Her first assignment was special services liaison officer, at the Marine Corps Air Station, Cherry Point. Subsequently she served as field operations officer at the Marine Corps Auxiliary Air Facility, Oak Grove, North Carolina, and assistant communications watch officer at the Marine Corps Air Station in Ewa, Honolulu. She returned to inactive status on 17 December 1945.

Following demobilization, she spent a year in graduate study at the University of Minnesota and later was employed as a veterans counselor by the U.S. Employment Services in Tacoma. Upon passage of the Women's Armed Services Integration Act in 1948, she accepted a Regular commission as a first lieutenant and reported to Headquarters in December.

Transferred to Parris Island the following month, she was assigned as executive officer of the newly formed 3d Recruit Training Battalion. From May to July 1950, she served temporarily as the executive officer of the Woman Officer Training Detachment at Quantico. The Korean War brought changes to the WM assignment policies, and she was one of the first to head west to assume duties at Camp Pendleton. Captain Sustad became the adjutant of the Marine Corps Base, perhaps the first postwar WM to be so assigned; and upon activation of the first post-World War II WM Company at Camp Pendleton, became its commanding officer, serving in that capacity until August 1952.

Col Jeanette I. Sustad, Director of Women Marines
31 January 1969-31 January 1973

The first woman Marine officer to be assigned duty in Europe, she served in the Staff Message Control Branch, Headquarters, United States European Command, Frankfurt, Germany. After her promotion to major in July 1953, she became assistant head of the branch and in the spring of 1954, when the Headquarters was moved to Paris, France, Major Sustad continued her assignment there.

Upon her return to the United States in September 1954, she served consecutive tours as the executive officer, Woman Recruit Training Battalion, Parris Island; officer-in-charge, Procurement Aids Branch, Headquarters, 9th Marine Corps Reserve District, Chicago; assistant to the executive officer and plans officer, G-I Division, Headquarters, U.S. Marine Corps; and as operations officer, Marine Corps Education Center, Quantico.

Lieutenant Colonel Sustad became the first fulltime Deputy Director of Women Marines in July 1965. Back at Camp Pendleton serving as the assistant G-l, in June 1968, she was one of the first Regular women Marines to be promoted to the rank of colonel after promotion restrictions were lifted by Congressional legislation.

Colonel Sustad was named Director of Women Marines in 1968, the same year she celebrated her 25th anniversary as a WM, and she assumed the top post on 1 February 1969- Wider assignment and training opportunities materialized under the guidance of Colonel Sustad, and she worked to either change or to set aside many outmoded regulations regarding grooming, marriage, pregnancy, and dependency.

Colonel Sustad retired on 31 January 1973. In the citation accompanying her Legion of Merit was written, "She worked tirelessly for the welfare of each individual under her purview ." a sentiment endorsed by many of the WMs who knew her.12

Brigadier General Margaret A. Brewer

Then-Colonel Margaret A. Brewer, seventh and last Director of Women Marines, was the only post-World War II woman to hold that position. She succeeded Colonel Sustad on 1 February 1973. Born in Durand, Michigan, she received her primary education in Michigan but graduated from the Catholic High School of Baltimore, Maryland, prior to entering the University of Michigan at Ann Arbor. She received a bachelor's degree in geography in January 1952 and was commissioned a Marine second lieutenant in March of that year.13

Candidate Brewer attended the Woman Officer Training Class as an undergraduate during the summers of 1950 and 1951 at the time of the Korean War. Although the policy was to offer Regular commissions to only a few women graduates of Officer Candidates School, and to release the remaining to inactive duty as Reserve officers, rumors were rampant during the summer of 1951 that all would be retained involuntarily—and undergraduates as candidate Brewer would be ordered to active duty in enlisted status. The scuttlebutt proved foundless and candidate Brewer returned to college to complete her last semester, expecting to graduate in January and attend the Woman Officer Indoctrination Course the following fall. She notified Headquarters of her graduation, and promptly received an unexpected set of orders to the Marine Corps Air Station, El Toro, where she served as a communications watch officer until June 1953. The personnel shortage was so acute that Lieutenant Brewer was assigned with no more than 12 weeks of officer candidate training. She attended neither the Woman Officer Indoctrination Course nor the Communications Officers School. Plans were made to send her to the WOIC in September, but when the time came she had already successfully served as an officer for six months and the command at El Toro declined to release her.14

She was then transferred to Brooklyn to activate the post-Korea WM Communications Platoon to be attached to the 2d Signal Company, USMCR. Lieutenant Brewer served as the assistant inspector-instructor until late summer 1955. From September 1955 until June 1958, in the rank of captain, she served as commanding officer of the Woman Marine companies at Norfolk, Virginia, and Camp Lejeune. During the 18 months following, she was a platoon commander for women officer candidates at Quantico, during summer training sessions, and a woman officer selection officer during winter and spring, with headquarters in Lexington, Kentucky. Transferred to Camp Pendleton in November 1959 for duty with the Commissioned Officers Mess, she was promoted to major in September 1961. In April 1963 she returned to Quantico to serve as executive officer and later, as commanding officer, of the Woman Officer School. From 1966 to February 1968, Major Brewer was assigned to the Public Affairs Office, 6th Marine Corps District, in Atlanta, Georgia, and she was promoted to lieutenant colonel in December 1966.

Lieutenant Colonel Brewer served as Deputy Director of Women Marines at Headquarters Marine Corps from March 1968 to March 1971. Reporting to Quantico, she assumed duty as special assistant to the Director, Marine Corps Education Center. Promoted to colonel in December 1970, she became chief of the Support Department, Marine Corps Education Center, in June 1972, and served in that capacity until she became the Director of Women Marines in February 1973.

During her last weeks as Director, Colonel Brewer spoke enthusiastically, not only of the increased opportunities for women in the Marine Corps, but of the notable change in attitude on the part of male Marines in positions of influence at Headquarters. For several years she had devoted her energies to effecting a smooth transfer of responsibility for women in the Marine Corps to the agencies at Headquarters where it rightly belonged. She confidently turned the reins over, certain that these agencies had come to recognize women Marines as Marines.15 Colonel Brewer was reassigned as the deputy director, Division of Information, Headquarters, Marine Corps on 1 July 1977.

General Brewer became the Marine Corps' first woman general officer when, on 11 May 1978, she was assigned as the Director of Information, Headquarters Marine Corps, and appointed a brigadier general.

At the time there was no legal provision for the routine selection and promotion of a woman to flag rank in either the Navy or the Marine Corps. Women could, however, be designated by the Secretary of the Navy for the billet of a rear admiral or brigadier general. A woman officer so designated could be appointed to that rank while so serving. A Navy woman of the time had previously been so appointed. A special board was convened at Headquarters to select the Director of Information. Four women colonels were considered.

The Position

As women became more accepted in the Marine Corps; as policies, law, and traditions were changed; as discriminatory restrictions fell; the position of the Director of Women Marines evolved from one of nearly complete control to one of an advisory nature. Although technically they were always considered advisors, the early Directors, with the exception of Colonel Streeter, were members of the Commandant's staff and were directly involved in recruiting, training, uniforming, and assigning women Marines. The careers of senior officers and enlisted women were managed by the Director and all were personally known to her.

The Director's stated mission belied her real influence. According to the Marine Corps Manual, "The Director of Women Marines advises the Commandant and staff agencies on all matters of policy and procedure concerning women in the Marine Corps and Marine Corps Reserve." The functions of the officer were listed as:

(1) Initiates policies and makes recommendations on all policies and procedures affecting women initiated by other divisions and departments.

(2) Advises and makes recommendations on duty assignments of Women Marines.

(3) Advises cognizant staff agencies in the execution of approved policies affecting Women Marines.

(4) Visits and assists in the inspection of activities where Women Marines are stationed.

(5) Maintains liaison with directors of women in the other Armed Services and with the Office of the Secretary of Defense in connection with the Defense Advisory Committee on Women in the Armed Services.16

As a result of a reorganization of Headquarters Marine Corps in October 1973, the Director was placed under the cognizance of the Manpower Department, which encompassed the major areas of concern to her. Colonel Brewer spent increasingly more time transferring the functions of her office to the appropriate Headquarters departments. The 26th Commandant, General Louis H. Wilson, Jr., had directed that women Marines were to be treated more truly as Marines; recruited, trained, and assigned as members of a single and united Corps.17

The news that there would no longer be a Director of Women Marines was made public on 16 June 1977 and on that day Colonel Brewer reaffirmed her confidence in the planned disestablishment of the position.18 The office created in 1943 and reinforced in 1948 was to be disbanded at a time when the Corps proposed to almost triple the women's strength of 3,700. Only the Army would be left with a director of women.

Ceremonies marking the dissolution of the Director's position were held on 30 June 1977 in the Commandant's office. Among the guests was retired Colonel Julia E. Hamblet, the woman who had held the position of Director of Women Marines longer than any other, and who additionally had served as Director of the Women's Reserve immediately after World War II. General Wilson traced the history and accomplishments of women Marines since World War II, and he recalled the often-told story that when General Thomas A. Holcomb authorized the acceptance of women into the Marine Corps, former Commandant Archibald Henderson's portrait fell from the wall. The 1977 Commandant gallantly added that if sometime in the future, the announcement should be made that there would no longer be women Marines, he hoped that his portrait too, would fall to the floor.

Col Margart A. Brewer, Director of Women Marines
31 January 1973-30 June 1977

Notes

INTRODUCTION

The primary source for material in this book is the Women Marines files, 1918-1973, 7 boxes, Headquarters U.S. Marine Corps Records (RG 127-76-36, Federal Records Center, Suitland, Maryland), hereafter WMs HQMC Records; Office of the Director of Women Marines files (Collections Section, Hist&MusDiv, HQMC), hereafter Dir WMs files; Women Marines Research File, (Hist&Mus Div, HQMC), hereafter WM Research file.

Unless otherwise noted, the material in this section is derived from: Postwar MCWR I file, box 3, WMs HQMC Records, hereafter Postwar MCWR I file; Col Julia E. Hamblet interview with Hist&MusDiv, HQMC, hereafter Hamblet Interview.

1. Gen Gerald C. Thomas memo to CMC, dtd 30Oct45 (Postwar MCWR I file).

2. Ibid.

3. Maj Julia E. Hamblet memo to CMC, dtd 4Feb48 (File 1527, Women Reserve & Regular, box 7, WMs HQMC Records).

4. Col Ruth C. Streeter interview with Hist&MusDiv, dtd 31May77 (WM Research file).

5. Col Ruth C. Streeter memo to Director of Personnel, Marine Corps, dtd 29Aug45 (Postwar MCWR I file)

6. Col Edward W. Snedeker memo to Director, Division of Plans and Policies, dtd 10Dec45 (Postwar MCWR I file)

CHAPTER 1

A TIME OF UNCERTAINTY, 1946-1948

Unless otherwise noted, the material in this chapter is derived from: File 2385-50-30, Organizations, Central Files, HQMC, hereafter Organizations file; Postwar MCWR I file; Hamblet interview; Muster rolls, Company E, 1st HqBn, HQMC, 19Apr46-31Jan47 (Ref-Sec, Hist&MusDiv, HQMC); Scrapbook loaned by Col Julia E. Hamblet to Hist&MusDiv, HQMC, hereafter Hamblet scrapbook; LtCol Mary J. Hale interview with Hist&MusDiv, dtd l4Dec77 (Oral Hist Collection, Hist&MusDiv, HQMC), hereafter Hale interview; Personal papers loaned by LtCol Emma H. Clowers to Hist&MusDiv, HQMC, hereafter Clowers papers; Scrapbook and papers loaned by Dorothy M. Munroe to Hist&MusDiv, HQMC, hereafter Munroe scrapbook; The Reserve Bulletin, Division of Reserve, HQMC, hereafter The Reserve Bulletin; WM Research File.

1. ChiefNavPer ltr to CMC, dtd 27Feb46 (Postwar MCWR I file).

2. CMC ltr to ChiefNavPer, dtd 12Mar46 (Organizations file).

3. Gen Gerald C. Thomas memo to CMC, dtd 19Nov45 (Postwar MCWR I file).

4. Col Joseph W. Knighton memo to CMC, dtd 13Mar46 (Organizations file).

5. Gen Gerald C. Thomas memo to CMC, dtd 15Mar46 (Organizations file).

6. CMC ltr to Col Randolph McC. Pate, dtd 28Mar46 (Postwar MCWR I file).

7. Board to recommend policy for administration of postwar MCWR, HQMC, dtd 17Apr46 (Postwar MCWR I file).

8. Col Joseph W. Knighton memo to Gen Allan H. Turnage, dtd 15May46 (Postwar MCWR I file).

9. Cited from Joy Hancock, Lady in the Navy (Annapolis: Naval Institute Press, 1972), p. 223, hereafter Hancock, Lady in the Navy.

10. Stevenson, Burton Egbert, The Home Book of Quotations: Classical and Modem (New York: David, Mead & Co., 1958), p. 2298.

11. Col Katherine A. Towle memo to Director of Personnel, dtd 6May46 (Postwar MCWR I file).

12. Col Katherine A. Towle memo to Director of Personnel, dtd 14Jun46 (Postwar MCWR I file).

13. Headquarters Memorandum No. 50-1946, dtd 7Aug46, Subj: Retention of WRs on active duty (Postwar MCWR I file).

14. Admin Div, CMC office memo to multiple addresses, Subj: Retention of WRs on active duty until 30Jun47 (Postwar MCWR I file).

15. Gen Alexander A. Vandegrift ltr to Maj Julia E. Hamblet, dtd 14Jun46 (Hamblet scrapbook).

16. Maj Julia E. Hamblet ltr to Gen Alexander A. Vandegrift, dtd 25Jun46 (Hamblet scrapbook).

17. CMC ltr to Maj Julia E. Hamblet, dtd 3Jul46 (Hamblet scrapbook).

18. Maj Julia E. Hamblet memo to Director, Division of Reserve, dtd 80ct46 (Postwar MCWR I file).

19. Headquarters Memorandum No. 80-1946, dtd 16Oct46, Subj: MCWR, policies for administration of (Postwar MCWR I file).

20. Maj Julia E. Hamblet memo to Director, Division of Reserve, dtd 8Oct46 (Postwar MCWR I file).

21. The Reserve Bulletin, Mar47.

22. Hale interview.

23. Maj Julia E. Hamblet ltr to Capt Emma H. Hendrickson, dtd 16Dec46 (Clowers papers).

24. Maj Julia E. Hamblet ltr to former WRs, dtd 9Jan47 (Munroe scrapbook).

25. Letter of Instruction 1397, dtd 9Jan47.

26. "Be a Marine And a Civilian Too," undtd Marine Corps Reserve pamphlet (Munroe scrapbook).

27. Capt Constance Risegari-Gai ltr to former WRs, undtd (Munroe scrapbook).

28. VTU 1-1 (WR), Notices for the week of 12Nov47, undtd (Munroe scrapbook).

29. VTU 3-1 admin records 1947-57, loaned by Bertha Santos to Hist&MusDiv, hereafter Santos papers.

30. The Reserve Bulletin, Nov47 and Dec54.

31. Santos papers.

32. PAU 4-1, The Marine Corps Reserve-A History (Washington: Division of Reserve, Headquarters, U.S. Marine Corps, 1966), p. 130.

33. LtCol Ben A. Munn ltr to Hist&MusDiv, dtd 26Jan77 (WM Research file).

34. CMC report to SecNav, Subj: MarCor Per Plan for Fiscal Yr49, dtd 18Jul47 (Postwar MCWR I file).

35. The Reserve Marine, Apr47.

36. Gen Lemuel C. Shepherd, Jr., memo to Gen Gerald C. Thomas, dtd 17Apr47 (Postwar MCWR I file).

37. Ibid.

38. Gen Lemuel C. Shepherd, Jr., memo to CMC, dtd 23Apr47, with CMC endorsement (Postwar MCWR I file).

39. Maj Julia E. Hamblet memo to Director, Division of Reserve, dtd 29Apr47 (Postwar MCWR I file).

40. Director of Aviation memo to CMC, dtd 27May47 (Postwar MCWR I file).

41. Gen William T. Clement memo to CMC, dtd 29May47 (Postwar MCWR I file).

42. AdminDiv, Office of CMC memo to multiple addresses, dtd 9Jun47 (Postwar MCWR I file).

43. Gen Gerald C. Thomas memo to CMC, dtd 11Jun47, with CMC endorsement (Postwar MCWR I file).

44. WMs HQMC Records.

45. CMC ltr to former WRs, dtd 27Oct47 (Munroe scrapbook).

46. Our World; A National Magazine for the People of Tupperware, Jan77, p.5 (WM Research file).

CHAPTER 2

WOMEN'S ARMED FORCES LEGISLATION: PUBLIC LAW 625

Unless otherwise noted, the material in this chapter is derived from: Hearings-WR Bill file (Dir WMs file), hereafter WM Bill file; Postwar MCWR I file; File 1527 Women Reserve & Regular file (Dir WMs file), hereafter Res&Reg file; and P.L. 625, 80th Congress.

1. Hancock, lady in the Navy, p. 223.

2. Col Katherine A. Towle statement before the House Naval Affairs Committee on H.R. 5915, undtd (WR Bill file).

3. House of Representatives Naval Affairs Committee, U.S. Congress, To Amend the Naval Reserve Act of1938, As Amended, So as to Establish the Women's Reserves on a Permanent Basis, and for Other Purposes, House Report 226, 79th Congress, 2nd Session (Washington, 1946), p. 33-35.

4. Ibid, p. 33-34.

5. Maj Julia E. Hamblet memo to Director, Division of Reserve, dtd 29Apr47 (Res&Reg file).

6. Senate Committee on Armed Services, U. S. Congress, A Bill to Establish the Women's Army Corps in the Regular Army, To Authorize the Enlistment and Appointment of Women in the Regular Navy and Marine Corps and the Naval and Marine Corps Reserve and for Other Purposes, Hearings on S. 1103, S. 1527, and S. 1641, 80th Congress, 1st Session (Washington, 1947), p. 10.

7. Ibid., p. 13.

8. Ibid., p. 68.

9. Col Joseph W. Knighton memo to Gen Lemuel C. Shepherd, Jr., dtd 8Jul47 (Res&Reg file).

10. Director, Division of Plans and Policies memo to CMC, Subj: Reg WMs, proposed program for (Women's Reg Service & Discharge file, Dir WMs file).

11. Capt Ira H. Nunn, USN, ltr to CMC, dtd 13 Feb48 (WR file).

12. Woman Veteran, Apr48 (Women Veterans file, Dir WMs file).

13. Cited from Hancock, lady in the Navy, p. 231.

14. Mrs. Ruth Streeter ltr to CMC, dtd 4Aug47 (Res&Reg file).

CHAPTER 3

GOING REGULAR

Unless otherwise noted, the material in this chapter is derived from: WMs HQMC Records; The Reserve Bulletin, 1948-1949; WM Research File; Old Studies Matters Women Marines, box 3, WMs HQMC Records, hereafter Old Studies; Clowers papers; Personal Papers, copies, donated by LtCol Doris V. Kleberger to Hist&MusDiv, HQMC, hereafter Kleberger papers; Hamblet interview; Col Margaret M. Henderson interview with Hist&MusDiv, dtd Oct76 (Oral Hist Collection, Hist&MusDiv, HQMC), hereafter Henderson interview; LtCol Elsie E. Hill interview with Hist&MusDiv, dtd 30Apr77 (WM Research file), hereafter Hill interview; Hale interview; LtCol Elaine T. Carville interview with Hist&MusDiv, dtd 1May77 (WM Research file), hereafter Carville interview; Pauline Riley Wilson interview with Hist&MusDiv, dtd 1Apr77 (Oral Hist Collection, Hist&MusDiv, HQMC), hereafter Wilson interview; SgtMaj Ruth Ryan interview with Hist&MusDiv, dtd 24Mar77 (WM Research file), hereafter Ryan interview; 1stSgt Bertha J. Schultz interview with Hist&MusDiv, dtd 10Feb77 (Oral Hist Collection, Hist&MusDiv, HQMC), hereafter Schultz interview; SSgt Jack W. Draughon interview with Hist&MusDiv, dtd 24Mar77 (WM Research file), hereafter Draughon interview; 1stSgt Esther D. Waclawski interview with Hist&MusDiv dtd Nov76 (WM Research file), hereafter Waclawski interview.

1. Col Katherine A. Towle, Women in the Marine Corps draft (File, Mission of Women Marines, box 3, WMs HQMC Records).

2. Hamblet interview.

3. Katherine A. Towle, Administration and Leadership (Berkeley: The University of California, 1970), pp. 122, 138-139.

4. Ibid., p. 139.

5. DP&P Study No. 12785, dtd 4Dec47 (Organizations file).

6. DirWM Study No. 1-48, dtd 29Nov48 (Old Studies).

7. CMC ltr to all enlisted women and former enlisted women, MCWR, dtd 15Jul48 (Munroe scrapbook).

8. CMC ltr to all officers and former officers, MCWR, dtd 12Jul48 (File, Requirement for WM, box 7, WMs HQMC Records).

9. DP&P Study No. 179-48, dtd 2Nov48 (File Women Reserve & Regular, box 7, WMs HQMC Records).

10. DP&P Study No. 152-48 (File, Requirement for WM, Box 7, WMs HQMC Records).

11. DirWM Study No. 1-48, dtd 29Nov48 (Old Studies).

12. Reserve Bulletin, Nov48.

13. Ruth Cheney Streeter, History of the Marine Corps Women's Reserve (Washington, 6Dec45), pp. 31-32.

14. Ibid., p. 52.

15. DP&P Study No. 171-48, dtd 20Oct48 (File, History of the Office of the Dir WMs, box 5, WMs HQMC Records).

16. Reserve Bulletin, Dec 48.

17. Waclawski interview.

18. WM Research file.

19. Henderson and Hill interviews.

20. Clowers papers.

21. Col Katherine A. Towle memo to LtCol Jackson, dtd 22Nov48 (File, Reindoctrination Training-WMs, USMCR to USMC, box 7, WMs HQMC Records).

22. Schultz interview.

23. Wilson interview.

24. Hamblet interview.

25. Ibid.

26. Clowers papers.

27. Col Katherine A. Towle ltr to MajGen Leroy P. Hunt, dtd 23Dec48 (File Al/8, Reserve, Division of, box 8, WMs HQMC Records).

28. Marine Corps Memorandum No. 7-48, dtd 16Nov48 (File 1300, Assignment & Distribution 1944-1956, box 3, WMs HQMC Records).

29. DirWM Study No 1A-1949, undtd (Old Studies).

30. Ibid., appd, 17Mar50.

31. Col Katherine A. Towle comments on proposed General Order, dtd 26Sep49 (File 1412, Promotions, box 5, WMs HQMC Records).

32. DirWM Study No 1-48, dtd 29Nov48 (Old Studies).

33. Henderson interview.

34. Hale interview.

35. Muster Roll, 3d Recruit Training Bn, Parris Island, S.C, Feb49.

36. Henderson interview.

37. Hq, MCRD, PISC, Post General Order, Subj: 3rdRTB, Organization of, draft (File P 11/2, Recruit Training, box 5, WMs HQMC Records).

38. Henderson, Hale, Ryan, and Schultz interviews.

39. Ryan interview.

40. Draughon interview.

41. Ibid.

42. Reserve Bulletin, Feb49.

43. Parris Island Boot, 26Feb49.

44. Ibid., 16Apr49.

45. Henderson interview.

46. Schultz interview.

47. Hale interview.

48. SSgt Ann Estelle Lamb's Case File (Manpower Department, HQMC).

49. Henderson interview.

50. Schultz interview.

51. Henderson interview.

52. Henry I. Shaw, Jr., and Ralph W. Donnelly, Blacks in the Marine Corps (Washington: History and Museums Division, HQMC, 1975), p. 57.

53. Reserve Bulletin, Apr49.

54. Carville interview.

55. Col Katherine A. Towle ltr to Doris V. Kleberger, dtd 30Mar49 (Kleberger papers).

56. Muster Rolls, Headquarters Battalion, Marine Corps Schools, Quantico, Virginia, Jul49.

57. Hill interview.

58. Ibid.

59- Quantico Sentry, 30Jun49.

60. Hill interview.

61. Reserve Bulletin, Oct49.

62. Kleberger papers.

63. Col Katherine A. Towle comments (Kleberger papers).

64. Kleberger papers.

65. Reserve Bulletin, Oct49.

66. Kleberger papers.

67. Hill interview.

68. Ibid.

CHAPTER 4

THE KOREAN WAR YEARS

Unless otherwise noted, the material in this chapter is derived from: Women's Organized Reserve Units, box 3, WM's HQMC

Records, hereafter WR Units file; File A 1/8 Reserve, Division of, box 7, WM's HQMC Records, hereafter DivRes file; File P 11/3-1, Organized Reserve, box 7, WM's HQMC Records, hereafter Organized Reserve file; Colonel Valeria F. Hilgart interview with Hist&MusDiv, dtd 23Mar77 (Oral Hist Collection, Hist&MusDiv, HQMC), hereafter Hilgart interview; Lieutenant Colonel Nita Bob Warner interview with Hist&MusDiv, dtd Mar77 (Oral Hist Collection, Hist&MusDiv, HQMC), hereafter Judge interview; GySgt Frances Curwen Bilski interview with Hist&MusDiv, dtd 23Mar77 (WM Research file), hereafter Bilski interview; Theresa "Sue" Sousa interview with Hist&MusDiv, dtd 31Mar77 (Oral Hist Collection, Hist&MusDiv, HQMC), hereafter Sousa interview; Personal papers loaned by Lieutenant Colonel Pauline B. Beckley to Hist&MusDiv, HQMC, hereafter Beckley papers; Clowers papers; Scrapbook donated by MSgt Julia Bennke Stacy to Hist&MusDiv, HQMC, hereafter Stacy scrapbook; Munroe scrapbook.

1. Hamblet interview.

2. WR Units file.

3. Reserve Bulletin, Mar49.

4. Ibid., undtd.

5. DivRes file.

6. Ibid.

7. Ibid.

8. Reserve Bulletin, Apr49.

9. Wilson interview.

10. Munroe scrapbook.

11. Judge and Bilski interviews.

12. Judge interview.

13. Munroe scrapbook.

14. Ibid.

15. Organized Reserve file.

16. MGySgt Rocita A. Martinez ltr to Hist&MusDiv, HQMC, dtd 18Apr77 (WM Research file).

17. Frances M. Exum interview with Hist&MusDiv, dtd 13Apr77 (WM Research file).

18. Organized Reserve file.

19. Stacy scrapbook.

20. Sousa interview.

21. Warner interview.

22. Kleberger papers.

23. Haie interview.

24. WR Units file.

25. Director of WMs scrapbook (WM Research file).

26. Carville interview.

27. WR Units file.

28. Beckley papers.

29. WR Units file.

30. The Reserve Marine (Division of Reserve, HQMC), hereafter Reserve Marine, Jan51.

31. SgtMaj Ethyl Wilcox interview with Hist&MusDiv, dtd 21Jan77 (Oral Hist Collection, Hist&MusDiv, HQMC).

32. Mary Sue Mock Milton interview with Hist&MusDiv, dtd 26Mar77 (WM Reserve file).

33. Maj Mary E. Roddy interview with Hist&MusDiv, dtd 17Mar77 (WM Research file).

34. WR Units file.

35- Reserve Marine, Nov51.

36. Beckley papers.

37. Stella Uhorczuk ltr to Hist&MusDiv, HQMC, dtd 7Mar77 (WM Research file).

38. Judge interview.

39. Waclawski interview.

40. WR Units file.

41. Judge interview.

42. Bilski interview.

43. Old Studies.

44. Pendleton Scout, 1Aug50.

45. Waclawski interview.

46. San Diego Chevron, 8Dec50.

47. Clowers papers.

48. Warner interview.

49. El Tow Flight Jacket, 20Oct50.

50. Quantico Sentry, 10Nov50.

51. Carville interview.

52. Katherine Keefe interview with Hist&MusDiv, HQMC, 3Aug77.

53. Cherry Point Windsock, 30Nov51.

54. Kleberger papers.

55. Anna Orlanda Hopkins ltr to Hist&MusDiv, HQMC, dtd 25Feb77 (WM Research file).

56. Hilgart interview, and Lieutenant Colonel Virginia Caley interview with Hist&MusDiv, dtd 17Feb77 (Oral Hist Collection, Hist&MusDiv, HQMC).

57. Hilgart interview.

58. Kleberger interview.

59. San Diego Chevron, undtd.

60. The Windward Marine, (Kaneohe, MCAS), 16Mar56.

61. File P 11/2, Recruit Training, box 5, WMs HQMC Records.

62. Hale interview.

63. Ardella Wheeler Butts interview with Hist&MusDiv, HQMC, dtd 23Mar77 (WM Research file).

64. Schultz interview.

65. Reserve 46, box 7, WMs HQMC Records.

66. Colonel Margaret A. Brewer interview with Hist&MusDiv, dtd 30Dec77 (Oral Hist Collection, Hist&MusDiv, HQMC).

CHAPTER 5

UTILIZATION AND NUMBERS, 1951-1963

Unless otherwise noted, the material in this chapter is derived from: "Maximum Utilization of Women in the Marine Corps," report by Procedures Analysis Office, Nov51, File, Approved Policies on Utilization, Assignment of WMs since 1943, box 1, WMs HQMC Records, hereafter Procedures Analysis Report Nov51; File 1300, Assignment & Distribution (1944-1956), box 3 WMs HQMC Records, hereafter Assignment file 44-56; File, Utilization of Women Marines, DirWMs files, hereafter Util WMs file; File Utilization of Women, box 7, WMs HQMC Records, hereafter Util of Women file; DirWM reports on Women on Active Duty By MOS compiled by author on chart, Utilization Section, box 1, WM Research File, hereafter MOS Chart; "Enlisted Jobs In the Marine Corps Which Can Be Performed By Women In the Event of Mobilization," a thesis by Major Julia E. Hamblet, Ohio State University, 1951 (File 1951, box 1, WM Research file), hereafter Hamblet thesis.

1. Procedures Analysis Report Nov51.

2. Newsclippings, unidentified, DirWMs scrapbook on Parris Island, box 4, WMs HQMC Records.

3. Administrative Officer memorandum to Director, Division of Plans and Policies, dtd 12Dec50 (Assignment File 44-56).

4. DirWM memorandum to Director, Plans and Policies, dtd 5Jan51 (Assignment file 44-56).

5. Ibid.

6. Procedures Analysis Report Nov51.

7. Ibid.

8. Ibid.

9. Util WMs file.

10. Marine Corps Memorandum Number 41-52, MOS's appropriate for enlisted women Marines, dtd 17Apr52 (Util WMs file).

11. MOS Chart.

12. Sousa interview.

13. MOS Chart.

14. Hilgart interview.

15. MOS Chart.

16. MGySgt Rocita A. Martinez ltr to Hist&MusDiv, dtd 18Apr77 (WM Response file, WM Research file).

17. MOS Chart.

18. Util WMs file.

19. Asst Chief of Staff memorandum to Director, Plans and Policies, dtd 26Jan53 (Util WMs file).

20. Head, Classification Section memorandum to Head, Detail Branch, dtd 9Mar53 (Util WMs file).

21. Personnel Control Branch memorandum to Asst Chief of Staff, G-I, dtd 26Feb53 (Util WMs file).

22. Head, Classification Section memorandum to Head, Detail Branch, dtd 9Mar53 (Util WMs file).

23. Dir Personnel memorandum to Asst Chief of Staff, G-I, dtd 24Mar53 (Util WMs file).

24. Asst Chief of Staff memorandum to Military Personnel Policy Division, Office of Asst SecDef, dtd 31Mar53 (File, Requirement for WMs, box 7, WMs, HQMC Records).

25. Women's Armed Forces Integration Act of 1948.

26. Hamblet thesis.

27. Hamblet interview.

28. Comments furnished by PIO for release by DOD to free-lance writer, dtd 21Mar55 (Util WMs file).

29. Lieutenant Colonel Gail M. Reals interview with Hist&MusDiv, HQMC, dtd 6Jan77 (Oral Hist Collection, Hist&MusDiv, HQMC), hereafter Reals interview.

30. Clowers papers.

31. LtCol Emma H. Clowers' Navy Commendation Citation (Manpower Department, HQMC).

32. Ryan interview.

33. Bilski interview.

34. DirWMs memorandum to Asst Chief of Staff, G-3, dtd 12May52 (File 1500, Training and Education, box 3, WMs HQMC Records), hereafter Training file.

35. DirWMs memorandum to Asst Chief of Staff, G-3, dtd 11 Aug52 (Training file).

36. Camp Lejeune Globe, 23Jan53.

37. Ibid., 8Jan53.

38. Unit Diary, WM Co, MBCL, 8Jan-13Feb 53.

39. MSgt Lillian J. West ltr to Hist&MusDiv, HQMC, dtd 22May77 (WM Response file, WM Research file).

40. DirWMs memorandum to Asst Chief of Staff, G-3, dtd 7May54 (File 1510, Enlisted Training, Box 3, WMs HQMC Records).

41. Camp Lejeune Globe newsclippings, undtd, loaned by GySgt Frances Curwen Bilski.

42. Carville interview.

CHAPTER 6

UTILIZATION AND NUMBERS: PEPPER BOARD, 1964-1972

Unless otherwise noted, the material in this chapter is derived from: File 5300, WM Program Study Group, box 6, WMs HQMC Records, hereafter WMPSG file; Notebook, Pepper Board Backup Material, box 2, WM Research file, hereafter Pepper Board notebook; File, Study No. 1-64, box 6, WMs, HQMC Records, hereafter Study 1-64 file; File, Major Accomplishments (Code AW) 1967-1973, box 1, WM Research file, hereafter Maj Accomplishment file; Woman Marine Newsletters, box 2, WM Research file, hereafter WM Newsletter, File, 1200 Classification and Designation, Box 3, WMs HQMC Records, hereafter Classification and Designation file; File, Assignment & Distribution (1957-1971), box 3, WMs HQMC Records, hereafter Assignment & Distribution file; File 5200, General Management file, box 5, WMs HQMC Records, hereafter General Management file; File, Assignment of WMs to WestPac, box 7, WMs HQMC Records, hereafter

WMs to WestPac file; File, Assignment of WMs Overseas Box 6, WMs HQMC Records; LtCol Jane L. Wallis interview with Hist&MusDiv, HQMC, dtd 9Mar77, hereafter Wallis interview; LtCol Vea J. Smith interview with Hist&MusDiv, dtd 2Feb77 (Oral Hist Collection, Hist&MusDiv, HQMC), hereafter Smith interview.

1. DirWMs comments on replies from MC Bulletin 5312 of 27Feb63, dtd 24Dec64 (WMPSG file).

2. Ibid.

3. Col Barbara J. Bishop ltr to Hist&MusDiv, HQMC, dtd 31Jul77 (WM Response file, WM Research file).

4. Study 1-64 file.

5. Ibid.

6. Ibid.

7. CMC ltr to LtGen Robert H. Pepper, dtd 3Aug64 (Pepper Board notebook).

8. Ibid.

9. Director of Personnel memorandum to CMC, dtd 18Dec64 (Pepper Board Notebook).

10. Ibid.

11. Ibid.

12. Ibid.

13. DirWMs memorandum to CMC, dtd 2Dec65 (WMPSG file).

14. Ibid.

15. CMC handwritten comments on memorandum from Asst Chief of Staff, G-1 to CMC, dtd 22Nov65 (WMPSG file).

16. Maj Accomplishment file.

17. Ibid.

18. Ibid.

19. Ibid.

20. Maj Accomplishments, 30Jun67 (Maj Accomplishment file).

21. WM Newsletter, Spring 67.

22. LtCol Lillian H. Gridley official biography (RefSec, Hist&MusDiv, HQMC).

23. WM Newsletter, Spring 67.

24. Dir WMs memorandum to Dir Policy Analysis Div, dtd 15Jan70 (File Miscellaneous White House/Ref Book Items/Fact Sheets, box 5, WMs HQMC Records), hereafter White House file.

25. DirWMs memorandum to Chief of Staff (AD), dtd 20Jan65 (White House File).

26. Maj Joan M. Collins interview with Hist&MusDiv, HQMC, dtd 7Jan77 (Oral Hist Collection, Hist&MusDiv, HQMC), hereafter Collins interview.

27. Maj Carol Vertalino Deliberto interview with Hist&MusDiv, dtd 25Apr77 (Oral Hist Collection, Hist&MusDiv, HQMC).

28. Maj Accomplishments, 30Jun69 (Maj Accomplishment file).

29. Dir WMs memorandum to Asst Chief of Staff, G-3, dtd 3Jan68 (File 1520, Officer Training, Box 5, WMs HQMC Records).

30. Ibid.

31. Asst Chief of Staff, G-3 memorandum to DirWMs, dtd 9Feb68 (Officer Training file).

32. Dir WMs memorandum to Dir Policy Analysis Div, dtd 15Jan70 (White House file).

33. Col Mary E. Bane interview with Hist&MusDiv, HQMC, dtd 30Dec76 (Oral Hist Collection, Hist&MusDiv, HQMC) hereafter Bane interview.

34. Ibid.

35. DirWMs memorandum to Dir Policy Analysis Div, dtd 22Aug66 (File 1080, Personnel, Box 5, WMs HQMC Records).

36. WM Newsletter, Winter 67.

37. DirWMs memorandum to Chief of Staff, G-l, dtd 7Jul66 (Classification and Designation file).

38. CMC ltr to CO, MAD, NATTC, Memphis, Tenn, dtd 21Jul66 (Classification and Designation file).

39- DirWMs comment, subj: Establishment of WM billet in Office of Dep Under Secretary Navy (Mpr), dtd 13Jan67 (Assignment & Distribution file).

40. Statement of Col Jeanette 1. Sustad before the Special Subcommittee, House of Representatives, Dec69 (Laws and Legal Matters file, box 5, WMs HQMC Records).

41. Pepper Board notebook.

42. Smith interview.

43. Desert Dispatch, Barstow, Calif., 21Jun66.

44. Command Chronology, MCSC, Barstow, Calif, 30Dec67 (Archives, Hist&MusDiv, HQMC).

45. Prospector, Barstow, Calif, 21Jul67.

46. Unit Diaries, MCSC, Barstow, Calif., 1967-1971 (RefSec, Hist&MusDiv, HQMC).

47. Public Info Office memorandum, MCSC, Albany, Ga., donated by LtCol Vea J. Smith (Albany file, box 1, WM Research file).

48. Albany Emblem, 21Mar69.

49. Ibid., 18Aug67.

50. Ibid., 9Feb68.

51. Unit Diary, MCSC, Albany, Ga., Nov72 (RefSec, Hist&MusDiv, HQMC).

52. DirWMs input for CMC Ref Book Items, dtd 28Nov66 (General Management file).

53. WM Newsletter, Autumn 66.

54. DirWMs report to Chief of Staff, dtd 16Sep66 (WMs to WestPac file).

55. Ibid.

56. Ibid.

57. Bishop letter.

58. Command Chronology, MCAS, Iwakuni, Japan, 1Jul-31Dec66 (Archives, Hist&MusDiv, HQMC).

59. Torii Teller, Iwakuni, Japan, 29Mar67.

60. WM Newsletter, Spring 67.

61. Torii Teller, 27Mar67.

62. WM Newsletter, Autumn 66.

63. Stars & Stripes, 23Oct66.

64. Maj Nancy A. Carroll ltr to Hist&MusDiv, HQMC, dtd 17Apr77 (Wm Response file, WM Research file).

65. Wallis interview.

66. Stars & Stripes, 19Jul67.

67. Wallis interview.

68. Ibid.

69. Ibid.

70. Ibid.

71. Sustad interview.

72. Connolly interview.

73. Quoted from MSgt B. J. Dulinsky ltr to DirWMs, dtd 18Mar67, WM Newsletter, Spring 67.

74. Quoted from Captain E. E. Filkins ltr to DirWMs, dtd 16Aug68, WM Newsletter, Summer 68.

75. Lieutenant Colonel E. E. Davis interview with Hist&MusDiv, HQMC, dtd 22Mar77 (Oral Hist Collection, Hist&MusDiv, HQMC).

76. LtCol Vera M. Jones interview with Hist&MusDiv, dtd 24Mar77 (Oral Hist Collection, Hist&MusDiv, HQMC).

77. "Information on Saigon," booklet by DirWMs (File Women Marines in Vietnam, box 1, WM Research file).

78. Quoted from Captain E. E. Filkins ltr to DirWMs, dtd 7jan69, WM Newsletter, Spring 69.

79. Quoted from Captain Vera M. Jones ltr to DirWMs, dtd 3Feb68, WM Newsletter, Winter 68.

80. Quoted from MSgt B. J. Dulinsky ltr to DirWMs, dtd 9Feb68.

81. Quoted from Captain E. E. Filkins ltr to DirWMs, dtd 15Aug68.

82. Quoted from SSgt E. Salazar ltr to GySgt H. Dowd, dtd 10Sep69, WM Newsletter, Winter 69.

83. ComUSMACV msg to CMC, dtd Jun70 (WM Research file).

84. Maj Charlene S. Itchawitch ltr to Hist&MusDiv, HQMC, dtd 19Jan77 (WM Response file, WM Research file).

85. Maj Accomplishment file, 30Jun67.

86. Woman Marine Geographical Assignments, 30Jun71 (Assignment & Distribution file).

CHAPTER 7

UTILIZATION AND NUMBERS: SNELL COMMITTEE, 1973-1977

Unless otherwise noted, the material in this chapter is derived from Ad Hoc Committee on Increased Effectiveness and Utilization of Women in the Marine Corps File, box 1, WM Research file, hereafter Ad Hoc Committee file; Speeches and articles by DirWMs, notebook, box 2, WM Research file, hereafter DirWMs speech notebook; File, WMs in FMF, Pilot Program, box 1, WM Research file, hereafter WMs in FMF file; Bane interview; Maj Kathleen V. Abbott Abies ltr to Hist&MusDiv, HQMC, dtd 7jul77 (WM Response file, WM Research file), hereafter Abies ltr; Biographies of WMs in the Marine Corps Band file, Box 1, WM Research file, hereafter Marine Corps Band file.

1. Ad Hoc Committee file.

2. Quoted from Deputy C/S (Manpower) ltr to Assistant C/S, et. al., dtd 18Sep72 (Ad Hoc Committee file).

3. Quoted from DirWMs memorandum to CMC, dtd 18Oct73 (Ad Hoc Committee file).

4. Senior Member, Ad Hoc Committee memorandum to Deputy C/S (Manpower), dtd 3Jul73 (Ad Hoc Committee file).

5. Recommendation No. 7, Report of Ad Hoc Committee (Ad Hoc Committee file).

6. Report of Ad Hoc Committee (Ad Hoc Committee file).

7. Remarks by Col Margaret A. Brewer, Defense Manpower Commission, dtd 15May75 (DirWMs speech notebook).

8. Parris Island Boot, 9Jul76.

9. Navy Times, 28Mar77.

10. Col Margaret A. Brewer, "The Marine Team," Marine Corps Gazette, Apr76.

11. Ibid.

12. Navy Times, 13Aug75.

13- Capt Charles Barber, Provost Marshal, Parris Island memorandum to Captain Weda, dtd 5Feb74 (WM Research file).

14. Headquarters Marine Corps Hotline, Apr75.

15. Cpl Mary F. Bungcayo interview with Hist&MusDiv, dtd 21Mar77 (Oral Hist Collection, Hist&MusDiv, HQMC).

16. Hilgart interview.

17. 2dLt Judith Cataldo ltr to Hist&MusDiv, dtd 22Mar77 (WM Response file, WM Research file).

18. Ibid.

19. Navy Times, 27Apr74.

20. Daily News, Jacksonville, N.C., 9Jan75.

21. Ibid.

22. DivInfo news release no. DLS-145-C2-77 (WM Research file).

23. MCRD Command Chronology, Jun-Dec73 (Archives, Hist&MusDiv, HQMC).

24. Quantico Sentry, 14jan74.

25. Twentynine Palms Observation Post, 14Mar75.

26. The Newport News (Va.) Times Herald, 1Jul75.

27. PIO, Camp Lejeune, N.C., news release no. 08-103-75, dtd 2Sep75.

28. Camp Lejeune Globe, 17Feb77.

29. Beaufort Jet Steam, 21Jan77.

30. Sgt Geneva Jones interview with Hist&MusDiv, dtd 21Mar77 (Oral Hist Collection, Hist&MusDiv, HQMC).

31. Camp Lejeune Globe, Apr77.

32. LCpl Katie Jones Dixon interview with Hist&MusDiv, dtd 21Mar77 (Oral Hist Collection, Hist&MusDiv, HQMC).

33. Cherry Point Windsock, 19Jul74.

34. WM Newsletter, Winter 68.

35. SgtMaj Jaunal ltr to Hist&MusDiv, dtd 1Feb77 (WM Response file, WM Research file).

36. Brewer interview.

37. Johnson biography (Marine Corps Band file).

38. Brewer interview.

39- Individual biographies, Women in the Marine Corps Band (Marine Corps Band file).

40. WMs in FMF file.

41. CMC msg to FMF commanders, dtd 19Feb74 (WMs in the FMF file).

42. Cherry Point Windsock, 19Jul74.

43. Ibid.

44. CG, lstMarDiv msg to CMC, dtd 4Nov74 (WMs in FMF file).

45. Ibid.

46. CG, 2d MAW ltr to CMC, dtd 25Nov74 (WMs in FMF file).

47. CG, FMFPac msg to CMC, dtd 30Oct74 (WMs in FMF file).

48. Los Angeles Times, 29Aug76.

49. Ibid.

50. Ibid.

51. Capt K. A. Gordon interviews with Hist&MusDiv, HQMC, dtd 9Sep77 (WM Research file).

52. Bane interview.

53. Ibid.

54. Ibid.

55. Abies ltr.

56. Ibid.

57. Col Margaret A. Brewer, "The Marine Team," Marine Corps Gazette, Apr76.

CHAPTER 8

RESERVES AFTER KOREA

Unless otherwise noted, the material in this chapter is derived from Files, Reserve 46, box 7, WMs HQMC Records, hereafter Reserve 46 file; File 1510/6, Reserves, box 6, WMs HQMC Records, hereafter Reserves file; File PII/3-1, Organized Reserve, box 7, WMs, HQMC Records; File, Reserves after Korea, box 1, WM Research file, hereafter Res after Korea file; Sousa interview; MSgt Laura J. Dennis interview with Hist&MusDiv, HQMC, hereafter Dennis interview. (The author was I&I, WM Platoon, Boston, 1957-1958, and in 1975-1976 prepared two staff studies for the Division of Reserve on the training of senior Women Reserve Officers.)

1. Reserve Memorandum 2-52, concept of the Woman Marine Platoons of the Organized Marine Corps Reserve, dtd 22Jan52 (Reserve 46 file).

2. Dennis interview.

3. Sousa interview.

4. Reserve Marine, Feb52.

5. Navy Times, 24Dec55.

6. Roster of Platoons (Reserve 46 file).

7. Reserve Structure Board, DivRes, dtd 6May58 (Res after Korea file).

8. LtCol Elsie E. Hill comments, dtd 14May58 (Reserve 46 file).

9. DirWMs memorandum to Division of Reserve, dtd 16May58 (Reserve 46 file).

10. DirWMs memorandum to Chief of Staff, dtd 30Jun58 (Reserve 46 file).

11. LtCol Mary E. Roddy scrapbook loaned to Hist&MusDiv.

12. DirWMs comments, dtd 28Jun67 (Reserve file).

13. Women Marines Reservists, Ad Hoc Committee Report, dtd 13Sep67 (Res after Korea file).

14. MCO 1001R.47, dtd 10Jun71 (Res after Korea file).

15. DivRes talking paper, dtd 3May76 (Res after Korea file).

16. MajGen Michael P. Ryan memorandum to CMC, dtd 23Jul75 (Res after Korea file).

17. CMC msg to CG 4th MarDiv and CG 4th MAW (Res after Korea file).

18. LtCol Patricia A. Hook interview with Hist&MusDiv, HQMC, dtd Jun77

19. News clipping, dateline Ft. Benning, Ga. (Ref Card, WM Research file).

20. Ibid.

21. Ibid.

22. Ibid.

CHAPTER 9

RECRUIT TRAINING

Unless otherwise noted, the material in this chapter is derived from WRTB Order 5000.3B, SOP for recruit training, 15Apr63, loaned by SgtMaj Eleanor E. Judge to the Hist&MusDiv, HQMC, hereafter SOP63; WRTB Order P5000.3D, SOP for recruit training, 15Sep71, loaned by Maj Joan M. Collins to Hist&MusDiv, HQMC, hereafter SOP71; MCRD Order P1510.26, SOP for female recruit training, dtd 20Dec76 (WM Research file), hereafter SOP76; File PII/2, Recruit Training, box 5, WMs HQMC Records, hereafter Recruit Training file; File 1510, Enlisted Training, box 3, WMs HQMC Records, hereafter Enlisted Training file; File 1103/1, New WM Complex, Woman Recruit Training Command files, PISC, hereafter WM Complex file; Hill interview; Judge interview; LtCol Vera M. Jones interview with Hist&MusDiv, HQMC, dtd 24Mar77 (Oral Hist Collection, Hist&MusDiv, HQMC) hereafter Jones interview; Capt Nancy A. Davis interview with Hist&MusDiv, HQMC, dtd 7Jun77 (WM Research file), hereafter Davis interview; CWO Virginia R. Painter interview with Hist&MusDiv, HQMC, dtd 22Mar77 (WM Research File), hereafter Painter interview; MSgt Bridget V. Connolly interview with Hist&MusDiv, HQMC, dtd 4Jan77 (Oral Hist Collection, Hist&MusDiv, HQMC), hereafter Connolly interview. (The author served as S-3, WRTB; commanding officer, Recruit Company; and executive officer, WRTB from Oct61-Aug63)

1. SOP76.

2. Ibid.

3. CO 3d RTB ltr to CMC, dtd 15Sep52 (Recruit Training file).

4. CO 3d RTB ltr to DirWMs, dtd 31May51 (Recruit Training file).

5. Ibid.

6. Col Katherine A. Towle, 2d endorsement on CO 3d RTB ltr to CMC, dtd 15Sep52 (Recruit Training file).

7. CMC msg to CG MCRD, PISC, dtd 18Aug52 (Recruit Training file).

8. CMC ltr to CG MCRD, PISC, dtd 24Apr58 (Enlisted Training file).

9. Leatherneck, Dec58, p. 35.

10. Ibid., p. 38.

11. Ibid., p. 39.

12. CG MCRD, PISC, ltr to CMC, dtd 6Mar61 (Enlisted Training file).

13. WM Newsletter, 1967-1969 (WM Research file); Maj Accomplishments file 1967-1970.

14. Input for DirWM newsletter from LtCol Jenny Wrenn, dtd 8Apr70 (WM Research file).

15. Judge interview.

16. Connolly interview.

17. Input for DirWM newsletter from LtCol Jenny Wrenn, dtd 8Apr70 (WM Research file).

18. Judge interview.

19. Collins interview.

20. Reals interview.

21. SOP71.

22. Quoted in Parade, 1958 (Hamblet scrapbook).

23. SOP63; SOP71; SOP76.

24. SOP76.

25. Painter interview.

26. SOP63; SOP71.

27. Davis interview.

28. Hill interview.

29. Parris Island Boot, 10Oct55.

30. Hill interview.

31. Parris Island Boot, 7May76.

32. SOP63; SOP71; SOP76.

33. Constance Shafter ltr to Hist&MusDiv, HQMC, dtd 4Mar77 (WM Research file).

34. SOP63; S0P71; SOP76.

35. Parris Island Boot, 16Mar68.

36. Jones interview; Davis interview.

37. Parris Island Boot, 4Nov50.

38. Marine Corps Gazette, Feb63, p. 74.

39. Parris Island Boot, 40ct64.

40. Public Works Officer ltr to CO WRTB, dtd 31Aug67 (WM Complex file).

41. CO WRTB ltr to CG MCRD, PISC, dtd 9Feb75 (WM Complex file).

42. Jones interview.

CHAPTER 10

OFFICER TRAINING

Unless otherwise noted, the material in this chapter is derived from File, Woman Officer School, MCDEC, MCB, Quantico, 20 December 1974, Disestablishment, WM Research file, hereafter WOS File; LtCol Barbara E. Dolyak interview with Hist&MusDiv, HQMC, dtd 13Sep77, hereafter Dolyak interview. (The author attended officer candidate training in 1953 and 1954, attended WOIC in 1955, and served on the staff as supply officer and instructor in 1957 and 1958. She served as instructor at WOS from 1965 until 1970.)

1. Clowers papers.

2. Hamblet interview.

3. CMC ltr A03C53-ch, dtd 14Sep71, referenced in Col Williams F. Saunders ltr to CG, MCDEC, dtd 31May72 (WOS file).

4. CMC ltr to CG, MCDEC, dtd 20Feb73 (WOS file).

5. Ibid.

6. Ibid.

7. CG, MCDEC ltr to CMC, dtd 160ct74 (WOS file).

8. Ibid.

9. Ibid.

10. Dolyak interview.

11. CMC ltr to multiple addresses, White letter No. 5-76, dtd 23Jun76 (WOS file).

12. Ibid.

13. Dolyak interview.

14. Basic School mission, quoted from briefing paper (WOS file).

15. Dolyak interview.

16. Ibid.

17. CG MCDEC ltr to CMC, dtd 20Dec76 (WOS file).

18. Ibid.

19. Ibid.

20. CMC ltr to CG, MCDEC, dtd 30Dec76 (WOS file).

21. Capt Robin L. Austin, quoted in Camp Lejeune Globe, 28Apr77.

22. CG MCDEC ltr to CMC, dtd 29Jun77 (WOS file).

23. BGen Paul X. Kelley, quoted in Quantico Sentry, 21Jun77.

24. Cruise Book BC 3-77 loaned to Hist&MusDiv, HQMC, by LtCol Barbara E. Dolyak.

CHAPTER 11

ADMINISTRATION OF WOMEN

Unless otherwise noted, the material in this chapter is derived from a compilation of information, oral, written, and taped, gathered by means of letters and interviews. All women Marines interviewed for this history, active and former, were asked to comment on the subject of WM companies, barracks, and regulations and the relationship between officers and enlisted women. Regulations vary from post to post so that the information presented in this chapter is representative of most WM commands but not necessarily all of them. In March 1977, the author visited the WM Company, Headquarters Battalion, HQMC; the WM

Barracks at Cherry Point, and Headquarters and Service Company, Base Material Battalion, MCB, Camp Lejeune, N.C.

1. Col Katherine A. Towle ltr to MajGen Leroy P. Hunt, dtd 23Dec48 (File Al/8, Reserve, Division of, box 7, WMs HQMC Records).

2. Col Julia E. Hamblet memo to Asst C/S G-I, dtd 14Nov48 (File 5321 Allowances T/Os, box 6, WMs HQMC Records).

3. Gen Louis H. Wilson, White Letter No. 5-76, to all General Officers, all Commanding Officers, and all Officers In Charge, dtd 23Jun76 (WM Research file).

4. Maj Gerald W. Sims interview with Hist&MusDiv, HQMC, upon visit of author to Base Material Battalion, Marine Corps Base, Camp Lejeune, N.C, 22Mar77.

5. Quantico Sentry, 25Mar77.

6. Sgt Carol Fox interview with Hist&MusDiv, HQMC, dtd 21Mar77 (Oral Hist Collection, Hist&MusDiv, HQMC).

7. Ibid.

8. LCpl Judith Coy and PFC Katie Dixon Jones interviews with Hist&MusDiv, HQMC, dtd 21Mar77 (Oral Hist Collection, Hist&MusDiv, HQMC), hereafter Coy interview and Dixon interview.

9. Col Margaret A. Brewer interview with Hist&MusDiv, dtd 16Jun77 (Oral Hist Collection, Hist&MusDiv, HQMC), hereafter Brewer interview.

10. Schultz interview.

11. Painter and Bilski interviews.

12. Hilgart interview.

13. Collins interview.

14. CWO-3 Eileen R. Scanlon interview with Hist&MusDiv, HQMC, dtd 12Jan77 (Oral Hist Collection, Hist&MusDiv, HQMC).

15. Woman Marine Program Study Group, dtd 30Nov64 (WM Research file).

16. Paula Wiltshire Sentipal ltr to Hist&MusDiv, HQMC, dtd 24Jan77 (WM Research file).

17. Lt Cathy A. Fremin interview with Hist&MusDiv, HQMC, dtd 20Jun77 (WM Research file).

18. LtCol Ruth F. Reinholz interview with Hist&MusDiv, HQMC, dtd 1Jan77 (Oral Hist Collection, Hist&MusDiv, HQMC), hereafter Reinholz interview.

19. Maj Ruth D. Woidyla interview with Hist&MusDiv, HQMC, dtd 20Jun77 (WM Research file).

20. Ibid.

CHAPTER 12

PROMOTIONS

Unless otherwise noted, the material in this chapter was derived from File 1412, Promotions, box 5, WMs HQMC Records, hereafter Promotions file; and Director of WMs Newsletters 1966-1970. All women Marines interviewed for this history were asked to comment on promotion policies and their effect on careers and on morale.

1. Public Law 90-130.

2. CWO-4 Ruth L. Wood ltr to Hist&MusDiv, HQMC, dtd 1Apr77 (Response file, WM Research file).

3. Dir WMs Newsletter, Winter 68 (WM Research file).

4. Remarks of the President upon signing H.R. 5894, Office of the White House Press Secretary (Promotions file).

5. Col Margaret A. Brewer, "The Marine Team," Marine Corps Gazette, Apr76.

6. WMs Newsletter, Spring68 (WM Research file).

7. Dir WMs comments on study to reevaluate the first sergeant/sergeant major program, dtd 21Sep56 (Promotions file).

8. Ibid.

9. Ibid.

10. Col Julia E. Hamblet memo to Chief of Staff, dtd 21Nov58, Subj: Report of conversation with the Commandant relative to the first sergeant/sergeant major program (Promotion file).

11. MCO 1421.6, dtd 3May60.

12. Parris Island Boot, 19Feb65.

13. Sergeant Major of the Marine Corps memo to the Commandant, dtd 1Nov71 (Promotion file).

14. Ibid.

15. Dir WMs comments, dtd 19Nov71 (Promotion file).

16. Asst Chief of Staff memo to Deputy Chief of Staff, Manpower, dtd 7Aug72 (Promotion file).

17. News article undtd, Dir of WMs scrapbook (WMs HQMC Records).

CHAPTER 13

MARRIAGE, MOTHERHOOD, AND DEPENDENT HUSBANDS

Unless otherwise noted, the material in this chapter was derived from File 5730, Congressional legislative liaison, box 5, WMs, HQMC Records; file, Marriage-Discharge/Transfers, box 3, WMs, HQMC Records, hereafter Marriage file; Dir WMs Newsletter, 1966-1970, WM Research file; File, Miscellaneous (White House/Ref Book items/Fact Sheet), box 5, WMs HQMC Records, hereafter Misc file; Col Jeanette I. Sustad interview with Hist&MusDiv, HQMC, dtd 20Jun77 (Oral Hist Collection, Hist&MusDiv, HQMC), hereafter Sustad interview; Capt Katherine A. Gordon, interview with Hist&MusDiv, dtd 29Jun77 (WM Research file), hereafter Gordon interview.

1. Dir WMs comment, dtd 21Sep59 (Marriage file).

2. WMs Newsletter, 16Aug66 (WM Research file).

3. Ibid.

4. Proposed Executive Order, Regulations Governing Discharge from the Armed Forces of Women Serving under the Army-Navy Nurses Act of 1947 and the Women's Armed Forces Integration Act of 1948 (Marriage file).

5. LtCol Margaret A. Brewer comments to Mary Ann Kuhn of the Washington Daily News, dtd 1Oct70 (Misc file).

6. Sustad interview.

7. Gordon interview.

8. Judge interview.

9. Sustad interview.

10. Maj Mary Sue League papers donated to the Hist&MusDiv, HQMC (WM Research file).

11. MCO 5000.12, dtd 16Jul75 (WM Research file).

12. Office of the Asst SecDef (Manpower, Reserve Affairs, and Logistics) Background Study, Use of Women in the Military, dtd May77 (WM Research file).

13. RAdm Clifford A. Swanson ltr to Office of the Judge Advocate General, dtd 5Jan49 (Marriage file).

14. Col Jeanette I. Sustad remarks to Special Subcommittee on Utilization of Manpower in the Military, House Armed Services Committee, dtd 6Mar72 (File Laws and Legal Matters, box 5, WMs HQMC Records).

15. Equal Opportunity Actions Affecting Military Women (1972-1976) (WM Research file).

16. B.J. Simmons, Jr., Department of Navy Bureau of Personnel memo to Deputy Under Secretary of Navy (Manpower), dtd 13Mar68 (File 5200, General Management, box 5, WM HQMC Records).

17. Clowers papers.

18. Dir WMs memo to Head, Career Planning Branch, dtd 10Aug72 (File 5600, Publications, box 5, WMs HQMC Records).

19. Equal Opportunity Actions Affecting Military Women (1972-1976) (WM Research file).

CHAPTER 14

UNIFORMS

Unless otherwise noted, the material in this chapter is derived from: Headquarters, U.S. Marine Corps, Uniform Regulations U.S. Marine Corps Women's Reserve, 1945, dtd 30Apr45 (Marine Corps Historical Library, Hist&MusDiv, HQMC), hereafter Uniform Regulations, 1945; Marine Corps Manual, 1949, with all changes (Marine Corps Historical Library, Hist&MusDiv, HQMC); Marine Corps Order P1020.34, dtd 2Jun6l, with all changes to include MCO P1020.34C, dtd 12Mar76 (Central Files, HQMC), hereafter MCO P1020.34; WM Newsletter, and Munn interview.

1. Uniform Regulations, 1945.

2. Warner interview.

3. Carville interview.

4. Maj Harry D. Elms interview with Hist&MusDiv, HQMC, Nov76, (WM Research file).

5. Munn interview.

6. Parris Island Boot, Nov50.

7. Munn interview.

8. Hamblet interview.

9. DirWMs memorandum to Secretary-Recorder, Permanent Marine Corps Uniform Board, dtd 13Mar62 (Uniform notebook, box 2, WM Research file), hereafter Uniform notebook.

10. DirWMs memorandum to President, Permanent Marine Corps Uniform Board, dtd 2Jul62 (Uniform notebook).

11. Col Mary E. Bane interview with Hist&MusDiv, HQMC, Nov76.

12. Ibid.

13. Munn interview.

14. Newsclippings marked Journal, 31Aug52, otherwise unidentified, donated by LtCol Munn (box 2, WM Research file).

15. "The Premier Presentation of Women Marines Uniforms designed by Mainbocker, Marine Barracks, Washington, DC," 28Aug52, program donated by LtCol Ben Alice Day Munn (box 2, WM Research file).

16. Henderson interview.

17. Parris Island Boot, 26Jan66.

18. WM Newsletter, Winter 68.

19. Col Jeanette L Sustad interview with Hist&MusDiv, HQMC, dtd Nov76.

20. Paula Wiltshire Sentipal interview with Hist&MusDiv, dtd Nov76.

21. MCO P1020.34C, dtd 12Mar76.

22. LtCol Elsie E. Hill ltr to Col Margaret M. Henderson, dtd 7Dec6l (File 1021, Clothing & Uniform, box 1, WMs HQMC Records).

23. MCO P1020.34A, Cl, dtd 4Nov63.

24. MCB 1020, dtd 22Sep75 (Central Files, HQMC).

25. Navy Times, 20Jun77.

CHAPTER 15

LAURELS AND TRADITIONS

Unless otherwise noted, the material in this chapter was derived from Laurels and Traditions Section, WM Research Notebook 3, box 2, WM Research file, hereafter Laurels file; WM Anniversary file, box 2, WM Research file, hereafter Ann file; and Molly Marine file, box 2, WM Research file, hereafter Molly Marine file.

1. Director of WMs File, box 2, WM Research file.

2. Col Hazel E. Benn's Legion of Merit citation (Manpower Dept, HQMC).

3. Col Hazel E. Benn interview with Hist&MusDiv, dtd 17Jan77 (Oral Hist Collection, Hist&MusDiv, HQMC).

4. Leatherneck, undated 19535. SSgt Barbara O. Barnwell's Navy and Marine Corps Medal citation (Manpower Dept, HQMC).

6. Syracuse (N.Y.) Herald-American, 9Aug53.

7. Navy Times, 17jul63.

8. GySgt D. L. Kearns' Navy and Marine Corps Medal citation (Manpower Dept, HQMC).

9. 1stLt V. K. Brame's Navy and Marine Corps Medal citation (Manpower Dept, HQMC).

10. Reidsville (N.C.) Review, undated (Laurels file).

11. Oceanside (Calif.) Breeze, 18Nov76.

12. LCpl Sheryl L. Young's Navy and Marine Corps Medal citation (Manpower Dept, HQMC).

13. Capt Leaverton, LtCol O'Hollern, and LtCol Reinholz' Bronze Star medal citations (Manpower Dept, HQMC).

14. Leatherneck, Jul64.

15. 1stSgt Josephine S. Davis letter and papers donated to Hist&MusDiv, dtd l4Dec76 (Response file, box 2, WM Research file), hereafter Davis papers.

16. SSgt J. Gebers ltr to SSgt Joan Ambrose, dtd 7May65 (Laurels file)

17. Davis papers.

18. Headquarters Marine Corps photo No. 12358, dtd 13Feb44.

19. Dir WMs memo to Col Dana C. Hart, dtd 7Mar51 (Ann file).

20. Brewer interview.

21. Mrs. John B. Cook telecon to Hist&MusDiv, dtd 18May77.

22. Hamblet interview.

23. Gen Clifton B. Cates ltr to Col Katherine A. Towle, dtd 13Feb51 (Ann File).

24. Memo for file, unsigned, dtd 21Jan54 (Ann file).

25. Gen Randolph McC. Pate ltr to Col Julia E. Hamblet, dtd 13Feb56 (Ann file).

26. Dir WMs memo to Chief of Staff, dtd 12Jan60 (Ann file).

27. Dir WMS comment on proposed CMC message on the occasion of the 31st anniversary of WMs, dtd 7Jan74 (Ann file).

28. Ibid.

29. Message from the Commandant, dtd 13Feb74 (Ann file).

30. Parris Island Boot, 20Feb70.

31. Ibid.

32. Molly Marine file.

33. WMA file, box 2, WM Research file.

CHAPTER 16

THE SERGEANTS MAJOR OF WOMEN MARINES

Unless otherwise noted, the material in this chapter is derived from the official biographies of the sergeants major (File Sergeant Major, WM Research file).

1. Qualification for Sergeant Major of Women Marines (File Sergeant Major, WM Research file).

2. Sergeant Major Grace A. Carle interview with Hist&MusDiv, dtd 15Mar77 (Oral Hist Collection, Hist&MusDiv, HQMC).

CHAPTER 17

THE DIRECTORS OF WOMEN MARINES

Unless otherwise noted, the material for this chapter was derived from the official biographies of each of the Directors of Women Marines and collected news articles filed under each one's name, Dir WMs File, box 2, WM Research file, hereafter Dir WMs file; and Women Marines File, RefSec, Hist&MusDiv, HQMC. (The author attended the ceremony marking the disestablishment of the Director of Women Marines office on 30Jun77.)

1. Katherine A. Towle File (Dir WMs file).

2. Oakland Tribune, 16May63-

3. Hamblet interview.

4. Munn interview.

5. Julia E. Hamblet File (Dir WMs file).

6. Boston Post, 19Apr53.

7. Judge interview.

8. Margaret M. Henderson File (Dir WMs file).

9- Col Ruth C. Streeter, Tales of an Ancient Marine (privately published), p. 56 (Hist&MusDiv, HQMC).

10. Barbara J. Bishop file (Dir WMs file).

11. Jeanette I. Sustad file (Dir WMs file).

12. Col Jeanette I. Sustad's Legion of Merit citation (Manpower Dept, HQMC).

13. Margaret A. Brewer file (Dir WMs file).

14. Brewer interview, 30Dec76.

15. Brewer interview, 16Jun77.

16. Col Margaret M. Henderson briefing of Indonesian WAVE officers, 20Nov63 (Speeches by Directors and CMC, box 2, WM Research file).

17. Brewer interview, 16Jun77.

18. Ibid.

Appendix A

Women Marines Strength, 1948-1977

DATE	OFFICERS	ENLISTED	TOTAL
30 June 48	8	159	167
30 June 49	31	322	353
30 June 50	45	535	580
30 June 51	63	2,002	2,065
30 June 52	115	2,347	2,462
30 June 53	160	2,502	2,662
30 June 54	163	2,339	2,502
30 June 55	135	2,113	2,248
30 June 56	113	1,634	1,747
30 June 57	107	1,510	1,617
30 June 58	115	1,530	1,645
30 June 59	123	1,703	1,826
30 June 60	123	1,488	1,611
30 June 61	117	1,495	1,612
30 June 62	121	1,576	1,697
30 June 63	135	1,563	1,698
30 June 64	128	1,320	1,448
30 June 65	140	1,441	1,581
30 June 66	153	1,697	1,832
30 June 67	189	2,122	2,311
30 June 68	228	2,555	2,780
30 June 69	284	2,443	2,727
30 June 70	299	2,119	2,418
30 June 71	277	1,981	2,258
30 June 72	282	2,066	2,348
30 June 73	315	1,973	2,288
30 June 74	336	2,402	2,738
30 June 75	345	2,841	3,186
30 June 76	386	3,133	3,519
30 June 77	407	3,423	3,830

Appendix B

Occupational Fields for Women Officers

Occupational fields in which women officers are eligible to serve, and percentages in each, as of 31 December 1976.*

	NO. WOMEN OFFICERS	PERCENTAGE OF WOMEN OFFICERS	PERCENTAGE OF USMC OFFICERS
01 PERSONNEL AND ADMINISTRATION	142	33.41	30.80
02 INTELLIGENCE	18	4.23	9.42
04 LOGISTICS	0	0.00	0.00
13 ENGINEER AND SHORE PARTY	4	0.94	0.56
14 DRAFTING, SURVEYING, AND MAPPING	0	0.00	0.00
15 PRINTING AND REPRODUCTION	0	0.00	0.00
21 ORDNANCE	0	0.00	0.00
23 EXPLOSIVES ORDNANCE DISPOSAL	0	0.00	0.00
25 OPERATIONAL COMMUNICATIONS	20	4.70	2.22
26 SIGNALS INTEL/GROUND ELECT WF	0	0.00	0.00
28 TELECOM MAINTENANCE	0	0.00	0.00
30 SUPPLY ADMINISTRATION/OPERATIONS	28	6.59	2.25
31 TRANSPORTATION	5	1.17	16.67
32 REPAIR SERVICES	0	0.00	0.00
33 FOOD SERVICES	8	1.90	20.51
34 AUDITING, FINANCE, AND ACCOUNTING	46	10.80	21.00
35 MOTOR TRANSPORT	6	1.40	4.41
40 DATA SYSTEMS	18	4.23	6.47
41 MC EXCHANGE	12	2.82	44.44
43 PUBLIC AFFAIRS	14	3.29	35.90
44 LEGAL SERVICES	26	6.11	5.21
46 PHOTOGRAPHY	5	1.17	5.26
49 TRAINING AND TRAINING AIDS	3	0.70	17.65
55 BAND	0	0.00	0.00
57 NUCLEAR, BIOLOGICAL, AND CHEMICAL	0	0.00	0.00
58 MILITARY POLICE AND CORRECTIONS	5	1.15	5.26
59 ELECTRONICS MAINTENANCE	1	0.23	0.71
60/61 AIRCRAFT MAINTENANCE	4	0.94	1.98
65 AVIATION ORDNANCE	0	0.00	0.00
66 AVIONICS	0	0.00	0.00
68 WEATHER SERVICE	3	0.70	21.43
70 AVIATION OPERATIONS	1	0.23	4.17
72 AIR CONTROL/SUPPORT/ANTIAIR WF	9	2.11	1.61
73 AIR TRAFFIC CONTROL	13	3.05	13.40
99 IDENTIFYING AND REPORTING MOS'S	34	8.00	3.01

03, 08, 18, 75—not eligible for assignment

*(*Source: WM Research file*)

Appendix C

Occupational Fields for Enlisted Women

Occupational fields in which enlisted women are eligible to serve, and percentages in each, as of 31 December 1976.*

	NO. ENLISTED WOMEN	PERCENTAGE OF ENLISTED WOMEN	PERCENTAGE OF ENLISTED MARINES
01 PERSONNEL AND ADMINISTRATION	950	30.42	9.05
02 INTELLIGENCE	4	0.12	0.33
04 LOGISTICS	22	0.70	1.84
00 UTILITIES	38	1.21	1.63
13 ENGINEER AND SHORE PARTY	31	0.99	0.37
14 DRAFTING, SURVEYING, AND MAPPING	5	0.16	1.59
15 PRINTING AND REPRODUCTION	14	0.44	6.90
21 ORDNANCE	2	0.06	0.07
23 EXPLOSIVES ORDNANCE DISPOSAL	0	0.00	0.00
25 OPERATIONAL COMMUNICATIONS	155	4.96	1.21
26 SIGNALS INTEL/GROUND ELECT WF	0	0.00	0.00
28 TELECOM MAINTENANCE	166	5.31	4.11
30 SUPPLY ADMINISTRATION/SUPPLY	443	14.18	3.87
31 TRANSPORTATION	69	2.21	8.59
32 REPAIR SERVICES	8	0.25	2.60
33 FOOD SERVICES	16	0.51	0.39
34 AUDITING, FINANCE, AND ACCOUNTING	139	4.45	8.17
35 MOTOR TRANSPORT	186	5.95	1.41
40 DATA SYSTEMS	101	3.23	6.18
41 MC EXCHANGE	75	2.40	12.02
43 PUBLIC AFFAIRS	53	1.69	15.19
44 LEGAL SERVICES	91	2.99	16.98
46 PHOTOGRAPHY	19	0.60	4.52
49 TRAINING AND TRAINING AIDS	47	1.50	14,78
55 BAND	28	0.89	3.76
57 NUCLEAR, BIOLOGICAL, AND CHEMICAL	0	0.00	0.00
58 MILITARY POLICE AND CORRECTIONS	90	2.88	2.12
59 ELECTRONICS MAINTENANCE	1	0.03	0.05
60/61 AIRCRAFT MAINTENANCE	13	0.41	0.12
65 AVIATION ORDNANCE	0	0.00	0.00
66 AVIONICS	57	1.84	0.81
68 WEATHER SERVICE	22	0.70	7.24
70 AVIATION OPERATIONS	25	0.80	1.27
72 AIR CONTROL/SUPPORT/ANTIAIR WF	0	0.00	0.00
73 AIR TRAFFIC CONTROL	15	0.48	1.86
98 U.S. MARINE CORPS BAND	11	0.35	7.59
99 IDENTIFYING AND REPORTING MOS'S	226	7.23	2.44

03, 08, 18, 75—not eligible for assignment

*(*Source: WM Research file*)

Appendix D

Women Marine Units, 1946-1977

Company E, Headquarters Battalion, Headquarters Marine Corps, Henderson Hall, Arlington, Virginia; activated 19 August 1946; disbanded 31 May 1950

COMMANDING OFFICERS

First Lieutenant Regina M. Durant 19 Aug 1946-30 Dec 1946

Captain Elizabeth J. Elrod 31 Dec 1946-19 Dec 1948

Captain Pauline B. Beckley .20 Dec 1948-31 May 1950

Officers carried on rolls of Company C, Headquarters Battalion; enlisted women carried on rolls of Companies D and E, Headquarters Battalion, according to their work section.

Company D, Headquarters Battalion, Headquarters Marine Corps, Henderson Hall, Arlington, Virginia, activated 1 July 1932

Redesignated Woman Marine Company, Headquarters Battalion, Headquarters Marine Corps, Henderson Hall, Arlington, Virginia, 20 May 1970; deactivated 4 August 1977

COMMANDING OFFICERS

First Lieutenant Elaine T. Carville .1 Jul 1952-7 Jul 1953

Major Jeanette Pearson 8 Jul 1953-2 Jun 1954

Captain Joyce M. Hamman .3 Jun 1954-9 Nov 1954

Second Lieutenant Elizabeth M. Faas 11 Nov 1954-1 Feb 1955

Second Lieutenant Florence E. Land 2 Feb 1955-6 Mar 1955

Second Lieutenant Valeria F. Hilgart .7 Mar 1955-19 Jan 1956

Captain Virginia Caley 31 Jan 1956-31 Jul 1957

Captain Patricia A. Maas .1 Aug 1957-9 Jun 1959

First Lieutenant Dorothy A. Olds 10 Jun 1959-5 Jan I960

Captain Patricia A. Watson 6 Jan 1960-25 Nov 1962

Captain Carol J. Carlson 26 Nov 1962-31 Jan 1964

Captain Gail M. Reals .3 Feb 1964-23 Dec 1966

Captain Nancy J. Mackie .24 Dec 1966-13 Jun 1968

Captain Melba J. Myers 14 Jun 1968-3 Jul 1968

First Lieutenant Mary G. Nitsch 4 Jul 1968-23 Jul 1968

Captain Jeanne A. Botwright .24 Jul 1968-1 Apr 1970

Captain Charlene M. Summers 2 Apr 1970-23 Jan 1972

First Lieutenant Karen I. Kelly 24 Jan 1972-7 Feb 1972

Captain Joan M. Collins 8 Feb 1972-11 Jul 1974

Captain Shelley B. Mayer 12 Jul 1974-18 Jul 1977

First Lieutenant Cathy A. Fremin 19 Jul 1977-30 Aug 1977

Woman Officer Training Detachment, Basic School, Marine Corps Schools, Quantico, Virginia: Captain Elsie E. Hill and staff attached to Headquarters Battalion; operational control under G-3, Basic School. Unit activated only when class in session during summers of 1949 and 1950. First class began 20 June 1949.

Woman Officer Training Detachment, Headquarters Battalion, Marine Corps Schools, Quantico, Virginia, activated 16 May 1952 as permanent unit under Basic School

Redesignated Women Marines Training Detachment, Headquarters Battalion, Marine Corps Schools, Quantico, Virginia

Redesignated Woman Marine Detachment, Marine Corps Schools, Quantico, Virginia, 17 December 1958

Redesignated Woman Officer School, Marine Corps Schools, Quantico, Virginia, 16 April 1965 Woman Officer School redesignated as a school under the Education Center, Marine Corps Schools, Quantico, Virginia 12 June 1973; disestablished 20 December 1974

COMMANDING OFFICERS

Captain Elsie E. Hill .20 Jun 1949-24 Sep 1951

Captain Emma H. Hendrickson .25 Sep 1951-30 Nov 1951

Lieutenant Colonel Julia E. Hamblet 16 May 1952-6 Apr 1953

Major Dorothy M. Knox 7 Apr 1953-31 May 1953

Major Margaret M. Henderson 1 Jun 1953-10 Dec 1954

Major Mary Janice Hale 11 Dec 1954-11 May 1955

Lieutenant Colonel Pauline B. Beckley 12 May 1955-10 Feb 1957

Major Nita Bob Warner 11 Feb 1957-15 May 1957

Lieutenant Colonel Emma Henderickson Clowers .16 May 1957-23 Mar 1959

Major Nita Bob Warner .24 Mar 1959-1 May 1959

Lieutenant Colonel Dorothy M. Knox .2 May 1959-11 Jun 1962

Lieutenant Colonel Doris V. Kleberger 12 Jun 1962-16 Jun 1965

Major Margaret A. Brewer .17 Jun 1965-30 Jul 1965

Lieutenant Colonel Elsie E. Hill 31 Jul 1965-31 Oct 1966

Major Ruth F. Reinholz .1 Nov 1966-31 Jan 1967

Lieutenant Colonel Valeria F. Hilgart .1 Feb 1967-9 Apr 1970

Lieutenant Colonel Theresa M. Hayes .10 Apr 1970-10 Jan 1972

Lieutenant Colonel Carolyn J. Auldridge Walsh .11 Jan 1972-10 Jul 1973

Lieutenant Colonel Roberta N. Roberts Patrick .12 Jul 1973-20 Dec 1974

3d Recruit Training Battalion, Marine Corps Recruit Depot, Parris Island, South Carolina, activated 23 February 1949

Redesignated Woman Recruit Training Battalion, Marine Corps Recruit Depot, Parris Island, South Carolina, 1 May 1954

Redesignated Woman Recruit Training Command, Marine Corps Recruit Depot, Parris Island, South Carolina, 28 May 1976

COMMANDING OFFICERS

Captain Margaret M. Henderson .23 Feb 1949-19 Jun 1950

Captain Mary J. Hale 29 Aug 1950-17 Sep 1950

Major Pauline B. Beckley .18 Sep 1950-25 Nov 1952

Major Helen M. Tatum .26 Nov 1952-11 Jan 1953

Major Nita Bob Warner 12 Jan 1953-7 Apr 1954

Lieutenant Colonel Elsie E. Hill .8 Apr 1954-2 Sep 1956

Major Jeanette I. Sustad .3 Sep 1956-21 Oct 1956

Lieutenant Colonel Barbara J. Bishop 22 Oct 1956-25 Jul 1959

Major Doris V. Kleberger .26 Jul 1959-2 Dec 1959

Lieutenant Colonel Elsie E. Hill 3 Dec 1959-15 May 1962

Lieutenant Colonel Julia E. Hamblet .16 May 1962-25 Apr 1965

Lieutenant Colonel Dorothy M. Knox .26 Apr 1965-4 Apr 1967

Major Mary E. Bane 5 Apr 1967-26 Oct 1967

Lieutenant Colonel Ruth J. O'Holleran 27 Oct 1967-15 Jul 1969

Lieutenant Colonel Jenny Wrenn 16 Jul 1969-9 Feb 1971

Lieutenant Colonel Roberta N. Roberts 10 Feb 1971-11 Jul 1972

Major Gail M. Reals 12 Jul 1972-15 Aug 1972

Lieutenant Colonel Ruth F. Reinholz 16 Aug 1972-20 Dec 1972

Major Gail M. Reals 21 Dec 1972-6 May 1973

Lieutenant Colonel Jenny Wrenn 7 May 1973-30 Jul 1975

Lieutenant Colonel Vera M. Jones .31 Jul 1975-14 Sep 1977

Lieutenant Colonel Gail M. Reals .15 Sep 1977-

Post Troops, 3d Recruit Training Battalion, Marine Corps Recruit Depot, Parris Island, South Carolina, activated 11 January 1950

SECTION COMMANDER

Second Lieutenant Mary S. Mock 11 Jan 1950-21 Aug 1951

Captain Emily Schultz .22 Aug 1951-14 Nov 1951

Company W, Marine Barracks, Camp Lejeune, North Carolina, activated 13 October 1950

Redesignated Camp Headquarters Women Marines Company, Headquarters and Service Battalion, Marine Barracks, Camp Lejeune, North Carolina, 29 November 1951

Redesignated Woman Marine Company, Headquarters Battalion, Marine Corps Base, Camp Lejeune, North Carolina, 1 June 1954

Redesignated Woman Marine Company, Headquarters and Service Battalion, Marine Corps Base, Camp Lejeune, North Carolina, 9 June 1961; deactivated 2 August 1977

COMMANDING OFFICERS

Captain Mary J. Fischer Elder .13 Oct 1950-5 Sep 1953

Captain Elaine T. Carville 6 Sep 1953-16 Oct 1953

Major Barbara J. Bishop 17 Oct 1953-11 Apr 1955

First Lieutenant Nancy L. White 12 Apr 1955-11 Jul 1955

Captain Mary Sue Mock 12 Jul 1955-4 Mar 1957

Captain Margaret A. Brewer .8 Mar 1957-12 May 1958

Captain Ellen B. Moroney 13 May 1958-11 Sep 1961

Captain Jane L. Wallis .12 Sep 1961-20 Mar 1964

Captain Carol A. Vertalino .21 Mar 1964-26 May 1966

Major Elsa L. Farman 27 May 1966-10 May 1967

Captain Jo H. Hall 11 May 1967-23 Jan 1969

Captain Delia J. Elden 24 Jan 1969-19 Jul 1970

Captain Ruby J. Chapman 20 Jul 1970-29 Nov 1971

Captain Juanka A. Lamb 30 Nov 1971- 20 Jun 1973

Captain Carol L. Pollack 21 Jun 1973-13 Nov 1975

Captain Linda Essex Edwards 14 Nov 1975-2 Aug 1977

Woman Marine Company, Service Battalion, Marine Barracks, Camp Joseph H. Pendleton, California, activated 1 June 1951

Redesignated Woman Marine Company, Headquarters Battalion, Marine Barracks, Camp Pendleton, California, 20 September 1952

Redesignated Woman Marine Company, Headquarters Battalion, Marine Corps Base, Camp Pendleton, California, 1954

Redesignated Woman Marine Company, Headquarters and Service Battalion, Marine Corps Base, Camp Pendleton, 21 January 1958

Redesignated WM Company, Headquarters Battalion, Headquarters Regiment, Marine Corps Base, Camp Pendleton, 1 July 1962; deactivated 1 April 1974

COMMANDING OFFICERS

Captain Jeanette I. Sustad .1 Jun 1951-27 Aug 1952

Second Lieutenant Valeria F. Hilgart .28 Aug 1952-29 Nov 1952

Second Lieutenant Catherine M. Gregory .30 Nov 1952-27 Mar 1953

Captain Frances M. Johnson 28 Mar 1953-6 Sep 1954

Second Lieutenant Ruth J. O'Holleran 7 Sep 1954-3 Dec 1955

Captain Jenny Wrenn .4 Dec 1955-28 Feb 1957

First Lieutenant Dorothy A. Olds .1 Mar 1957-10 Mar 1957

Captain Marguerita C. Russell .11 Mar 1957-26 Jan 1958

Captain Clarabelle M. Merntt 27 Jan 1958-10 Jan i960

Captain Martha A. Cox .11 Jan 1960-19 Sep 1961

Captain Shirley L. Mink .20 Sep 1961-9 Oct 1963

Major Florence E. Land .10 Oct 1963-4 Jul 1964

First Lieutenant Carla H. Bednar .5 Jul 1964-1 Dec 1964

First Lieutenant Sara R. Beauchamp 2 Dec 1964-1 Mar 1965

First Lieutenant Jolana Johnson 2 Mar 1965-1 Oct 1966

Captain Estella C Rhodes 2 Oct 1966-30 Jun 1967

Captain Mary S. Stevens League 1 Jul 1967-2 Dec 1968

Captain Anna H. Williams 3 Dec 1968-2 Jul 1969

Captain Sharyll A. B. Plato 3 Jul 1969-9 Sep 1969

Captain Anna H. Williams .10 Sep 1969-19 Nov 1969

Second Lieutenant Alice F. Jones 20 Nov 1969-30 Dec 1969

Captain Barbara A. Schmidt 31 Dec 1969-29 Nov 1970

Major Georgia L. Swickheimer .30 Nov 1970-6 Apr 1971

First Lieutenant Sue E. Vanhaastert 7 Apr 1971-19 Jul 1971

Second Lieutenant Roberta M. Baro .20 Jul 1971-2 Aug 1971

Captain Lillian Hagener 3 Aug 1971-16 Aug 1973

Captain Nancy J. Lewis Hackert .17 Aug 1973-12 Jan 1974

First Lieutenant Donna M. Hug 11 Jan 1974-10 Feb 1974

First Lieutenant Maria T. Hernandez 11 Feb 1974-1 Apr 1974

Post Personnel Company, 3d Recruit Training Battalion, Marine Corps Recruit Depot, Parris Island, South Carolina, activated 15 November 1951

Redesignated Permanent Personnel Company, Woman Recruit Training Battalion, Marine Corps Recruit Depot, Parris Island, South Carolina, 1 May 1954

Redesignated Headquarters Company, Woman Recruit Training Battalion, Marine Corps Recruit Depot, Parris Island, South Carolina (date unknown)

Redesignated Permanent Personnel Company, Woman Recruit Training Battalion, Marine Corps Recruit Depot, Parris Island, South Carolina, 1 April 1958

Redesignated Headquarters Company, Woman Marine Training Battalion, Marine Corps Recruit Depot, Parris Island, South Carolina, 27 April 1964; deactivated 25 May 1976

COMMANDING OFFICERS

Captain Emily Schultz .15 Nov 1951-25 Nov 1952

Second Lieutenant Phyllis J. Young 26 Nov 1952-26 Jun 1953

First Lieutenant Muriel J. Katschker .27 Jun 1953-18 Jul 1954

Captain Essie M. Lucas 19 Jul 1954-12 Mar 1955

First Lieutenant Ruth F. Reinholz 14 Mar 1955-12 Jun 1956

Second Lieutenant Francis B. Newman 13 Jun 1956-7 Jul 1956

Captain Constance Baker 8 Jul 1956-1 Nov 1957

Captain Gussie R. Calhoun .2 Nov 1957-2 Mar 1959

Major Doris V. Kleberger 3 Mar 1959-5 Jul 1959

Captain Donrue Wever .6 Jul 1959-11 Jun I960

First Lieutenant Betty L. Leonard 12 Jun 1960-20 Aug I960

Captain Patsy A. Twilley .21 Aug 1960-22 Mar 1962

First Lieutenant Jo Ann Kilday 23 Mar 1962-10 Sep 1962

Captain Leah M. Draper 12 Sep 1962-30 Jun 1963

First Lieutenant Jacqueline Leffler White 1 Jul 1963-31 Jan 1964

Second Lieutenant Barbara J. Oliver .1 Feb 1964-16 Feb 1964

First Lieutenant Vera M. Jones 17 Feb 1964-3 Jan 1965

Captain Mary S. Stevens .4 Jan 1965-15 Aug 1966

First Lieutenant Johnena J. Cochran .15 Aug 1966-6 Feb 1967

First Lieutenant Suellen A. Beaulieu .7 Feb 1967-1 Aug 1967

Captain Loretta J. Ross .2 Aug 1967-17 Mar 1968

First Lieutenant Marie L. Arnold .18 Mar 1968-22 Dec 1968

Captain Jean M. Panzer 23 Dec 1968-23 Sep 1969

Major Karen G. Wheeler .24 Sep 1969-31 Oct 1969

First Lieutenant Bonnie J. Tervo .1 Nov 1969-21 May 1970

Second Lieutenant Elizabeth T. Agaisse 24 May 1970-3 Jul 1970

Captain Emma G. Ramsey 5 Jul 1970-28 Feb 1971

First Lieutenant Elizabeth T. Agaisse 1 Mar 1971-15 Apr 1971

First Lieutenant Cheryl J. McCauley 18 Apr 1971-20 May 1971

Captain Shirley E. Leaverton .21 May 1971-16 Jul 1973

First Lieutenant Barbara J. Gard 17 Jul 1973-11 Sep 1973

Captain Carolyn Bever Wiseman .12 Sep 1973-23 Apr 1974

First Lieutenant Susan V. Wagner 24 Apr 1974-26 Sep 1974

Captain Carol A. Barber. .30 Sep 1974-9 Jul 1975

Second Lieutenant Bonnie L. Duphiney 10 Jul 1975-2 Aug 1975

Captain Barbara A. Martin 3 Aug 1975-25 May 1976

Woman Marine Detachment-1, Marine Corps Air Station, El Toro, California, activated 15 May 1951

Woman Marine Detachment-1 redesignated Sub Unit-2, Headquarters Squadron, Marine Corps Air Station, upon reorganization of the air station on 15 March 1972; deactivated 20 February 1974

COMMANDING OFFICERS

Captain Nita Bob Warner 15 May 1951-15 Dec 1952

Major Shirley J. Fuetsch 16 Dec 1952-8 Jan 1953

First Lieutenant Wilma Morris .9 Jan 1953-4 Feb 1953

Major Ben Alice Day 5 Feb 1953-30 Dec 1954

First Lieutenant Shirley A. Tate .1 Jan 1955-14 Mar 1955

Major Helen A. Tatum .15 Mar 1955-29 Apr 1955

Major Dorothy M. Knox .30 Apr 1955-3 Apr 1958

Captain Valeria F. Hilgart .4 Apr 1958-17 Oct I960

First Lieutenant Sonia Rivera-Cuevas 18 Oct 1960-16 Jan 1961

Captain Marie J. Halvorsen 17 Jan 1961-11 Feb 1962

First Lieutenant Nancy Talbot Rick .12 Feb 1962-13 Nov 1963

Captain Nanette L. Beavers 14 Nov 1963-5 Nov 1966

Major Roberta N. Roberts .6 Nov 1966-20 Aug 1967

Captain Judith K. Lund .21 Aug 1967-26 Nov 1969

First Lieutenant Eleanor J. McElroy .27 Nov 1969-22 Sep 1970

Lieutenant Colonel Jane L. Wallis .23 Sep 1970-8 Mar 1971

Major Barbara E. Dolyak .9 Mar 1971-1 May 1972

Captain Marcia A. Biddleman 1 Jul 1972-1 Mar 1973

CWO-3 June R. Doberstein 2 Mar 1973-20 Feb 1974

Woman Marine Detachment-2, Marine Corps Air Station, Cherry Point, North Carolina, activated 1 March 1951; deactivated 31 December 1974

COMMANDING OFFICERS

Major Helen A. Wilson 1 Mar 1951-3 May 1951

First Lieutenant Nancy J. Mecartney 4 May 1951-8 Sep 1953

Captain Emily Schultz 9 Sep 1953-17 May 1954

First Lieutenant Louise M. Snyder 18 May 1954-12 Sep 1954

Captain Sara F. Hanan 13 Sep 1954-24 Jan 1955

Captain Jeanne Fleming 25 Jan 1955-25 May 1956

Captain Ruth F. Reinholz 16 Jun 1956-25 Nov 1957

Captain Ruth J. O'Holleran 26 Nov 1957-24 May 1959

Captain Inger R. Beaumont .25 May 1959-19 Jul 1959

Major Anne S. Ritter .20 Jul 1959-17 Mar 1962

Captain Martha A. Cox 18 Mar 1962-10 Dec 1964

Captain Carolyn J. Auldridge .11 Dec 1964-15 Oct 1966

First Lieutenant Elizabeth D. Doize 1 Nov 1966-28 May 1968

Captain LorettaJ. Liehs 29 May 1968-16 Jan 1969

Major Nanette L. Beavers 17 Jan 1969-14 Jan 1970

Captain Donna J. Sherwood .15 Jan 1970-23 Aug 1970

Captain Sara A. Beauchamp 24 Aug 1970-25 Mar 1972

Captain Sharon L. Sherer .28 Mar 1972-31 May 1973

Captain Marguerite K. Campbell .16 Jul 1973-31 Dec 1974

Woman Marine Company, Headquarters and Service Battalion, Fleet Marine Force, Atlantic, Camp Elmore, Norfolk, Virginia; activated 1 April 1952; deactivated 15 April 1977

SUPERVISOR OF WOMEN

Second Lieutenant Doris V. Kleberger Nov 1950

First Lieutenant Joan McCormick Nov 1951

COMMANDING OFFICERS

Second Lieutenant Mary E. Sullivan .1 Apr 1952-25 Jun 1952

First Lieutenant Natalie Noble .4 Aug 1952-29 May 1953

Captain Dolores A. Thorning 13 Jun 1953-23 Jan 1955

Second Lieutenant Rita A. Ciotti 24 Jan 1955-13 Aug 1955

Second Lieutenant Martha A. Cox 14 Aug 1955-4 Oct 1955

Captain Margaret A. Brewer .5 Oct 1955-6 Feb 1957

First Lieutenant Shirley J. Gifford .7 Feb 1957-30 Jun 1958

First Lieutenant Eleanor H. Bispham .1 Jul 1958-26 Aug 1958

Captain Margaret R. Pruett .27 Aug 1958-3 Aug 1960

First Lieutenant Valeria M. Dayton .4 Aug 1960-25 May 1962

Captain Georgia L. Swickheimer .26 May 1962-20 Dec 1965

First Lieutenant Mary L. Howard .21 Dec 1965-30 Oct 1967

First Lieutenant Lois J. Bertram 31 Oct 1967-13 Mar 1969

First Lieutenant Mary J. Stoakes 14 Mar 1969-6 Aug 1970

First Lieutenant Carolyn K. Bever Wiseman 7 Aug 1970-24 Nov 1971

First Lieutenant Patricia A. Perkins .25 Nov 1971-13 Feb 1974

First Lieutenant Mary E. Mitchell 14 Feb 1974-12 Dec 1974

Captain Kathryn A. Jacob MacKinney 13 Dec 1974-15 Apr 1977

Company D, Headquarters Battalion, Marine Corps Schools, Quantico, Virginia, activated 1 March 1952

Redesignated Headquarters Company, Women Marines Detachment, Marine Corps Schools, Quantico, Virginia, 1 May 1959

Reorganized, Headquarters Company, Woman Officer School, Marine Corps Schools, Quantico, Virginia, 16 April 1965

Redesignated Headquarters Company, Woman Officer School, Marine Corps Development and Education Command, Quantico, Virginia, 1 January 1968; deactivated 12 June 1973

OFFICER IN CHARGE, WM BARRACKS

Second Lieutenant Elaine T. Carville 7 Nov 1950-31 Jan 1951

First Lieutenant Marion R. Moore .1 Feb 1951-28 Feb 1952

COMMANDING OFFICERS

First Lieutenant Marion R. Moore .1 Mar 1952-20 Dec 1952

Second Lieutenant Ruth F. Reinholz 23 Dec 1952-11 Jan 1953

Captain Bernice M. Pitman 12 Jan 1953-20 Apr 1954

First Lieutenant Ruth F. Reinholz 21 Apr 1954-30 Apr 1954

Captain Jeanne Fleming 1 Mar 1954-9 Aug 1954

First Lieutenant Anne S. Ritter .10 Aug 1954-6 Dec 1955

First Lieutenant Ellen B. Moroney 7 Dec 1955-19 Nov 1956

Captain Eileen F. Parker .20 Nov 1956-31 Dec 1956

Second Lieutenant Marion L. Call 1 Jan 1957-22 Jan 1957

Captain Virginia A. Hajek .23 Jan 1957-3 Aug 1958

Second Lieutenant Grace Ann Entriken .6 Aug 1958-7 Sep 1958

Captain Beverly Schofield Love .8 Sep 1958-31 May 1960

First Lieutenant Shirley N. Arnold 1 Jun 1960-5 Jul 1960

Second Lieutenant Nanette L. Beavers .6 Jul 1960-31 Jul 1960

Captain Jane L. Wallis .1 Aug 1960-11 Aug 1961

Captain Grace A. Overholser .21 Aug 1961-5 Jun 1962

Captain Margaret R. Pruett 6 Jun 1962-18 Nov 1962

First Lieutenant Gail M. Reals 7 Feb 1963-24 Mar 1963

First Lieutenant Nancy A. Carroll 26 Mar 1963-21 Apr 1964

First Lieutenant Vea J. Smith 22 Apr 1964-5 Dec 1965

Captain Jo Anne Kilday 6 Dec 1965-5 Dec 1966

Captain Vera M. Jones .6 Dec 1966-20 Jan 1967

First Lieutenant Dolores R. Noguera .21 Jan 1967-7 Aug 1967

First Lieutenant Ruth D. Walsh 8 Aug 1967-12 Nov 1968

First Lieutenant Barbara A. Schmidt .13 Nov 1968-30 Nov 1969

Captain Janice C. Scott 1 Dec 1969-11 Oct 1971

First Lieutenant Sharon F. Daugherty .12 Oct 1971-30 Apr 1973

Captain Shirley L. Bowen 1 May 1973-11 Jun 1973

Woman Marine Company, Headquarters and Service Battalion, Marine Corps Recruit Depot, San Diego, California, activated 16 June 1952; deactivated 24 February 1977

COMMANDING OFFICERS

Major Emma H. Clowers 16 Jun 1952-23 Apr 1953

First Lieutenant Eileen F. Parker .24 Apr 1953-31 May 1953

Major Helen A. Wilson .1 Jun 1953-2 Jun 1954

Major Shirley J. Fuetsch 3 Jun 1954-31 Oct 1955

Captain Donrue Wever .1 Nov 1955-30 Nov 1956

Captain Mary L. Voight 2 Dec 1956-8 Apr 1958

Second Lieutenant Margaret H. Frank .9 Apr 1958-17 Apr 1958

First Lieutenant Katherine M. Donohue .18 Apr 1958-12 Jun 1958

Captain Patricia A. Watson .13 Jun 1958-17 Dec 1959

Major Theresa M. Hayes 18 Dec 1959-15 Jan 1963

Captain Marilyn F. Day 16 Jan 1963-8 Feb 1965

Captain Winifred B. Paul 9 Feb 1965-24 Jul 1965

Major Barbara J. Lee 26 Jul 1965-26 Dec 1966

Second Lieutenant Elizabeth A. Wilson 27 Dec 1966-4 Feb 1967

Captain Gail A. Waugh 5 Feb 1967-7 Aug 1968

Captain Susan Sommers .13 Aug 1968-29 Aug 1969

Captain Mane J. Halvorsen 30 Aug 1969-1 Feb 1970

Captain Lillian Hagener 2 Feb 1970-31 Jul 1971

Captain Barbara Weinberger 3 Sep 1971-25 Jan 1974

Captain Eleanor F. Pekala 26 Jan 1974-2 Sep 1975

First Lieutenant Mary K. P. Lowery .25 Sep 1975-9 May 1976

First Lieutenant Candice A. Lewis 10 May 1976-24 Feb 1977

Woman Recruit Training Company, Women Recruit Training Battalion, Marine Corps Recruit Depot, Parris Island, South Carolina

The company was never a reporting unit. What information is recorded here has been gained through personal interviews and a review of various records, recruit platoon books, newspaper articles, etc.

COMMANDING OFFICERS

Second Lieutenant Margaret L. Grammer Brown 1 Jan 1952-4 Sep 1952

First Lieutenant Virginia Caley .11 Oct 1952-31 Jul 1953

Captain Essie M. Lucas .1 Aug 1953-23 Aug 1954

Captain Elaine T. Carville .24 Aug 1954-6 Nov 1956

Captain Theresa M. Hayes .7 Nov 1956-22 Dec 1957

Captain Mary E. Bane 21 Jan 1958-11 Jun I960

First Lieutenant Georgia Swickheimer .6 Aug 1960-29 Sep I960

First Lieutenant Mary A. Johnson 30 Sep 1960-27 Mar 1961

First Lieutenant Betty L. Leonard .22 Jun 1961-30 Jul 1961

First Lieutenant Dolores A. Schleichert 31 Jul 1961-29 Apr 1962

Captain Mary L. Vertalino 30 Apr 1962-24 Jun 1963

Captain Annie Muriel Trowsdale 25 June 1963-3 Jan 1965

Captain Vera M. Jones 4 Jan 1965-23 May 1966

Captain Eleanor Elaine Filkins 8 Jul 1966-5 Apr 1968

First Lieutenant Suellen A. Beaulieu .May 1968

Captain Joan M. Collins 17 Jul 1969-17 Aug 1971

Captain Vanda K. Brame .18 Aug 1971-13 Jun 1972

Major Gail M. Reals 14 Jun 1972-27 Jun 1972

Captain Carolyn K. Bever Wiseman 28 Jun 1972-11 Sep 1973

Captain Linda K. Adams Priest 12 Sep 1973-31 Oct 1975

Captain Nancy A. Davis .1 Nov 1975-June 1977

Company A, Headquarters and Service Battalion, FMFPac, U.S. Naval Base, Pearl Harbor, Oahu, Hawaii, activated 24 June 1952

Redesignated Woman Marine Company, Headquarters and Service Battalion, FMFPac, Camp H. M. Smith, Oahu, Hawaii, 10 July 1956; deactivated 12 February 1976

COMMANDING OFFICERS

Second Lieutenant Margaret M. Schafer .24 Jun 1952-22 Dec 1952

Captain Valeria F. Hilgart .23 Dec 1952-13 Jan 1955

Captain Virginia Caley .14 Jan 1955-2 Dec 1955

First Lieutenant Theresa M. Hayes 3 Dec 1955-6 Jan 1956

Captain Doris V. Kleberger .7 Jan 1956-25 Feb 1957

Captain Jenny Wrenn .10 Apr 1957-5 Apr 1959

First Lieutenant Nancy J. Durkin 6 May 1959-15 Jul 1959

Captain Ruth J. O'Holleran 16 Jul 1959-30 Oct 1961

Captain Ellen B. Moroney .2 Nov 1961-18 Nov 1962

Captain Carol A. Vertalino 19 Nov 1962-1 Feb 1964

Captain Elaine E. Filkins 2 Feb 1964-14 Dec 1965

Captain Roberta N. Roberts .15 Dec 1965-30 Dec 1966

Captain Jeanne A. Botwright .31 Dec 1966-5 Dec 1967

Captain Judybeth D. Barnett .6 Dec 1967-16 Dec 1970

First Lieutenant Cheryl S. Gillespie .21 Dec 1970-16 Jun 1972

Captain Antoinette Meenach .17 Jun 1972-1 May 1974

Captain Karen S. De Wolf 2 May 1974-12 Feb 1976

Woman Marine Detachment-3, Marine Corps Air Station, Kaneohe, Hawaii, activated 2 November 1953; deactivated 1 September 1956

COMMANDING OFFICERS

Captain Phyllis J. Young .2 Nov 1953-2 Oct 1954

Captain Patricia A. Maas .10 Oct 1954-1 Sep 1956

Woman Marine Company, Headquarters Battalion, Marine Corps Supply Center, Barstow, California; activated 1 July 1967; deactivated August 1971

COMMANDING OFFICERS

Captain Rebecca M. Kraft .1 Jul 1967-8 Sep 1967

Captain Joan Hammond .9 Sep 1967-26 Oct 1968

First Lieutenant Diane L. Hamel 27 Oct 1968-4 Nov 1969

Captain Alice K. Kurashige .5 Nov 1969-14 May 1970

First Lieutenant Geraldine E. Peeler 15 May 1970-15 Jul 1970

First Lieutenant Vanda K. Brame .16 Jul 1970-31 Apr 1971

First Lieutenant Linda J. Lenhart .7 Jul 1971-31 Jul 1971

Woman Marine Company, Headquarters Battalion, Marine Corps Supply Center, Albany, Georgia, activated 13 September 1967; deactivated August 1971

COMMANDING OFFICERS

First Lieutenant Emma G. Ramsey during forming

Captain Sara R. Beauchamp 13 Sep 1967-5 Jan 1969

Captain Mary S. League .6 Jan 1969-20 Mar 1970

Captain Bonnie J. Allman .May 1970-May 1971

Appendix E

Women Marines Who Served in Vietnam

1967-1973

Officers

First Lieutenant Lois J. Bertram Captain Elaine E. Filkins (Davies) Captain Vera M. Jones CWO-2 Ernestine A. Koch

First Lieutenant Shirley E. Leaverton Lieutenant Colonel Ruth J. O'Holleran Lieutenant Colonel Ruth F. Reinholz First Lieutenant Lila Jean Sharpsteen

Enlisted Women

Sergeant Barbara J. Aaron (Avant)

Staff Sergeant Bridget V. Connolly

Sergeant Doris L. Denton

Staff Sergeant Adelina Diaz (Torres)

Lance Corporal Teresa A. Dickerson

Corporal Marilyn L. Dorsey

Master Sergeant Barbara J. Dulinsky

Corporal Andrea L. Edwards

Corporal Jeanne L. Francoeur (Bell)

Corporal M. R. Gehant

Sergeant Mary E. Glaudel

Staff Sergeant Frances I. Gonzales (Shore)

Staff Sergeant Donna L. Hollowell (Murray)

Corporal Alaine K. Ivy

Sergeant Carol E. Lester

Lance Corporal Jeanette I. Hensley

Corporal Nellie Mach (Perkins)

Corporal M. Del Martinez

Corporal Nola E. Mackinster

Staff Sergeant Loretta M. Morrison

Sergeant Ella L. Netherton

Corporal Diane L. Potter

Sergeant Jacqueline K. Roach

Staff Sergeant Ermelinda Salazar (Esquibel)

Corporal Sandra Spaatz

Sergeant Helen J. Varden

Sergeant Mary P. Walsh (McDermott)

Corporal Pauline W. Wilson

Appendix F

Enlisted Women Marines Retained After World War II Who Served Until Retirement

List provided by Master Sergeant Annette Parziale. She titles it, "Chronological listing of continuous active duty retirees fortunate enough to be in the right place, at the right time, and holding the right SSN number to be retained after WW II" (MSgt Parziale ltr to Hist&MusDiv, WM Research file).

Catherine G. Murray E-7 29Mar43-30Nov62

Geraldine M. Moran E-9 .22Feb43-31Mar63

Ruth M. Haungs .E-7 .25Jun43-31Mar63

Annette Parziale E-7 2Jul43-31Mar63

Bertha J. Schultz .E-8 29Oct43-31Jul63

Helen Gardner Redmond E-6 25Mar43-25Dec63

Myrtle Butler Borg Stinson .E-7 .21Sep43-31Jan64

Bettye R. Hollis E-7 8Oct43-29Feb64

Beatrice M. Kent .E-6 .9May44-31Mar64

Martha E. Kirchman E-7 .6Apr44-31May64

Lucy Cozzi E-7 .20Feb45-30Sep64

Marion O. Ahearn E-8 .9Nov43-31Oct64

Dorthea E. Hard .E-6 26May44-31Oct64

Esther D. Waclawski E-8 10Oct44-30Nov64

Alice J. Connolly .E-8 9Jun43-28Feb65

Juel C. Pensock E-7 .15Nov43-6May66

Elizabeth Pinter E-8 20Sep43-31May66

Dorothy L. Kearns E-7 16Oct44-31May66

Betty J. Alley E-6 .18Jun45-31Jan67

Jessie L. Van Dyke E-9 6May43-31Jul68

Anna Peregrim .E-8 .1Feb45-22Aug68

Martha J. Clark . .E-8 .1Mar45-31Aug69

Vera E. Piippo .E-8 17Jul43-30Sep69

Catherine L. Quinlan .E-9 .16Oct43-30Sep69

Margaret H. Crowel .E-8 18May45-31May70

Loraine G. Bruso .E-8 .15Dec43-31Jan71

Elizabeth M. Tarte E-8 .1Oct43-23Nov71

Bertha Peters Billeb .E-9 .5Mar43-30Apr73

June V. Andler E-9 .9Mar44-30Apr74

Sarah N. Thornton .E-9 .11Dec43-31Jul74

* * * * * * * * * * * * *

Made in the
USA
Monee, IL

15856045R00157